Deferrals of Domain

Deferrals of Domain

□□

Contemporary Women Novelists and the State

Martine Watson Brownley

St. Martin's Press
New York

Excerpts from *Daughters:* Reprinted with the permission of Scribner, a Division of Simon & Schuster Inc. from *Daughters* by Paule Marshall. Copyright © 1991 Paule Marshall. Published in hardcover by Atheneum, 1991. Published in paperback by Plume, 1992.

Reprinted with the permission of Paule Marshall, published by Atheneum, 1991. Copyright © 1991 Paule Marshall.

Excerpts from *A Sport of Nature* by Nadine Gordimer Copyright © 1987 by Nadine Gordimer. Reprinted by permission of Alfred A. Knopf, Inc.

Reprinted with the permission of A. P. Watt Ltd. on behalf of Felix Licensing BV.

Excerpts from *The Gates of Ivory* by Margaret Drabble. Copyright © 1991 by Margaret Drabble. Used by permission of Viking Penguin, a division of Penguin Putnam Inc.

Reprinted by permission of Sterling Lord Literistic, Inc. Copyright by Margaret Drabble.

Excerpts from *Bodily Harm* reprinted with the permission of Simon & Schuster from *Bodily Harm* by Margaret Atwood. Copyright © 1981 by O. W. Toad, Ltd.

Reprinted with permission of Jonathan Cape.

Used by permission, McClelland & Stewart, Inc. *The Canadian Publishers.*

Deferrals of Domain

ISBN 0-312-22811-2

Library of Congress Cataloging-in-Publication Data
Brownley, Martine Watson.
   Deferrals of domain: contemporary women novelists and the state / Martine Watson Brownley.
      p.   cm.
   Includes bibliographical references and index.
   ISBN 0-312-22811-2 (cloth)
   1. Commonwealth fiction (English)—20th century—History and criticism.   2. Literature and state—English-speaking countries—History—20th century.   3. Women and literature—English-speaking countries—History—20th century.   4. Commonwealth fiction (English)—Women authors—History and criticism.   5. Atwood, Margaret Eleanor, 1939– Bodily harm.   6. Drabble, Margaret, 1939– Gates of ivory.   7. Marshall, Paule, 1929– Daughters. 8. Gordimer, Nadine. Sport of nature.   9. State, The in literature.   I. Title.
PR9084.B76   2000
823'.9109171241—dc21   99–43175
                                                                                           CIP

Internal design and typesetting by Letra Libre

First edition: April 2000
10 9 8 7 6 5 4 3 2 1

To Margaret W. Pepperdene

Contents

Acknowledgments

It is a pleasure to acknowledge the assistance that I have received from a number of institutions and individuals while I worked on this study. The Emory University Research Committee provided leave that enabled me to complete it. Lectures at the University of Georgia, Ohio University, and Dekalb College allowed me to receive responses to different parts of my work, and I am grateful to Jeffrey Portnoy, Loreen L. Giese, and Barbara McCaskill, and to the audiences at each institution who challenged and encouraged me. As for the individuals who have helped me in many different ways at various times, the lack of specificity in an alphabetical list without titles in no way reflects the extent of the deep gratitude that I feel to each one of them for the generous assistance she or he offered when I needed it: Paula R. Backscheider; Nancy Baltus and Lee Ann Lloyd; Karen R. Bloom; David Bright; Amy Benson Brown; Laura Callanan; Linda Calloway; Alan Cattier; Angela L. Cotten; Rick Delaney; Cheri and Jim Demmers; William B. Dillingham; Frances Smith Foster; Elizabeth Fox-Genovese; Ralph Freedman; Tiffany and Diego Gallina; Ann Geneva; Carole L. Hahn; Sarah Herbert; Elizabeth Kraft; Kristi S. Long; the late Lore Metzger; Carole Meyers; Jessica Rabin; Walter L. Reed; Laura L. Runge; and an anonymous reader for St. Martin's Press. All of these people enabled me to complete this book, but the extent of the help offered by Emilia Navarro was especially crucial to the project, as was that of Karen and J. B. Jolly. My greatest debt has long been to the teacher and scholar to whom it is dedicated.

Quotations and Abbreviations

All italics within quotations are those of the author quoted, unless otherwise specified within the text.

Dictionary definitions are from the *Oxford English Dictionary* and *Webster's New World College Dictionary* (3rd ed., 1988).

AtN	*Newsletter of the Margaret Atwood Society*
BFT	Collins, *Black Feminist Thought*
BH	Atwood, *Bodily Harm*
B & S	Bazin and Seymour, *Conversations with Nadine Gordimer*
D	Marshall, *Daughters*
DP	Foucault, *Discipline and Punish*
FCB	Ferguson, *Feminist Case Against Bureaucracy*
G & S	Graulich and Sisco, "Meditations on Language and the Self"
GI	Drabble, *The Gates of Ivory*
GT	Butler, *Gender Trouble*
IR	Irigaray, *Irigaray Reader*
KR	Kristeva, *Kristeva Reader*
MAF	S. Wilson, *Margaret Atwood's Fairy-Tale Sexual Politics*
MP	W. Brown, *Manhood and Politics*
P/K	Foucault, *Power/Knowledge*
PMPW	Elshtain, *Public Man, Private Woman*
SC	Pateman, *Sexual Contract*
SG	Irigaray, *Sexes and Geneologies*
SI	W. Brown, *States of Injury*
SN	Gordimer, *A Sport of Nature*
"*SN* & B"	Clingman, "*A Sport of Nature* and the Boundaries of Fiction"
SS	Zimmerman, *Safe Sea of Women*
WE	J. Mitchell, *Woman's Estate*
WLR	J. Mitchell, *Women: The Longest Revolution*

Preface: Hobbes's Fish

> *Can you draw out Leviathan. . . .*
> *Will you play with him as with a bird,*
> *or will you put him on leash for your*
> *maidens?*
>
> —Job 41: 1, 5 (RSV)

For a long time this study of Margaret Atwood's, Paule Marshall's, Nadine Gordimer's, and Margaret Drabble's representations of relationships between women and the state lumbered along under the working title "Facing Leviathan: Contemporary Women Novelists and the State." Unfortunately, beyond the screen of my word processor that title fared poorly. Blank looks from friends who heard it were discouraging, as were more searching questions from aficionados of Thomas Hobbes. At the very end, unwilling to mislead Hobbesians as well as library catalogers, I reluctantly abandoned "Facing Leviathan."

I briefly resurrect this fragment of textual history because Hobbes's mythical beast sums up so well the kind of state power with which this study is concerned: hierarchical, centralized, and militarized political might.[1] The focus is on what has traditionally been called "high" politics: governmental affairs at the national level and the traditional public sphere in its most limited configuration. Politics, and even state politics, is thus defined in the most restricted conventional sense, and is much more narrowly defined than is usually the case in current feminist and literary discussions. This narrowing is a deliberate strategy in order to focus on various ramifications of the feminist contention that everything is ultimately political, which is itself one aspect of the "impulse to totalize politics and power" that Gerald Graff has noted in contemporary literary criticism (158). My interest is in just what happens with this kind of totalizing move when the politics at issue are state politics.

For the women characters in the novels in this study, the personal is often the political, although not inevitably. The obverse is less often true. The political in the traditional sense in which I use it rarely turns out to be the personal for these characters. Adrienne Rich is correct that at times "even ordinary pronouns become a political problem" ("Notes" 16), but that particular kind of problem is not the focus here. In addition, the focus is on politics as direct action rather than as discursive or symbolic system. The primary concern is not so much with how the state structures the everyday lives of women as with how women can—and cannot—intervene directly in the state, although the two are of course inevitably related.

In few areas of intellectual analysis has the contemporary "methodological shift away from the notion of structure and toward a notion of process" (de Lauretis, *Alice* 105) been clearer than in the works of feminist and other theorists of the modern state. As process rather than product, as the creator as well as the arbiter of interests, the state emerges in the writings of these theorists not as a monolithic institution but as a heterogeneous site of contest. For example, Davina Cooper defines the state as "a contingently articulated, multifaceted phenomena with no fixed form, essence or core" (60–61), while Wendy Brown terms it "a significantly unbounded terrain of powers and techniques, an ensemble of discourses, rules, and practices, cohabiting in limited, tension-ridden, often contradictory relation with one another" (*SI* 174).[2]

For many reasons the representations of the state by the novelists in this study do not directly reflect this kind of complexity. In part their portrayals are more simplified because they are still working primarily within realistic conventions, and, as Michel Foucault has shown, modern state power, like all power, seeks to mask itself (*History* 86). Brown writes that the state's "power and privilege operate increasingly through disavowal of potency, repudiation of responsibility, and diffusion of sites and operations of control" (*SI* 194; see also 179). But representations of the state in these novels are not simplified primarily because the states are wily postmodern camouflagers of their own power. In the novels the women characters who become involved in high politics usually do so at so great a remove from the sources of state power that the novelists find it unnecessary to go into detail about the particular governmental forms that these characters confront. Whatever the actual complexity and heterogeneity of contemporary states, the women in the novels are not close enough to observe or understand them.

Thus the novelists' states remain indistinct entities. Theorists have objected to the term "the state" as vague, emphasizing its elision of multiple and sometimes contradictory governmental functions and its suppression of historical specificity.[3] For theoretical purposes they are correct; welfare and warfare bureaucracies are very different entities, and many diverse state forms have emerged, evolved, and disappeared over the centuries. But for the literary analysis of these novels that is my primary concern, the term "the state" works well enough, because the novelists themselves are vague about specifics of the states they represent.

The novels show various contemporary state forms, from the dissolving welfare state in Great Britain and the Khmer Rouge tyranny in Cambodia, to postcolonial state configurations in Africa and the Caribbean and the ménage of democracy and neoimperialism that marks the United States. Governmental operations in these countries obviously differ in many ways. However, in assessing the women characters' relationships to their respective states, the particular state formation in the novel is usually not the determining factor. For example, while due process of law is available to women in Canada but not on Atwood's Caribbean islands of Ste. Agathe and Ste. Anthony, the same is true for the men in both countries. Whether the given state is capitalist or communist, dictatorial or democratic, in most cases the novels represent the relationships of women to the state as severely limited. Nor are these limitations usually a matter of choice on the women's parts. In most cases they are not engaged in intentional withdrawal,[4] the evasion of state control that Henrietta Moore has seen as a female survival strategy: "Many women try to work around the state rather than to work with it." Moore concludes that "The politics of the modern state are becoming ever more exclusive as they seek to become ever more inclusive" (183). The novelists in this study concur, but not for the same reasons.

Like the state itself, women are constructed and positioned as state subjects very differently in theoretical as compared to novelistic discourses. The novelists' generally dismal presentations of women's relationships to the state are in stark contrast to the more optimistic visions of many contemporary theorists. The characters in the novels seldom behave as most theorists suggest that they could—or should. For example, while many theorists tend to focus on what Ernesto Laclau and Chantal Mouffe describe as "that infinite intertextuality of emancipatory discourses in which the plurality of the social takes shape" (5), the novelists see mainly repressive and oppressive discourses, with few options for the woman who wants to combat either. A number of theorists urge the construction of new political identities and more egalitarian forms of citizenship[5]; the novelists show that women are barely citizens at all in any meaningful sense. Anna Yeatman is typical of many theorists who have urged women to develop "contestatory political and public spaces . . . in relation to existing systems of governance" (*Postmodern* ix).[6] In contrast,

the novelists see women as having minimal access to public space and little ability or even will to claim any. Most theorists worry about the possible deradicalization of women who engage in state politics.[7] The
novelists suggest that such fears are groundless. They depict women with
so few avenues of access to the public world that the women's infrequent
and limited participation in politics can change neither them nor the
state. Finally, most theorists' accounts focus mainly on horizontal power.
They work with power in terms of networks of relations, particularly
emphasizing its productive aspects and discursive forms of power. The
novelists tend to treat vertical power, direct force exerted from the top
down.[8]

It is these kinds of differences of perspective between the theorists and
the novelists that this study explores. Katherine Payant has written that
the feminism in American mainstream women's fiction is often less radical than that in feminist theory (219). But the most significant points at
issue in the differing theoretical and novelistic assessments are not really
those concerning political or historical correctness—questions about
which group more satisfactorily deploys a particular ideology or which
vantage point produces the more accurate reflection of historical reality.
Both offer valuable perspectives, and their differences of emphasis, read
against each other, can measure the usefulness and validity of each for
contemporary women.

For example, the theorists do not entirely ignore contemporary
shades of the Leviathan. Brown is typical in admitting that while the state
is "an incoherent, multifaceted ensemble of power relations," it is at the
same time "a vehicle of massive domination" (*SI* 174). But the major emphasis of most theorists has not fallen on the domination, while the novelists have consistently represented this kind of raw power as central to
women's experience of the state. These differing foci, and the reasons for
them, have ramifications for the kinds of relationships that contemporary
women are evolving with state politics. Or, to take another example of
differing emphases, Varda Burstyn writes that

> When we discuss the state as a manifestation of social relations, as a rela-
> tion of production, as the major organiser of class hegemony, as the site of
> conflict mediation, we are using conceptual terms which enable us to ex-
> press real attributes and functions. But these terms, though absolutely nec-
> essary, also tend to depersonalise the state, to hide the fact that it is created
> by, made up of, and maintained by real people. . . . (72)[9]

The novel resists such depersonalization, because a concern with "real
people," with the representation of actual human beings as individuals,

traditionally has been a primary characteristic of the genre. Within the context of a novel, even a committed communist discussing the freezing weather on the German-Russian front during World War II can sympathize with the enemy. Doris Lessing's Marie keeps "thinking of those German boys, poor sods, fascists or no fascists, they're human beings" (*Ripple* 250).[10] The levels of the theoretical and novelistic critiques differ, and these differences in perspective can help in evolving more balanced views of the relationships of contemporary women to the state than either genre alone can provide.

Nancy Hewitt has written of the need to "shape a human history that captures both the messy multiplicity of lived experience and the power relations within which those lived experiences are played out" (317). Looking at the differences between "the messy multiplicity of lived experience" that the novelists portray and "the power relations" molding and molded by that multiplicity that the theorists depict can contribute to such a history. To do so, chapter 1 surveys some of the general questions raised by the differing assessments of the relationships between women and the state offered by theorists and novelists. Chapter 2 offers a more specific kind of overview, comparing theoretical and novelistic treatments of three recurring feminist themes, which I have called the Outsider Narrative, the Coalition Narration, and the Salvation Narrative of Politics.

Subsequent chapters provide detailed individual analyses of each of the four novelists. *Bodily Harm, Daughters, A Sport of Nature,* and *The Gates of Ivory* offer a range of representations of women and the state, and thus each affords opportunities for different critical and theoretical perspectives on these relationships. Because this study centers on literary analysis, it tends to highlight elements of state power that theorists currently occlude, ranging from women's still-minimal access to state politics, to the violence exercised by modern states. At the same time, however, feminist theory also clarifies major elements of many contemporary women's lives about which the novels are ambivalent or misleading, such as romance or the role of sexuality in state politics. In the first two chapters of background material, critique of the theorists dominates; the four chapters on the novelists both deploy and critique theory within specific literary contexts.

Significantly, in one important area the theorists agree with the novelists. Both see the contemporary state as primarily a male preserve, in most cases as uncompromisingly masculine as the Leviathan. Hobbes's introduction to his work explained that man's art created the Leviathan in his own image, as "an Artificiall Man" (9). In this respect little has changed in the centuries since the philosopher from Malmesbury wrote.

Brown points out that "more than any other kind of human activity, *politics* has historically borne an explicitly masculine identity." Despite a footnote admitting war as a possible exception, her text claims politics as "more exclusively limited to men than any other realm of endeavor" and as "more intensely, self-consciously masculine than most other social practices" (*MP* 4).[11] In this case what is true of politics in general is exponentially true of state politics. In the novels considered here, the scope of male power in the state is huge, whether in the prison cells of a Caribbean dictator, in hearings before U.S. Congressional committees, in the South African intelligence and police services, or in the refugee camps created by Pol Pot's genocide.

Finally, I regretted losing the reference to the Leviathan in my original title for some implied positive reasons as well as the overtly negative ones. If Hobbes produced a nightmare state that excluded women from power in the public sphere, he also clearly revealed the artificiality of that exclusion. Although thoroughly masculine, Hobbes's state is male simply by virtue of tradition, not because of nature or merit. In writing of power over children, he admitted that "whereas some have attributed the Dominion to the Man onely, as being of the more excellent Sex; they misreckon in it. For there is not always that difference of strength, or prudence between the man and the woman, as that the right can be determined without War" (139). In commonwealths, too, Hobbes noted that "for the most part, (but not alwayes) the sentence is in favour of the Father; because for the most part Common-wealths have been erected by the Fathers, not by the Mothers of families" (139–40). The repetition of "for the most part" reflects textually the strain in his assertions. Later in the *Leviathan* Hobbes would claim that fathers were "before the Institution of Common-wealth, absolute Soveraigns in their own Families" (163). But this patriarchialism contradicts his own earlier discussion. As Susan Moller Okin points out, "The mother, with her original sovereignty over both herself and her children, and with no good reason to relinquish either, has disappeared from the story" (198).[12]

Women facing the kind of state power that Hobbes represented thus confront not only an authoritarian political force but also their own potentially equal rights in claiming their share of "Dominion." Contemporary monster states have evolved as they have and functioned as they do in part because of their traditional exclusions of women. For women, then, facing Leviathan involves thinking about how—or whether—to assert their theoretical rights to active political roles in today's states in order to try to leash these contemporary Leviathans for themselves. The alternative is continuing to wait, as the writer in Job puts it, for someone to "put him on leash" for them, a wait that past history suggests will be a long one.

I

□□□□□□□□□□□□□□□□□□□□□□□□□□□□□

Introduction: Women and
Fictions of the State

[S]ince the dawn of feminism, and certainly before, the political activity of exceptional women, and thus in a certain sense of liberated women, has taken the form of murder, conspiracy and crime.

—Julia Kristeva, *Kristeva Reader,* 204

[W]hen a subject is highly controversial . . . one cannot hope to tell the truth. . . . Fiction here is likely to contain more truth than fact.

—Virginia Woolf, *A Room of One's Own,* 4

One of the most interesting areas annexed by the post-war novel is the area of the woman's novel. . . . Women today, women writers today, are living lives that are very different from those of their nineteenth-century counterparts, more different than the lives of Snow and Amis from the life of Trollope. . . .

—Margaret Drabble, "Mimesis," 7

Some people think a woman's novel is anything without politics in it.

—Margaret Atwood, "Women's Novels," 29

L iterature in the western canon offers relatively few stories about women and the state. Moreover, if one identifies in any way with the women characters in these narratives, most of them make unsavory reading. In classical Greek drama women who became embroiled with the state usually died. At Aulis and in Thebes, Iphigenia and Antigone showed what could happen to women when the needs of the state conflicted with the bonds of the family. Only in the comic world of Aristophanes did women move to mold state policy to their wills— and even then they succeeded mainly by relying on their sexuality.

That same sexuality, however, also destroyed the few female rulers of the state who strayed into early literature. Misled by passion, Virgil's Dido and Shakespeare's Cleopatra, capable and canny queens both, perished for love. Their wicked female counterparts who preferred ambition, ruthless rulers manqué like Lady MacBeth, fared no better in their stories. Even a good queen like Hecuba, whose nineteen sons and daughters became in the Trojan world of war an exponential example of women's state service through reproduction, ended as, literally, a dead bitch.

The worlds of epic poetry and classical and Shakespearean drama thus offered a few women of the ruling class narrative space in which to die. The advent of the novel wrought a slight democratic expansion of that space. The new genre allowed women from the middle and lower classes also to suffer at the hands of the state, although there were still not very many of them. Moll Flanders in Newgate, Hester Prynne on the scaffold, and Tess of the D'Urbervilles were typical, but Madame DuFarge showed that the novel was not entirely alien space for women in state service. However, DuFarge is the exception rather than the rule, and even she came to a bad end. Although punishment was the norm when eighteenth- and nineteenth-century novelists brought women into contact with the state, in contrast to the portrayals in earlier literature, female characters in these novels often survived their encounters with state power. Nevertheless, only in the late twentieth-century novel did the majority of women characters who dealt with state power live and, on occasion, thrive.

This rapid summary obviously reflects schematic oversimplifications. Yet even when one moves beyond canonical novels to include a wider selection, the portrayals of the relationships between women and the state remain predominantly negative until the later twentieth century. It was not until the mid-twentieth century that a major woman novelist emerged who made women and state politics central in a number of her narratives. But Doris Lessing ultimately left such politics behind as a subject, moving into the realm of science fiction. Ever the pioneer, Lessing presaged the proliferation of feminist speculative fiction, particularly utopias and dystopias, among late twentieth-century women writers.[1]

Although dystopias have tended to predominate, reflecting the negative relationship between women and the state that characterized the novel from its beginnings, a number of the utopias reflected what Kathleen B. Jones has termed a "woman-friendly polity" ("Citizenship" 781).

Utopian novels in which women play central roles in egalitarian states where traditional gender constraints are removed offer intriguing political possibilities for the future—and very few connections with the present. Functioning as contemporary myths of women's empowerment, these novels elide history. Government is absent or minimal in them (Russ, "Recent" 73). Seldom does any text satisfactorily explain how the given utopia emerged; the origins of the ideal states tend to be vague and sometimes ominous. Jael, the warrior in Joanna Russ's *The Female Man,* informs the other women that Whileaway developed not from a plague that killed all males but from women's struggles: "I and the war I fought built your world for you, I and those like me, we gave you a thousand years of peace and love and the Whileawayan flowers nourish themselves on the bones of the men we have slain" (211; cf. Marks and de Courtivron 119). Both within and outside of the texts, the gap between the woman-friendly politics of the utopias and the contemporary state and its historical antecedents is wide.

Less of a gap is apparent in some other contemporary novels that deal with women and the state. Among these, a number of critics have contrasted novels written by women in the late 1960s and the 1970s with women's novels from the 1980s on. The precise dates and details chosen by individual critics to differentiate the two sets of novels vary, and most of them admit the permeability of their divisions.[2] Nevertheless, the basic terms of the binary are similar in all of them. The novels of the late 1960s and 1970s are almost always termed "feminist novels," while the later fiction is described in terms of its retreat from direct engagement with feminist concerns. For example, Deborah Rosenfelt and Gayle Greene call the novels of the 1980s and after "postfeminist,"[3] while Maria Lauret labels them "backlash fictions" (165).

Many of the characteristics that critics adumbrate to contrast the two sets of novels have little direct connection with traditional state politics. The closest correlations are in attitudes toward the roles of political action and the prospects for social change. Critics note the optimism and the utopianism, along with the direct political engagement, in the novels of the 1970s. Rosenfelt is typical in describing them as marked by ultimate triumph, with plots of salvation that narrate "the feminist dream, the myth of a progress toward liberation surely attainable within the immediate future" (287). Lauret analyzes their powerful "oppositional cultural practice" and their strong engagement with the women's movement (7, 88). Militancy marks these novels. Tracing the powerful "mythography" of lesbian novels of the period, Bonnie Zimmerman notes that these works "seriously propose that Lesbian Nation must be established through armed struggle" (*SS* 207, 64). The close connections with the community that Zimmerman emphasizes in these novels (207) were typical of most novels written by women during the period.

In contrast to the visionary optimism and political engagement of the feminist novels, women's novels of the 1980s are marked by a retreat from feminist concerns and from any kind of community. Elinor Langer writes that in these novels "Not only ideology but society itself is oddly absent" (35). Greene accuses the later novelists of "losing sight of the connections between individual and collective" in the "privatization and depoliticization of their concerns" and their "resignation to things as they are" (200–1). Zimmerman, too, emphasizes the turn from "community and triumph" to "loss, compromise, and accommodation" (*SS* 209). All of the critics describe the novels of the 1980s as marked by ambiguities and contradictions.

The loss of political immediacy and engagement in the 1980s novels obviously reflects the increasingly conservative political climate of the period, the ebbing of second-wave feminist confidence, and the turn by many women from direct political action to individual and cultural concerns.[4] Rosenfelt points out that these novels implicitly find feminist analysis "insufficient as an account of the diversity of women's experiences or naively optimistic about the possibilities for change, given the disheartening evidence in the eighties of patriarchy's staying power" (270). One result is a greater tendency toward certain kinds of realism in the postfeminist novels. Katherine Payant describes these novels as offering "an accurate reflection of the lives and consciousnesses of many women in the 1980s" (214). Redeploying some distinctions drawn by Elayne Rapping can suggest the different levels of realism functioning in the two sets of novels. Because the early novels remain focused primarily on "gender relations as power struggle," they are generally not concerned with portraying "the myriad other forces and factors which define female life in modern times" (13). It is these other contexts on which the different realisms characteristic of the postfeminist novels are focused. Even Rosenfelt, whose valorization of and nostalgia for the feminist novels is clear, admits a greater "complexity of vision" in the postfeminist works (280).

One of the things that most critics do not say is that on the whole, the postfeminist novels tend to be more skillfully crafted than the feminist ones. The purity of the politics in the feminist models is seldom matched by the literary artistry of their prose. Awkward plotting, particularly the overuse of melodrama, abounds, and too often the characters are cardboard, stereotyped with men as villains and women as victims. In many of them, art retreats before propaganda, one of many reasons why some of the feminist novels played important roles in the early women's movement.[5] Substantially less satisfying in politically feminist terms, the postfeminist novels offer more artistic complexity and, in general, smaller gaps between the texts and actual contemporary politics.

Because of this artistic complexity and realism, this study focuses on selected examples of the novels of the 1980s and 1990s. I begin in 1981 with Margaret Atwood's *Bodily Harm,* a transitional novel that queries the optimism of early feminist politics even while reflecting it in other ways. The other three novels—Nadine Gordimer's *A Sport of Nature* (1987), Paule Marshall's *Daughters* (1991), and Margaret Drabble's *The Gates of Ivory* (1991)—fall solidly into the postfeminist category. The artistic complexity of all of these novels is important for this study because my primary purpose is literary, to offer a series of analyses of one element in these texts: their representations of relationships between women and the state.

The differently focused realism of the postfeminist novels as opposed to the feminist ones is also useful for my purposes because analyses of these novels in terms of state politics have ramifications for feminist theory. Many of the novels of the late 1960s and 1970s have close connections to various feminist theories. The direct reflections of Shulamith Firestone's work in Marge Piercy's *Woman on the Edge of Time* are the most obvious example, but there are a number of others. With the postfeminist novels, however, establishing connections to theory is often more difficult, particularly in the cases of novelists and theorists who deal with women's relationships to the state. These difficulties create salutary barriers against a Procrustean tendency too common in feminist literary studies: appropriating attractive concepts from feminist theory and slapping them wholesale on unsuspecting literary texts. But the distances between the available theory and the novels can be puzzling as well as frustrating. As Paul Veyne has noted, "A theory is only the summary of a plot" (118). Contemporary women novelists and feminist theorists have emplotted very different stories about women and the state.

Feminist theoretical writers reflect gaps reminiscent of those in the feminist utopias between the future politics they envision and the politics that exist now. Many of these gaps occur because of what Ann Snitow terms the "central feminist divide," which she locates "between the need to build the identity 'woman' and give it solid political meaning and the need to tear down the very category 'woman' and dismantle its all-too-solid history" ("Gender" 9). Although Snitow analyzes the divide in most of the major binaries that historically have marked feminism, from equality vs. difference to social constructionism vs. essentialism (14–16, 19, 24), the place in which it most persistently surfaces is in the split between theory and activism. Over fifteen years ago Jane Marcus wrote that the division between practice and theory was "the most serious issue facing feminist critics today" (218), and her statement is just as true now.[6] This persisting division has serious ramifications for feminism and the state.

It is a commonplace of most feminist theory that theory and practice must go together. Nevertheless, again and again theorists find themselves in the position of admitting that their political formulations are inadequate for or inapplicable to current politics. For example, in the midst of questioning why "the very category, the subject, . . . that is supposed to be presumed for the purpose of solidarity, produces the very factionalization it is supposed to quell," Judith Butler halts to insist that "Within feminism, it seems as if there is some political necessity to speak as and for *women,* and I would not contest that necessity." Butler continues: "Surely, that is the way in which representational politics operates, and in this country, lobbying efforts are virtually impossible without recourse to identity politics. So we agree that demonstrations and legislative efforts and radical movements need to make claims in the name of women." With that bow to practical politics, she then proceeds with her argument about the need to "deconstruct the subject of feminism" in order to "release the term into a future of multiple significations" ("Contingent" 14–16). Butler's brief textual swerve into and out of practical politics is a reflection of the gap that exists between prevailing theoretical constructions of women as subjects and current feminist politics.

Here, as in so many areas of contemporary feminist theory, Butler represents the rule, not the exception. Similar rhetorical moves constantly reappear as increasingly complex analyses of the indeterminacy of "woman" coexist uneasily with a "strategic essentialism" considered good enough for political purposes but hopelessly outdated in theory.[7] Basically, the theorists are urging action on the basis of premises that they prove are false—a contemporary political rendition of the Platonic "noble lie." Like all strategies of condescension, this rhetoric reinforces extant hierarchies (Thompson 52),[8] in this case the implicit valorization of theory over practice. The resulting gap—what Teresa de Lauretis describes in another context as the contradiction between "the positivity of political action, on one front, and the negativity of critical theory, on the other" (*Technologies* 36)—has been lauded as a productive tension by some theorists.[9] Nevertheless, just as in the feminist utopias, the theoretical texts postulate positions far beyond any politics we know without much specific indication of how to bridge the gaps between those positions and the present.

In any discourse gaps between theory and practice are inevitable. But in the case of woman as political subject, at the moment the hiatus is particularly wide. In the abstract, feminist theory is clear about the kind of politics it wants. Certain adjectives recur in feminist political descriptions: "decentralized"; "egalitarian"; "antihierarchical" or "nonhierarchical"; "participatory"; "collective"; "pluralist." Significantly, these adjectives could not be used to describe any currently existing governmental system. Feminist goals, however praiseworthy, are similarly distant from current state formations. Typical formulations, which could be replicated at length, include:

> [A] radically democratic polity which also furthers the values of ecology, nonmilitarism, and solidarity of peoples.
>
> —Benhabib, "Feminism" 30

> [D]ecentered organizations in which the grassroots units are connected and coordinated within a federated structure through the selection of delegates from below.
>
> —K. E. Ferguson, *FCB* 211

> [A] state that facilitates nurturing instead of one that promotes the sovereign self.
>
> —Boris 20

> [T]he replacement of our current model of self-interested and antagonistic individualism with a model of community, "cooperative sociality," or "imaginative collectivity."
>
> —Miner and Longino 178

> [A] democratic polity that is respectful not just of our *interests* but of the fullness of our relationships and of our integrity as people.
>
> —Ackelsberg, "Communities" 309

Although many theorists can imagine rich political futures, most offer few connections with the present.[10]

Among the major forces blocking the way to the kind of future they envision is the contemporary nation-state. Here yet another gap in feminist theory occurs—indeed, a major absence. Complaints about the paucity of feminist theories connected with the state are ubiquitous.[11] In part feminist theorists are simply reflecting a larger academic trend. Linda Weiss points out that with a "few notable exceptions, the state was an analytical object which social scientists in the English-speaking world were trained either to ignore or to conceptualize in reductionist terms" (1). She writes that after a "long history of state trivialism," scholars are now pursuing a course of "state denial" (2).[12] But more than following academic fashion seems to be involved. Noting that not only contemporary theorists but the classic feminist writers from Simone de Beauvoir to Kate Millett seldom dealt with the state, Suzanne Franzway, Dianne Court, and R. W. Connell remark that "It is almost as if there were a motivated avoidance of the problem of the state" (27). Feminists have for years written a great deal on specific issues involving women and the state, from abortion and affirmative action to pornography and rape.[13] But the state itself remains seriously undertheorized.

The state is of course particularly resistant to theoretical treatment because of the multiplicity of state forms, their complexity, their historical differences, and their continuing evolutions and revolutions over time. The 1970s debates in anthropology over how the rise of the centralized state influenced women's status highlighted many of these issues.[14] Following Friedrich Engels, many argued that the state destroyed women's relatively equal status in earlier communally organized cultures. Sherry Ortner and other theorists insisted that women's status rose with more complex state formations. Still others saw the state as irrelevant, contending that the oppression of women was universal, cutting through state and nonstate cultures alike. These debates remain unresolved, although, as Irene Silverblatt notes, there is no longer any "unambiguously clear evolutionary narrative of women's degradation with the rise of the state" (141). Most contemporary theorists agree with Davina Cooper that the relationship between the state and women's status is "a contradictory one" (78, n. 18).

In many cases feminist theorists' neglect of the state has been due not to hesitancy before complexity but to deliberate choice. They intentionally avoid high politics. For example, Naomi Black writes that "as a political scientist I fear excessive concentration on the state, given what we know about the lack of autonomy and also the lack of representativeness of the state" (100). Jodi Dean promotes her discursive model of civil society by arguing that "it provides a conception of democracy no longer focused on the state" (9). Judith Allen's well-known essay "Does Feminism Need a Theory of 'The State'?" answers its titular question negatively, ending with the assertion that "There are more useful tasks to be done" (35). Other tasks can seem "more useful" partly because of the vast range of issues that contemporary feminism confronts, given its goal of a total transformation of society. Working to change cultural structures as well as human consciousness itself, the feminist movement has never been concerned only or even predominantly with gaining political power or redressing political grievances. In the millennial context of evolving a revolutionary new system of life, current states can seem merely superannuated forms, not worth the effort required to understand or change them. Of course, in the meantime, everyone has to live in them.

Aside from the sheer complexity of the issues, there are a number of other reasons for contemporary feminist theory's neglect of the state. Some of these, such as women's traditional outsider status in the political sphere and problems generated by conceptions of the personal as political, will be taken up in the next chapter. This section and the two next ones briefly review several other causes for feminist theoretical neglect of the state, including the historical patterns of women's political participation and prevailing intellectual trends that have shaped feminist and other contemporary theories.

Historically, women's political activism has flourished primarily in local rather than national venues. Indeed, studies have shown that at the grass-roots level, contemporary women's political participation is equal to that of men.[15] Oriented toward their immediate communities, women's activism has generally been ad hoc—limited in scope, improvisational, and short-term.[16] Women have usually been most successful politically when they organized in terms of single issues.[17]

Contemporary feminist politics have reflected all of these traditional patterns. Mary Fainsod Katzenstein points out that in the West, "significant sections of the feminist movement in every country have opted to ignore electoral politics at some cost to movement goals" ("Comparing" 13). The U.S. women's movement initially developed and had its major impact outside of mainstream politics.[18] Anne N. Costain emphasizes that second-wave successes were "largely independent of political resources, strong allies, or very effective political tactics" (*Inviting* xiv). European feminists began to consider existing political parties as possible venues for action only in the late 1970s.[19] Studies of feminist activism in West Germany and Great Britain have shown the continuing reluctance on the part of these women to deal with state politics.[20] A major exception to this widespread trend is Australia, where during the 1970s and early 1980s feminists increasingly worked at the state level. By the mid-1980s Franzway, Court, and Connell described feminist participation in the state as not only "extensive" but "accepted" (11); their official roles led to the new designation "femocrat." Canadian anglophone feminism, too, has been committed to action within state structures (Vickers 51).

Other operating characteristics of feminist politics also limited their impact on the state. Feminist ideals of participatory and communal politics, with leadership and decision making shared, work best with small groups and with specific and limited goals. However, as Jo Freeman notes, the ethic of participatory democracy does not give organizational efficiency. She writes that many feminists "accepted the ideology of 'structurelessness' without realizing the limitations of its uses" (*Politics* 119).[21] The large-scale organization imperative for effective intervention in the state has been difficult for feminists to justify in theory and sustain in practice. Iris Marion Young concedes that "feminists have developed little in the way of models of political organizing that can serve as alternatives to interest group bureaucracy, on the one hand, or the small personalized task group, on the other" ("Ideal" 301). The resulting weakness in institutional building left feminists with few formal resources for confronting the state. Nor in any case did a good many feminists want to do so.

In the particular case of the United States, divisions within the feminist movement from the beginning meant that a substantial amount of energy and creativity was never directed toward mainstream politics at the state level. Various early splits among liberal, socialist, and radical feminists in the late 1960s, followed by the gradual eclipse of the radicals by cultural feminism during the mid-1970s,[22] left mainly the liberal branch of the movement to contend with the state.

The rigid insistence of many forms of socialist and radical feminism that all cooperation with current power is necessarily co-optation discouraged feminist interventions in the state. As Ti-Grace Atkinson explained, radical feminists refused to deal with state politics because in a democracy they saw only two options: "to be an accomplice or to be a revolutionary." Atkinson was more honest than many in acknowledging the paralysis produced by this binary. She admitted that such radical absolutism left little possibility for individual action: "[I]n order to avoid either having blood on our hands or blood on our heads, [we] deny that we as individuals *can,* much less *ought,* to do anything at all" (118). Although the desire for radical change does not necessarily preclude working for current reform, deradicalization was considered inevitable in any entry into traditional politics. Hester Eisenstein has noted how Australian femocrats working within the state were disdained by many radical activists ("Femocrats" 89). Feminists from Charlotte Bunch to Diana Fuss have questioned the rigid binary maintained by too many feminists between revolution and reform,[23] but their voices have remained in the minority.

The result of the prevailing equivalence of participation in traditional politics with co-optation was a focus of radical feminist efforts at the individual or community level rather than in the state. As early as 1975 Karen Kollias complained that instead of attacking power structures, the women's movement was focusing mainly on "sex-role oppression, consciousness raising, and supportive services" (133).[24] The drift toward cultural feminism in the mid- to late 1970s and its predominance in the 1980s exacerbated such tendencies, as did the national political climate during that period. Joyce Gelb and Marian Lief Palley connect the growing fiscal conservatism and hostility toward affirmative action and civil rights in Washington with the general feminist move toward local rather than national politics (213).

A number of commentators have noted the blurring of boundaries between liberal and more radical forms of feminism that began in the late 1970s and has continued since that time.[25] Significantly, however, this convergence has taken place primarily among feminist activists. In the academy, another major site for the development of feminism,[26] more radical forms of feminism dominated. Very early in the second wave of feminist activism that began during the 1960s, theorists recognized and thoroughly analyzed the serious limitations of liberal political theory for feminism.[27] Thus liberal feminists have never been a vocal presence in the university, particularly among theorists, the most influential academic feminists. Judith Grant points out that "there are virtually no second wave liberal feminist theorists" (18).[28] As a result liberal feminism, the branch which both by ideology and by default was conducting much of feminism's business with the state, lacked theory for what it was doing.

Early second-wave feminist theory was generated from both Marxist/socialist and radical feminist stances. However, many later radical feminists turned away from formal theoretical writing.[29] Therefore, the great majority of academic theorists in both England and the United States now represent varieties of socialist feminism,[30] ranging from unreconstructed Marxism to radical democracy, the updated kinder, gentler version of socialism. Karl Marx, who viewed the state as the vehicle of ruling class interests, expected its demise and focused on political economy; he had no reason to theorize government in detail.[31] Socialist feminists, influenced also by the general antistatism of the New Left in the 1960s, tended to follow suit. The state as an object of academic theoretical study suffered accordingly.

This situation was exacerbated by the status of contemporary socialist feminism in the United States as almost entirely an intellectual endeavor, with few activists beyond the university. Karen V. Hansen and
Ilene J. Philipson date the turning point for the demise of the U.S. socialist feminist movement in 1975.[32] (Writing from a Canadian perspective, Lorna Weir notes the same "strongly academic and weakly activist
formation of socialist feminism" in England as in the United States [93],
but this conflation understates continuing English socialist feminist activism.) One result, as numerous commentators have noted, was that
feminist academic theory became increasingly separated from the political practice of the women's movement.[33] Hansen and Philipson write
that with the waning of the activism from which socialist-feminist writing originated, much of the theory became "more abstract and removed
from the realities of present-day life in the United States" (25). As this
kind of intellectual elitism spread, few commentators on feminist politics
failed to decry these developments, which were not limited to the
United States. Noël Sturgeon is typical in complaining of the "invisible
moat" created by feminist theory between "its most sophisticated and
complex political critiques and various kinds of social movement practices" (6–7).

Actually, Sturgeon's "moat" is not really "invisible." It is clearly reflected in the rhetorical gaps between future political vision and current
politics in the passage from Butler analyzed earlier and equally apparent
in other theorists. And "moat" is probably not the best metaphor for the
division; it is more like a chasm. This theory-practice split is particularly
problematical at the state level in the West, where a predominantly socialist feminist theory confronts political circumstances in which liberal
feminism is the only viable activist option. Zillah R. Eisenstein points
out that what now remains of "the women's movement's visibility are
multiple liberal feminist agencies and lobbying groups." Noting that
"most feminist national strategy today remains liberal feminist," Eisenstein emphasizes that "women are still forced to turn to the liberal reforms that can affect their lives in dealing with their everyday problems"
(*Radical* xv, 197).

Ultimately, most commentators will acknowledge, however grudgingly, that feminists must deal not only with future possibilities but also
with the public world as it currently exists.[34] At this point that public
world at best will respond to liberal politics, not radical initiatives.[35] Ann
Snitow describes the resulting feminist dilemma: "It's not that we haven't
gotten beyond classical liberalism in theory but that in practice we cannot *live* beyond it" ("Gender" 27). Alice Jardine terms it always "working
at two speeds." She writes that she finds herself functioning as a liberal

within her own university context to change the institution, while "every term of [her] daily practice is put into question" in her research. She admits that "any feminist working within a Western context and who is attempting to change things at whatever speed or at whatever level has to somewhat identify with the liberal tradition" (qted. in H. Eisenstein, *Gender* 69). What this identification should be, and its ramifications, remain almost entirely untheorized. Kathy Ferguson points out the need to evaluate liberal reforms on the basis of their ability to challenge rather than simply extend the status quo (*FCB* 180), but feminists have yet to begin theorizing the grounds for such differentiations.

Splits between liberals and radicals have historically damaged the women's movement. Emma Goldman, for example, dismissed women's suffrage as irrelevant (Falk 81–82). The liberal-radical division, which resurfaced with particular virulence when much of early second-wave feminism embraced the hostility to liberalism characteristic of the political radicalism of the 1960s (Echols, "Nothing" 459), continues to flourish in the academy today. There liberal feminism remains under fire on personal as well as political grounds,[36] as degrees of individual radicalness are painstakingly calibrated. Precisely why so many academic feminists place a premium on the radical label remains unclear, although like most academics, who today have minimal political influence, they may be seeking to compensate with the virulence of their political purity for their lack of actual political impact. This academic recension of the longtime radical-liberal split is especially pernicious—and pointless—at a time when even the best theorists like Butler and Jardine are admitting that practical political action requires liberalism. In terms of politics at the state level, Hester Eisenstein connects the prevalence of the "more radical than thou" stance among feminists with their failure to understand "the strategic importance of feminist intervention in the state apparatus" (*Gender* 25).

No one expects theoretical physicists in the academy to produce working bicycles, and at one level it is past time for academic feminist theorists to admit that what they do is not directly tied to everyday political practice. But the refusal of most to do so[37] is not simply a laudable desire to maintain the connections with the activist movement out of which academic feminism developed and a recognition of the vital contemporary importance of feminist politics in the larger world. The current gaps between theory and practice suggest that from the beginning, feminists were right to insist on a dialectical relationship between the two. Dealing with the state in particular requires input from both theorists and activists. A major problem has been that both lacked the necessary practical experience with the state. Neither had working knowledge of state institutions. Even in Australia, where the femocrats have extensive experience with the state, feminist activists have produced little theory.[38]

❑   ❑   ❑

For theorists, the general lack of interest in the state that historically characterized activist radical feminism and academic socialist feminism was encouraged by prevailing intellectual trends. Whatever the specific political allegiances of academic feminist theorists, with very few exceptions the major ones are overwhelmingly postmodernists and/or poststructuralists.[39] In postmodern theory fragmentation ruled as interest turned to the local, the decentered, the particular, and the margins. High politics were left behind along with discredited master narratives. What Nancy Hartsock and others have criticized as the "anemic" politics of postmodernism ("Postmodernism" 16) also discouraged interest in the state in some theoretical quarters. Among various prevailing critical emphases in feminist and other theory that have contributed to the neglect of the state, three major ones are Foucauldian concerns with micropolitics, the focus on discourse, and the prevalence of psychoanalytic theory.

Michel Foucault set out to correct Hobbes's political emphasis, to "eschew the model of Leviathan in the study of power" (*P/K* 102; see also 97). He believed that "the representation of power has remained under the spell of monarchy": "In political thought and analysis, we still have not cut off the head of the king" (*History* 88–89). In his work he proceeded to perform just such a decapitation by analyzing localized power networks—the "micro-physics of power"; the "capillary form of power"; the "micro-relations of power" (*DP* 26; *P/K* 39, 199). Foucault was also concerned that focusing primarily on the state meant that power was viewed only as repressive and defined in terms of prohibition; he preferred to emphasize power as both relational and productive. Foucault's enormous influence shaped many fields as scholars abandoned the state to deal primarily with micropolitical concerns. Judith Walkowitz notes that feminists in particular found his "decentered, localized understanding of power in many ways compatible with the decentered, localized insights of second-wave feminism" (29).

In their rush into Foucauldian micropolitics, scholars sometimes forgot that Foucault himself fully recognized the significance of the state. He repeatedly emphasized that he did not intend "in any way to minimise the importance and effectiveness of State power" (*P/K* 72; see also 60, 122). Among contemporary manifestations of power, he ranked the state as "the most important," noting that "in a certain way all other forms of power relation must refer to it" ("Afterword" 224).[40] In addressing decentralized power networks, he was simply trying to correct errors that had arisen from earlier theorists' overly exclusive state foci.

The emphasis on language and discourse in contemporary criticism, fueled by Foucault as well as by deconstructive theorists, also contributed to theoretical neglect of the state. Seyla Benhabib complains that "Contemporary feminism has shifted its attention from social analysis to discourse analysis, from power itself to the politics of its representation." Although she emphasizes that each mode must inform the other, she warns that "from the perspective of discourse analysis macroinstitutions like the state, the economy, the legal system, and international relations tend to disappear and are replaced by 'micro' practices the sum of which does not add up to these larger wholes" ("On Contemporary" 370).

Theoretical analyses of the state as a major site and producer of discursive practices have made vital contributions, for such practices are obviously fundamental in state construction and operation. The problem with criticism's discursive focus, as with the emphasis on micropolitics inspired by Foucault, was not that these approaches were wrong, but that their predominance frequently occluded equally important concerns. Invoked to correct intellectual overemphasis on one dimension, they replicated it in another. Predominantly linguistic concerns repeatedly subsumed the social and historical dimensions of discourse. Typical were overstatements such as "*The* project of modern feminism . . . is to bring more female experience into the net of language" (Ireland 137, emphasis added). Eager expectations that linguistic freedom alone would suffice as a liberatory force failed to take into account the "highly mediated" effects of language on relations of domination (Flax, *Disputed* 141). In addition, as Wendy Brown points out, "discursive power is legitimating or coercive power, not liberating power" (*MP* 197). Those with excessive confidence in language as an agent of political change sometimes neglected its role as a precondition, treating it simply as an end in itself.[41]

In the realm of the state, poststructuralist treatments of language as a component of political power have too often been reductive. Frederick Crews castigates Roland Barthes, Jacques Derrida, and Foucault himself for conflating "quasi-libidinal linguistic play with political liberty, as if a carnival of unconstrained textuality could somehow serve as a proxy for the actual release of oppressed social groups from neglect and exploitation" (xix). Indeed, those who actually exercise power in contemporary states seldom share the confidence many theorists have in the political efficacy of language. Sergei Kovalyov, a former political prisoner who is now a Russian human rights commissioner, touched on the issue in discussing those who committed human rights violations in Chechnya. He commented in an interview:

> "I knew these people before, in places like the Interior Ministry police, and they cannot change suddenly. . . . At the start, they swore there would be no more inhuman persecution, especially for political reasons. They swore we were now becoming a law-abiding state. But it's the same people. That is the terrible thing. *You cannot remake an entire country with words.*" (Remnick 49, emphasis added)

Although some feminist critics objected to the privileging of symbolic struggles over social ones through "discursive reductionism" (Ebert 40),[42] micropolitical and discursive foci were enormously appealing to many academics as a compensatory form of political activity. At a time when their own extramural authority was negligible, language at least was amenable to the kinds of power that intellectuals could exert, particularly after deconstructive methods had significantly enhanced that power.

Finally, Paulina Palmer describes the split between politics and psychoanalysis as "one of the chief problems confronting feminism at the moment, one which shows little sign of achieving a satisfactory solution" (162). The centrality of psychoanalytic approaches in much feminist theoretical work has tended to divert attention from the state. Rosalind Coward states flatly that "psychoanalysis has nothing to say about the workings of the state, the economy and politics as they are traditionally conceived." Implicitly conceding her overstatement, however, she adds that as a theory and practice psychoanalysis has "implications" for these areas, although she goes on to recommend critiques that displace traditional conceptions of the political ("Sexual" 186). Various feminist theorists have pointed out the political problems produced by the isolation of the psychic from the social in psychoanalytic thought and its support of the patriarchal social order.[43] Jean Bethke Elshtain, for example, sees feminist psychoanalytic theorists as unwittingly constructing "a patina of defenses against politics": "Political history gets overassimilated to domestic dynamics and family history" ("Feminist Discourse" 618).[44]

At the same time that Foucauldian, discursive, and psychoanalytical emphases were leading some critics to abandon analysis of the state, others turned away from it because of contemporary historical developments. Today many assert the increasing irrelevance of the state, as nations dissolve into tribalism or are subsumed into multinational political or economic formations, particularly corporate ones. But those penning the state's obituary may be premature. In the case of the "stateless corporations and borderless finance" postulated by theorists of globalization, for example, Weiss argues that globalization has actually in crucial instances been advanced through nation-states and that the two kinds of power currently may be reinforcing each other. While admitting that states face new constraints on their policymaking, she finds contemporary states remarkably adaptable as they evolve to maintain their functions (189, 195, 204).[45] Even those like Stuart Hall, who see a "decline or erosion" of the nation-state, usually concede its continuing contemporary importance.[46] Others committed to decentering the state in their work find it an annoyingly resilient form. Warren Magnusson admits that such "decentering moves have had remarkably little effect on the way we—not just ordinary people and workaday social scientists, but the great social thinkers themselves—tend to think about social, political, and economic phenomena" (71).[47] Magnusson finds this pervasive difficulty in thinking beyond the state "testimony indeed to the power of statist categories" (71).

Feminist writers are also starting to recognize that the state remains a major focus of power, too strong and ubiquitous to be ignored with impunity.[48] Anna Yeatman concedes that "the administrative state is here to stay" (*Bureaucrats* 39), while Cynthia Adcock locates "the ultimate power of patriarchy [in] the organized, legitimized violence of the nation-state" (210). Franzway, Court, and Connell insist that "For practical politics the state is not just important, it is unavoidable," and emphasize that feminist political strategies will depend on how states are theorized (x; see also 54, 129). Wendy Brown concurs that the state "mediates or deploys almost all the powers shaping women's lives," noting that "*male* social power and the production of female subjects appears to be increasingly concentrated in the state" (*SI* 194). In the case of women of color, Chandra Mohanty points out that state institutions usually mediate their relationships to white men, and thus any feminist politics requires dealing with this mediation ("Introduction" 11). No one expects one universal theory of *the* state to emerge, but a consensus is forming that theoretical studies of historical states, their systems, and their operations are crucial in understanding the power relations of gender. Recognizing the difficulties in failing to theorize high politics, the state-centered realm, feminist theorists recently have turned to focus on it.

As theoretical attention shifts, and while theorists are in the process of evolving paradigms, literary representations can play a role in focusing attention on the relationships between women and the state. Contemporary women novelists are depicting these relationships in various ways that raise questions and highlight issues with which any effective feminist theory of the state will ultimately have to grapple. Although political theory cannot be generated directly from these novels, they can indicate some useful parameters for such theory.

Most of the great historical changes that the novel both reflected and helped to create, such as the rise of capitalism and the development of a restricted and feminized domestic sphere, led generally to a generic emphasis on private concerns. Although the novel has been connected with empirical and ideological elements ranging from questions of truth and virtue to the shifting parameters of factual and fictional fields and of canonical and non-canonical discourse, it has tended to mediate these concerns mainly through the stories of individuals and their personal lives.[49]

The many formal dislocations of the postmodern novel are of course altering this traditional perspective. But women writers have by and large remained loyal to realistic modes and techniques, even in their speculative fictions.[50] When they write of women and the state, their stories remain focused in terms of representations of everyday reality. They depict the high politics of the state in quotidian contexts, rendering the lived experiences of such politics in individual lives. Thus the kinds of insights that novels can offer to current discussions are in certain ways limited both because of their form—the ideological occlusions of realistic literary conventions—and because of their content, their focus on the particular, the local, and the everyday. At the same time, however, as long as such limitations are recognized, the restricted content of the novels is also their uniquely important contribution to the debates. It is these limitations, for example, that highlight the limitations of the efficacy of politics.

In discussing kinds of history, Claude Lévi-Strauss differentiated between "low-powered history," such as biographical and anecdotal accounts that are rich in information and weak in explanation, and "histories of progressively greater 'power,'" which schematize the information offered in lower-powered forms, first putting it in the background and finally eliminating it entirely. Noting that at each level "the historian loses in information what he gains in comprehension or vice versa," he points out that the historian's choice is "between history which teaches us more and explains less, and history which explains more and teaches less." The "logic of the concrete" that Lévi-Strauss connects with low-powered history, which "considers individuals in their particularity and details for each of them the shades of character, the twists and turns of their motives, the phases of their deliberations" (261–62), also characterizes novels.

Lévi-Strauss noted that one cannot reconstitute a complete history by successively dovetailing lower-powered histories into histories of higher power. Emphasizing the integrity of each separate historical domain, he writes that "any gain on one side is offset by a loss on the other" (261). In the absence of a body of theory on women and the state, some of the knowledge conveyed via the "logic of the concrete" in novels can illuminate aspects of the practical political concerns that create the gaps in Butler and other theorists. Martha Nussbaum points out that "It seems appropriate . . . for any form of collective action to bear in mind, as an ideal, the full accountability to the needs and particular circumstances of the individual that the novel recommends, in its form as well as its content" (71). The novels could be described in a sense as offering useful Derridean supplements to theory, both supplementing theoretical abstraction with their "logic of the concrete" and simultaneously substituting their particularity for its more encompassing formulations. Within the continuing interplay between the two dimensions, as the supplement adds and the substitute replaces, some of the difficulties that theorists must address can emerge from analysis of the novelists' accounts.

Aristotle's separation of the political realm from the domestic and long-term traditional theoretical acceptance of the distinction have come to reflect a crucial psychological truth in terms of the ways that western life has historically been perceived. As Wendy Brown notes, "Politics and manhood thrive in the realm of the 'extraordinary,' above the realm of ordinary life and cares, routine needs, human necessity" (*MP* 183). The realm of "ordinary life," in contrast, is the domain of the novel, which, not coincidentally, has from the beginning been connected with women, who themselves have traditionally been associated with "routine needs" and "human necessity." The majority of early English novelists were women, as were the novel's readers; moreover, several contemporary theorists find a female subjectivity central to or inherent in the novel.[51] The relationships of women, both historical and fictional, to the production and the reception of the novel are complex, and literary theorists and historians are only beginning to analyze women's roles in the emergence and development of the genre.[52]

In addition to divergent values, in terms of perceptions of the public and the private, two different time scales are involved. E. M. Forster long ago wrote that the novel centers on "life in time" (28–29, 41), giving additional impetus to its generally private emphases. For the public sphere, Vaclav Havel notes that "political time is different from everyday time": "Nothing can be assessed in politics immediately; everything unfolds at its own speed" (90). Thus as a topic in novels, high politics enters a literary context primarily composed of elements that traditionally have been considered alien to it, particularly domestic time and values.

This novelistic juxtaposition of the two realms that Aristotle's theory separated highlights some barriers feminists face to wide public acceptance of their theoretical approaches to politics, along with difficulties in the theories themselves. For example, at the level of state politics, feminist insistences that the personal is the political are interrogated by the representations in these novels, as the writers reflect the vast distance between the state politics and the women's lives that they depict. Certain difficulties in integrating the perspectives of this sophisticated theory into the everyday rounds of many women's lives emerge clearly.

Almost 250 years ago Samuel Johnson expressed the sense of incommensurability between high politics and diurnal routine in one of his couplets: "How small of all that human hearts endure, / That part which laws or kings can cause or cure" (*Poems* 356). Johnson could perhaps be dismissed as a retrograde high Tory by contemporary radical theorists. But Jesse Jackson cannot, and he speaks similarly: "Because, get right down to it, most people's lives [are] not about ideology, left wing, right wing, any of that—they hurt, hope, rejoice mostly about the same personal things. For instance, feel good when their children are growing up right, don't want broken hearts because their children went astray" (Frady 57).

Prevailing intellectual trends, particularly the thoroughgoing politicization characteristic of contemporary criticism and the anti-essentialism central to current theoretical approaches dominated by emphasis on human differences, do not favor Johnson's and Jackson's viewpoints. For many, their words are simply reflections of their own or others' false consciousness. Such critics can easily show, for example, that how children grow up is determined in crucial ways by the access that the prevailing ideology allows them to have to education, medical care, a safe environment, and other privileges. These critics would be correct, although intellectual accuracy is not necessarily the determining factor in matters of politics. Moreover, as with Foucauldian micropolitics and discursive foci, problems result from compensatory overemphasis. An alternative view would suggest that the ubiquitous politicization of criticism has obscured dimensions of human experience that can be treated most effectively not—or at least not only—in political terms, and that the single-minded focus on differences characteristic of feminist and postmodern theory for almost two decades obscures crucial similarities among human beings.

Finally, the consciousness depicted by Johnson and Jackson, whether false or not, is that of the majority of western people. To dismiss it out of hand is to dismiss the way that most people live their lives and to denigrate what most people value; the arrogance of such dismissals in part explains the continuing problems that Marxism and feminism have had in gaining widespread acceptance in the West. As Sheila Radford-Hill notes, "Movements that are too far ahead of the people are always elitist and often reactionary" (166).[53] The widespread perspective represented in Johnson's and Jackson's words must be dealt with by any theorists who want to connect the political power of the contemporary state with individual lives. In their different ways the eighteenth-century writer and the twentieth-century political activist emphasize the human perceptions of reality to which any effective politics, which shapes and is shaped by those perceptions, must be related.

More than most revolutionary movements, feminism has from the beginning emphasized such human realities and tried to ground its theory and politics directly in them. Such connections became more tenuous as academic feminist theory became increasingly separated from movement practice. At the same time that the gap between theory and practice widened, as feminist theory began generally to "shift away from analysis of the actually existing world" (di Leonardo, *Gender* 37, n. 18), the prestige of theory increased exponentially, in part because it offered one of the few venues in which feminists continued to be successful. Alice Echols points out that since 1975 theoretical rather than political accomplishments have characterized feminism (*Daring* 293).[54] The result has been, as Judith Grant writes, that "in both Marxism and feminism, the importance of theory is exaggerated in the absence of a large, radical movement" (115). The stellar theoretical advances thus have been made at a time when theory and its academic practitioners have been increasingly detached from the everyday lives of most women.

Linda Nicholson writes of "the gap between the fantasies and images of Woman allowed to us and the complexities of the lives we lead" ("Introduction" 9).[55] Her point is the inadequacy of traditional conceptions of "Woman" to the lived experiences of contemporary women. Today, however, some feminist theories are creating "fantasies and images" of women that also can be distant from many contemporary women's experiences. This is the gap reflected in the rhetorical moves that Butler and other theorists have to make to exempt practical political actions from their theoretical constructions. Looking at how novels represent women and state politics, and particularly at their depictions of the distance between the two, provides a salutary reminder of some of the problems in prevailing perceptions of politics in current feminist theory.

Analyzing these novels also brings into question some other dominant beliefs in feminist and other contemporary theory. In the novels the split subject, in whom many theorists see great political potential, creates serious difficulties in the context of state politics. Similarly, the viability of subversion and quasi-guerilla tactics emerges as questionable, as do claims for maternal peace politics. The tendency of feminist theory to valorize outsider status—the nomad, the marginal individual—appears more dubious within larger formal political contexts. Some of these constructs are questioned in individual novels, while in other cases they recur in all the novels analyzed.

If contemporary novels about women and the state offer a "reality check" of sorts for feminist theory, it nevertheless remains a *literary* reality check. Nancy Miller writes that the plots of women's literature are not supposed to provide therapeutic solutions: "They are about the plots of literature itself, about the constraints . . . on rendering a female life in fiction" (*Subject to Change* 43). These constraints emerge with particular clarity in novels depicting the relationships between women and the state, where relatively few plot lines are currently being deployed. Moreover, these literary conventions have human consequences. While late twentieth-century criticism has abandoned reductive mimetic claims for literature, it has also left behind equally reductive denials of any connection between literature and life. Feminist critics have made persuasive cases for the powerful influences of contemporary fiction on both individuals and society, insisting that we learn about ourselves and our world through narratives.[56] In this connection much recent feminist criticism has moved to analyze what Patricia Yeager calls "emancipatory strategies" in women writers, particularly their subversion and disruption of old patterns to make way for new narratives.[57] The novelists in this study instead emphasize the strength and persistence of old patterns when women confront the state. If, as Carolyn Heilbrun writes, stories "serve as models" (*Writing* 37), they serve as negative and monitory models as well as empowering ones. In contemporary novels portraying women and the state, the paucity of plots and the persistent limitations of female agency that they represent remind us how far women have yet to go.

The four novelists for this study were chosen in part because all have achieved some popular success, along with considerable critical recognition. Atwood, Marshall, Gordimer, and Drabble enjoy international reputations. By now, a new novel by any of them is a major publishing event, with extensive press coverage and public interest; their works regularly appear on best-seller lists. At the same time, these authors are widely taught in universities, and a growing body of criticism exists on each. All of them would be included in the canon of contemporary literature that is gradually being shaped today in universities by informal consensus.[58] Their status both inside and outside of the academy suggests the accessibility of their stories to a relatively wide spectrum of the reading public. In addition, by now they all have been writing for a long time. Gordimer's first novel appeared in 1953; Marshall followed in 1959, Drabble in 1962, and Atwood in 1969. Their writings thus can claim the public validation reflected by satisfying a variety of readers over time, suggesting that what they say about women and the state has resonated in various ways in the popular and critical imagination.

Aesthetic criteria were also important in choosing these particular writers. Although the emphasis on literary excellence obviously stems partly from my own training, I also believe that complex literary texts most effectively render the ambiguities inherent in the difficult issues involved in representations of the relationships between women and the state. Feminist aesthetics continues to be a relatively underdeveloped area.[59] Early treatments of literary works too often valorized political progressiveness while disregarding formal considerations, and by the time some critics were ready to advance artistic claims, compelling arguments about the arbitrary, elitist, and culturally bound bases of aesthetic standards had emerged. But the fact that aesthetic criteria are historically contingent does not necessarily render them irrelevant or valueless. Michèle Barrett insisted well over a decade ago that we can "rehabilitate a category of objectively judged aesthetic value" in terms of the imagination and the skill displayed in works of art: "Within specific aesthetic forms and conventions we may be able to identify different levels of skill as well as the expression of particular fictional, or imaginative, constructions of reality" ("Feminism" 50, 52). Few theorists have developed Barrett's points, which offer intriguing possibilities for evaluating literary texts.

With these criteria in mind, I sought works with treatments of women and state politics that were marked by imaginative scope and constructed with a high level of literary craftsmanship—texts of formal complexity composed with artistic skill. Margaret Atwood's requirements for a successful novel suggest the basic parameters. She says that to be a success, a novel first has to hold the reader's attention and second "has to function on the level of the language in which it's composed." As Atwood puts it, "If the use of the language is terrible you're going to have a poor novel regardless of the consciousness it's reflecting or focusing" (Ingersoll 111). These formal requirements narrowed the field of novels for this study considerably. A number of contemporary novels by women—perhaps the majority—that treated high politics were awkwardly written, while many of the best women writers do not depict politics at that level in their works. In discussing recent lesbian fiction, for example, Zimmerman notes the absence of "overtly political fiction" (*SS* 226). In addition, because the feminist theory employed in this analysis is predominantly western and has proved most applicable to works produced from within that context, I limited this study to writers who were educated in the western literary tradition and who, whatever their varied cultural influences might be, wrote primarily out of that tradition.[60]

One limitation of this study for which I offer no apology is its focus mainly on middle-class women, both in terms of the characters in the novels and the novelists themselves. The whole question of the relationship of middle-class women to feminist activism needs some perspective. Juliet Mitchell long ago noted that "It is far too crude to claim in an unqualified way that the Women's Liberation Movement is middle-class, but this is always done" (*WE* 36; cf. "Reflections" 47). Those in positions to know the facts dispute such claims. As early as 1970, Robin Morgan was insisting that "the women's movement *is* diverse in class origins": "[A] large percentage of the movement comes from working-class backgrounds" (*Sisterhood* xxx-xxxi).[61] Almost two decades later, Catharine MacKinnon wrote that she had seen no "empirical documentation supporting the assertion that feminists are predominantly from, or currently of, the middle class" and that her own experience belied it (*Toward* 262, n. 27). Given the persistence of these claims of homogeneity, the question is just whose interests are being served by them. Significantly, some of the earliest attacks on feminism as bourgeois originated from male radicals of the 1960s, who were unhappy with women coworkers for asserting their own rights.[62] Since that time a number of other interests that in one way or another benefit from the status quo have found it advantageous to emphasize class divisions among women.

From the beginning, many voices spoke for inclusiveness in the women's movement. The *Redstockings Manifesto* of the late 1960s is typical:

> We identify with all women. We define our best interest as that of the poorest, most brutally exploited woman.
>   We repudiate all economic, racial, educational or status privileges that divide us from other women. (Morgan, *Sisterhood* 600)

Most early feminist theory was inclusive, whatever its shortcomings in practice. Many of the critiques by lesbians and women of color that broadened the women's movement were launched on the basis of the movement's own claims about itself and its goals.

These theoretical ideals in no way excuse those in the early move-ment who did not live up to them. Their failures to see beyond the con-cerns of middle-class women and white women were grievous errors that never should have been committed. But they are also errors for which many feminists have continued to try to make amends, in some cases for almost three decades now. The only true reparation remains the ongoing progress toward greater inclusiveness that is a hallmark of most current feminisms. Remembering the past is of crucial importance to in-sure that previous wrongs will not recur. But continuing recriminations against those who have admitted their mistakes and are trying to atone for them serve little purpose except fostering ill will. Ironically, many who would never patronize people because of their color feel free to condescend to others because of their class. Such behavior, as Christine Delphy notes in another context, suggests that "Many women (like most men) think that class outweighs gender" (*Close* 128).[63]

In the case of women and the state, the middle-class emphases of these novels are an important element of their realism. Historically, middle-class women have been advantageously positioned for political action. Mitchell notes that although the traditional contradiction "in the social relations between men and women [is] differently expressed in different societies and social classes," this contradiction "intensifies for the middle classes and makes them the first to focus on the issue" (*WLR* 102–3). This emergence of feminist consciousness in middle-class women is in part due to what Chantal Mouffe describes as their "contradictory inter-pellation," their situatedness as "subjects constructed in subordination by a set of discourses [who] are, at the same time, interpellated as equal by other discourses" ("Hegemony" 95).

The popular imagination often connects revolution with the lower classes, but in most cases this is a romanticization. Alison Jaggar points out that "historically, the middle class has always been a source of radical ideas, from liberalism to feminism to Marxism itself" (241). She notes the relatively privileged backgrounds of Karl Marx, Friedrich Engels, Vladimir Lenin, Leon Trotsky, and Mao Zedong; in this study, the Khmer Rouge leaders who haunt *The Gates of Ivory* were also from the middle class. Mitchell, too, emphasizes that revolutionary ideology is "likely *to come initially from within the ideologically dominant class,*" which in the cap-italist West has been the bourgeoisie (*WE* 34).[64] With the increasingly great disparities between incomes that have developed in the industrial-ized West, the major impetus for change has tended to emerge from the middle rather than the upper class.

The same position that heightens middle-class women's awareness of gender discrimination also allows them the means to fight it. Participation by the poor in formal political activity tends to be low.[65] Marilyn Frye notes that "revolution may in fact *be* something of a luxury—its moment is not to be found among the absolutely destitute" (*Willful* 28).[66] Freed from concern over obtaining the basic necessities for survival, women of the middle class have had resources to devote to political struggles. Their education, time, and energy were crucial in the first-wave women's rights activism of the later nineteenth and early twentieth centuries (Randall 215).[67] Like many of their second-wave successors, these women have been rightly criticized for opposing oppression only in terms of their own interests. At the same time, their contemporary critics have sometimes forgotten the lesson that early second-wave writers from Monique Wittig (16) to the Combahee River Collective emphasized: "[T]he most profound and potentially the most radical politics come directly out of our own identity, as opposed to working to end somebody else's oppression" (275).[68]

In general, E. Ann Kaplan points out that evaluating "white middle-class discourses is important as registering dominant social codes that in turn implicate (indeed themselves construct) other classes and ethnic groups" (184). In the case of the state, middle-class discourses predominate, whatever the actual class interests that are being served. To understand the state's inclusions and exclusions of women, it is necessary to deal with these discourses and their functions. Joanna de Groot and Mary Maynard write that "the current emphasis on diversity focuses attention away from a supposed norm to those who are different from it, without always making the norm visible and subject to critical scrutiny. We think it important to study privilege and how it works" (167). High politics is a venue that at this point demands this kind of study.

Finally, this book makes no claim to comprehensiveness in its analysis of the chosen novels. Its primary focus deliberately remains only on elements of high politics. Marshall, for example, claims in an interview that *Daughters* is "in many ways a meditation on language" (G & S), and the novel is certainly a stunning example of the "multivocality" that Mae Gwendolyn Henderson connects with black women writers (36). However, it is not from that perspective that I consider Marshall's novel, and central elements in the other novels are similarly omitted. What is admittedly lost in these areas, however, can perhaps be gained in the primary one. Because these novels have by and large not been read in terms of state politics, several of them have been taken to represent political successes for women. The focus on the state thus allows correction of some earlier critical misreadings. My intent was not to be encyclopedic or inclusive but to use novels that provided a range of representations of women's relation to the state. The chosen texts offer four very different cases, suggesting the variety of identities that women can currently assume in high politics.

Historically, women have generally been limited to two roles in state politics, that of witness or victim. From the time that Aphra Behn depicted colonial politics gone awry in *Oroonoko* (1688), female novelists also have reflected these two basic political identities for women. Women appear as victims of state politics, casualties of the public realm, to a greater or lesser extent in all of the novels in this study. All the novels also show women as witnesses, observing state processes without directly participating themselves. Although the historical significance of the role of witness can be large, and witnessing has often endowed women with moral stature, its impact on the state remains a heavily mediated one. Significantly, in *The Gates of Ivory* western women find it difficult even to witness effectively in the realm of international politics.

The other novels offer three contemporary options for female political identity beyond the witness and victim positions. The order in which the novels are analyzed here traces a movement from passivity to action, albeit in most cases limited action. The initial options range from victimhood within the state to subversion of the state, along a spectrum of increasingly efficacious activities. In *Bodily Harm* a woman becomes an active critic and subversive observer of state power, waiting with the potential for action. *Daughters* extends the range of action, depicting a woman as a subversive actor within the state, as occasional terrorist. Finally, Gordimer in *A Sport of Nature* portrays a woman as a direct participant in high politics. Ironically, that moment of greatest triumph for a woman in the state also relies on the most traditional and stereotypical female political behavior portrayed in any of the novels. I thus chose to end not with Gordimer but with Drabble, who poses questions not only about the roles of women in high politics, but also about the capacity of the novel as a genre to portray them.

Under prevailing protocols for much current feminist (and increasingly also literary) criticism, well before now I should have situated myself and my politics at length, up to and including a mini-autobiography. However, in my opinion one contribution that analyses of literary works might make to understanding the relationships between women and the state is to dilute and displace some of the autobiographical excess that has come to mark contemporary criticism. The resulting generic distancing could be salutary. Gérard Genette has noted that narrative inserted into discourse becomes discourse, while discourse inserted into narrative remains discourse (141). Autobiography functions similarly. In a sense it currently operates almost as a kind of master genre, a textual formation so powerful that it tends to dominate other narratives or discourses into which it is inserted. Late twentieth-century readers, whether of high deconstruction or *People* magazine, are autobiography junkies, and its Siren song drowns out other textual demands for our attention.

Samuel Johnson once claimed that "there has rarely passed a life of which a judicious and faithful narrative would not be useful" (*Rambler* 320). What is true for biography may not be as apropos for autobiographical literary criticism. Johnson himself of course produced classic combinations of biography and literary criticism, but in the case of autobiography some contemporary critics have not managed this volatile mixture so felicitously. For the purposes of this study, the most salient biographical details are the political opinions of the four authors on which it focuses, since these views have ramifications for their representations of women and the state. As background for analysis of their literary treatments, this and the next section survey their attitudes to situate them politically as well as artistically.

This study focuses on a white Jewish South African, an African American whose parents were Bajan immigrants, and two WASPs, one English and one Canadian. All of them share a basic commitment to some kind of progressive and liberatory politics. Beyond that commitment, their different backgrounds and experiences have given them varied attitudes toward women and state politics. In some cases the evolution of these attitudes can be traced over time; in others their views on specific issues have been recorded infrequently. All of these women highlight some of the potential difficulties for the artist in dealing with politics. Their attitudes on women, politics, art, and feminism—and various combinations thereof—show many similarities, along with important differences, particularly in the cases of Gordimer and Marshall.

All of the novelists considered have shown strong interests in national and often international politics, and with the exception of Drabble, each has at one time or another been actively involved in such politics. Marshall participated in the U.S. Civil Rights Movement in the 1950s and 1960s,[69] while Gordimer has long worked with antiapartheid groups in South Africa. Atwood, who has been very active in Amnesty International and other humanitarian and civil rights organizations, is constantly in the thick of contemporary political agitation of all kinds.[70] Even Drabble, who has not been active in organized politics, describes herself as someone who has "always been interested in social and political questions" (Lauritzen 245).[71]

Gordimer identifies herself as "socialist in my general outlook" (B & S 184). Drabble, who calls herself "a strong supporter of the Welfare State," wrote in 1970 that "on most major issues the official Labour line represents my views quite adequately" (Packer 97, #327; Drabble, "Minority View" 10).[72] Atwood, who in the past has been connected with Canadian nationalist groups, currently describes herself as a "Red Tory" (*AtN* 20 [Spring/Summer 1998]: 10). Recently, in a comment deleted by a *New York Times* editor from a letter she sent to the paper, she described certain Canadian government premiers as "lobotimized, slavering trolls" (*AtN* 16 [Spring/Summer 1996]: 10). Marshall has also been fiery. In 1973 she expressed her personal commitment to a "new world of African, Asian and Afro-American dimensions," speaking of this world in terms of "a vision . . . which sees the rise through revolutionary struggle of the darker peoples of the world, and, as a necessary corollary, the decline and eclipse of America and the West" ("Shaping" 108).

Committed in various ways in their lives, all of these writers openly acknowledge the political dimensions of their works. Their early comments were clearly intended to controvert the strict separation between political and aesthetic concerns that dominated literary criticism during the 1950s and 1960s when they began writing. Gordimer firmly asserts that a writer "uses the substance of the life around him [*sic*] . . . and if he does so truthfully, then of course political things come into it, especially in South Africa. Politics, the effects of politics, permeate even the most private sector of people's lives, and this comes into your writing if you're an honest writer, which I hope I am" (B & S 43; see also 114, 217, 242, 282). Marshall, too, emphasizes the importance of the political in her work.[73] What she says in connection with *Daughters* is true of all of her fiction: "On the surface the stories are personal, about people. I'm a storyteller after all. But my people are defined by the world they live in, which is basically a political world, so there is always that link between the personal and the political in the work" (G & S 296).

Atwood has described Drabble as "a writer who has always been aware of the political dimensions to a character's life" ("Margaret Atwood Talks" 124). Drabble herself emphasizes that the "area of personal relationships verges constantly on the political: it is not a narrow backwater of introversion, it is the main current which is changing the daily quality of our lives" ("A Woman Writer" 159). Atwood, who has been described as "among the most telling political writers in the West today," insists that "Political engagement can give a writer tremendous energy" (Stimpson 764; Atwood and Students 241). Terming the novel "a moral instrument," she goes on to claim that "*Moral* implies political": "The novelist, at any rate, still sees a connection between politics and the moral sense, even if politicians gave that up some time ago" (*Second* 353).

All of these writers' insistence on the importance of politics situates them in accordance with current feminist theoretical views. However, on associated political questions they diverge from many theorists. In part the differences are a matter of emphasis; for example, the novelists are especially sensitive to the relationship of art to propaganda. But in other areas the writers' divergences are more crucial, particularly in their views of the limitations of politics and political explanations.

During the period when prevailing critical dogma strictly segregated art and politics, these novelists emphasized confluences of the two. But as the critical climate changed and political concerns came to dominate many critical approaches, these writers turned to draw certain distinctions between their aesthetic and ideological concerns. Acknowledging politics as an integral part of the contexts they seek to represent, they nevertheless insisted that political concerns should not limit their representations by dictating or dominating those contexts. Their comments on the role of the political in their fiction are reminiscent of Johnson's and Jackson's remarks about the way most people live their lives. Marshall, for example, says that "the political is always there in my work, but as subtext": "I'm always seeking to treat my characters and their lives by writing about them as people rather than as representatives-of-whatever" (Baer 24). Similarly, Gordimer's comment that she came "to the abstractions of politics through the flesh and blood of individual behaviour" (B & S 35) is reminiscent of Lévi-Strauss's comments on the levels of increasing abstraction in historical writing. Gordimer draws a careful distinction to show the role of political elements in her novels and short stories: "I don't write about apartheid. I write about people who happen to live under that system" (B & S 210).

All of these writers emphasize that they will not reduce their materials in accordance with specific political contexts. The question is primarily one of focus; they stress that they shape their works according to the demands of their characters and stories, not in terms of any explicitly imposed ideology.[74] Thus their remarks about the roles of politics in their works usually invoke their independence as artists. A crucial similarity among the four women is their insistence on the importance of their works as art. Gordimer asserts that "As a writer, I feel that my first duty is integrity as an artist" (B & S 187). Atwood speaks similarly: "If you are a writer you have a loyalty to your art that transcends your loyalty to any sexual or other ideology" (Draine 372).[75] The ideological independence they demand in creating their works is often expressed in terms of their artistic priorities. For example, when asked if she thinks of herself as a political writer or activist, Marshall deflected the question with a reference to art. Her answer emphasizes her literary priorities: "I don't sit down to my [personal computer] thinking about myself in those terms. I'm too busy struggling to find the right words and to shape the sentences" (G & S 291).

The novelists' remarks on politics implicitly and explicitly recognize that all writing is marked in various ways by ideology. What they object to is the deliberate importation of specific ideologies that they consider extrinsic to the narrative demands of the work itself. Drabble notes: "I think that political theory can produce very great works of art, but *I* can't do it" (Firchow 107). Pointing out that "all ideologies have trouble with writers" (Atwood and Students 241), Atwood writes that "in any revolution, writers have been among the first to be lined up against the wall, perhaps for their intransigence, their insistence on saying what they perceive, not what, according to the ideology, ought to exist" (*Second* 203–4). The independence that all four writers demand as artists is based on a distinction between politics as one element of their subject matter and politics as the structuring principle dictating their fictions.

It is primarily to maintain this distinction that all four women so strongly differentiate art and propaganda. Firmly, even fiercely, they maintain the distinction between art and polemic. In interviews Gordimer again and again contrasts the novelist with the preacher, the politician, the reporter, and the journalist, but above all, she separates novelists from propagandists.[76] Atwood voices exactly the same sentiments. She emphasizes that "Writers, as writers, are not propagandists or examples of social trends or preachers or politicians": "The aim of propaganda is to convince, and to spur people to action; the aim of writing is to create a plausible and moving imaginative world" (*Second* 203).[77]

The commitments of all four of these writers to artistic independence is among a complex of reasons that has led to their often uneasy or negative relationships to feminism over the years. Much ink has been spilled over the feminism of Gordimer, Drabble, and Atwood, and each has been strongly attacked for not being sufficiently feminist in her works.[78] Part of the difficulty is definitional. Beyond some generalized connection with women's rights, "feminism" has always been a notoriously difficult word to define in specific terms. By now the range of views that claim or are claimed to be "feminist" is far too disparate to produce any single satisfactory definition. With so many varieties of "feminism" currently in play, feminist critics often find it useful to refer to "feminisms," using the plural to avoid necessarily exclusory definitions.

While many supporters of feminism have attempted to keep the term open, opponents have sought to propagate narrow definitions to discredit feminist politics. The usual tactics have been trying to limit feminism by connecting it with man-haters, or with lesbians, or with white middle-class women, or with a concern for women's rights only rather than the rights of all. Problems with polemical misuses of the word have a long and depressing history. In 1938 Virginia Woolf, condemning "feminist" as "a vicious and corrupt word that has done much harm in its day," called for women to "write that word in large black letters on a sheet of foolscap" and burn the paper. Woolf demanded the ritual burning because she considered the word "now obsolete" (*Three* 101). But Woolf's diagnosis of obsolescence turned out to be premature. Women's rights were far from being securely established, and the word "feminist" endured, along with too many of the economic, social, political, and psychological limitations on women that had originally produced it.

The well-known "I'm not a feminist, but—" phenomenon among younger women today, with the "but" followed by assertions of support for many of the positions initially introduced and long championed by feminisms, reflects the current success of opponents in weighting the word with negative connotations. A closely related development has been the derogatory associations fastened on the term "feminist writer." Early definitions were either too wide—Rosalind Coward's "Are Women's Novels Feminist Novels?" was an early essay seeking to establish some distinctions—or too narrow. Narrow definitions derived mainly from the practices of major polemical women novelists of the 1960s and 1970s, such as Marilyn French and Alix Kates Shulman. Most of the narrow definitions centered on the appearance of or emphasis on doctrinaire radical feminist politics in a writer's texts—as Gordimer puts it, "something *conceived* with the idea of proving something about women" (Kenyon, *Women Writers* 107; see also B & S 297).[79]

Just as with the word "feminism" itself, currently in the media and the popular mind the narrow—and derogatory—definition of "feminist writer" has prevailed. Practicing feminist critics have had minimal control over its widespread negative signification. Its current pejorative connotations are clear in the uneasiness that all four novelists have with being labeled a "feminist writer" and the grounds for their various objections.

Of the four writers in this study, Drabble and Atwood have been the most involved in discussions of feminism, in part because their early work was taken up enthusiastically by participants in the women's movement or commentators on it. In both cases, however, the relevant novels actually predated second-wave feminist activism. Drabble emphasizes that "the women's movement is a phenomenon that got started after I got started" (Preussner 570). She has explained that when she wrote her early novels, she saw them not so much in terms of women's issues as of "the problems of a specific section of women that I happened to know about, middle-class women with ambition." She adds that at that time, no one talked about "the women's novel": "[I]t was considered bad form to mention that people were women at all" (Creighton, "Interview" 25). Atwood, too, has stressed that her first novel, *The Edible Woman,* which was heralded as a feminist work, anticipated rather than reflected such trends. The novel was actually written in 1964 and appeared in 1969 only because the publisher lost the manuscript for two years. "I don't wish to take credit where credit is not due: I did not initiate the movement, I did not even join it when it came along because I was living in Edmonton and there wasn't any there at that time" ("ATLANTIS" 205).[80]

Atwood's refusal of unearned credit also reflects the dislike of being what she calls "a mouthpiece for anybody" ("ATLANTIS" 210) that is characteristic of artists generally. The prescriptive criticism that surfaced in certain feminist critical circles during the early and mid-1970s, which has periodically resurfaced at various times since, sought to evaluate works in terms of their reflection of feminist beliefs and goals.[81] This kind of criticism infuriated many writers. Drabble described it as "a new sort of censorship, you could call it positive thinking" ("Women and Literature" 25). She and Atwood objected to what they saw as feminist demands to produce only positive portrayals of women. Atwood opposed "role model books" ("ATLANTIS" 208), while Drabble complained that "I don't like the way the feminists think I ought to be writing a blueprint for everybody's life" (Hannay 148). Another revealing remark from Drabble, however, suggests that the pressure was not entirely external. In a lecture on "Women and Literature," she confessed that "in a way the more feminist criticism there is, the more difficult it becomes, because the more self-conscious the writer becomes about the political implications of his or her characters' action" (26).

Other comments of Drabble and Atwood reflected concerns that the feminist label would skewer the reading and reception of their works. By and large, the potential feminist limitations on their art that they disliked stemmed from popular constructions of "feminist" in narrow terms. Such constructions almost inevitably led to the reduction of art solely to politics that they opposed. Atwood insisted that her art was "not exclusively feminist," emphasizing that although she supported women's right to equality, "it's not the only thing I support" ("ATLANTIS" 205). Drabble commented that the only problem with being described as a feminist writer is that "people tend not to notice anything else in one's work at all. They seize only on the feminist issues" (Lauritzen 254–55).

Despite their complaints about some of the literary problems they saw feminism as creating, Drabble and Atwood are the only authors among the four who have identified themselves as feminists. Atwood has been consistently outspoken; typical is her assertion in 1990 that she has "supported women's efforts to improve their shoddy lot in this world which is, globally, dangerous for women, biased against them, and at the moment, in a state of reaction against their efforts" ("If You Can't" 21). Drabble's comments on her relationship as a writer to feminism have become increasingly positive, probably because she was initially much less comfortable than Atwood with being termed a "feminist writer." In 1969 she told an interviewer: "I'm a feminist only when I have certain accusations flung at me" (Le Franc 20). Nine years later, however, she commented in passing in a newspaper article that she considered herself a feminist ("Rape" 9). By 1985 she was asserting that she was "very happy to be called a feminist novelist," explaining that "the background of a lot of my thought is feminist and always has been" (Lauritzen 254–55).[82]

In contrast to Drabble and Atwood, both Gordimer and Marshall have pointed out the irrelevancy of feminism to the worlds they depict. Marshall has made few direct comments on feminism per se. Her most extended statements occurred in a 1982 interview, where she dismissed it. She asserted that "the whole business of the feminist movement, in many instances doesn't apply to Black women, to the Black community, because Black women have always had another kind of experience, and another kind of life." Marshall's observations reflected the failure of the early women's movement to include women of color and their concerns; she noted that "what Friedan is saying in large measure doesn't apply to Black women" (Bröck 205). However, the comments were made over a decade and a half ago, and she has not commented on the women's movement's subsequent attempts to address these issues.

Like Marshall, Gordimer dismisses the relevancy of feminism for the politics that she knows and portrays. She asserts that she "is not a feminist writer" and has had harsh things to say about feminism (B & S 295).[83] She has described "Women's Liberation" as "a farce in South Africa" because there "the basis of color [cuts] right through the sisterhood or brotherhood of sex" (B & S 203). That Gordimer sees some role for feminism elsewhere is shown by her remark that the women's movement "doesn't seem irrelevant to me in other places in the world, but it does seem at the present time to be kind of a luxury in South Africa" (B & S 277). In addition, in discussing the need for black South African women's priority to be racial oppression, she adds that "the feminist battle must come afterwards" (B & S 167). Gordimer's general socialist slant probably also contributes to her predominantly negative stance toward feminism. For example, in one interview she expresses the old Marxist view (without identifying it as such) that if the "real battle for human rights is won, the kingdom of . . . feminine liberation follows. Because if we are all free individuals, that's all we need" (B & S 168).[84]

Like Marshall, Gordimer objects to feminism as limited. Her objections reflect the recurring problems resulting from narrow definitions of feminism. Gordimer consistently connects feminism only with white women. She also emphasizes that "so far as politics is concerned, I am concerned with the liberation of the individual no matter what sex or color" (B & S 295). Despite its initial problems with inclusiveness, from the beginning feminism was in theory exactly the kind of broad liberatory movement that Gordimer describes. By the early 1980s both black and white feminists were clear in their support for wide goals. In 1981, for example, bell hooks defined feminism as not just a belief in ending women's oppression but "a commitment to eradicating the ideology of domination that permeates Western culture" (*Ain't I* 194), while Mary O'Brien expanded the task of feminism to "the regeneration and reintegration of historical and natural worlds" (195). Such support has continued into the 1990s. Teresa Ebert is typical in writing that "feminism should not be about simply shifting the allocation of resources but should seek to increase access to resources for all people: regardless of gender, race, sexuality" (11). The conservative political agendas served by many antifeminists who eagerly propagate narrowly polemical definitions of feminism are clear. Why someone with Gordimer's socialist politics would espouse such views remains an open question.

A further difficulty for women writers was that although the feminist movement substantially increased public interest in their work, in some cases it was a kind of interest undesired by the writers themselves. As Atwood points out, few writers want to be defined only by gender ("Introduction" xii). In some cases feminist recovery efforts intersected only too well with the marginalizing moves of mainstream culture. Rosalind Delmar has noted "the easy slippage from 'feminist' to 'woman' and back" (27), and "feminist writer" has become the major contemporary recension of the historically charged term "woman writer."[85] Ostensibly descriptive, "woman writer" has usually implied "women's writer," suggesting limited scope and subject matter appealing primarily to a female audience. The hesitancy about being designated a "woman writer" expressed in different ways by most of these authors clearly reflects fears that the term fails to do justice to the scope of their achievements.

Gordimer says flatly that "For myself, I don't see a particular role as a woman writer" (B & S 295). Atwood was so infuriated at a *Maclean's Magazine* review claiming that she had written a "women's novel" that she wanted to sue the reviewer. She contented herself instead with emphasizing that the reviewer was defining "woman's novel" in "a way that would include most of the mainstream realistic novels since 1800 up to the present day: a novel in which the main interest was the relationships among the characters in the books" (Amiel 67; "ATLANTIS" 203).

Drabble from the beginning was hailed by critics as a "woman's novelist" (Poland 262). Initially comfortable with the designation, she wrote in 1968 that she "freely admitted" that she was "a writer more interested in women than in men" ("Fairy-Tales" 441). The next year, however, other remarks suggest some uneasiness with the connection; she told an interviewer that "I don't think I write particularly for women. I just happen to be one" (Le Franc 20). By 1977 she was explaining that she wrote *The Ice Age,* with its male protagonist, as a conscious attempt on her part to lose the designation "woman's writer": "I was fed up with women—slightly" (Gussow 41).[86] It is a critical commonplace that after five early "women's novels" Drabble moved from the domestic to the social, and from the private to the public, to focus on larger issues of welfare-state Britain.[87] Significantly, however, Bruce Stovel has pointed out that the earlier novels reflect substantially greater understanding of social change than the later ones (57–58)—yet another indication that the lingering denigratory associations of the term "woman's novel" are misplaced. By the mid-1980s Drabble herself had made her peace with the designation, as she had with "feminist writer." In 1985, while she told one interviewer that she thought she had "moved from women's issues" ("in a way, one becomes less of a woman as one gets older" [Satz 190]), she firmly denied to another that she ever felt any need to reject descriptions of her as a "woman writer." "I am very happy to be called a woman writer," she insisted (Lauritzen 254).

Finally, whatever their personal views of feminism and the category of "woman writer," the fact is that women are central in the works of all these authors. Atwood, who from the beginning has been the most positive about women's and feminist issues, has never written a novel with a male protagonist.[88] Even Gordimer, the most consistently negative on any literary connections with women ("By and large, I don't think it matters a damn what sex a writer is"), admits that "I'm a woman, and obviously what I write is influenced by the fact that I'm a woman" (Plimpton 260; B & S 295). The majority of her best novels are those with female protagonists.[89]

Marshall in particular has emphasized that women are "central" to her writing (Ascher 25). She has reiterated that her goal is to create "a body of work that will offer black women . . . a chance to see ourselves reflected truthfully in fiction" (Seaman 411).[90] In interviews she has explained that when she was a girl, none of the literature available reflected the experiences of young African American women like her, and that she started writing novels to remedy that lack.[91] Again and again she mentions writing for an "ideal reader," a young woman like she was who is trying to understand herself and her community and who can attain through literature a sense "of her right to be in the world" (Seaman 411).[92] From that sense of entitlement instilled in individual women Marshall sees the future possibility of rescuing the black community. She emphasizes her concern with "not only releasing self in personal terms but in larger political and historical terms" (Russell 16). Nevertheless, the base of her work remains epidectic as well as deliberative, a celebration of "the life of women who had been simply dismissed by society" (Bröck 195).

While Marshall has focused on the formative role of literature for contemporary young black women, Drabble has emphasized the importance of female literary traditions. As editor of the *Oxford Companion to English Literature,* she insisted that feminist criticism be included in it (Berkley 60); one of her lectures emphasizes the strong female tradition in the English novel available to women writers ("Women and Literature" 15). Drabble has eloquently made the case for the importance of contemporary fiction written about women by women. In interviews she has pointed out that she "and most women are writing about things that have never been written about, really" (Cooper-Clark 22). She sees contemporary women's novels as especially interesting because they are charting new ground (Poland 263). In a 1983 speech entitled "A Woman Writer," she noted that it was common to decry the lack of heroic issues in contemporary England. But she went on to point out that "women have causes still—plenty of them, as the growing interest in Women's Liberation demonstrates. And the novel is the ideal place to voice them, discuss them, try them out." She spoke of the numerous subjects available to women writers because of the need for "patterns or images of a possible future" and "a new blueprint": "[N]ever before, perhaps, have women had so much to say, and so great a hope of speaking to some effect" (158–59).[93]

Thus Atwood, Marshall, Gordimer, and Drabble agree both in recognizing the role of political elements in literature and in resolutely refusing to privilege that role above others, while their views differ on feminism and on the position of the woman writer. But most of their divergences share a common motivation: artistic independence that accepts no externally imposed limitations. Their views are that literature should not be restricted by artificially excluding political material; at the same time, the artistic process should not be confined by gender or by any ideology, even an ideology the writer personally supports.

The treatments of women and the state by these four authors, however, exhibit many limitations, limitations not reflected in current feminist theory on the state. The ranges of both forms of discourse, and particularly the reasons for the different fictional scope as compared to the theoretical, are the subject of the next chapter.

II

□□□□□□□□□□□□□□□□□□□□□□□□□□□□□

Three Political Narratives

> *Since political structures and political ideas shape and set the boundaries of public discourse and of all aspects of life, even those excluded from participation in politics are defined by them.*
>
> —Joan Scott, *Gender and the Politics of History*, 24

> *How States are Ruined on Account of Women*
>
> —Section Title in Machiavelli's *Discourses* (III.26)

> *[T]he outsider will say, "in fact, as a woman I have no country. As a woman I want no country. As a woman my country is the whole world."*
>
> —Virginia Woolf, *Three Guineas*, 109

> *As a woman I have a country; as a woman I cannot divest myself of that country merely by condemning its government.*
>
> —Adrienne Rich, "Notes Toward a Politics of Location," 8

Although feminist theorists are still in relatively early stages of constructing accounts of the state, a number of different narrative strands are emerging. In some instances the rudimentary narratives of the theorists overlap with the full-blown stories created by contemporary women novelists. Other theoretical stories are missing from the literary ones. But in almost every case in which the two overlap, the narratives of the novelists critique those of the theorists, either explicitly by offering different versions of the same story or implicitly by constructing alternative stories.

In general, the novelists' narratives of women and the state are sobering in the narrowness of their range and the strictness of their limitations. Audre Lorde saw poetry as an important vehicle for women to articulate ideas for change, pointing out that poems "help give name to the nameless so it can be thought" (*Sister* 37). For Lorde poetry enabled women to formulate visionary possibilities only barely imagined. Among the contemporary women novelists and theorists analyzed here, however, it is the theorists who lean toward visionary potential and the novelists who remain closer to the way most western women live today. In discussing narratives of politics, Jean Bethke Elshtain points out that they "structure individual and collective experience in ways that set the horizon for human expectations in later epochs" (*Women* 48). The narratives of contemporary theorists and novelists are structuring very different horizons of expectations for their readers.

The four novelists in this study offer varying perspectives on the relationships between women and the state, perspectives that correlate in diverse ways with the positions of contemporary feminist theorists. As background for the individual analyses of each novelist, this chapter will provide general overviews of certain differences between the novelists and the theorists. It will examine three of the most prominent narratives evolved by feminist theorists to compare them with the stories the novelists have told about women and state power. I have designated these three narratives the Outsider Narrative, the Coalition Narrative, and the Salvation Narrative of Politics. First, however, a brief overview of traditional theoretical narratives about women and high politics can provide some context against which to situate the three contemporary feminist theoretical narratives.

In traditional political theory the initial story of women and the state is a narrative of exclusion, followed by successive displacements as women seemed to be moving closer to the realm of high politics during certain historical periods. Linda Kerber writes that "Surveys of the history of political thought have shown that the habit of contrasting the 'worlds' of men and of women, the allocation of the public sector to men and the private sector (still under men's control) to women is older than western civilization" ("Separate" 18). In the West, with the exception of Plato, early political theorists allowed women little direct access to the state. Indeed, Aristotle created the polis by bifurcating the public realm of men from the domestic realm of women. In the centuries that followed, the expression "public woman" was an oxymoron, used finally to refer to the prostitute, a woman defined by males as bringing behavior properly domestic into the public marketplace.

As the status of women altered in various ways over time, their exile from high politics was maintained by a series of theoretical displacements. Theorists strategically shifted the boundaries of the public and the political in ways that excluded women. For example, at the time when a few highborn Renaissance women were beginning to exercise some power in certain Italian city-states, Niccolò Machiavelli focused on citizenship in terms of the capacity to bear arms, thereby effectively barring women. Later, John Locke established property as a primary qualification for political participation, another exclusionary move against women. In the early history of the United States, Kenneth Lockridge has shown how "new public arguments had to be constructed for politically disqualifying women in an age that increasingly seemed to qualify them for public life." He notes the roles of republican mother and republican wife as examples of particularly clever modes of limited participation that were evolved (113). Kerber has also studied how the ideology of republican womanhood functioned "to bring the older version of the separation of spheres into rough conformity with the new politics that valued autonomy and individualism" ("Separate" 20). Such ideological maneuvers insured that wherever women were, high politics were not.

In classical accounts the public was the realm of the citizen in his political capacity; the private encompassed everything else, from the household to the market (Elshtain, *PMPW* 241–42). During the later eighteenth and early nineteenth centuries new theoretical constructions emerged that functioned in part to blur the classic bifurcation. The term "civil society," originally used in the seventeenth century in contrast to the "state of nature," was developed in different ways by Adam Ferguson, Georg Hegel, Karl Marx, and other theorists to demarcate an economic realm of commercial association in which property rights were central.[1]

The various versions of an economic sphere configuring and configured by capitalism and the nation-state, an independent realm that nevertheless made claims for state regulation and protection of the marketplace, were initially hostile to women and by and large continued that way.[2] In contrast, during the nineteenth century the emerging public realm of "the social," where questions of health, poverty, delinquency, and other formerly familial problems were adjudicated, was feminized in its original conception. Women played important roles in the social sphere, initially in their work for social reforms and later as consumers of public assistance and state employees in the health and welfare areas.

Even as large numbers of women entered this expanded public sphere, they found scant access to traditional legal and governmental activities of the state. Denise Riley has traced how the social sphere—which she terms a "second form of apartheid"—was constructed "so as to dislocate the political" (66). She writes that at the time when the social was being conceptualized, the political assumed

> an intensified air of privacy and invulnerability, of "high politics" associated with juridical and governmental power in a restricted manner. The question of poverty, for instance, becomes divorced from politics and assigned . . . to the social sphere. The associations of "women" with this sphere accompany a displacement and a permanent erosion of older distinctions between the "public" and the "private," at the same time as the constriction of the "political" is refined. "Women" are overwhelmingly sociological and therefore, given these new definitions, not political entities. . . . (51)[3]

Thus, even as the variously defined civil, economic, and social spheres eroded the older public-private binary with their ambiguous relationships to both parts of it,[4] they continued to block women from the state. In particular, the social sphere protected high politics as a male enclave by providing what was in effect an adjunct public sphere for women—and for what in politics are still generally termed "women's issues." Subsequent reformulations, ranging from those of Antonio Gramsci to Jürgen Habermas's famous "public sphere" and Edward Shils's update of "civil society," have reflected the same patterns of implicitly or explicitly preserving a space for high politics that is gendered male.[5] In the United States and parts of Western Europe, current moves to reconfigure the social sphere by privatizing government social services suggest that this sphere has once again evolved to a point where it threatens to bring women uncomfortably close to the realm of high politics.

In addition to gendered spatial metaphors, gendered definition is a related tactic used to isolate women from high politics. Janet Siltanen and Michelle Stanworth point out that in political sociology, the use of the male as norm is linked to a tendency to arbitrarily differentiate the "political" from the "social" or "moral" in terms of sex. They enumerate various examples:

> [W]hen [one researcher] finds that girls score higher than boys on measures of citizen duty and political efficacy he does not revise his assertions

about apolitical females; but instead re-labels these attitudes as "moral" rather than "political." In a similar manoeuvre, [two other researchers] dismiss the similarities in the attitudes of women and men towards capital punishment and birth control as a "moral" rather than a "political" overlap, while [a third study] differentiates men's approach to voting from women's "moral route to the polls."

Their final example of this kind of gendered definition among researchers is the tendency to consider women workers' concerns as "social" while regarding men's labor issues as "political" (192).[6]

Gendered spaces and manipulation of definitions are only two discursive examples of the range of tactics that have insulated high politics from women. Male vigilance in protecting this public space suggests not just negative views of female influence and capacities but a deep and pervasive fear of female power.[7] Historically, women have gained access to politics mainly through their relationships to men—usually as wives or lovers, although occasionally as daughters or mothers. One of the most potentially powerful roles has traditionally been that of the political widow.[8] But the political roles available to such women have remained limited and primarily ceremonial. Amy Richlin and Suzanne Dixon have shown how traditional stereotypes of women powerful in the state, such as the "*meretrix augusta,*" the "scheming concubine," the "domineering dowager," and the "pious wife" or "first lady icon" reflect or assuage widespread public fears of women close to high politics (Richlin 65–66; Dixon 215–19).

Even in the social sphere, which has been carefully demarcated to keep women segregated from high politics, men have not hesitated to intervene if women seemed to be veering too close to high political turf. Ynestra King writes that at the United Nations Decade on Women in Nairobi in 1985, the women at the conference always knew before discussions began whether the issue to be debated was considered politically significant; if so, almost all the national delegations would replace their female representatives with males. She concludes that "The governments of the world did not trust women to speak for themselves even when the issues under consideration related to the welfare of women" (292).[9]

A great deal of effort in many areas has thus been expended to insure that the sphere of high politics would consist primarily of relationships between men. Its procedures, operations, and values have remained predominantly homosocial; it has been viewed by women and men alike as a realm set apart from women and their values. Anne Phillips points out that women have historically been socialized to consider politics as an "alien affair" (*Engendering* 79). The result has been a pervasive female distrust of politics in general, and particularly high politics.

Nowhere was this distrust clearer than in second-wave feminisms, which from the beginning showed substantial skepticism toward mainstream politics.[10] By the 1980s sectors of the women's movement, particularly in the United States, had became more involved in legislative and electoral politics.[11] Joyce Gelb and Marian Lief Palley note that feminist successes in attaining policy goals have been "due in large measure to keen understanding of the realities of the American political system" (199). But despite this increasing activism and its successes, skepticism about state politics continued largely unabated among feminist theorists.[12] Frances Fox Piven noted in 1985 that "Much of the feminist literature of the last few years evinces an almost categorical antipathy to the state" (265). The 1990s brought little change.

The strength of the prevailing negative theoretical views is particularly ironic given the strong cases that Piven, Anne N. Costain, and a few other critics have made for viewing the western state as an ally for women.[13] Historically, women have long been associated with interventionist state policies.[14] Suzanne Franzway, Dianne Court, and R. W. Connell emphasize that "modern feminism has developed in very close relation to the state." Pointing out the lack of substantial feminist movements in the former Soviet Union, China, Indonesia, and Saudi Arabia, they note that such movements have emerged "only under certain kinds of state structure—broadly, liberal capitalist states."[15] Within the Australian context they add that "Many feminist activists, perhaps a majority, are state employees" (ix). During the initial emergence of second-wave feminisms in the United States, Costain describes the government as "centrally involved in facilitating" the movement and playing "an unusually early, active, and supportive role" (25; see also F. Davis 47–48).

The state powerfully influences the lives of contemporary western women in a number of ways. Commentators from Scandinavia and the United States as well as Australia have emphasized how the welfare state has made many women significantly more dependent than men on national policies.[16] More privileged women also depend on the state for protection and advancement. Franzway and her coauthors emphasize the need "to register the extent to which the state has been the vehicle for advances in the position of women" (28–29). Katie King writes that in the United States today, "much of the work of fighting sexism is often given to the government" (129), while Ernesto Laclau and Chantelle Mouffe point out that for European feminists, "the state is an important means for effecting an advance, frequently *against* civil society, in legislation which combats sexism" (180). Nevertheless, theoretical biases against the state remain predominant in feminist political writing.

❑   ❑   ❑

Kept at a distance from the state by varied male theoretical displacements and redefinitions as well as feminist antistate theorists, some women responded by valorizing this enforced distance. One result has been the Outsider Narrative of women's relationship to politics. Through the Outsider Narrative, instead of fighting their exclusion from high politics, women capitalize on its benefits. As Luce Irigaray explains, "If women allow themselves to be caught in the trap of power, in the game of authority, if they allow themselves to be contaminated by the 'paranoid' operations of masculine politics, they have nothing more to say or do *as women*" (*This Sex* 166). Choice is central in this narrative; women actively seek and vigilantly maintain outsider status. Virginia Woolf's account in *Three Guineas* of a "Society of Outsiders" for women is one of the best-known examples of this narrative. Refusing among other things to join men's political groups, the society seeks to further "freedom, equality, [and] peace" by experimenting "with private means in private" rather than "public means in public" (113).

The Outsider Narrative is a compensatory story, and like most compensatory narratives, it shows a dangerous dependence on stereotypes. Metaphorically or literally, the "purity" of women and their altruistic views are represented as endangered by the "dirty" politics of self-interested men. Women thus keep their distance in order to maintain their own virtuous ideology and use it to save a sordid polity. A redemptive version of this narrative was used by nineteenth-century feminists to argue that voting rights for women would infuse positive female values into the public sphere.

Feminist embrace of the Outsider Narrative may reflect psychological needs as well as historical realities for women. Helena Michie has explored feminism's "unease with otherness" (18).[17] Whether from the lack of strong personal boundaries postulated by Nancy Chodorow and others or from brutal historical experience, women often tend to find otherness and difference threatening. Significantly, Michie connects this unease in part with women's hesitancy to claim entitlement, which is of course a primary element of traditional politics. Michie critiques the belief that "within feminism there is no Other, or rather that Otherness can be enveloped in feminism's fertile and nurturant embrace" (20).[18] Politics, however, evolved in order to deal with the other and with others, to adjudicate differences between people. To "envelop" otherness is to effectively eliminate the need for such politics. Michie notes feminism's tendencies to control otherness "either by its displacement or removal from the speaking subject . . . or by the incorporation of the other into the family, into sameness" (18). In feminist politics the Outsider Narrative effects the displacement, while other narratives, such as that of sisterhood, produce the incorporation.[19]

The Outsider Narrative exists in hard and soft versions. Hard versions would include most gender-separatist politics. In soft versions the isolation is primarily psychological, as when Adrienne Rich urges women in the legal and medical professions to "zealously preserve the outsider's view and the outsider's consciousness" ("Adrienne Rich" 43). The "outsider-within perspective" that Patricia Hill Collins connects with African American women functions in similar ways (*BFT* 11). A variation of the soft version occurs in the widespread emphasis of contemporary theorists on self-reflexive politics. A combination of consciousness-raising and social activism, self-reflexive politics focus on taking political action while simultaneously interrogating all such actions. Among other things it addresses feminist difficulties with reform politics, particularly the ubiquitous fears of co-optation. Leslie Rabine describes self-reflexive politics in terms of "a deconstructive strategy" that questions conventional political activities while they are being performed ("Feminist" 28). The participant is thus involved and at the same time distanced from the involvement—in effect situated outside of it through self-conscious interrogation.

In whatever version, the Outsider Narrative has been a major influence on feminist theory in almost every area. In literature, for example, Elizabeth Meese urges "rejection of the insider's role, the place at the center of the literary establishment," through strategies of displacement, disruption, and contradiction (147–48). Feminist theorists valorize a number of outsider figures for disparate purposes, picking up the nomad from Gilles Deleuze and Félix Guattari and ranging from the migrant and the *mestiza* to the immigrant and the diasporic subject.[20] Seyla Benhabib connects the social critic with "the social exile and the expatriate" ("Feminism" 28); Michelle Wallace describes postmodern critiques as reflecting "the outsider's or the migrant's or the nomad's sense of being in the world" ("Politics" 53). The prevailing contemporary consensus, as Kate Gilbert summarizes it, is that "some kind of outsider status is necessary for a woman's work to be politically useful and morally defensible" (21).

The novelists in this study all reflect women's political status as outsiders. As the novels open, almost all the characters are represented as basically apolitical, or at least not consciously political. All the novels are realistic in showing women's connections with high politics as initially mediated through males. The protagonists are born or marry into political families, like Ursa and Estelle in *Daughters* and Hillela in *A Sport of Nature,* or are in other ways brought into contact with politics by male friends or lovers, as are Elizabeth in *The Gates of Ivory* and Rennie in *Bodily Harm.*

In the novels female encounters with high politics are never portrayed as naturally developing ones. Adrienne Rich has written of "a woman's life vaguely unfolding until shocked out of innocence into politics" (*What* 146),[21] and that is the version of the Outsider Narrative that recurs in the novels. Women come into contact with the state abruptly, when something out of the ordinary occurs or in times of crisis. None of the characters initially seeks out high politics on her own volition. Many, like Atwood's Rennie and Marshall's Ursa, do their best to avoid them. Only a minority directly choose political action themselves; most have politics thrust upon them. For this reason self-reflexive politics are seldom depicted. Faced with a crisis, the characters recognize that action is imperative, and both the time and the opportunity for thoughtful, self-critical evaluation are lacking.

Instead of valorizing the outsider's role, the novels highlight its limits in high politics. The fiction uses the Outsider Narrative to suggest that the most pressing political problem for women is access. Drabble's Elizabeth, for example, can get no closer to Cambodia than the Thai border in *The Gates of Ivory.* The U. S. S. *Woodrow Wilson,* anchored offshore with its guns aimed at Triunion during every election in *Daughters,* is another symbol of the overwhelming difficulties facing women who seek to intervene in the state. From the outsider position, women characters in the novels often cannot locate even minor representatives of state power, much less engage in resistance. *Bodily Harm* is typical, when all the characters suspect each other of being the CIA agent on the islands. With any access at all to high politics so difficult for women, struggling to maintain outsider status emerges in the novels as an exercise in futility. Although being an outsider does give women characters useful perspectives on politics, the resulting insight is not represented as compensating for their concomitant lack of power. The Outsider Narrative in the novels is primarily a story of impotence.

In addition to perspective, the Outsider Narrative has other positive elements for women in their dealing with the state, particularly the flexibility that it offers them. But what Tania Modleski writes of feminist literary theorists is equally applicable to theorists of the state: "[T]here is something profoundly depressing in the spectacle of feminist critics' avowing their eagerness to relinquish a mastery that they have never possessed" ("Feminism" 127). This enthusiastic renunciation of what one does not have and is unlikely to get is not the only irony of the Outsider Narrative. Various quasi-nomadic figures that theorists do *not* valorize—the refugee, the evacuee, the displaced person, the deportee—offer a different perspective on valorization of the migrant figure. These other figures emphasize the extent to which migration and nomadism are desirable positions only when they are freely chosen—and sometimes not even then. Actual émigrés and exiles are seldom gladdened by their lot. Nor are migrant labor camps prime real estate choices for those seeking to relocate. The hardships and tenuousness of such existences bring into question not only the accuracy but also the appropriateness of nomadic metaphorizations.

Sneja Gunew differentiates "being a migrant" from "writing from a migrant position" by emphasizing the conscious election involved in the latter. "Writing from a migrant position" involves "choosing to interrogate—a will to alienation" (168). However, the option of such willed alienation is a luxury. Diana Fuss emphasizes that "in order to idealize the outside we must already be, to some degree, comfortably entrenched on the inside": "We really only have the leisure to idealize the subversive potential of the power of the marginal when our place of enunciation is quite central" (*inside/out* 5).[22] The resources and leisure that Fuss invokes suggest that critics who valorize nomadism actually can be more closely identified with another itinerant figure, the tourist.[23] The tourist figure highlights the avoidance of everyday engagement and long-term responsibility that the nomad figure partially elides. Like the tourist, too, critics valorizing migrancy have homes.

Various feminist writers have emphasized that denials of personal situatedness are in essence refusals of history, as Adrienne Rich does in the final epigraph for this chapter. Biddy Martin and Chandra Mohanty have shown how "The claim to a lack of identity or positionality is itself based on privilege, on a refusal to accept responsibility for one's implication in actual historical or social relations, on a denial that positionalities exist or that they matter, the denial of one's own personal history and the claim to a total separation from it" (208).[24] As Fuss emphasizes, the truth is "that most of us are both inside and outside at the same time" (*inside/out* 5). The Outsider Narrative seeks to deny the connections with the inside that those privileged enough to seek outsiderhood almost inevitably possess. Fuss objects to recommending positions of outsiderhood as "a viable political program, especially when, for so many gay and lesbian subjects, it is less a question of political tactics than everyday lived experience" (*inside/out* 5). Her point is equally valid for others who have historically been excluded from traditional politics.

If the Outsider Narrative is always a luxury, it seems a particularly ironic luxury at a time in western state politics when women are finally becoming a significant electoral presence in some nations. In the United States Carol McClurg Mueller describes the increasing number of women elected to public office after 1970 as "a dramatic change in the representativeness of the American electoral system" and points out that after 1975, in elections "gender was no longer a significant factor once incumbency and party were controlled" ("Collective" 102–3).[25] By the middle of the 1980s, more women than men were voting in the United States (E. Klein, "Diffusion" 29).[26] In addition to the femocrats in Australia,[27] gains in Scandinavia have been especially impressive. Helga Hernes notes that these countries have the "world's highest rates of parliamentary representation for women" (89). In 1991 Anne Phillips wrote that "The number of women now elected in Norway or Sweden or Denmark has reached levels that are almost inconceivable in Britain or the United States" (*Engendering* 19).[28]

A final extratextual irony in connection with these novels that reflects the extent of critical enthusiasm for the Outsider Narrative appears in many treatments of the novelists themselves. Much has been made of the "marginality" of all these writers, except for Drabble.[29] Atwood is credited with double marginality, as a woman and a colonial subject. Marshall enjoys triple marginalization as an African American woman of Caribbean immigrant stock. Gordimer, however, wins the sweepstakes as quintuply marginalized: a white liberal colonial woman, and a Jew to boot.

None of this facetiousness is intended to deny the difficulties that these women have faced. From Marshall's eloquence over the racism she has experienced to Atwood's responses to vicious attacks on her as a woman writer and Gordimer's speeches and writings against apartheid, each of them commands respect. Moreover, that as writers they have benefited from the broader perspectives forced on them by their various positions outside of powerful majorities is unquestionable. The problem is both larger and less specific: the unthinking valorization of the outsider and the marginal that too often marks contemporary criticism.

The fact is that once a critic is committed to authorial recensions of the Outsider Narrative, he or she can find it anywhere. Every woman is finally an island, as is every man. Even Drabble has occasionally had a minor marginality of sorts bestowed on her by critics because of her childhood in northern England and her Quaker schooling.[30] Significantly, despite their various marginalities, all of these writers are firmly ensconced in their own cultures and recognize themselves as belonging there. Gordimer insists that South Africa is her country and refuses to immigrate. Nor has Marshall followed the path of her first heroine Selena in *Brown Girl, Brownstones* back to the islands. Despite the nasty attacks on Atwood as a woman, her sex did not prevent her from becoming Canada's premier literary figure when she was very young. As successful authors for decades, all four of these women now write from powerful literary positions. Unthinking valorization of marginality ignores the human capacity for growth, change, and assimilation—and its inevitability.

The overvalorization of the marginal individual, like that of the migrant, too often reflects a naive romanticism on the part of contemporary criticism. Just as Marx romanticized the proletariat and some 1960s radicals romanticized the simple life of the poor, current criticism romanticizes marginal people. The basic idea of the marginal individual's greater access to different viewpoints is, in theory, a good one; the reality is not always so. In life the marginal individual, like the migrant, is all too often the subsistence individual, with no time for ideas at all. Marginality also can enforce ignorance by curtailing access to information. André Malraux writes that "The intelligentsia always has a tremendous sympathy for the outlaw; out of generosity, or because they appreciate his cleverness" (393–94). In fact, the basic motivation for the contemporary valorization of such individuals may be narcissistic. Intellectuals and artists tend to consider themselves marginal to the dominant culture, whether or not their economic and social status actually substantiates such beliefs. For critics who consider themselves intellectuals or artists or both, lauding the marginal can be a way of lauding the self.

The second contemporary political narrative, the Coalition Narrative, is something of a growth industry in feminist theory. Few current feminist writers on politics neglect to mention coalition politics as a priority for women. The best-known version, although not at base feminist, is the articulations constructed by Mouffe and Laclau. But Iris Marion Young's "Rainbow Coalition" ("Impartiality" 75–76; "Polity" 131–32), Jodi Dean's "Reflective Solidarity," and Ann Ferguson's "pluralist coalitionist politics" (*Sexual* 2) are also examples, along with widespread exhortations to the joys of coalition by countless critics who do not attach specific names to their formulations.[31] Significantly, Braidotti connects nomadic politics with coalitions (*Nomadic* 35). Although a few writers have analyzed the difficulties of engaging in coalition work—Bernice Johnson Reagon's exemplary treatment terms coalition both "necessary" and "a monster," describing it as "some of the most dangerous work you can do" (362, 361, 359)[32]—the feminist view of coalition has remained overwhelmingly positive. Indeed, Jane Gallop claims that "the reigning discourse about collectivity so minimizes the difficulties that it makes it harder for collectivity to work" (Gallop, Hirsch, and Miller 367).

The Coalition Narrative is a laudable story, and a generous one. It is a positive alternative to some of the exclusionary politics of the early women's movement of the 1960s and 1970s, both the unwillingness of some branches to work with men and the failure of the movement as a whole to adequately represent the concerns of lesbians and women of color. The Coalition Narrative also emerged as a reaction to the failure of identity politics, after feminists recognized the theoretical shortcomings of such politics and their practical difficulties in a world where individual women bear multiple identities. The best theorists have constructed the Coalition Narrative as a way to deal with difference. Judith Butler explores the concept of coalitional politics as "a set of dialogic encounters by which variously positioned women articulate separate identities within the framework of an emergent coalition" (*GT* 14). Ann Ferguson theorizes a coalition "looking to add rather than subtract differences from the group's agenda," which would determine common interest "not by the least common denominator but by the most common divisions" (*Sexual* 242).

As theory Butler's and Ferguson's ideas—which are characteristic of most feminist theorists who propose coalition politics—are exemplary. At the level of state politics they present certain difficulties in execution. From a practical perspective, the strong self-reflexive element in this kind of politics can produce internal negotiations that immobilize a group, predominating in a way that hinders activity outside the coalition. The women's movement has learned from bitter experience that difference is important, but full ventilation of all the ramifications of individual women's differences can hinder political efficacy.

Feminist theorizing of coalitions is typical of the welcome and necessary complexity that the theorists continue to infuse into traditional political thinking. These kinds of approaches are important in dealing with a multicultural and multinational world. At the same time, however, the gap between these approaches and traditional politics is substantial. Historically, the most effective politics have been binary ones. As Malraux writes in *Man's Hope*, "Every true revolutionary is a born Manichean. The same is true of politics, all politics" (393). Mouffe's point that every community necessarily produces a "constitutive outside," "an exterior to the community that is the very condition of its existence" ("Feminism" 379),[33] suggests that binaries may be inherent in any political process, no matter how inclusive its aims. Furthermore, despite the intellectual limitations of binary constructions, political binaries are not always negative. Postcolonial theorists have pointed out that the colonizer/colonized binary, which is "encoded in colonialist language as a dichotomy necessary to domination," is "differently inscribed in the discourse of liberation as a dialectic of conflict and a call to arms" (Parry 29).

Whatever the unquestionable virtues of a multidimensional politics that can do justice to complex issues, the fact is that again and again candidates, leaders, parties, and movements have been most successful when they can construct strong binaries. Even coalition politics have worked best with single-issue campaigns, when temporary alliances directed toward a limited goal produce such binaries. Particularly at the state level where large numbers of people are involved, multifaceted discussion is extremely difficult to conduct. Feminists have rightly worked to establish a richer and more nuanced public life at every level. But they have not satisfactorily confronted the problems presented by political reductiveness, particularly the binary simplifications that have historically marked successful politics.

The Coalition Narrative also ignores the rather dismal history of actual coalitions among women. This history reflects Evelyn Fox Keller and Helene Moglen's description of collectivity as "a myth that seems ever more remote from our actual experience" (30). Both first- and second-wave feminist activism shows the proliferating divisions endemic to radical political movements. The history of the second-wave women's movement in the United States is typical in being a history of divisions, not coalitions.[34] Born from a split during the 1960s between the "politicos" who wanted continued cooperation with the male-dominated left and the "radical feminists" who preferred to focus on women's issues, the early movement fragmented into small independent groups and the National Organization for Women (NOW). Participation in the small groups declined through the 1970s, mainly because of internal dissension; Barbara Ryan writes that "by 1975 the original radical feminist sector had all but disappeared" (69). NOW in turn was splintered by the formation of the Women's Equity Action League (WEAL) and other organizations. Internecine battles were fierce as continuing divisions over sexual orientation, race, and class split various parts of the movement. The infighting at the 1990 conference of the National Women's Studies Association, which almost destroyed the organization, replicates the same patterns.

Despite such experiences, U.S. feminisms have long emphasized coalitions[35] and have achieved occasional successes with them. (European

feminists have experienced more difficulty in forging coalitions with political parties [Katzenstein 6–7,11].) Ann Ferguson notes the origins of
first-wave feminism in the United States in a coalition between middle-
class white women and ex-slaves working as abolitionists (*Sexual* 125). A
century later Congress passed the Pregnancy Disability Act in 1978 because of a broad-based coalition in which women's groups joined with
civil rights, labor, antiabortion, and civil liberties organizations (Costain
and Costain 203). However, such successes were the exception, while division was the rule. The outrage among many women's groups over
coalitions between radical feminists and right-wing groups to oppose
pornography was more typical. Ethel Klein writes that "the proliferation
of organizations aimed at addressing the concerns of diverse groups of
women has made the passage of a feminist policy agenda more difficult."
Her analysis of the ways that racial and class divisions among women
have limited effective feminist political action shows how differing priorities have made coalitions harder to forge and sustain (see also Gelb,
"Social" 274). Klein's disturbing conclusion is that despite "a broad-based
constituency for feminist politics," the women's movement "lacks an organizational base that penetrates these various communities of women
and is therefore currently incapable of aggregating and consolidating
policy preferences across these groups" ("Diffusion" 32).

In contrast to the theorists' enthusiasm for the Coalition Narrative,
contemporary novelists seldom employ it. What they emphasize instead
is the role of individualism in women's participation in state politics.
Women characters gain access to high politics through their connections
with men, but only when alone do the women take action. To act politically in the novels they have to break from others, particularly men, and
to abandon their old dependencies and the mind-sets that allow politics
as usual. Gordimer's Hillela devotes herself to politics only after her first
husband's assassination ends her dreams of a large "rainbow family" (*SN*
360). In all four novels, leaving home, both literally and metaphorically,
is required before the protagonists engage with the state. Atwood's Rennie flees Canada for the Caribbean, while Drabble's Elizabeth travels to
Cambodia. Political action demands emotional independence. Again and
again in the novels, renunciation of romance and the conventional family is necessary for political action. Ursa in *Daughters* finally acts only after
she has freed herself from her father's paralyzing influence.

In this connection it is significant that women characters in the novels enter high politics not only by acting alone but also by acting as relatively unified subjects. The Split Subject Narrative, beloved of literary
theorists but also increasingly influencing political theory, plays a role in
the novels before, not after, women move toward interventions in the

state. Characters become involved in high politics only after facing and coming to terms with their major inner conflicts. As split subjects, all the characters in the novels remain immobilized in the self, unable to take any political action at all. While Atwood's Rennie and Marshall's Ursa continue to be torn by divided loyalties from their childhoods, they stay passive. Also relevant here are the connections of the Split Subject Narrative with the Outsider Narrative, since in important ways the split subject functions as, in effect, a collection of outsiders in terms of agency.

A number of theorists have pointed out problems with the concept of the split subject.[36] From the perspective of the social sciences, Joanna de Groot and Mary Maynard complain that postmodernist accounts of individual multiplicity lack "both an evidential and an experiential base" (171). Although supporting "decentered forms of subjectivity," Jane Flax from a psychoanalytical perspective warns of the risks of fragmentation as "inappropriate, useless, or harmful" in many contexts: "Lacking an ability to sustain coherence, one slides into the endless terror, emptiness, desolate loneliness, and fear of annihilation that pervade borderline subjectivity" (*Disputed* 102–103). Politically, Teresa Ebert argues that fragmented subjectivity is simply one more concept that late capitalism has appropriated to protect its hegemony, as it discards dysfunctional elements in its ideology (259). That Ebert is on target is suggested by Sheila Jeffreys's insight that those who are responding to calls to become "radically uncertain" are mainly members of minority groups, not those who currently hold power. Pointing out the difficulties that oppressed people experience in gaining confidence and assertiveness, Jeffreys insists that the best way to fight the powerful "is to have some certainty ourselves about who we are and what we are doing" (370).[37] Similarly, Bonnie Zimmerman finds that many lesbians consider fragmentation "a sign of oppression, not liberation" and experience split identity as "alienating and disempowering" (*SS* 199).

As with Foucauldian localizations of power and the roles of discourse in politics, difficulties with the split subject usually arise more from critical overstatements than from the basic concept itself. The great writers of the Enlightenment from Dryden to Voltaire, most of whom had a keen sense of the powerfully divisive psychic forces that impel and imperil individuals, would not recognize the putatively unified subject of the Enlightenment created by too many postmodernist critics. One pervasive problem is some critics' failure to differentiate the multiplicity inherent in the human condition from psychosis. Critical excesses such as the contemporary valorization of schizophrenia are another.[38] For those who suffer from it, schizophrenia is a terrifying affliction that is trivialized when it is appropriated for metaphorical use. Although most human beings assume multiple roles in a number of communities over time, the fact is that most of them retain enough of a sense of coherent identity to recognize themselves when they get up in the morning and to brush their own rather than someone else's teeth.

Although the characters in the novels act alone, the impetus and support for their actions tend to be some familial or quasi-familial connection. For instance, after Elizabeth decides to leave for Cambodia in *The Gates of Ivory*, she parodically postulates a quasi-uxorial role for herself with Stephen. Often, but not always, the ties are female ones, although the rich political possibilities in female friendship that feminist theorists have explored[39] seldom appear in the novels. The suggestion seems to be that individualism is a necessary, although not sufficient, condition for participation in the state. After individualism, the reestablishment of at least rudimentary ties to others is needed to intervene in high politics, but the ties shown tend to be marginal ones.

In contrast to the feminist theorists, the novelists seldom depict coalition politics, in part because they focus on fairly early stages in the various processes of women's politicization. Even on the linguistic level coalition is connected with maturity; one root of the word is the Latin *alescere,* "to grow up." Recognition of the importance of coalition and the desire for it tend to be relatively late developments in consciousness about feminist politics. Katzenstein has noted three progressive phases in feminist political development: (1) a "receptivity to feminist ideas"; (2) an actual "feminist consciousness"; and (3) a choice among "particular feminist ideologies" (8). Only in the second phase, feminist consciousness, does identification with women as a group occur, and particular strategies for action are not involved until the third phase of ideological adherence. Similarly, "Group Feminism" is the third and final stage in Mueller's study of the course of changes in consciousness among women who ran for public office ("Collective" 100).[40]

The formal limitations of the novel as a genre also play a role in the failure of the novelists to portray coalitions. Generically the novel's focus has always been on the individual rather than the group; it incessantly personalizes. It deals most effectively with single human beings rather than with systems or institutions in part because, as Robert Boyers notes, "the forces that together produce the dominant modes of behavior and of production within a society are resistant to the reductions in scale and diversity that an organized narrative will require" (21). Depicting the world in terms of individuals makes effective representation of coalitions of any size difficult.

Gayle Greene has pointed out that pervasive American myths of individualism make it difficult for American writers "to conceive of character as enmeshed within and formed by social relations" (23). But the American case is only a particularly clear example of the basic ideological posture of the novel as a genre. Given the historical circumstances of the rise of the novel to literary prominence, its generic content and form shaped and were shaped by individualistic ideology. This individualism is another aspect of the antagonism toward institutions that Walter L. Reed has analyzed as a basic element of the genre. Discursively counterinstitutional, in content also the novel falters before the collective.

Brook Thomas writes that although the novel "demands individualized characters, it also provides within itself the potential ironically to undercut its individualistically based narratives" (150). But typically this undercutting itself relies on individuals. For example, because the novel usually shows individuals in their social contexts, it can depict community, but in formal terms that community functions primarily as background. The novel may also use representative individuals to symbolize a community, but a representative individual is still finally an individual. Moreover, sequential intersecting portrayals of individuals do not necessarily add up to a community; the operative analogy would be to prosopography in historical writing. Those who have argued the novel's connections with European nationalism, suggesting that it "allowed people to imagine the special community that was the nation," have been most convincing in terms of its linguistic variety and complexity rather than its direct representation of the collective (Brennan 49).

The individualism of the novel is a major element connecting it to Lévi-Strauss's lower-powered levels of explanation. It is also one reason that the "political novel" is a difficult genre in which to write. The problem is partly the sheer numbers of people involved. Even Tolstoy could convey the effects of a cast of thousands only through such techniques as sweeping descriptive overviews. But Martha Nussbaum locates some of the resulting problems when she calls it "no accident that mass movements frequently fare badly in the novel, to the extent that they neglect the separate agency of their members, their privacy, and their qualitative differences" (70).

In addition to the numbers involved in portraying political groups, the ideological abstractions of politics also fare poorly in novels. For instance, representations of questions of political rights, long a major subject for feminist theorists, are infrequent in works by these novelists. Rights seldom appear in the novels because, as Wendy Brown points out, the discourse of rights is "necessarily abstract and ahistoricizing," with a "decontextualizing force [that] deprives political consciousness of recognition of the histories, relations, and modalities of power that produce and situate us as human" (*SI* 127).

Irving Howe has defined the political novel as one in which political ideas or the political milieu dominate (17).[41] But for a novel with this kind of structure to be successful, the political ideas have to in effect take on a life of their own and function as characters. Too often the result, as Boyers points out, is that "the very possibility of [private] life must be seen to be a function of political arrangements that impinge on it or tolerate it" (25; cf. Howe 20). Under such conditions generic slippage, particularly the reduction of the novel to allegory, becomes likely.

The weakness of the novel as a genre in depicting the collective is one of the reasons that contemporary women novelists seldom reflect the importance of the community and the workplace as routes for women's entrance into politics, two options for access that Martha Ackelsberg has analyzed in detail ("Communities" 303–8). (In addition, of course, community and workplace politics are often fairly far removed from traditional high politics.) But this limitation of the novel as a genre also has its uses as feminists try to evolve a balanced perspective on women and their actual and potential roles in the state. The novelists' emphases on the importance of individualism and integrated personal identity for women's intervention in the state are a salutary reminder of some of the difficulties that theories of coalition politics occasionally gloss over. For example, coalition politics can generate broad-based support, but ideological agreement has historically become more elusive as coalitions expand.[42] Canadian women's success in constructing long-term national coalitions has not translated into political effectiveness because, according to Naomi Black, "their coalition structure makes it virtually impossible for them to mobilize resources or even agreement to the necessary degree" (108).

The drawbacks of coalitions also raise questions about whether feminists need to rethink ramifications of identity politics. Just because the early formulations were insufficient does not mean that conceptions more satisfactory than "strategic essentialism" cannot be evolved for practical political purposes. Some problems that have arisen as the concept of "feminism" has been expanded to include opposition to many varied forms of domination beyond simply the oppression of women suggest that feminists may have abandoned identity politics prematurely. As women have brought their feminist politics into the peace and antinuclear movements, environmental activism, and other efforts against exploitation of all kinds, some commentators have voiced concern about the dilution of gender focus inevitable in such coalitions. Charlotte Bunch quotes the warning of a group of nonwestern women researchers and activists in a document prepared for the Nairobi Conference. After defining feminism as including "the struggle against all forms of oppression," they caution: "[A]t the same time, the struggle against gender subordination cannot be compromised in the struggle against other forms of oppression, or be relegated to a future when they may be wiped out" ("Global" 178). Eleanor Smeal was more blunt: "[I]f we don't make women the number one issue, our issue, who will? I'll tell you who, nobody" (qted. in Ryan 133).

Additional theoretical consideration of possible relationships between identity politics and coalition politics might be useful. Effective coalition demands strong identities at the level of both the individual and the group. Significantly, African American women, for whom the barriers to both individualism and to women's movement participation have been formidable, are the feminist theorists and writers who have treated these problems most perceptively. Audre Lorde has pointed out that coalition "means the coming together of whole, self-actualized human beings" (*Sister* 142), while bell hooks has similarly noted that effective group action in politics requires people who are "self-actualized or working towards that end," not "wounded individuals" (*Sisters* 5). At the collective level Patricia Hill Collins has emphasized "the group autonomy that must precede effective coalitions with other groups" (*BFT* 35). From the beginning, the women's movement has been unable to construct this kind of solidarity, and its efforts have become increasingly dispersed. Without a stronger group identity than women have so far been able to construct, coalition politics remain problematical. Finally, as Reagon warns, activists cannot stay in coalitions all the time; it is psychologically necessary to move dialectically between "home and coalition" and not confuse the two (359–60). With no formulations of acceptable identity politics currently available, feminists have no "home" to which to return.

The distance between the coalition politics predominant in the ideas of theorists and the individualism and lack of group connections that characterize the novels is also an indirect reflection of the tendency in feminist theory to move far beyond historical precedent and current practice without taking into account necessary intervening stages for political action. Bill Ashcroft, Gareth Griffiths, and Helen Tiffin have noted the future orientations of feminist and postcolonial discourse, both of which tend to deal with politics in terms of societies where major hegemonic shifts have already taken place (177). For example, while feminisms have prospered in local politics, many theorists and activists have primarily emphasized the importance of global thinking. Virginia Woolf's proclamation that as a woman she has and wants no country, which claims the entire world as her country, is the prototype for this approach (*Three Guineas* 109). Among contemporary theorists Micaela di Leonardo terms it unreasonable "to build a theory of political action on only part of the world's population" ("Morals" 613), while Kathleen Jones urges feminism to shift "the boundaries of citizenship away from nationalism toward multicultural community" ("Citizenship" 812).

Although the importance of global thinking in an increasingly inter-dependent world is clear, the barriers to international endeavors in the context of a plethora of cultures and many feminisms are formidable. The same kind of insufficiently realistic political assessment that has fueled enthusiastic feminist endorsement of Laclau and Mouffe's "radical dem-ocracy," at a time in the United States when the percentage of eligible voters who actually cast ballots has often fallen far below 50 percent, has led to unthinking paeans to globalism. The problem is the huge gap be-tween the idea, laudable as it is, and its implementation. In the cases of both globalism and radical democracy, a number of complex intermedi-ate steps would be required to realize the potential of the concepts. In addition, feminist theorists' tendency to think either very big or very small, to focus on either the global or the local, is yet another reason for their neglect of the state, which in the context of such thinking is an in-termediate level of action.

The last theoretical narrative to be considered here pervades not just feminist theory but almost all contemporary theory: the Salvation Nar-rative of Politics. This narrative asserts the ubiquity of the ideological, the idea that everything is political and therefore, by extension, that only the political can save us. In this kind of monological overreading, politics and political discourse become, as Kristeva warned they might, "our modern religion: the final explanation" (*KR* 304).

Brook Thomas has drawn parallels between political criticism and de-construction: "The belated discovery by literary critics in this country that literature is ideological is similar to their belated discovery two decades ago that literature is after all made up of words. At that time nu-merous critics abandoned their studies of character, action, and plot and began to see all literature as commenting on its status as language." Thomas emphasizes that each trend provided important correctives to earlier critical reductiveness, while at the same time carrying potential dangers of other kinds of simplification (166). The excessive expansion of politics and overemphasis on the political in the Salvation Narrative of Politics constitute one of these simplifications.

The ubiquity of theoretical concern with power and politics both fos-tered and was fostered by redefinitions of the two terms that extended their meanings. In these expansions Foucault was the major influence, particularly his objections to reductive conceptions of power as interdiction (*History* 86), but feminist theorists also played a central role. Instead of focusing on power as domination and prohibition, they explored power as creative and transformative. Power was described as enabling and productive, as "energy, strength, and effectiveness" or as "ability," "competence," and "the capacity to produce a change."[43] These redirections of emphasis were in many ways useful, but at the same time they encouraged a certain domestication of the concept of power. Frances Bartkowski notes that until recently feminist theory "has tried to deal with questions of power in ways that have avoided the complexities and contradictions in that realm" (55). As with the Foucauldian approaches, in many cases the tendency was to neglect vertical power as horizontal power was analyzed and to overlook national and international forms of power in the focus on the local.

As part of the general redefining of power, feminists also expanded traditional definitions of politics. Beginning with Kate Millett's *Sexual Politics* (31–32), politics became defined as any power relationship or structure of domination, whether it directly related to community or governmental concerns or not. Typical is Joan Scott's call for a "broader notion" of politics. She stresses the need for a conception that includes "all unequal relationships as somehow 'political' because involving unequal distributions of power" (*Gender* 26). Kay Boals's definition is even wider; she seeks "to define as political any human relationship, at any level from the intrapsychic to the international, provided it can be shaped and altered by human decision and action" (172).

The various redefinitions of politics by feminist theorists have been some of their most important contributions, allowing concerns that traditionally had been ignored as private to be placed on the public agenda. These theorists also redefined as political many traditional women's community activities, such as volunteer work and local initiatives.[44] Piven emphasizes just how revolutionary such transformations have been:

> [T]he public articulation and *politicization* of formerly insular female values may even be comparable to such historic developments as the emergence of the idea of personal freedom among a bonded European peasantry, or the spread of the idea of democratic rights among the small farmers of the American colonies and the preindustrial workers of England and France, or the emergence of the conviction among industrial workers at different times and places of their right to organize and strike. (267)

At the same time, the pervasiveness of politics in such definitions created other difficulties. Other feminist theorists remain concerned over the excessive widening of the political field. Matters of public policy are inadequately differentiated from matters of sexual desire when, as Fuss writes, "one can be engaged in political praxis without ever leaving the confines of the bedroom" (*Essentially* 101). Elshtain argues that "if all relationships and activities, including our most intimate ones, are political in their essence, if politics is everything and everywhere, then no genuine political action and purpose is possible, as we can never distinguish the political from anything else" (*PMPW* 104).[45]

For Aristotle, the essence of the truly human was to be found solely in the public sphere. The Romantics reversed that binary, seeing the essence of the human being only in what was personal and private. The continuing post-Romantic valorization of the private led naturally to efforts to extend the provenance of that sphere into the public, and the well-known feminist maxim that "the personal is the political" is one result of such extensions. This famous slogan, the best-known feminist example of the Salvation Narrative of Politics, highlights some of the problems with overly wide definitions of power and politics. Again and again critics have pointed out the shortcomings of this formulation, but it retains its appeal in part because of its powerful expression of a limited truth.

Critics have explicated this slogan in a number of ways, emphasizing the relationship between the two terms as paradigmatic, interdependent, or symbolic, and seeking to differentiate them.[46] The problem remains that literally the statement asserts their identity. Claiming such identity combines two disparate forms of power that Foucault has distinguished as "political power" and "pastoral power." Political power focuses on "the relation between the one and the many in the framework of the city and its citizens." The function of pastoral power is "to constantly ensure, sustain, and improve the lives of each and every one." Foucault points out that the two are difficult to calibrate, noting "the extremely numerous reappearances of the tricky adjustment between political power wielded over legal subjects and pastoral power wielded over live individuals" (*Politics* 67).

Feminists have continued to find this adjustment difficult. In practice the "personal" side of the formulation tended to overwhelm the "political," as therapeutic moves displaced traditional political ones. Changes of consciousness were in many cases valorized over public interventions. Such a focus could easily mislead women about the kind and extent of power—particularly political power—they actually possessed.[47] Connecting the personal transformations that are unquestionably necessary for a nonsexist future with institutional changes at the state level has proven difficult. Women also were substantially more successful in politicizing the private than in privatizing the public, particularly the realm of high politics.

The novelists' emphasis falls not on the pervasiveness of the political but on its limitations. Again and again they suggest what politics *cannot* do. One common indication of the limits of politics occurs in the endings of the four novels, all of which show crucial gaps in the action. Pivotal events, particularly those connected with political transactions, are occluded, displaced, or elided. Atwood moves into the future tense, with questionable ramifications for the actual fate of her protagonist. Gordimer switches into a utopian mode, while Drabble invokes a dystopian one. Marshall fails to depict the climactic act of betrayal around which her entire novel is structured. The displacements of central political actions from the text suggest the almost insurmountable difficulties that women encounter in finding satisfactory political solutions under current conditions. But perhaps more important, in each case the occlusion of action also marks the writer's refusal to allow politics to dominate her novel.

These problematic endings emphasize the very real limitations not only to what women can accomplish in the public sphere, but also to what accomplishment in the public sphere can mean for women. The novelists show in different ways a lesson that both first- and second-wave feminist activism had already painfully taught. First-wave feminists learned that their confidence that voting rights would secure women's positions as full citizens was misplaced, while second-wave activists found that civil rights were also not enough. Formal legal rights and powers were insufficient to protect women in a society structured by basic economic and social inequalities. Ironically, this discovery seems simply to have broadened the overtly political agenda, rather than leading to careful consideration of exactly what politics can and cannot do. High politics in particular can be too limited a venue for the revolutionary transformations that some forms of feminism seek.

Despite important connections between the public and private spheres, a number of feminist theorists have begun to emphasize differences between the two that were frequently elided in earlier criticism. Kathy E. Ferguson writes:

> The two realms are unlike in that relations in the larger public arena cannot be based on the intimate knowledge that sustains the personal realm, but on a more distant knowledge based on respect and equality. The conflict and confrontation and compromise necessary to any vital political realm are not simple echoes of the private; they are aspects of a specifically public civility and citizenship in a participatory, democratic polity. (*FCB* 201)

Kathleen Jones agrees that "applying the logic of intimate relations to the organization of political life is fraught with contradictions." She points out that "the shared principles of equality, mutuality of respect, and consensual decision making in face-to-face contexts are called upon to serve the apparently divided purposes of maintaining community and protecting individual interests from erasure" ("Citizenship" 787). For the novelists who treat high politics, the differences between the public and the private are much more important than the intersections. The gulf depicted between the two spheres is wide, and if the personal intersects the political at all, the confluence remains local, below the level of the state.

Obviously, all phenomena have political implications and can be analyzed in those terms. The problem is again one of emphasis. Rendering everything only in terms of politics is in many cases reductive. Although everything is at some level or another political, many things are not only political, and in such cases analyses solely on political grounds necessarily oversimplify. Nor is everything in life amenable to solution by political means.

Even so acute a student of the ubiquity of power as Foucault recognized the limits of politics. In a lengthy discussion he draws careful distinctions about the relationships of madness, crime, and sexuality to politics. He begins with questions of psychological disorders: "I don't think that in regard to madness and mental illness there is any 'politics' that can contain the just and definitive solution. But I think that in madness, in derangement, in behavior problems, there are reasons for questioning politics; and politics must answer these questions, but it never answers them completely." He adds that the situation with crime and punishment is the same: "[N]aturally it would be wrong to imagine that politics has nothing to do with the prevention and punishment of crime, and therefore nothing to do with a certain number of elements that modify its form, its meaning, its frequency." But, Foucault continues, "it would be just as wrong to think that there is a political formula likely to resolve the question of crime and put an end to it." Finally, he speaks similarly about sexuality: "[I]t doesn't exist apart from a relationship to political structures, requirements, laws, and regulations, . . . and yet one can't expect politics to provide the forms in which sexuality would cease to be a problem." Foucault sums up the political ramifications of madness, crime, and sexuality by urging thought "about the relations of these different experiences to politics, which doesn't mean that one will seek in politics the main constituent of these experiences or the solution that will definitively settle their fate" (*Foucault Reader* 384–85). Feminist theorists would do well to take this perspective into account as they turn to evolve more comprehensive analyses of state politics.

❑   ❑   ❑

In their novels Atwood, Marshall, Gordimer, and Drabble are not very sanguine about the three narratives of contemporary feminist theorists. They reverse theoretical valorization of the Outsider Narrative, largely ignore the Coalition Narrative, and smash the Salvation Narrative of Politics. What is more interesting, however, is what all three of these theoretical narratives have in common. In terms of narrative structure, all three are romance narratives. The outsider, whether the Byronic hero or the celluloid cowboy loner, is a figure from romance. (Connections between the outsider and the outlaw, another favorite figure in contemporary theory,[48] are suggestive here.) Coalition reflects the union characteristic of romance, while all salvation narratives are ultimately romances.

The novelists, on the other hand, overtly refuse the romance narrative. Drabble parodies it, while Gordimer undercuts it at one level with a protagonist who energetically sleeps her way to state power. Atwood's hero systematically exhausts popular romance configurations by having affairs with and ultimately refusing three different types of putative male rescuers: the equal partner, the father figure, and the handsome, mysterious stranger. Marshall's novel ends with the main character looking forward to returning home alone. Such refusals of romance are characteristic of most contemporary women novelists. Rachel DuPlessis has described both the centrality of the romance in earlier women's writing and the many strategies that twentieth-century women have used to write beyond the conventional romance ending. Indeed, she sees "the project of twentieth-century women writers" as the examination and delegitimation of various gendered cultural conventions, particularly those of romance (*Writing* ix).

As feminist theorists evolve ever more complex and compelling narratives to explain the situations of women, they have shown a certain susceptibility to the romance in various forms. Gallop has noted that feminists seem to be "attracted to matrimonial metaphor"; she has also criticized the feminist tendency to read "everything through the family romance" (*Around* 195, 239).[49] Susan Bordo has pointed out how some Lacanian treatments of hysteria by feminists romanticize "the hysteric's symbolic subversion of the phallocentric order while confined to her bed" (*Unbearable* 181)—yet another version of the Outsider Narrative.

Almost thirty years ago some of the earliest theorists in second-wave feminisms—Kate Millett, Germaine Greer, Shulamith Firestone, and Ti-Grace Atkinson—provided powerful critiques of romantic love and its ideology. Emphasizing how romantic love masks inequalities in power between men and women, they traced the development of romance as a mystification of unpalatable political as well as sexual realities. Not enough has been done in the intervening decades to further their analyses of this powerful cultural script. Current feminist theorists might well learn something from contemporary women novelists about ways to avoid the romance paradigm. Whatever its virtues might or might not be, the romance narrative is always at some level escapist. And escapist is exactly what contemporary feminist theory cannot afford to be.

III

☐☐☐☐☐☐☐☐☐☐☐☐☐☐☐☐☐☐☐☐☐☐☐☐☐☐☐☐☐☐☐

Fantasies of Power:
Margaret Atwood's *Bodily Harm*

Politics originates in "senseless violence"—organized plunder, pillage, and rape—male bonding to appropriate and devastate bodies and the fruits of bodily labor. It pauses to construe itself as the telos of human existence, and proceeds to develop as institutions of domestic domination and foreign aggression.

—Wendy Brown, *Manhood and Politics*, 182

Last Week I saw a Woman flay'd, and you will hardly believe, how much it altered her Person for the worse.

—Jonathan Swift, *Tale of a Tub*, 109

In spite of everything, I suspect those who are fond of pronouncing the women's movement dead of sharing the pornographers' love for dead women, especially dead feminists.

—Catharine MacKinnon, *Feminism Unmodified*, 227

I did have a number of men say that they liked Bodily Harm the best [among her novels], and I have the sneaking suspicion that the reason was that it had guns and war in it. Could that be?

—Margaret Atwood, 1983 Interview (Ingersoll 162)

B odily Harm is the product of a crucial cultural moment in the history of second-wave North American feminisms, and as such it bears the imprint of that moment. The novel remains more than a historical curiosity, however, because the conflicts of that period continue to complicate the relationships of feminisms to the state. *Bodily Harm* appeared in 1982, during the period when the energy and commitment that fueled early feminist efforts had waned and when the influence of what would be termed "postfeminism" was beginning its ascendancy. By satirizing the postfeminist stance, the novel affirms the validity of the feminist political commitments of the 1960s and 1970s. At the same time *Bodily Harm* reveals some of the shortcomings of these early feminisms. In showing both the value of 1960s feminisms and their limitations, the novel gives the state a key role, with state violence precipitating various critiques of both positions. As Atwood tests feminist consciousness against the violence of the state, her portrayal of state power brings to the fore questions about the relationship between changing individual consciousness and changing the world. In addition, when read against contemporary theoretical treatments of power, the novel emphasizes the formative role of violence in the state as well as the limits of violence as a political signifier.

In certain ways *Bodily Harm* appears to offer a quintessential Salvation Narrative of Politics. Even the name of the protagonist, Renata ("reborn"), reflects the salvation motif, as do the religious associations of the islands' names and the names, descriptions, and activities of other characters.[1] Rennie is one of the refugees whom Jean Baudrillard describes as living in a "*post-orgy world,* the world left behind after the great social and sexual convulsions" (*America* 46). A Canadian journalist who has abandoned her early idealism and commitment to substantive issues for articles on "lifestyles," she begins as apolitical and cynical, an "expert on surfaces" who prefers being a "spectator" (*BH* 29, 114). Shaken by a diagnosis of breast cancer and subsequent surgery, she finagles a Caribbean assignment, only to be caught up in an abortive revolution on the wretched little islands she visits for her travel piece. When Rennie is thrown into jail as a suspected foreign agent connected with the uprisings, her conversations with the woman who shares her cell result in a new understanding of power politics, both sexual and international.

Bodily Harm is composed of these conversations about the two women's past experiences, along with Rennie's thoughts. The novel in a sense replicates an extended consciousness-raising session[2] as Atwood portrays the production of political awareness in Rennie. Although this awareness is never identified in the novel specifically as feminist, much of what Rennie comes to understand and the ways that she understands reflect the phenomenology of feminist consciousness that Sandra Lee Bartky has traced. Rennie moves from an initial "consciousness of *victimization*" to a "joyous consciousness of [her] own power, of the possibility of unprecedented personal growth and the release of energy long suppressed." By the end of the novel she faces "the transformation of day-to-day living into a series of invitations to struggle" (Bartky 15–16, 20).

In *Bodily Harm* the Outsider Narrative complements the Salvation Narrative of Politics. Because of what is in effect a conversion experience during her imprisonment, Rennie vows to change her life and to return to serious journalism. Originally an outsider, intentionally isolated in every way from politics, after her experiences on the islands Rennie journeys back to Canada as a subversive determined to use her writing to expose political evils. She is still an outsider, but a different kind of outsider.

Two major textual maneuvers undermine this redemptive reading of the novel. One is the indeterminacy of the conclusion. Eight pages before the end, with Rennie still incarcerated, Atwood switches to a projective future tense: "This is what will happen" (*BH* 258). She then continues sporadically in that tense: "Then the plane will take off. It will be a 707. Rennie will sit halfway down, it will not be full . . ." (*BH* 264). In context the ending can be read as an accurate prolepsis or as a fantasy of Rennie's—merely wish fulfillment—about her future.[3] Atwood herself agreed with an interviewer that because of Rennie's new consciousness, whether or not she actually escapes is not crucial: "It makes a difference in a way, but whether she gets out or not, she has still undergone an experience that has changed her way of seeing" (Ingersoll 228). However, in terms of Rennie's relationship to the state, it makes a great deal of difference whether she actually returns to Canada or stays locked up in prison. A jailed subversive in her situation presents a negligible threat to any state. *Bodily Harm* raises questions about what the relationship between the personal and the political could actually be under such conditions. The problem becomes the efficacy of raised consciousness in the face of the armed state—the complex relationships of belief, knowledge, and power.

The second stylistic maneuver that complicates a straightforward salvational reading of the novel is its excess of analogical associations. Typical is the depiction of one of Rennie's key moments of recognition in the jail, as she watches the guards tormenting prisoners whose hair they are cutting:

> It's indecent, it's not done with ketchup, nothing is inconceivable here, no rats in the vagina but only because they haven't thought of it yet, they're still amateurs. She's afraid of men and it's simple, it's rational, she's afraid of men because men are frightening. She's seen the man with the rope, now

she knows what he looks like. She has been turned inside out, there's no longer a *here* and a *there*. (*BH* 256)

In this passage Rennie connects the state violence against the prisoners with the unknown man who broke into her Toronto apartment and left a rope behind on her bed and with the rat in the Canadian police pornography collection she once saw. The moment also connects with a number of thematic elements in the novel: Rennie's fear of becoming known as a man-hater or turning into "the sort of woman who was afraid of men" (*BH* 41–42; see also 189); her growing sense of various public and private violations of her own and other women's bodily boundaries; her idea that as a tourist, she can remain a spectator, exempt from the life around her; and the remark by Dr. Minnow, who takes Rennie on her first sightseeing tour, that on the islands "nothing is inconceivable" (*BH* 121).

In fact, the passage connects to so many other elements in *Bodily Harm* that its proliferating implications become in a sense textual excess, with a range of reference widening beyond authorial control and readerly comprehension. Similar sweeping verbal, imagistic, and thematic connections riddle the novel. In some cases they work well. The image of the "faceless stranger," for example, applied to a number of characters ranging from the man who broke into Rennie's apartment, to Paul, and finally to Rennie herself, works because one important lesson that she has to learn is her connectedness to other human beings. She also must accept her own implication in the victimization of others: "[T]here's no such thing as a faceless stranger, every face is someone's, it has a name" (*BH* 263).[4] Similarly, the repeated phrase "massive involvement" (*BH* 37, 208, 261) moves beyond its diagnostic associations with cancer to suggest the new commitment that Rennie develops to an active life linked with other people.

In other instances, particularly when the analogies involve politics, the connections Atwood postulates are less effective. Her basic move is to illustrate how the personal is the political by linking Rennie's actual cancer to public forms of corruption through the metaphor of cancer. One critic writes that the cancer metaphor "reveals the connections between the larger political systems of power in the world (Royal Canadian Mounted Police, CIA, repressive third-world governments, drug racketeers) and the systems of power which oppress women (pornography, patriarchal control of medical practices, advertising), thus making visible the relationship between sexual and political oppression" (Patton 151).[5] Obviously, all of the examples involve forms of power, and it is also true that these forms of power have historically oppressed women in various ways. Thus such analogies produce generalized emotional effects through fear and a sinister atmosphere in the novel. Deployed in excess throughout *Bodily Harm,* they depict a dangerous world overwhelmingly hostile to women.

Beyond these generalized negative effects, however, the analogies create certain difficulties. Susan Sontag has analyzed in detail figurative misuses of cancer, emphasizing that "only in the most limited sense is any historical event or problem like an illness" (85). Within *Bodily Harm* itself, Atwood depicts this view when Daniel, Rennie's doctor, insists that cancer "isn't a symbol, it's a disease" (78). More problematical than the basic metaphor, however, are its analogical extensions in the novel. What, for example, do cancer and pornography actually have in common? Or cancer and political torture? To what extent does juxtaposing them through metaphor add substantively to the understanding of each? In addition, since in the novel the analogies operate not only between the basic disease metaphor and the public systems but also suggest relationships among the public systems themselves, how are the oppressions of women by advertising and drug racketeering similar?

To consider a specific stylistic example, the word "*Malignant,*" italicized and capitalized, recurs in the text. It is used to refer to Rennie's cancer, to the hotel manager's "look of pure enjoyment" at Rennie's arrest, and to the pleasure that a policeman takes in tormenting his prisoners (*BH* 35, 232, 255). But whatever their similarities, a potentially fatal disease, a spiteful individual, and institutionalized brutality have crucial differences. When examined, again and again the novel's sweeping metaphorical and thematic analogies emerge as vague and unconvincing. Strong disanalogies dilute their impact. Violence against women by the medical profession, in pornography, and by the state could be viewed as existing across a spectrum of sorts, but surgery in a modern hospital is finally a different experience from torture under a totalitarian regime (torture that in any case has historically been inflicted more frequently on men than on women). Analogizing these disparate forms of violence obscures as much as it reveals—and, in the case of state power, perhaps more. In jail Rennie's illness finally "seems of minor interest, even to her": "She may be dying, true, but if so she's doing it slowly, relatively speaking. Other people are doing it faster: At night there are screams" (*BH* 251).

In interpreting *Bodily Harm* most critics have eagerly accepted Atwood's analogies and added their own. Typical is a description of the secession movement in the islands as "the political counterpart of mastectomy" (Goodwin 114), perhaps suggesting hitherto unrecognized links between Fort Sumter and breast surgery. Another describes "the prison, the island, and the larger world to which Rennie might return" as "different versions of the same thing" (Davidson, "Poetics" 7). But few people would have trouble choosing between urban life in Toronto and imprisonment under a totalitarian regime. As too often happens in contemporary deployment of analogy, metonymy masquerades as synecdoche. That critical commentary replicates features of the texts analyzed is well known. More troubling is that the misuse of analogy which appears in criticism of *Bodily Harm* seems symptomatic as much of general contemporary critical trends as of peculiarities of the text itself.

From its role as the workhorse of cultural studies, analogy has moved into both literary criticism and feminist criticism as a major technique. A primary characteristic of current criticism is the kind of analogies that Atwood sprinkles so liberally through *Bodily Harm* and that her commentators echo. The widespread misuse of analogy in such criticism has also been similar. For example, Laura Doyle points out that literary critics who deal with the relationship between sex and race in terms of analogy obscure the "inextricability of racial and sexual practices": "[H]ierarchies of race and gender *require* one another as co-originating and co-dependent forms of oppression rather than merely parallel, compounded, or intersecting forms" (21). The problems experienced by early socialist feminists who tried to adapt Marxist categories by analogy for feminist purposes have been traced by a number of critics.[6] A final example particularly relevant to the case of *Bodily Harm* is the elaborate arguments that some feminist critics have constructed based on the traditional analogy of the body politic. Too often such arguments take scant account of the fact that the metaphor of the body politic was from its inception steeped in patriarchalism and ignore the ways that these masculine associations impact its viability for feminist counterdeployment. Various authoritarian connotations of the figure are also frequently overlooked.

The point here is not a blanket condemnation of analogy. A staple of inductive argument, analogy has long played useful roles in criticism. But contemporary critics often disregard its limitations as a technique. Gérard Genette warns of our "natural" tendency to valorize analogical relations, pointing out that "the first movement of the mind, confronted by any semantic relation, is to regard it as analogical, even if it is of a quite different kind and even if it is purely 'arbitrary'" (120). One irony is that analogy should abound at exactly the time when criticism is focused on revealing and interpreting difference. As Mary Jacobus notes, analogy "sustains and screens the defining of difference as sameness." She explains: "Analogy is a means of denying difference; since it really works to superimpose likeness, difference becomes the blind spot of analogy" (283).

Contemporary literary and cultural criticism is increasingly allowing analogy a range and an authority that it has never historically possessed. Analogy has always been used in explanation, to make the unfamiliar intelligible, and also in description, to enliven a discussion (Copi 379). But analogy does not function in these instances as it does in argument. The problem in much current criticism is that descriptive analogies and explanatory analogies are too often functioning textually as argumentative analogies.

In *Bodily Harm* Atwood's overly sweeping analogies function thematically. They simultaneously reflect and critique a particular kind of thinking that characterized elements of the early feminist movement and that remains prominent today in certain segments of it, notably among some feminist opponents of pornography. One of Atwood's achievements in the novel is to convey the emotional power and suggestiveness of this rhetoric while also indicating its limitations.

Pierre Macherey points out that a literary work "never 'arrives unaccompanied': it is always determined by the existence of other works, which can belong to different areas of production" (100). *Bodily Harm* arrived in the early 1980s accompanied by a plethora of works arising from the feminist movement's campaigns against rape and other forms of sexual violence against women during the 1970s.[7] Along with the activism—the Take Back the Night marches, the establishment of rape crisis centers and shelters for battered women, the self-defense courses, and the efforts to reform rape laws—texts played a central role. Susan Brownmiller's *Against Our Will: Men, Women, and Rape* in 1975 opened the debate. Other books followed, such as Andrea Dworkin's *Pornography: Men Possessing Women* (1979) and Susan Griffin's *Pornography and Silence: Culture's Revenge Against Nature* in 1981—the year of the publication of *Bodily Harm* in Canada.[8] The following year, when Atwood's novel was published in the United States, was also the year of the famous—and infamous—conference at Barnard College ("The Feminist and the Scholar IX: Towards a Politics of Sexuality") that ignited the internecine "Porn Wars" or "Sex Wars" among feminists.[9] A year later Minneapolis held the first hearings on antipornography legislation, followed by NOW's sponsorship of public hearings on pornography in four cities in 1984.[10] By the mid-1980s the U.S. Attorney General's Commission on Pornography directly linked sexual violence and pornography. But even as the commission was convened in 1985, antipornography ordinances failed in both Los Angeles and Cambridge, Massachusetts. In 1986, the year that the commission's final report was issued, the Supreme Court ruled such legislation unconstitutional. Lisa Duggan and Nan D. Hunter consider the feminist pornography debates essentially over by 1986 or 1987, by which time the majority opinion had turned against laws as a vehicle for fighting pornography (16). Nevertheless, today antipornography feminists survive as a vocal minority within the contemporary women's movement.

The feminist campaign against pornography has done a great deal of good for many women. From the beginning it has been hard-hitting and uncompromising. Like any foray into practical politics, the crusade against sexual violence relied on powerful rhetoric that functioned more effectively in the street than in the study. Strong binaries marked this discourse, with male aggressors and female victims, male power and female passivity. The tendency was for logic to give way to powerful analogy, as in Robin Morgan's famous formulation "Pornography is the theory, and rape the practice" ("Theory" 139).[11] Metonymy, the trope of reduction, buttressed analogy; Dworkin wrote that "the male is the penis" and "sex is the penis" (*Pornography* 55, 23). Reducing rape to an issue of violence rather than sex was also a metonymic move. Like many deployments of binaries and other reductive techniques, this rhetoric produced a collective antagonist, in this case men. Claiming all men as potential rapists, Brownmiller wrote that rape "is nothing more or less than a conscious process of intimidation by which *all* men keep *all* women in a state of fear" (15). What Rachel DuPlessis writes of a collective protagonist can be equally true of a group antagonist: It can "imply that problems or issues that we see as individually based are in fact social in cause and in cure," and its effectiveness is in part dramatic (179). The rhetoric of many of the antipornography feminists positioned men as women's oppressors, with male oppression basic to the structure of all society.

This particular rhetoric carries certain liabilities, in part because of its disturbing associations. Like most critiques, it replicates some of the techniques central to its object of attack. Angela Carter has noted pornography's "directly frontal assault upon the senses of the reader, its straightforward engagement of him at a non-intellectual level, its *sensationalism*" (15). The binaries and analogies of feminist antipornography discourse operate similarly. Wendy Brown has brilliantly analyzed pornographic rhetorical structures in Catharine MacKinnon's speeches and writings, which Brown locates in "the insistent and pounding quality of her prose," in "an over-burdened syllogistic structure," and in "the literalism and force of her abstract claims." Brown argues that "MacKinnon's theory of gender transpires within a pornographic genre, suspending us in a complex pornographical experience in which MacKinnon is both purveyor and object of desire and her analysis is proffered as substitute for the sex she abuses us for wanting" (*SI* 90–91).[12]

The rhetoric of many antipornography feminists and pornographic discourse also share strong mythic elements. Carter discusses the direct derivation of pornography from myth (6). The attackers of pornography in turn produced their own myths, based on the radical feminist position that the root cause of women's oppression is sexual and that male sexuality and violence are inseparable. Reducing sex to "acts of dominance," MacKinnon termed sexuality "a social sphere of male power to which forced sex is paradigmatic" (*Toward* 127, 173). Women are always and only victims. Like almost all myths, those constructed by MacKinnon and many antipornography crusaders were static and heterosexist, essentialized stories that elided historical particulars and refused crucial differences.

Not surprisingly, given the proclivity of academics for studying rather than practicing sexual behavior, the critical literature on pornography is huge.[13] Again and again this research has shown that pornography, like sexuality itself, is far more complex than the formulations of many antipornography feminists allow. Although the issues remain fiercely contested, on the whole the scholarship has undermined the antipornography crusaders' more monolithic constructions. For example, a number of critics have linked pornography to male anxieties and fears rather than to masculine power and dominance. Berkeley Kaite finds that in contemporary pornographic photographs the "normative boundaries of masculinity and femininity are transgressed rather than reinforced" (vii). In hard-core pornographic films Linda Williams sees "remarkable uncertainty and instability" rather than "unrelieved and unchallenged dominance of the phallus" (x).[14] Gay and lesbian pornography further complicates the issues. Critics have also emphasized that crucial questions about the relationship of representation to reality and of fantasy to action are elided in elements of the feminist case against pornography.

Thus irrefutable proof of the connections between pornography and discrimination against and violence toward women has been difficult to find. Analogy has been so prominent in the pornography debates in part because logical connections of cause and effect have been elusive. Rather than the logical appeal, the pathetic appeal and, particularly in the case of MacKinnon, the ethical appeal have marked the rhetoric of antipornography feminists. The emotional impact of this rhetoric depends in part on the logical limitations of the stance, the refusal of complexity and differentiation in order to evoke a visceral antipathy. (Once again, the techniques replicate those of pornography itself; Patricia Mann notes pornography's "deceptive simplicity" and the "visceral level" on which pornographic images function [67, 86].) Unfortunately, as Susanne Kappeler observes, "the gut reaction against pornography is too blunt to be politically effective" (35). Difficult enough as a moral or aesthetic question, pornography proved a nightmare as a political one. As debate widened in the public sphere, the complexity of the issues became increasingly apparent and the need to draw distinctions concomitantly more important.

In *Bodily Harm* Atwood shows the importance of recognizing these differences, while simultaneously emphasizing the general cogency of the stance of the feminists of the 1960s and 1970s. To highlight the continuing relevance of many elements of early feminist ideology, she removes Rennie from her white middle-class environment in Toronto, where despite the clear threats to female integrity represented by pornography and the man with the rope, postfeminism can be entertained by women like Rennie as a possible reaction. On the islands the threats to women are direct and unmediated and can be seen for what they are. With her powerful analogies, along with liberal use of metonymic and binary constructions, Atwood permeates *Bodily Harm* with early feminist rhetoric, constructing a sweeping indictment of a male monopoly on power systematically misused. She thus suggests the applicability of this position in a generalized way.

At the same time, Atwood shows the limits of this kind of thinking. As Rennie comes to understand the ubiquity and danger of male power, her insights reflect the pervasive sense of victimization that Bartky emphasizes in her phenomenology of feminist consciousness. However, along with this recognition of victimization, Bartky finds feminist consciousness "often afflicted with category confusion, an inability to know how to classify things" (18). Atwood also depicts this kind of "category confusion" in *Bodily Harm* by critiquing the feminist rhetoric she deploys. She portrays its inadequacies through its essentialism, its pervasive failure to make salient distinctions.

Rennie is the perfect vehicle through which to embody this kind of essentialist thinking and highlight its limitations. Various commentators have pilloried Atwood for her unidimensional female characters,[15] and Rennie is no exception. What some of these writers fail to take into account, however, are salient generic limitations. Atwood is a masterful manipulator of genre. For example, while writing *Bodily Harm* she described it as an "anti-thriller" marked by both comedy and tragedy (Draine 379). Critics have not rested there. Coral Ann Howells notes elements of the Gothic romance, murder mystery, and spy thriller (106); Sharon Rose Wilson adds the ghost story, the detective story, and the "doctor/vacation romance," while also describing it as "metafiction," "metaromance," an "anti-romance," and an "anti-comedy" (*MAF* 205–6).[16]

But in *Bodily Harm* as in all of her novels, whatever the various genres she deploys, Atwood is preeminently a satirist.[17] Satire depends on restricted characterization, strictly limiting character development for didactic purposes. It requires flat characters because for readers to learn from it, the protagonist must remain at some level naive. Rennie, like Swift's Gulliver an average individual of moderately good intentions, is an excellent satirical vehicle because of her limitations. Like Gulliver, she is willfully stupid and blind; like him, she is an unreliable narrator because she constantly misreads situations. Inevitably overreading events or interpreting them too literally, she either fails to learn from her experiences or learns the wrong things.

Atwood emphasizes Rennie's unreliability as a narrator by various splits in narrative voice in *Bodily Harm*.[18] Although Rennie speaks in the first person, Atwood also uses a third-person narrator, who is not omniscient but is limited to Rennie's point of view. This narrative fragmentation of Rennie's consciousness suggests her inability to synthesize and understand her experiences. The inadequacies of Rennie's account alone are also reflected by passages with Lora and Jocasta as first-person narrators. In part, Atwood is emphasizing that adequate representation of the diversity of women's experiences requires more than one female voice. At the same time, the other two narrators also highlight Rennie's personal shortsightedness.

Given the limitations of perception she displays throughout *Bodily Harm,* Rennie's culminating moment when she recognizes her fear of men emerges as suspect, despite its rhetorical power. She has seldom before been right in the novel; why should this particular perception be privileged? The problem is not that her insight is entirely wrong but that its truth is a limited one. Given that substantive power in the contemporary world is overwhelmingly exercised by males, men can indeed be frightening. But not all men have access to power, and not all men misuse it. Rennie's moment of recognition, after all, occurs as she sees *male* prisoners being tortured.[19] And Atwood herself noted in an interview that the only good character in *Bodily Harm* is a man (*Second* 425). In the context of the novel, Rennie's blanket condemnation of men is a regression to her earlier ways of thinking, the limitations of which have been clear throughout the story: "She used to think she knew what most men were like, she used to think she knew what most men wanted and how most men would respond. She used to think there was such a thing as most men, and now she doesn't" (*BH* 214).

The politics of sexual relations and state politics obviously have similarities. Like Rennie, the antipornography feminists connect the two:

The private world of sexual dominance that men demand as their right and their freedom is the mirror image of the public world of sadism and atrocity that men consistently and self-righteously deplore. (Dworkin, *Pornography* 69)

What is called sexuality is the dynamic of control by which male dominance . . . eroticizes and thus defines man and woman, gender identity and sexual pleasure. It is also that which maintains and defines male supremacy as a political system. (MacKinnon, *Toward* 137)

But the differences between the two systems are also very important, and these are elided in the sweeping analogies in *Bodily Harm* and in the rhetoric of some antipornography feminists. Powerful in their emotional appeal and thus ideal for polemical use, the analogies mislead even as they inspire. But the inspiration is the point; Chaim Perelman notes that "analogy quite often leads, not to an empirically verifiable theoretical hypothesis, but to a rule of conduct" (qted. in Genette xi).

No matter how much moral discourse is produced through analogy, the problem of satisfactorily connecting the individual's experience with the collective remains. Johannes Fabian expresses concern over analogical overexpansion, emphasizing that one will "not get from insights about individual experience to an understanding of collective narratives by way of 'analogy'" (203). In their campaigns the antipornography feminists have repeatedly failed to institutionalize such connections. For example, Kappeler writes that such attempts as the well-known Minneapolis ordinance, made "on the basis that pornography and its use are degrading to women as a gender, constitute an attempt to establish the connection between the individual victim and a class of potential victims" (14). The U.S. courts have so far refused to accept the connection, just as Atwood ultimately refuses to do in *Bodily Harm*—although she shows its power as a partial truth.

Another major element in *Bodily Harm* that undercuts the deployment of the Salvation Narrative of Politics and the Outsider Narrative is the violence that marks the novel. Atwood's focus on state violence is in marked contrast to current theoretical practice. Contemporary theorists, including feminists, have tended to focus on the state as a contradictory set of power relations, usually with particular emphasis on its discursive formations and its institutional and organizational practices.

Such approaches have resulted in more complex and satisfactory analyses than earlier treatments of the state as a monolithic unity. At the same time, they have tended to obscure the centrality of violence in establishing and maintaining state power. Rosemary Pringle and Sophie Watson find it "strange that theories of the state tend to focus on government and administration and treat the military as an optional extra, there to obey civilian orders." They contend that "Historically, it may be more accurate to view the military as the first element in state formation, 'with the addition of warfare onto hunting as a masculine specialization'" ("Fathers" 240).[20]

Traditional political theory has always emphasized the key roles of military force and violence in the state. Machiavelli, for example, who maintained that "the foundation of states is a good military organization," believed that a prince should "have no other aim or thought, nor take up any other thing for his study, but war and its organisation and discipline" (503, 53).[21] The best-known part of Max Weber's famous definition of the state focuses on its "*monopoly* of the *legitimate* use of physical force" in its territory (I: 54).[22] As Stewart R. Clegg points out, even the rule of law ultimately depends on the state's monopoly on violence (266).

The general failure of contemporary theorists to focus on violence is primarily a question of emphasis. Most social scientists agree that a "state's most important institution is that of the means of violence and coercion" (Hall and Ikenberry 1–2).[23] Taking this basic violence for granted, however, creates other difficulties. This tendency among theorists is one manifestation of a wider critical shift from conceptualizing power as domination and repression to studying it as ability and competence. Violent power and force have given way to productive power and energy, while decentered power has replaced the centralized power characteristic of sovereignty. A characteristic critical move in this work is to separate power from violence, as Hannah Arendt does in *On Violence*. Among contemporary theorists Foucault is the best known of those who draw this distinction, and examples from his analyses reflect some of the problems in doing so.

On the one hand, in writing of power Foucault points out "the violence which must have been its primitive form, its permanent secret and its last resource, that which in the final analysis appears as *its real nature* when it is forced to throw aside its mask and to show itself as it really is" (emphasis added). In the next paragraph, however, describing violence as an instrument or a result of power, he indicates that it does "not constitute the principle or *the basic nature* of power" (emphasis added). Foucault defines a relationship of power as "a mode of action which does not act directly and immediately on others" ("Afterword" 220). Violence, in his view, acts directly on the body, while a power relationship requires another who can act, not the passivity that is usually the only option for victims of violence. Having limited the exercise of power to situations of freedom ("Power is exercised only over free subjects, and only insofar as they are free"), Foucault ends up in the position of denying that slavery is a power relationship. Explaining that "slavery is not a power relationship when man is in chains," he terms it "a question of a physical relationship of constraint" ("Afterword" 221). If the problem of some antipornography feminists has been a failure to differentiate forms of power properly, Foucault in this case errs in the opposite direction, drawing overly fine distinctions. His exclusion of violence from power relations emerges as primarily an academic distinction, useful for the kinds of disciplinary and discursive power on which his best work focuses.[24]

The work of Foucault and other theorists on power has made landmark contributions, particularly in analyzing the multiple forms that power can take. At the same time, the intricate and nuanced treatments of productive power in contemporary criticism have tended to overshadow and occlude the continuing centrality of direct and violent power.[25] Too often what emerges is a kind of sanitized and domesticated power. When Bob Jessop suggests that power should be looked at "as a complex social relation reflecting the balance of forces in a given situation" (253), the phrasing carries connotations of association or even fellowship ("social relation") and equipose ("balance"), with only the single word "forces" indicating violent potential. Similarly, although it is useful to see power as in part "a pervasive social resource" and "an artifact of the creative faculty of the moral imagination" (Arens and Karp xxi, xxv), the positive descriptive language can be misleading. This contemporary critical sanitizing of power reflects the prejudices and predilections of academics as well as the society in which they function. The subtlety of the forms of disciplinary and discursive power that Foucault has explicated obviously offers greater depth and scope to academic analysis than power as force. In addition, many scholars are personally accustomed to discipline and surveillance as pervasive forms of power in the academy.

Clegg notes that as state organizations become more formally complex, the monopoly on violence that establishes states recedes into the background. Under normal conditions these states become less likely to employ violence routinely against citizens. This process, which Clegg terms a "growing trend toward civility in the spheres of public life" (267), impacts contemporary theories about power in part for the same reason. With rare exceptions, state violence is displaced for white middle-class citizens in the West; for them it is usually enacted in or against nations other than their own. As much of the direct western experience of state violence has become discursive, through news coverage, it has become easier to disregard.

However, in its focus on the forms of power that produce and maintain the docile bodies needed by most western societies, current theory elides both the violence behind western civility and the continuing overt violence in nations where state structures are still in initial stages of development. Joy James, for example, criticizes Foucault's *Discipline and Punish* for presenting the modern western state "as a nonpractitioner of torture" (25). Pointing out that "the violent state punishments that Foucault generalizes as past phenomena resurface in our postmodern-era policies," she objects to his implication that "manifestations of power or spectacles of violence have been extinguished." James notes that in the United States such tactics "are held on reserve where the threat and promise of state violence makes surveillance effective" (28). For those in many nonwestern nations, this violence is direct and unmediated.

Women critics on power have participated in the general intellectual shift toward treating power as productive rather than repressive. Nancy Hartsock writes that both feminist and nonfeminist female theoreticians have tended to move away from analyzing domination (*Money* 225–26). However, in the case of the state, eliding violence obscures the extent to which the state itself is a male formation. It is through the state as a medium of domination that its masculine elements most clearly emerge. Carole Pateman has explicated the patriarchal and fraternal violence inherent in the social contract. Equally important is the connection of citizenship with arms and military service. Jean Bethke Elshtain points out that the civic republican tradition, a central influence in western political practice, "assimilates civic and martial virtues and, in so doing, guarantees the civic incapacity of women" (*Meditations* 51). Kathleen B. Jones analyzes how representations of citizenship "exclude a body that does not easily fit military-corporate uniforms" ("Citizenship" 794). Much public rhetoric about citizenship today remains focused on the role of the citizen-warrior and militarized sacrifice in the state. Linda Kerber also notes that in the United States, the Second Amendment has encouraged a male monopoly on "agencies of state violence." She writes that "among the social implications of this monopoly has been the valorization of male violence outside formal military institutions" (*No* 300). More than any other state function or institution, the violence basic to state formation operates to separate women from power and participation in the state.[26]

In contrast to the lack of feminist theoretical interest in domination noted by Hartsock, feminist activists have compiled a long and distinguished record of opposing both state and nonstate violence against women. In few areas of feminist endeavor have theory and practice merged more successfully. The bulk of feminist theoretical treatments of violence has originated from activists associated with either the antipornography campaigns or the peace (and antinuclear) movements. Since such conjunctions of theory and practice have been relatively rare, it is worth seeing why they have surfaced in these two areas. Dealing with violence is obviously inherent in the goals of both movements, but their joint histories also are suggestive.

The feminist roots of the peace and antipornography movements run deep. Both originated in the early days of second-wave feminism, and both have maintained ties to the traditions of that period that are substantially stronger and more direct than the connections developed by contemporary theory. The early theories on which both movements relied were essentialist, and subsequent work has at best complicated and at worst discredited various assumptions under which they operated. Proponents of lesbian sadomasochism and female consumers of pornography undermined the antipornographers' case against males, just as the records of women's historical complicity in and support for war undercut the stereotype of the naturally peaceful woman. Nevertheless, in both cases the basic points retain a certain validity. Historically, more men than women have begun and fought wars, and more men than women have produced and read pornography.

Unsure of what to do with these kinds of facts, theorists in an age of difference feminisms have preferred dealing with other concerns. The tendency to avoid the ramifications of such quasi-essentialist issues has coincided with an occlusion of other uncomfortable facts about early second-wave feminism, most notably the traces of violence clear in its own history. Like state violence, that violence receives little attention now.

The violent rhetoric of the antipornographers reflects the violence, both rhetorical and actual, supported by some in the early movement. For example, in 1969 Mary Anne Weathers argued that the women's movement should prepare to merge with "the entire revolutionary movement": "We are now speaking of real revolution (armed). If you can not accept this fact purely and without problems examine your reactions closely. We are playing to win and so are they. Viet Nam is simply a matter of time and geography" (qted. in K. King 25). Or Sally Miller Gearhart proposed that in order to destroy the violence of patriarchy and capitalism, "*The proportion of men must be reduced and maintained at approximately 10% of the human race*" (271). Gearhart did explicitly eschew violent means, dismissing war and execution as methods for implementing her plan and ultimately rejecting male infanticide.[27]

Others were less hesitant about endorsing direct violence. Susan Cavin, who also advocated lower ratios of men to women at every level of society, included "open, direct sexual warfare" and "all-female armies fighting for the military overthrow of patriarchy" among her "practical solutions" for overcoming women's oppression (169). Some of the literature of the period reflected a belief in the efficacy of violence. Bonnie Zimmerman points out that in contrast to lesbian novels of the 1980s, novels of the 1970s supported the establishment of Lesbian Nation by armed struggle. The woman warrior is a major archetype in this fiction (*SS* 64–65).

The point here is not the viability or the widespread acceptance of such attitudes in the early women's movement, but the fact that such attitudes were expressed—and appeared in print—at all. By 1983 the hesitancy of the editor who reprinted Gearhart's essay reflected the prevailing viewpoint. She commented that "it is the word 'maintained' that disturbs even those of us otherwise intrigued by her proposal" (267). The violence that was an element in some early second-wave feminisms was a potential part of its heritage that was left behind when "women's liberation" became the "women's movement." The changes of style that ensued directly reflected more substantive changes. Contemporary theoretical occlusions of violence are thus part of a larger occlusion by many feminisms of their own past. In both cases, violence is something that most feminisms have hesitated to confront in all of its ramifications.

Bodily Harm brings violent state power to the fore. Colonial and postcolonial situations often offer overt examples of the violence inherent in all states. Frantz Fanon has described decolonization as "always a violent phenomenon" because colonialism, which is "violence in its natural state," yields only to greater violence (*Wretched* 35, 61). To highlight such violence Atwood positions Rennie in the Caribbean, during the first election after the British have left the islands of Ste. Anthony and Ste. Agathe. There Rennie sees traces of British violence such as the fort/jail, but the emphasis is on neocolonial violence. Critics may romanticize the inhabitants of Ste. Antoine and Ste. Agathe as "an island people with no exploitive motives" (Patton 161), but Atwood does not. With the exception of Dr. Minnow, the political conscience of the novel, she portrays the islanders as a fairly sorry lot. Significantly, Minnow, who cogently criticizes British colonialism, is nevertheless described as truly believing in "democracy and fair play and all those ideas the British left here" (*BH*

219; see also 32–33). Although the government uses techniques of surveillance (the modern telescope mounted on the jail; the men in mirrored sunglasses monitoring the people), it is the physical violence—public police brutality and the beating, torturing, and killing of political opponents and prisoners—on which Atwood focuses.

The depiction of the state in *Bodily Harm* reflects some of the concerns important to contemporary theorists. In fine Foucauldian fashion, Atwood emphasizes the relational aspects of power by carefully situating her two little islands in both local and international contexts. Locally she shows quasi-tribal loyalties and feuds ("everyone's related to everyone else around here" [*BH* 237]). These in turn are manipulated by multinational political and financial forces ranging from drug traffickers to superpower hostilities. For the period before the dissolution of the Soviet Union, Fanon points out that the competition between capitalism and socialism gave "an almost universal dimension to even the most localized demands" (*Wretched* 75), and all four of the novelists in this study pay particular attention to the international contexts of the national events they portray. In Atwood's novel, again as in Foucault's work, power is ubiquitous. In a world of clashing superpowers and their clients, where Cuban construction of an airport in Grenada attracts both the CIA and the KGB, political space is reconfigured and remapped accordingly. Minnow emphasizes that "There is no longer any place that is not of general interest" (*BH* 122). "Everyone is in politics here," he explains to Rennie. "All the time" (*BH* 113).

As the personal thus becomes political, neutrality disappears as a viable option, both for individuals like Rennie who want to remain uninvolved and for nations. Along with her characteristically virulent anti-Americanism, Atwood in *Bodily Harm* repeatedly slams the "sweet Canadians" (*BH* 32, 113, 169, 203, etc.) for the international havoc wreaked by their good intentions and naiveté. Atwood has called Canada "an economic and cultural colony" and has said that "women as well as Canadians have been colonized or have been the victims of cultural imperialism" (Ingersoll 35, 94; see also 119). Significantly, however, when dealing with an actual postcolonial situation in *Bodily Harm,* she eschews such analogies for Canadians as well as women. Although not imperialists themselves, the Canadians end up abetting international imperialism in the islands.

Complementing the Foucauldian ubiquity of power in *Bodily Harm* is power's Foucauldian elusiveness. Foucault noted that secrecy is indispensable for the operation of power, which he described as "tolerable only on condition that it mask a substantial part of itself." He added that the success of any power "is proportional to its ability to hide its own mechanisms" (*History* 86). Amid the multiple networks of power, it is difficult to locate agency in any state, to ascertain the ultimate sources of and responsibility for the powers wielded in that state's name. In a novel in which seeing is portrayed as a form of power,[28] substantive power remains invisible. The anonymity of state power is represented by the prime minister, Ellis, whose full name is never given. The islanders never see him. Literally one of the "faceless strangers" who haunt *Bodily Harm*, Ellis has not left his house for twenty years (*BH* 73–74). His unstable identity is replicated in the novel by the ongoing farce of attempted identifications of the CIA operatives on the islands, a series of comic mistakes that, like the situation with Ellis, have tragic consequences.

This elusiveness of state power is reflected in the violence that is its instrument. The drive to dominate that many feminist theorists have connected with male alienation from the body[29] has as one of its natural techniques torture, which reduces the victim to body while the torturer maintains his own alienation. But when state power is involved, the physical specificity of violent actions and the bodies on which they are enacted can be misleading. Violence marks the presence of power, but it does not necessarily identify any source beyond the immediate agent. Clegg highlights as "the central paradox of power" the fact that although in principle the power of an agency increases by delegating authority, such delegation requires rules, which in turn entail discretion that can then empower delegates. Clegg's sanitization of power is clear in his insistence that "the delegation of authority can *only* proceed by rules" (201, emphasis added). One of Atwood's points in *Bodily Harm* is that in the polity rules cannot necessarily constrain the violence of individuals.

Atwood shows that when violence is involved in the state, the political often becomes the personal. Paul dismisses political issues as simply excuses for "getting rid of people you don't like" (*BH* 213). Similarly, Lora comments that the revolt gives Ellis "an excuse to do it to everybody he doesn't like" (*BH* 237). As soon as state violence surfaces, the personal is difficult to separate from the ostensibly political. After Marsden talks about political "sacrifice for the good of all," Lora responds: "I know what you really want. You want to shoot people and feel really good about it and have everyone tell you you're doing the right thing" (*BH* 235). The policemen who brutally beat Lora in the jail act not under government orders but for self-protection, to stop her from exposing their drug dealing. Public rhetoric covers private interests in the state; local aspirants to political power are smeared as communists to encourage U.S. intervention and aid.

Historically, states have never been able to completely control the violence on which their power depends. The massive delegations of authority required in the modern bureaucratic state compound the difficulties. In public spectacles of torture or hanging, Foucault read the power of the sovereign written directly on the criminal's body (*DP* 47–50). Atwood shows that contemporary state violence allows no such direct inscription of authority. It is in the context of this opaqueness of individual acts involving state power as violence, and the tendency for violence to allow the political to become the personal, that certain questions Foucault omitted become salient. Refusing to ask "why certain people want to dominate, what they seek," he preferred to study power "at the point where its intention, if it has one, is completely invested in its real and effective practices." Foucault called for "a study of power in its external visage, at the point where it is in direct and immediate relationship with that which we can provisionally call its object, its target, its field of application, there—that is to say—where it installs itself and produces its real effects" (*P/K* 97). This approach, fruitful for state forms of disciplinary power, cannot necessarily reveal as much when applied to direct state violence, given the dispersions of agency almost always involved.

Foucauldian criticism has accustomed us to think in terms of connections between knowledge and power, but violence also refigures these connections. One morning in the jail Rennie and Lora discover that their tea has salt in it rather than sugar. Rennie suggests that they inform the guards of the mistake with the salt.

> "Hell, no," says Lora. "That wasn't a mistake, that was orders. They're doing it on purpose."
> "Why would they do that?" says Rennie. The poor food she can understand, but this seems gratuitous. Malicious.
> Lora shrugs. "Because they can," she says. (*BH* 247)

The exchange highlights the mindlessness of power as potential for force, the inexorable pointlessness of mere ability. State violence tends to be an unstable signifier, limited in what it can reveal.

In no single area has *Bodily Harm* been more overread by analogy than in criticism focused on the body.[30] But the violated body, which seems to reveal power so directly, tends within the state context to be only a distant signifier of actual political power. Foucault in this instance offers crucial guidance. Regarding power exercised on the body, he writes that such power relations "do not merely reproduce, at the level of individuals, bodies, gestures and behaviour, the general form of the law or government." He explains that "although there is continuity (they are indeed articulated on this form through a whole series of complex mechanisms), there is neither analogy nor homology" (*DP* 27).

From the beginning, second-wave feminist campaigns against violence relied on signifying violence and militarization as male. In line with her purpose of showing the importance as well as the limitations of the approaches of this early feminism, in *Bodily Harm* Atwood both underwrites and undercuts these traditional gendered associations. Aside from female self-defense, almost all of the violence connected with the state in the novel is perpetrated by males, reflecting the historical preponderance of male political violence. In Marsden and also in Paul, Atwood portrays male pleasure in violence. When the revolt breaks out and Paul enters the action, he seems "younger, alive in a way he hasn't been before. He loves it, thinks Rennie. That's why we get into these messes: because they love it" (*BH* 226).

To place the male propensity for violence in perspective, however, Atwood depicts Minnow—a male and also the major repository of positive values in the novel—as thinking that in politics, "guns are playing dirty" (*BH* 219). She also emphasizes the complicity of women in enabling state violence. Depicting the homosociality of traditional political power through male bonding, violent and otherwise, Atwood at the same time shows that women are thoroughly implicated in it. Women's work underpins the system generally; among the islanders, Lora explains that "This whole place runs on grandmothers" (*BH* 205).[31] Elva, who dominates her extended family as well as passing tourists, heals but also helps the men illegally import guns. She returns violence for violence, nearly strangling the justice minister when her son Prince is beaten (*BH* 204).

The two North American women in the novel repeatedly infantilize men, and in the process they misread the violence of male politics. Seeing the small machine gun Paul carries "casually, like a lunch pail," Rennie dismisses it as "a toy, the kind you aren't supposed to give little boys for Christmas": "She doesn't believe it could go off, and surely if it did nothing would come out of it but rubber bullets" (*BH* 226; see also 214). Similarly, she misreads the outbreak of the revolt as "juvenile delinquency" and reduces Paul's drug dealing to "Boys playing with guns, that's all it is" (*BH* 224, 216). That such infantilization is more than Rennie's usual misreadings is shown by its repetition in Lora, who generally functions to correct Rennie's misperceptions. Commenting that she probably should have left the islands when she saw the men preparing for revolution, Lora admits: "[T]he truth is I thought they were just having a good time, sneaking around at night, having secrets, sort of like the Shriners, you know? I never thought they'd *do* anything" (*BH* 235).

Any infantilization of men recalls the only time that most women have access to substantial power over males, in their roles as mothers of young children. It also recalls the connections that numerous feminist

theorists from Dorothy Dinnerstein on have made between male aggression and the initial male experience of female power, the desire of
the male to break from his attachment to a powerful woman. As in that
period, when any familial power a woman has is checked by the ultimate
power of patriarchy, such infantilization misperceives the locations of
substantive power.[32] Dismissing male violence via infantilization, Rennie
and Lora misunderstand situations and endanger themselves and others.
Critical attention usually has focused on colonizers as infantilizing indigenes and men as infantilizing women. The emphasis has been on the
damage done to the subjects who are treated this way; in *Bodily Harm* this
stance is reflected by the Canadian government envoy's feminized infantilization of the islands (260). In all of these cases, infantilization occludes
violence. But as women infantilize men, Atwood also reverses the stereotypes, showing that violence is also occluded when the less powerful assume the stance of those with actual power.

Finally, in this novel satirizing romance, Atwood emphasizes the roles
of both men and women in perpetuating the romance of violence. Criticizing "the male romanticization of violence," Dworkin terms the legend
of male violence "the most celebrated legend of mankind" (*Pornography*
52, 16).[33] But the romance of violence is by no means only male. The
criminal—Robin Hood, MacHeath—has frequently been a romantic figure beloved by women.[34] The romantic hero, who is regularly associated
with violence (Cranny-Francis 182), often has had overtones of the criminal, as in the case of the Byronic hero. In *Bodily Harm* Atwood literalizes
such conventions by casting a drug dealer as the putative romantic hero.
Through Paul's unsavory occupation, the illegitimacy of the element of
eroticized domination present in romantic love is made overt, as is its attraction for many women. When Paul matter-of-factly discusses the importance of guns in drug running, Rennie finds herself "trying very hard
not to find any of this romantic." Nevertheless, "she can't help wondering
whether Paul has any bullet holes in him. If he has, she'd like to see" (*BH*
216–17).

Like most women in contemporary novels and life, Rennie comes
into contact with the state by accident, primarily because of her association with a man. But her stay with Paul during the abortive rebellion
on Ste. Agathe positions her only as a subordinate within the male-dominated state and its violence. She recognizes her actual status as Paul bargains with Marsden to let her leave the island. The two men's
negotiation, a version of Gayle Rubin's famous "traffic in women,"[35]
shows Rennie the reality behind the romance and politics of violence.
She suddenly realizes the "truth about knights": "The maidens were only
an excuse. The dragon was the real business. So much for vacation ro

mances, she thinks" (*BH* 228).[36] Insofar as women enter politics through relationships with men, particularly romantic ones, they are interpellated as dependents, even as, in Rennie's case, pawns. They can have no independent political life of their own.

To take an active political stance, Rennie has to leave behind romance and dependency on males. Significantly, it is her ties to Lora, to another woman, that lead Rennie to the more positive politics that she espouses at the end of the novel. Rennie has never liked Lora as an individual; from the beginning she disapproves of Lora's conduct, her values, even her appearance. Rey Chow writes that "to the extent that it is our own limit that we encounter when we encounter another," often people simply "render the other as the negative of what they are and what they do" (34). Rennie continues to treat Lora as her negative other even in the jail cell. Although she comes to grudgingly appreciate some of Lora's strengths, she still feels no affinity with her.

At the end of the novel, when Lora is beaten by the prison guards almost beyond recognition, Rennie hesitates to aid her. Initially thinking that "it's no one she recognizes, she has no connection with this," she finally moves to save Lora because "every face is someone's" (*BH* 263). What Rennie understands at that moment is that Lora is not simply her own negative other but a fellow human being, and she also realizes that shared humanity entails shared responsibilities. For the first time in the novel, she sees another human being as an individual rather than as a positive or negative extension of herself. Personal affinities and freely chosen emotional ties are one thing; basic human bonds are another. Although the relationships that result from the two kinds of association are very different, through her experience with Lora in the jail Rennie learns that both are important.

In *Bodily Harm* romantic love impedes female citizenship by positioning women as secondary actants in male pursuits. In contrast, relationships between women liberate. However, Rennie's initiation into politics via her experience of shared humanity with Lora raises questions about certain directions in feminist theorists' ongoing attempts to redefine citizenship. These writers have done important work in showing the centrality of the gendered body to traditional conceptions of citizenship, in which the abstract individual turns out to be a propertied male. More problematical have been moves to model citizenship on friendship or even familial relationships.[37] The basic argument has been that historically, women's restriction to the private sphere has not socialized them to be comfortable in the kind of distanced relationships that have traditionally characterized citizenship (even in Aristotle, where friendship is central to civic relationships). Without the ability to form such relationships, women are hampered in the public sphere as it currently exists, whatever the civic possibilities of affective ties for a utopian future. In *Bodily Harm* Rennie's experiences with Lora suggest that not even friendship, much less a sororal or other familial model, is required for responsible political relationships. Shared circumstances—simply shared humanity—suffices, even for two women who dislike one another. The political orientation that results from the minimal relationship between the two women in the novel suggests that feminist criticism may be overemphasizing the usefulness of personal ties and affinities in citizenship.

The island women put even these minimal ties into a larger perspective, suggesting the difficulties in forging any kind of international feminism. Paul explains that the island women dislike white women for being rich and for spoiling the local men, a comment that reflects white women's historical connections to the rewards of western imperialism and their complicity with western men in its practices.[38] Equally important are racial divisions among women. The islanders' opinion of white women as "naturally lazy" for hiring black women to do their work for them reflects the racial divisions in early feminism, which Atwood makes overt in Paul's comment that the island women view "that Women's Lib stuff" as "for the white women" (*BH* 134). As a whole *Bodily Harm* focuses more on issues of gender and class than on racial concerns, but the points that Atwood does make are telling. She herself has emphasized that the only good person in the novel is black (*Second* 425). In addition, Judith Grant is one of a number of critics who have noted "the remarkable extent to which the sexuality debates are unself-consciously a debate among white feminists," despite the many racial components of the sex industry (80).[39] In her analysis of these components Patricia Hill Collins has shown how African American women "form a key pillar on which contemporary pornography itself rests" (*BFT* 168).[40] Atwood highlights this racial context by making the actress in the pornographic film black.

The power of *Bodily Harm* lies in its refusal of easy answers. While graphically depicting the cultural differences that are obstacles to any global women's movement, Atwood at the same time shows the need for such a movement through details of the lives of the local women. For these women the role of mother offers the only status; Lora explains that "Around here, if you don't have kids you're nothing" (*BH* 165). Male domestic violence against women is not only accepted but endorsed. Women's distance from the state is shown by their position just before the revolt, when they remain indoors while the men make political plans outside (*BH* 223). While Atwood reveals the shortcomings of early feminisms throughout *Bodily Harm,* she is careful to show that the alternatives are worse.

❑   ❑   ❑

Rennie's experiences clearly show the importance of recognizing that the personal is the political. Beyond that basic recognition, however, *Bodily Harm* suggests some of the problems in relating changes in consciousness to actual governmental change. Atwood makes a strong case for what change of consciousness in an individual can do against the state—and also for the limits of that change. In the same way she explores the roles of the imagination and of language in resisting the state.

The consciousness of the oppressed can be a crucial element in opposing state power. Elizabeth Janeway has analyzed how important mistrust of power is for the politically oppressed (206). Feminist consciousness relies on similar attitudes; Bartky mentions wariness and suspicion as characteristic of it (18). Rebellion of the intellect is important because, in the end, no government can rule by force alone. Janeway writes that "State terror is a tool used to frighten people into policing themselves. It magnifies physical force by invading the mind" (205).

Minnow speaks for the important role that imagination can play in state resistance. When Rennie asks the doctor why he even tries to oppose the government, given Ellis's overwhelming political power, Minnow agrees that resistance may seem illogical and futile. He continues: "But this is why you do it. You do it because everyone tell [*sic*] you it is not possible. They cannot imagine things being different. It is my duty to imagine, and they know that for even one person to imagine is very dangerous to them, my friend" (*BH* 203; cf. *Second* 396–97). The political function of the imagination has generally been treated in terms of its symbolic and discursive role in forming and mobilizing communities (Anderson; Beverley and Zimmerman x). *Bodily Harm* suggests that the imagination is equally important in constructing the political individual as a preliminary to community. Janeway points out that without solitary intellectual dissent, the community necessary for resistance cannot take shape (215). By the end of the novel, Rennie is following Minnow's advice, using her imagination to project a political future. Redirecting the imaginative powers she has previously squandered on her lifestyles journalism in Toronto, she creates a new political reality for herself.

Closely tied to the power of the imagination in *Bodily Harm* is the power of language. Like Atwood, Rennie is a writer; indeed, Atwood has suggested that Rennie herself could be the author of *Bodily Harm*.[41] As a journalist Rennie has already used her imagination to create reality. When women in Toronto start wearing the chain-drain jewelry that she has falsely reported as a trend, she sees life imitating lifestyles journalism.[42]

Through imagination, discursive reality prevails, and the usually complex relationship between representation and reality is reduced to one of cause and effect. Even as caricature the incident suggests the power of the written word via the media, a power that Minnow will reiterate to Rennie in the islands. There foreign press coverage can shape more crucial political realities because of the government's concern about foreign aid. Minnow explains that journalism can "stop excesses" because newspaper articles from abroad warn Ellis's corrupt government that "they are being watched" (*BH* 122).

Bodily Harm affirms the power of language and the imagination in many ways, not the least of which is through its own construction. Critics make much of Atwood's postmodernism,[43] and *Bodily Harm* does treat time and sometimes space surrealistically. However, in terms of politics, Jerome Rosenberg is correct that the novel is a work of realism (130). Atwood has discussed aspects of the actual rebellion on which the novel is based, although she refused to reveal the names of the islands (Castro 222).[44] She emphasized that the events in the novel are "all out there in the real world": "I find that I have to invent less and less. Most of the stuff in *Bodily Harm* is straight reality" (Adachi F17; Harpur D1). The phrase "straight reality" is somewhat misleading, for the editing and rewriting that Atwood admits—including changing several mice into one rat in the scene from the pornographic film (Adachi F17)[45]—reflect the imaginative manipulations through which she molds history to highlight moral and political implications that bare historical fact does not necessarily convey.

The realistic elements that ground not only *Bodily Harm* but all of Atwood's novels suggest that her postmodernism may have been overrated by critics. In her novels postmodernism is primarily a matter of certain techniques rather than of content or ideology. Even at the level of technique, Atwood has noted that some of her favorites, such as indeterminate endings, are actually traditional literary devices (Castro 221).[46] Her remarks and her practice suggest that contemporary critics may be too often embracing as new what is merely a return to older methods; the ghost of Laurence Sterne tends to resurface sporadically in literary history. Insofar as Atwood moves into postmodern modes, she does so because in an age of excess, realism is no longer adequate to convey the actual. In *Bodily Harm* the Toronto sculptor explains to Rennie that art "takes what society deals out and makes it visible" (*BH* 186). Creating this visibility in the contemporary world can be challenging; Atwood has commented on the problems of writing satire in a society where reality outdoes fiction in "absurdity or ghastliness" (Ingersoll 55). Under such conditions only the surreal can make the real visible and meaningful.

Thus *Bodily Harm* affirms the power of individual consciousness, the human imagination, and language to resist and try to change the state. But if Atwood shows their power, she also shows their limitations, and this emphasis is an important aspect of the novel's realism. For example, the distrust necessary in dealing with state power can become paranoia. (Significantly, Bartky also finds feminist consciousness "a little like paranoia," particularly at the beginning [18].) For all Minnow's eloquence about the importance of imagination in dealing with the state, his real threat to Ellis's government comes not only from his ability to imagine, but also from his insistence on acting on what he imagines. The imagination is an important form of Foucauldian local resistance, but like that resistance it has serious limitations. Imagination can veer into fantasy, and while imagination can impact reality, fantasy generally remains individual and cannot. As Janeway emphasizes, only group action can finally produce effective political intervention; individual dissent is merely preparatory (215). The differences between fantasy and reality, explored in tourism, voyeurism, and pornography, are a major focus throughout *Bodily Harm*. Distinguishing between the two is a particular problem for Rennie, with her tendency to misread. Atwood highlights the dangers of fantasy by leaving Rennie in jail at the end of the novel, keeping her reformation at the psychological level. Imagination is not all; whether or not Rennie can realize her imaginative vision in political terms will depend on external forces.

Bodily Harm thus offers a corrective to the continuing feminist tendency to overvalue consciousness change. In an interview Andrea Dworkin angrily attacked "the insane optimism in [the United States]—and it has been translated into every serious political movement I've seen in my lifetime—that it's all, ultimately, a matter of your attitude" (K. Abel 350). Although Dworkin connects this stance with a number of political movements, feminisms have been particularly marked by it. Consciousness-raising was a major target of attacks by early second-wave feminists who believed personal emphases were diverting energy and commitment from political efforts.[47] Originally intended as a preparatory mode, a preliminary exercise before political engagement, consciousness-raising too often became an end in itself. bell hooks is typical of numerous critics who emphasize the importance of connecting psychological foci to larger political issues: "In most cases, naming one's personal pain was not sufficiently linked to overall education for critical consciousness of collective political resistance" (*Talking* 32).

In *Bodily Harm* Paul ridicules the efficacy of feminist consciousness against the political order, attacking its focus on the personal: "When you've spent years watching people dying, women, kids, men, everyone, because they're starving or because someone kills them for complaining about it, you don't have time for a lot of healthy women sitting around arguing whether or not they should shave their legs" (*BH* 213). His overstatement does not negate the political impact of the point. Lora, too, points out the limits of consciousness-raising. In jail she complains to Rennie that all they are doing is "sitting around on our asses talking about men." "If it was two guys in here," Lora says, "you think they'd be talking about women? They'd be digging a tunnel or strangling guards from behind . . ." (*BH* 240). The fact that Rennie, not Lora, is the one who learns from and is changed by their discussions in the cell reflects the class connections that consciousness-raising has carried in second-wave feminism, its association with middle-class women.

Just as *Bodily Harm* shows the limitations both of early feminisms and of changes of consciousness, it also reveals the limits of discourse in dealing with the state. Language obviously can obscure as well as elucidate reality. If the corrective political power of the contemporary media is enormous, so are its shortcomings. Feminist and postcolonial critics have shown the unreliability of western media representations of both violence in nonwestern states and violence against women.[48] Minnow points out the metonymic relationship of news to violence, telling Rennie that journalists "always wait for the blood" (*BH* 121).

Equally troubling is the inadequacy of language in the face of violence. Elaine Scarry has analyzed the resistance of physical pain to language, pointing out that "pain does not simply resist language but actively destroys it, bringing about an immediate reversion to a state anterior to language, to the sounds and cries a human being makes before language is learned" (4).[49] Atwood confronts this kind of linguistic destruction in the torture of the deaf and dumb man, who "has a voice but no words," and her description falters. All that she can write is that his scream is "Not human" (*BH* 256). Setting off the two short words alone, at the end of a paragraph of brutal description, suggests their insufficiency to convey the reality of his experience. *Bodily Harm* shows the need for language to represent state violence, but it also shows the resistance of that violence to language. As in classical drama, actual killing in Atwood's novel always occurs offstage.

Just as cancer as metaphor can obscure the reality of cancer as disease, the pain of state violence can be obscured by language. Scarry writes that

> in order to express pain one must *both* objectify its felt-characteristics *and* hold steadily visible the referent for those characteristics. That is, the image . . . only enables us to see *the attributes* of pain if it is clear that the attributes we are seeing are the attributes *of pain* (and not of something

else). The deeply problematic character of this language, its inherent instability, arises precisely because it permits a break in the identification of the
referent and thus a misidentification of the thing to which the attributes
belong. While the advantage of the sign is its proximity to the body, its dis-
advantage is the ease with which it can then be spatially separated from
the body. (17)

In the face of the enormous capacity of the contemporary state to inflict
violence, language remains a limited weapon. As Foucault notes, "The
history which bears and determines us has the form of a war rather than
that of a language: relations of power, not relations of meaning" (*P/K*
114). Atwood's insistence on this history in *Bodily Harm* puts contemporary critical emphasis on the power of discourse into perspective. One
critic writes that "the chief form of violence depicted" in the novel is "si-
lencing language, either literally through denying it speech or more sub-
tly through trivializing its use" (Brydon 183). The deaf and dumb man,
Lora lying inert in the jail cell after her beating, and the dead Minnow
and Prince bring into question that assessment.

Gayle Greene has correctly emphasized that "issues of power in contemporary women's fiction center on questions of language" (17). The
novelists in this study who deal with the state, however, are an exception
to this generalization. Of the four, only Atwood gives extended consideration to the political power of language, and her treatment emphasizes
its limitations as much as its power. It is these limitations, along with an
acute sense of the complexity of the relationships between discourse and
action where the state is involved, that lead these novelists to largely ignore language as a force for change. Facing a culture that tends to un-
derrate the constitutive powers of language, academic critics have
provided needed instruction while at the same time following their own
predilections in emphasizing discursive power. They have not been so
eager to recognize its limits. The state unquestionably involves a "plurality of discursive forums" (Yeatman, *Bureaucrats* 170), but it also rests on
individuals bearing arms. The emphasis by the novelists in this study on
the men with the guns provides a corrective to the tendency to overvalue linguistic capacities in the face of the armed nation-state.

Finally, for all Rennie gains from her changed consciousness and all
her potential to influence politics through her writing, the emphasis in
Bodily Harm remains on the limits that any individual confronts in dealing with the state. The ending of Atwood's earlier novel *Surfacing* is fa-
mously upbeat: "This above all, to refuse to be a victim" (222). Obviously
reacting to optimistic overreadings of it, Atwood has several times emphasized that "you have to look at the context": "You can't simply refuse.

You can refuse to define yourself that way, but it's not quite so simple as that" (Castro 219; see also Ingersoll 43).[50] Referring to her treatment of victims and victimizers in *Survival,* she has also insisted that "You cannot create a character who is fully liberated in every sense of the word in a society which is not" (Ingersoll 189).

Similarly, in *Bodily Harm* Atwood ultimately refuses the Salvation Narrative of Politics. Without the presence of the state and its violence, the novel would be a Salvation Narrative. Rennie has learned the values of political consciousness, imagination, and words, and she is willing to use them. *Bodily Harm* affirms that all of these can change the individual and the individual's understanding of the world. The transition to actually changing the world, however, is left unclear. Rennie remains in prison. And even if she is released, given the limitations of discourse and consciousness against the violence of the contemporary nation-state, she may well remain in the same position vis-à-vis the state as the man with the rope was with her: a voyeur, looking on, wanting to do harm. The power of the outsider, even with the best subversive intentions, remains in question.

IV

□□□□□□□□□□□□□□□□□□□□□□□□□□□

The Romance of Politics:
Paule Marshall's *Daughters*

Perhaps we have reached a period in history when this question of the father's dominance can no longer be avoided.

—Luce Irigaray, *Sexes and Genealogies,* 11

The psychological toll of being a Black woman and the difficulties this presents in reaching political consciousness and doing political work can never be underestimated.

—Combahee River Collective, 277

Against all the odds (social, political, intellectual) the desire *for romance has survived.*

—Jackie Stacey and Lynne Pearce, "The Heart," 11

Until a strong line of love, confirmation, and example stretches from mother to daughter, from woman to woman across the generations, women will still be wandering in the wilderness.

—Adrienne Rich, *Of Woman Born,* 246

In an interview just after the publication of *Daughters* in 1991, Paule Marshall emphasized that one of its major themes was "the need for black men and women to come together in wholeness and unity" (Dance, "Interview" 20).[1] She described the novel as "a plea" to blacks "for dialogue, for a willingness to reach out and support and save each other." The kind of "reconciliation" that Marshall desires (Dance, "Interview" 4) obviously extends far beyond mere political collaboration. However, politics has a role in that reunification and is a crucial element in the novel.[2] Interpreted on the political level, Marshall's words invoke both the Coalition Narrative and the Salvation Narrative of Politics. "Come together," "support," "save"—in effect, she calls for salvation through coalition for black women and men. Just as in *Bodily Harm,* however, *Daughters* ultimately resists an entirely positive reading in redemptive political terms.

To embody her theme of reconciliation, one of the dominant symbols in Marshall's narrative, derived from a slave uprising on the Caribbean island of Triunion, is Congo Jane—or rather, Congo Jane and Will Cudjoe, "Coleaders, coconspirators, consorts, lovers, friends" (*D* 14; see also 138, 376).[3] Just as this description of their relationship recurs three times in the text, their inseparability is thrice emphasized by recalling Triunion's old saying: "You can't call her name or his without calling or at least thinking of the other, they were so close" (*D* 377; see also 14, 94). The pair represents an ideal of revolutionary equality, of sexual difference without hierarchy and of love and politics indissolubly fused. Like Toni Morrison, particularly in *Beloved,* Marshall draws on the slave past, "for all its horrors," as "a time when black men and women had it together, were together, stood together" (*D* 94). As Lowell Carruthers, the occasional lover of the novel's protagonist Ursa Mackenzie, notes, "We need to get back to thinking like that, being like that again, if we're ever going to make it" (*D* 94).

On the political level *Daughters* is an account of the obstacles that black men and women face to "being like that again"—and various alternatives to such cooperation. A major technique that Marshall uses to reveal both the obstacles and the alternatives is significant silences in her text. Pierre Macherey points out the need to "question the work as to what it does not and cannot say, in those silences for which it has been made":

> The order which it professes is merely an imagined order, projected on to disorder, the fictive resolution of ideological conflicts, a resolution so precarious that it is obvious in the very letter of the text where incoherence and completeness burst forth. . . . The work derives its form from this incompleteness which enables us to identify the active presence of a conflict at its borders. (155)[4]

Marshall's silences reflect conflicts that cannot be satisfactorily resolved given the conventions of the realistic novel, and the contemporary political realities that those conventions reflect, which shape *Daughters.*

The first of Marshall's silences that reveals "a conflict at [the text's] borders" involves Congo Jane and Will Cudjoe. Ursa's imagination has been captivated by the couple since her childhood in Triunion, when she stood on her mother's shoulders to touch the toes of their statues on the massive "Monument of Heroes." She wants to write about the pair but has been twice thwarted. In college in the United States her white male adviser refused to approve the project; Ursa speculates that the professor "probably can't stand the thought that those two actually existed" (*D* 14). Years later she cannot overcome a writing block to complete a Master's thesis on them.[5]

Significantly, Ursa is not the only one unable to portray Jane and Will. Triunion's old saying is that one could not be named without the other, but in *Daughters,* Jane is usually mentioned alone. Marshall herself constructs the couple through assertion—particularly the triple repetitions—rather than through narration or detailed description. The text offers little information about Will. In this way the focus of the narrative remains on women's political agency. However, because Marshall also does not depict either the relationship between the two or their joint revolutionary actions, the couple remains an ideal asserted by the author rather than produced by the narrative. Until Jane is hanged for rebellion, she herself is constructed primarily in personal terms and through stereotypical female roles: as a lover of "pretty things" (*D* 139); as a victim (of the slave system in general and her mistress in particular); as the nurse for Will's wound. Even the story of her hanging focuses on her famous lace shawl.

Representations of Jane and Will carry various potential dangers. The postcolonial government of Triunion recognized the political dangers of their story by locating the Monument of Heroes out in Morlands, the poor country district that has long elected Ursa's father Primus Mackenzie (nicknamed "the PM") as their representative. Even there, far from the white people in the capital, the monument was placed well back from the road, out of the sight of any passersby. The literary dangers of Jane and Will's story are both simpler and more subtle. With few models for the details of so revolutionary a fusion of the personal and the political, one risk is that a portrayal of the relationship in depth will not be believable. Moreover, Jane and Will's status as a political ideal is suggested by the other political couples whom Marshall does depict in detail in *Daughters.*

The most fully developed portrayal of such a couple is the PM and his wife, Estelle, on Triunion. The Mackenzies' romantic as well as political ties position them as the closest parallels in the novel to Jane and

Will. However, the relationship of Mae Ryland, an older community organizer in Midland City, New Jersey, and Sandy Lawson, the young mayor whose election campaign Mae organized, offers additional perspectives on the political potential of pairs. In both cases the women are directly compared to Congo Jane (*D* 280, 316), but in contrast to the text's assertions about Jane and Will, the two contemporary relationships show almost insoluble problems. Instead of equality, the traditional bifurcation of a public sphere gendered male and a feminized private sphere, with occasional opportunities for women in the social sphere, appears in both relationships. Given the difficulties they experience, the implication is that Jane and Will's relationship is not portrayed within the novel because the details of it are not entirely imaginable.

The problems of Estelle and the PM and Mae and Sandy directly reflect historical patterns that have limited women's direct power in the state. Both political pairs show the traditional mediation of women's relationship to the state through males. Also characteristic is that the women's political participation occurs mainly at the local level. The African American situation, where women predominate in community work while the leadership of national movements is almost entirely male,[6] replicates what Jenny Chapman describes as "the virtually universal pattern of male dominance in the recruitment of political elites" (xiv).

Estelle and Mae each occupy two roles that have often given women access to state politics, the traditional one of family member and the later nineteenth- and twentieth-century role of volunteer. Estelle on the Arts Council and Mae in the community as a whole reflect the long-term prominence of women's voluntarism in politics[7] that was encouraged by the demarcation of the social sphere from that of high politics. Estelle's familial connection to politics is through marriage to the PM, while Mae's reflects the extended families in many black communities. Mae functions as a community othermother, a woman who from the common role of othermother, one who shares mothering tasks with a bloodmother, has come to "feel accountable to all the Black community's children" (Collins, *BFT* 129).[8] In the novel everyone in the South Ward, even the old people, call Mae "Mother Ryland"; she herself explains that "The Lord didn't see fit to give me no babies of my own but I got me more grands and great-grands than I can count" (*D* 281). Mae claims Sandy as "once one of my grands," while Sandy himself describes Mae as "like family" to him (*D* 298, 279).

In *Daughters* Marshall emphasizes how the displacement of white women from a direct relationship to the state can become a double displacement for women of color. Even as these women have to work through their men to influence the state, the men in turn have to work through power structures that are mainly white. The PM and Sandy are decent men with ideals whose political careers were originally predicated on helping their communities. However, once in office, they find themselves powerless to chart their own political courses. After Triunion's triple colonization by Britain, France, and Spain, the island, "Independent in name only" (*D* 268), is triply recolonized by the corruption of the local ruling party, the requirements of international capitalism, and U.S. military might, with the U. S. S. *Woodrow Wilson* outside the harbor during every election. It is only a slight overstatement to say that Midland City under Sandy experiences similar colonization by wealthy suburbs, both black and white.

Marshall endows Triunion with a history that reflects a typical colonial-to-neocolonial pattern. Edward Said writes that after independence, "the triumphant natives soon enough found that . . . the idea of *total* independence was a nationalist fiction designed mainly for what [Frantz] Fanon calls the 'nationalist bourgeoisie,' who in turn often ran the new countries with a callous, exploitative tyranny reminiscent of the departed masters" (*Culture* 19).[9] Traitors to their own people and to the interests of the nation as a whole, to powerful foreigners the nationalist bourgeoisie are exemplary—and useful—capitalists. Neither the PM's background nor his financial status situates him as a member of this class, but he aspires to be, and he aids and abets their activities. Much of Fanon's description of the nationalist bourgeoisie reflects the PM's character and career. Primus "identifies" with the nationalist bourgeoisie, and like them he takes on "the role of the Western bourgeoisie's business agent"; he "turns [his] back more and more on the interior" where his district is located; he shares the "spirit of indulgence . . . dominant at the core of the bourgeoisie" (*Wretched* 152–53; 165). Even the resort scheme he supports for Morlands fits the pattern, for it represents a local recension of the "centers of rest and relaxation and pleasure resorts" that this class organizes "to meet the wishes of the Western bourgeoisie" (*Wretched* 153). In Midland City many of Sandy's attitudes toward politics also connect him with this class. He turns away from his black inner-city constituents to identify with whites and suburban blacks. His equivalent of the proposed resort in Morlands is a huge highway that will bisect poorer parts of the city, allowing those who come from the suburbs to bypass decaying urban areas entirely.

The PM and Sandy increasingly acquiesce in the political ineffectuality enforced on them by circumstances. Marshall plots their governmental careers as trajectories of feminization that are congruent with their secondary relationships to white power structures. Mae indicates that "In no time [Sandy] got to acting like some simpleminded woman a man can sweet-talk into throwing open her legs before she knows what's she getting into" (*D* 295). Estelle objects to the lack of initiative clear in every area of the PM's life: "Why does he just stand and wait for things to be done for him?" (*D* 149; see also 232). The political reliance of both men on their magnetic charm, particularly their smiles, is emphasized throughout the novel.

Marshall's depictions of the PM and Sandy reflect the extent to which feminization of any kind is a political process. Kathy Ferguson explains:

> As long as one group of people is primarily concerned with maintaining and exercising power, others will of necessity be primarily concerned with coping with that power held over them. They will need the skills of femininity to accomplish this. Thus as long as people's lives are constrained by radically unequal power relations, whether they are racial, sexual, economic, administrative, or some other, there will be femininity in the sense described here. (*FCB* 121–22; see also 173)

Both men are left with only the trappings of politics—Sandy's lunches, the PM's receptions—rather than substantive political power. Such activities suggest their relegation to the personal sphere. Ferguson notes that the "feminine role is inherently depoliticizing, in that it requires women to internalize an image of themselves as private rather than public beings" (*FCB* 94). The completeness of this process of internalization in Sandy and the PM is shown by the fact that for each of them, even the social sphere becomes mainly personal. The two men fail to operate successfully not only in the realm of traditional high politics but even in the social realm adjacent to it, where the women in the novel manage to function with great energy and at least some effectiveness.

Politics in *Daughters* is marked by male passivity and corruption, in contrast to female activity and idealism despite the limited spheres of action available to the women. Because of their political feminization, Sandy and the PM involuntarily participate in the Outsider Narrative, but they resist such positioning and persist in trying to become insiders at any cost. Both are also seduced by their attraction to the perks of their positions, abandoning the unyielding adherence to principle that constitutes the major justification for the Outsider Narrative. In contrast, Estelle and Mae spurn the trappings of power and consistently affirm their positions as outsiders. Like Congo Jane, whose love of "pretty things" is never shown distracting her from her primary political allegiances, the women refuse to be co-opted by power systems. Fiercely maintaining the ideological purity basic to the Outsider Narrative, both manage to make the best of the mediatory role to which high politics has traditionally assigned women.[10] Despite their admirable integrity, the fact is that with no substantive power and thus in a sense nothing to lose, the women in the novel can *afford* to stand for uncompromising rectitude in a way that the men cannot. What the Outsider Narrative ignores is that if politics is the realm of power, it is also the realm of compromise. In practical politics the ideological purity represented by the outsider position usually is sustained only at the cost of substantial political effectiveness, as Estelle's and Mae's experiences indicate. Ideological purity can possess a certain nobility, but in everyday political life it seldom has been an entirely satisfactory substitute for constructive political action.

In *Daughters* the two couples' bifurcation of ideological purity and access (although limited) to actual power, gendered female and male respectively, functions to insure the political status quo. The PM and Sandy in effect metonymically reduce Estelle and Mae to parts of themselves and then, personally reassured, ignore them. The PM dubs Estelle his conscience, "who'll see to it that this country boy in his donkey cart keeps to the straight and narrow" (*D* 133; see also 244). Sandy connects Mae with his origins in the South Ward, as opposed to proper mayoral concern for the city as a whole: "[S]he only thought about the Ward" (*D* 283). In both cases what the women represent is for all practical purposes consigned to the personal areas of the men's lives rather than becoming an active element in their politics.

Estelle and Mae, more dangerously for their own political efficacy, fail to separate the personal and the political that the men so thoroughly sever. The same personal ties that allow the women indirect access to male political power limit their willingness to oppose the ways that the PM and Sandy use that power. In essence, they play central roles in enabling the men to continue compromising the political values they themselves stalwartly uphold; it is in part the women's emotional dependencies that allow the men to act as they do. Estelle's love for the PM leaves her incapable of taking the action necessary to block the resort scheme he supports (*D* 363). She and Mae remain loyal to the PM and Sandy despite their betrayals, and both continue to believe in the men despite mounting negative evidence. Metonymically reduced by the men, the women in their turn reduce the men metaphorically. To maintain their faith, they end up infantilizing the men, in ways reminiscent of Rennie and Lora in *Bodily Harm*. Mae says of Sandy, "He's young. Maybe he can learn" (*D* 299). To all the women around him, the PM is "the boychild none can resist" (*D* 391).

❑   ❑   ❑

Marshall shows that both Estelle and Mae sacrifice their own political effectiveness because they make personal elements too central. The two women protect the PM and Sandy for many reasons: because the men are decent (although weak) human beings in truly bad circumstances; because of the traditional minority hesitancy to publicly attack their own given the overwhelming power of the majority; but above all, because they love them. Significantly, one of the major discourses in which the binary of pure women and corrupt men prominently figures is that of heterosexual romantic love. In effect, the women in *Daughters* ultimately view politics in terms of the romance plot.

Their misreading is particularly clear in Mae and Sandy's case, where traditional romantic love has no overt role. A telling remark at the end of a long monologue emphasizing that she is not yet ready to give up on Sandy reveals Mae's basic attitude. After making every possible excuse for him, she concludes:

> But if we find he can't learn and keeps on doing like he's doing . . . we'll vote his little gap-toothed self outta there the same way we voted him in, and find us another grand. And if that one don't do right neither, we'll vote his butt out too, and just keep on till we find us the right one. *The right one's got to be out there somewheres.* . . . (D 299, emphasis added)

"The right one"—the one perfect man or woman—is of course the primary trope of romance.[11] With both Mae and Estelle, the ideology, and therefore the power imbalances, of the traditional heterosexual romantic couple color their attitudes toward politics. That much of this association on both their parts is unconscious suggests the pervasive power of the romance paradigm over many women.

Congo Jane and Will Cudjoe's story is presented as a fusion of the romantic and the political, but the contemporary couples in *Daughters* show that transpositions of the romantic plot into the political arena hamper women's political efforts. The romance has traditionally discouraged female action. Janice Radway terms passivity "the heart of the romance experience" (97), while Alison Light emphasizes that all romances are about adolescence (25, n. 4).[12] Thinking in terms of the romance plot, the women in the novel lack the emotional independence necessary for effective intervention in politics.

Focusing on the romantic paradigm of the traditional heterosexual couple in connection with politics occludes crucial social and historical realities. First, within romantic emplotment individuals rather than institutions and systems necessarily predominate. Thus, as Radway points out, "the romance avoids questioning the institutionalized basis of patriarchal control over women" (217). Moreover, focus on the heterosexual couple ignores the homosocial relationships on which traditional politics rest.

The heterosexual romantic paradigm also ignores other past experiences. Historically, aside from courtship rituals, only in revolutionary situations (or, alternatively, in slavery[13]) have men and women functioned in at least quasi-equal relationships. For example, women played important roles in armed revolutionary struggles in Russia, Nicaragua, and other socialist countries.[14] But after the postrevolutionary regimes were established, interest in women's emancipation dissipated and women returned to their former unequal social and political status.[15] The same patterns held in national liberation struggles in Algeria, Iran, and Palestine.[16] Ruth Roach Pierson also points out the Israeli example. There, women participated

> as combatants in the defence of Jewish pioneer settlements before, during and after the First World War, in the anti-British struggle during and immediately after the Second World War, as well as in the war of independence of 1948–9. Once the state of Israel came into existence . . . and the Israeli Defence Forces were unified and regularised, women were excluded from "All jobs involving combat. . . ." (222)

Most important, the paradigm of romantic love is dangerous in political relationships because the paradigm itself evolved primarily to cover inequalities in power between men and women. Jane Gallop, following Lacan's discussion of chivalry in *Encore,* writes that "Courtly love obstructs the sight of the absence of a relation between the sexes"; it masks "the glaring absence" of any sexual relations. She goes on to quote Lacan that romantic love appears "at the level of political degeneracy [when] it had to become evident that on the woman's side . . . there was something that could no longer work at all" (*Daughter's* 44). The "something that could no longer work at all" was women's felt recognition of inequality. Heterosexual romantic love developed in part as a mystification of unpalatable political as well as sexual realities.

The most detailed feminist critiques of romantic love, following Simone de Beauvoir's analyses in *The Second Sex,* came from early radical writers in the late 1960s and early 1970s, such as Kate Millett, Germaine Greer, and Shulamith Firestone. Their treatments of romance are powerful political polemics and as such are marked by the tendencies to overstatement and reductiveness that insure the genre's effectiveness. For example, love is not always a "psychopathological condition" (Atkinson 62), nor is it simply the "opiate of a trapped sexual object" (Mitchell, *WLR* 108)—although it certainly can be either or both. This kind of rhetoric sometimes obscured the target of their attacks, which was never love per se, the deep human feelings of passionate connection and commitment that sustain individuals, but the institutional contexts that forced those feelings into destructive personal and social patterns.

Despite the early second wave's occasional rhetorical excesses, little has been written since that alters or expands these theorists' basic insights and social analyses.[17] Their impact spanned a generation, but by the late 1980s books extolling romantic love began to reappear (Baruch 5–7). This continuing resistance to critiques of romance suggests a deep-seated unwillingness or inability to confront and sustain them, even on the part of feminist theorists. As Ann Snitow points out, "romance is a primary category of the female imagination," and she criticizes the women's movement for leaving "this fact of female consciousness largely untouched" ("Mass" 261).[18] The one area in which a number of important critiques have appeared, studies of mass-market romantic novels by publishers such as Harlequin and Mills and Boon,[19] is the exception that proves the generalization. This popular fiction and its readers, although treated respectfully by most researchers studying them, tend to be viewed as fairly regressive by most academic feminists.[20]

Early second-wave feminists argued that heterosexual romantic love played a crucial role in the secondary status of women. To Firestone, love was "the pivot of women's oppression today" (121); Ti-Grace Atkinson described love as "the psychological pivot in the persecution of women" (43). These theorists were particularly interested in how the heterosexual romantic paradigm functioned to mask female powerlessness in the larger culture. Firestone explained romance as the result of the inevitable perversions of mutual love in a system where men wield greater power than women. Romance develops because love "becomes complicated, corrupted, or obstructed by *an unequal balance of power*": "[L]ove demands a mutual vulnerability or it turns destructive: the destructive effects of love occur only in a context of inequality. But because sexual inequality has remained a constant . . . the corruption 'romantic' love became characteristic of love between the sexes" (124).[21]

Atkinson analyzes the psychology of the heterosexual romantic paradigm in political terms. She explores how a woman attempts by means of love to gain access to some of the power of males, "instinctively trying to recoup her definitional and political losses by fusing" (44).[22] Atkinson's emphasis falls on "the striking grotesqueness of the one-to-one political units 'pairing' the Oppressor and the Oppressed, the hostile and the powerless, and thereby severing the Oppressed from any kind of political aid" (43).[23]

Marshall depicts the dangers of romantic paradigms in politics through the two contemporary couples in *Daughters*. She shows why relationships predicated on inequality cannot insure genuine political cooperation between the sexes or equal female participation in politics. At the same time, Marshall shows that some realities that the paradigm was evolved to hide compel women's continuing complicity with it.

After the police illegally arrest Robeson Daniels, his mother, Viney, Ursa's best friend, discusses her treatment by the precinct captain. A capable and successful businesswoman who has created a good life for herself and her son against great odds, Viney says that the captain "let me know that, yes, I might be a hotshot VP at Metropolitan, I might make twice his salary, but I was still in his book just another welfare mother standing there with her little ADC child and no father in sight." Viney goes on to admit to Ursa:

> "I would've given anything to have had a Mr. Somebody standing beside Robeson and me in that police station this afternoon. I felt this awful space, Ursa, this hole the size of me next to me, could even feel the wind pouring through it. . . . [It was] the outline, the space where some decent, halfway-together black man should have been. . . . And it's not that I can't manage on my own. Hey, I'm doing it every day! It's about dealing with what's still out there. . . ." (*D* 330–31)[24]

Although Viney's experience reflects certain unique pressures that black women face, it is also the case that the power realities of the current male-dominated system pressure many women toward the romantic paradigm as the best among grim alternatives. Most critics focus on women's romanticism as compensatory, with economic pressures a major concern.[25] Nancy Chodorow is typical in describing such romanticism as "an emotional and ideological mask for their very real economic dependence" (74). Rachel DuPlessis provides specific historical context, suggesting that "when middle-class women lose economic power in the transition from precapitalist economies and are dispossessed of certain functions, the romance script may be a compensatory social and narrative practice" (2). But even when direct economic dependence is not involved, serious problems remain. Effective intervention in political systems for financially independent women like Viney does not absolutely *require* a male partner; as a matter of fact, Viney manages to deal quite effectively with Robeson's arrest. But the psychological costs, as her comments to Ursa make clear, are enormous.

In *Daughters* "dealing with what's still out there" is frightening for all of the characters—for men as well as women, for whites as well as blacks—in the United States just as much as on Triunion. Marshall's bleak portrayals of corrupt systems in New York and Midlands City crumbling into chaos through poverty and violence bring into question the viability of any state politics to salvage them. Mae's call for a "regular Marshall Plan" to save the South Ward (*D* 299) parallels U.S. urban devastation with wartime destruction (and the resources of an entire nation, coordinated by a man who received the Nobel Peace Prize for his efforts). Ursa's lover Lowell dreams of running a program to recruit inner-city young people for college and help them succeed there. But he worries that he will be too late, because "things have gotten so bad for us, the mean streets have gotten so much meaner" (*D* 268). Significantly, Lowell recognizes that the problems are not only African American ones. He articulates what Marshall describes as "a hard truth others refused to see": "[M]aybe there was no escaping Harlem, not even for the white folks" (*D* 256; see also 96).

The international scope of the problems emerges as Ursa begins "seeing double" (*D* 290). She keeps seeing scenes from Triunion superimposed on her everyday experiences in the United States: "Inseparable. Inescapable. The same things repeated everywhere she turned" (*D* 333). Marshall has said that she finds working with the West Indies a technical advantage, because with the small islands as a "manageable landscape," she can use Caribbean settings to say what she wishes "about the larger landscapes, the metropoles" (Pettis, "*MELUS*" 119; see also Ogundipe-Leslie 20–21). In *Daughters,* however, she works not by analogy but through identity. Throughout the novel Ursa repeatedly questions her location— "Where am I? Which place? Which country? Is there no escaping that island?" (*D* 292)—only to discover that there can be no escape, because the two places are in a terrifying sense the same.[26] The colony and the metropolis merge in one nightmare vision. This vision grows in scope with other comparisons, such as Ursa's seeing first Dresden and then Beirut as she views the South Ward (*D* 298).

A number of contemporary critical approaches that analyze the perspectives of the less powerful have deployed various formulations of double vision. Almost all of them are directly or indirectly indebted to W. E. B. Du Bois's well-known concept of the "double-consciousness" of black Americans.[27] Henry Louis Gates locates a "double heritage, two-toned" from European or American as well as black traditions behind every western black text ("Criticism" 4). Patricia Hill Collins studies the unique perspective of the black woman as an "outsider-within" (*BFT* 11). In an essay on lesbian literary criticism Bonnie Zimmerman connects "double-vision" with disenfranchised groups and urges such vision on the privileged ("What" 219). Postcolonial theorists link the "double vision" of the native to traditional distinctions between colony and metropolis (Ashcroft et al. 37).

Above all, feminist theorists revel in doubleness.[28] From Adrienne Rich's *"double-life . . .* characteristic of female experience" to Nancy Miller's "double bind" faced by women writers, from Elaine Showalter's "double-voiced discourse"—or Elizabeth Meese's "double discourse"— of feminist criticism to Sidonie Smith's "double-voiced structuring" of women's autobiographies, and from Joan Kelly's "doubled vision" of feminist theory to the "double consciousness" formed in mothers (A. Ferguson) and also produced by utopias and fetishes (Neely), doubleness does yeowoman's service.[29] (A culmination of sorts is reached in Alice Jardine's description of the "doubly other" woman who writes as translating a "double message" and experiencing "a kind of double vision" in her "double practice" ["Pre-Texts" 229].) In addition to the usual academic bandwagon effect, the popularity of doubleness with feminist theorists derives partly from the fact that duality is almost always connected in one way or another with outsider status. Ursa's fused vision in *Daughters* implicitly or explicitly invokes all of these doubling formations.

A persistent problem in most of these paradigms is accurate positioning of women of color. Angela Bowen writes that "if we accept W. E. B. Du Bois' concept of the 'two-ness' of Black folks' vision, we must then accept that Black women bring a 'three-ness' of vision to all societal relations" (and she adds that Black lesbians "carry a 'four-ness' of vision") (64). Black women's ties with and differences from black men and white women have produced complex constructions of identity that offer unique angles of vision. It is this kind of perspective that Marshall, adding postcoloniality to Ursa's status as a black woman, deploys to advantage in *Daughters.*

Michelle Wallace has written that "the undermining of facile dualisms or binary oppositions of class, race, and sex is a priority in fiction by black women" ("Variations" 63). In *Daughters* Marshall participates in this ongoing deconstructive literary project, and adds her own unique slant to it. Like most theorists of doubleness, Marshall shows that hybrid traditions and the points of view that they foster are crucial in understanding and dealing with the chaos of contemporary culture. But in *Daughters* Marshall's distinctive contribution to current formulations is her portrayal of the resulting vision not as the bifurcated double exposure characteristic of most theory, but as an ironically unified vision created by samenesses superimposed. Doubling constructions usually rely on putative norms from the dominant culture. Marshall shows that no such norms from *any* culture can be found in the deadly similarities between Triunion and the United States that Ursa's "seeing double" reveals. Ursa's double vision deconstructs the obvious differences on which conventional critical binaries of doubleness have relied and reveals underlying identity. Marshall's warning is that contemporary societal crises may be in crucial ways deconstructing long-standing racial and postcolonial double formations.

From this perspective Marshall unflinchingly portrays her political pairs in terms of the obstacles posed to them by both unequal power divisions and hostile contemporary environments. Despite this realistic assessment, Marshall ultimately refuses to relinquish the ideal of the political couple in the novel. In an interview she referred to Viney's son Robeson and his friend Dee Dee as "the modern-day counterparts of Congo Jane and Will Cudjoe" (Dance, "Interview" 11). But the children are only eight years old, too young to be very convincing prototypes.

More interesting is a pair Marshall does not mention in the interview: Justin Beaufils, the young teacher who wins the PM's seat in an electoral upset at the end of the novel, and his wife, a Cuban-educated agronomist.[30] Various characters comment on Justin and his wife's teamwork during his political campaign, while Estelle wistfully compares them to herself and the PM in their younger days (*D* 360–61). Significantly, however, Beaufils and his wife are never directly depicted in the text. What we know of them is mediated entirely through others' descriptions, and we never even learn the woman's name. The partners equal in love and politics thus remain only an ideal in *Daughters,* never fully incarnated, but compelling despite their illusiveness. As such the silences about them in the novel reflect the conflict that Ann Rosalind Jones has noted "between feminism as emergent ideology and romance as residual genre" ("Mills" 204). However, *Daughters* also raises questions about just how "residual" the romance paradigm and its powers actually are.

❑   ❑   ❑

Marshall's couples, then, are the utopian goal for effective political action in the state. Recognizing and realistically depicting current obstacles to achieving such relationships, Marshall in *Daughters* also offers another avenue for political influence for women. She broadens her focus from the couple to the family to show the possibilities in female bonding for empowerment and resistance. Like its putative product the heterosexual romance, the family romance in its various recensions also impacts women's relationship to the state.

The power of the heterosexual romance paradigm to limit women to the private sphere derives in part from its concentration of all of a woman's emotional needs on one man. This emotional limitation to a single object has a prototype in the (at least stereotypically) close ties between mother and daughter. Significantly, Radway explains the romance as "a quest for motherly nurturance" (124), while Michele Roberts suggests that romances compensate for women's loss of "the nurturing mother" (228). After the daughter leaves the mother, paradigms of the heterosexual romance continue to insure that, as Firestone writes, "women are not creating culture because they are preoccupied with love" (121). To move beyond the attitudes that foster these paradigms requires increasing women's emotional independence. The emotional needs of the female, traditionally satisfied through an exclusive relationship first with one woman and then with one man, require more objects and differing levels of intensity to allow women to take action in the public sphere.

From the beginning, feminist theorists have been clear regarding the central role played by the traditional nuclear family in the oppression of women. Irigaray termed it "the privileged locus of women's exploitation" (*This Sex* 142). Atkinson found the family as corrupt an institution as slavery was and, like many feminists before and since, called for its abolition (5). The Editorial Collective of *Questions féministes* traced the key structural role of the family in women's secondary positions in society: "The economic inferiority of women in the work force, their exclusion from power positions, including politics, and their restricted access to knowledge must be linked with the division of labor between the sexes, which itself is based on the family as an institution" (217).[31] On the theoretical level, Susan Moller Okin writes that "the equality of women cannot be achieved in any political theory without the radical restructuring of the family" (289). Like the feminist attacks on romantic love, their critiques of the family have been widely, and undoubtedly deliberately, misread. Their objections have been focused primarily at the institutional level, directed not so much against basic familial feelings as against the social and economic structures that distort substantive human ties.

Feminist theorists have long sought alternative models and methods to rethink and restructure the nuclear family, for which the dominant metaphor has usually been sisterhood. In Marshall's novel Ursa describes Viney as her "sister/friend" (*D* 16, 40).[32] However, despite the potentially powerful combination of such sisterhood with the female friendship that recent theorists have proposed as an alternate political base for women, Ursa and Viney's relationship is primarily a source of emotional support rather than political action. Marshall's interest in the female bonds required for political power lies elsewhere.

Helena Michie writes: "Sisterhood projects a series of daughters who usurp the function and privilege of the father by reproducing themselves.

In choosing sisterhood over daughterhood, feminists have turned their gaze horizontally and have chosen—or tried to choose—to mirror each other and not the father." Despite these changes, Michie emphasizes that the "syntax, word, and language remain familial matters; the new grammar is still the grammar of the family" (16). Like the ideology of romance, that of sisterhood mystifies important patriarchal realities. Even more telling is another omission. In this sisterly projection, and particularly in the attempted autogenesis ("reproducing themselves"), the family member who is occluded in the attempt to usurp the power of the father is the mother.[33]

Nor is Michie's maternal occlusion in this passage unique. Claiming that "our society and our culture operate on the basis of an original matricide," Irigaray writes: "When Freud, notably in *Totem and Taboo,* describes and theorizes about the murder of the father as the founding act for the primal horde, he is forgetting an even more ancient murder, that of the woman-mother, which was necessary to the foundation of a specific order in the city." To show how "our imaginary still works according to the schema set in place by Greek mythology and tragedy" (*SG* 11), Irigaray analyzes the *Oresteia,* and particularly Clytemnestra's role in it. In Irigaray's reading, Clytemnestra's tragedy begins when she tries to protect her daughter Iphigenia from her husband. It ends when another daughter, Electra, takes her son's side against her, assuring the triumph of the patriarchal power of the city-state over the ancient order of the earth mother. This triumph insures the silence (and in some cases, as Irigaray notes, the madness) of most women, along with the "emergence of some useful Athenas, who spring whole from the brain of the Father-King, dedicated solely to his service and that of the men in power" (*SG* 12).

In another analysis of the Oresteian myth, Mary O'Brien comes to related conclusions. She analyzes Clytemnestra's offence in terms of gender roles, pointing out her actions "as a woman who loves her daughter, while she also acts sexually and politically like a man." In so doing,

> Clytemnestra becomes the agent of death, while the son born of her reproductive labour transforms his birth relationship to a death relationship, murdering his certain parent for the dubious sexual honour of his uncertain father. It is only *after* this male supremacy over natural relationships has been established that the public realm of rational/legal politics can be developed.

O'Brien emphasizes that this public realm rests "absolutely and resolutely on the negation of femininity, in the symbolic person of motherless Athene, and the banishment of the Furies to the perpetual privacy of an

Eternal Maternity Unit under the earth" (155–56).[34] Thus O'Brien and Irigaray interpret classical myth and literature to show that denying and banishing the maternal constitute the base on which the state and the homosocial relationships that create and sustain it are erected.

To subvert that political order and those relationships, Irigaray seeks to reestablish the bonds that the state must keep severed in order to insure its own survival: ties between women, particularly those between mother and daughter. She warns that women must take care "not again to kill the mother who was immolated at the birth of our culture" (*SG* 18). One of her solutions is the establishment of "a woman-to-woman relationship of reciprocity with our mothers" as "an indispensable precondition for our emancipation from the authority of fathers" (*IR* 50).

The story of the establishment of such relationships and the emancipation that they enable is central to the political plot of *Daughters*. From the beginning Ursa's primary parental focus has been her father, with "Her life set to his agenda" (*D* 250). Primus Mackenzie has insured that her identity has been largely constructed in terms of being his daughter, and she has, with a few notable exceptions, accepted that position. However, as Judith Butler points out, "the position articulated by the subject is always in some way constituted by what must be displaced for that position to take hold" ("Contingent" 8). In Ursa's case, what has been displaced is any substantive connection with her mother. As she explains to Viney, "I've just never known how to take her. . . . I'm still trying to figure out Estelle. Don't get me wrong. I love her. I'd do anything for her and she knows that, but she's a puzzle" (*D* 255). In the novel Ursa finally begins to experience the maternal relationship that both her father and her mother have denied her.

Estelle has struggled fiercely to make her daughter independent. To do so she has opposed not only the PM but also Celestine Bellegarde, the family servant who has taken care of both the PM and Ursa since infancy and who encourages Ursa's identification with her father. Writing to her family in the United States about the Civil Rights Movement, Estelle reveals her plans to send Ursa there "to take my place at the barricades as soon as she's old enough." Estelle explains that "Nobody here knows it, but I've already got her in training" (*D* 223). Her mother replaces the pretty dresses that the PM gives Ursa with coveralls, cuts her hair in an Afro, and pushes the child to take care of herself. Celestine fumes that Estelle is an "unnatural mother" (*D* 306, 397). Ursa herself describes Estelle as "*that strangest of mothers*" and repeatedly imagines her own life as a "small rowboat," which "Estelle had launched her in before she knew how to work the oars properly or could read the stars well enough to know which way was north" (*D* 335, 82; see also 254, 390).

Estelle represents one aspect of the various contradictions that Collins and other theorists have analyzed in the complex relationships between black mothers and daughters.[35] Estelle inculcates independence without the over-protectiveness that a number of these theorists have connected with African American mothers, although the end result is the same. As Gloria Wade-Gayles notes, the fictional mothers created by black women writers tend to be "strong and devoted," but "rarely affectionate" ("Truths" 10).[36] Estelle's attitudes and actions read like an almost perfect reversal of the white middle-class child-rearing practices that Nancy Chodorow and others connect with closeness and dependency in relationships between mothers and daughters. Such a reversal is appropriate. Gloria I. Joseph, who specifically cites Chodorow as a problematical example, writes that the second-wave feminist social scientists who theorized mothering "produced literature which in general was/is inapplicable to the relationships between Black mothers and daughters" (17).[37]

Most important, Estelle's tactics work. As Ursa grows up and the 1960s give way to the 1980s, her life in the United States reverses the materialistic trajectory of the culture, as she leaves a prestigious, high-paying corporate job for sporadic consulting work for nonprofit organizations and another attempt to write her thesis on Jane and Will. Evading the powerful ideological systems that so often entrap women, she resists assimilation by capitalism and romantic love. Far from Triunion, Ursa can give up whatever is necessary—her job, her lover—in order to maintain her integrity.

One system that Ursa has avoided confronting directly is the patriarchal one, represented by her father and his politics. For four years she has refused to return to Triunion because she cannot face what her father is and what he has done. Like Nadine Gordimer's Rosa in *Burger's Daughter,* Ursa needs to reconstruct her identity independently of her father's overwhelming influence, and also like Rosa, she does so by a return to the maternal. Her transformation begins when Estelle, unable to fight the resort plan on her own, summons Ursa home to help. It is Ursa who hands over the prospectus for the proposed resort to her father's opponent, causing the PM to lose the election. Her act is a classic Foucauldian localized disruption of power.

On the surface, then, the novel seems to suggest a fairly straightforward approach to producing women who can function effectively in the state. Stop the child-rearing practices that produce the kind of women described in the studies of Chodorow and particularly Carol Gilligan—women who value relationships and empathy over autonomy and justice, women in whom, as Gilligan writes, "identity is defined in a context of relationship and judged by a standard of responsibility and care" (160). *Daughters* offers no conventional biological mothers. Does the novel offer a Salvation Narrative of Politics through legions of Estelles rearing legions of Ursas?

This particular redemptive reading, like an uncomplicated valorizing of Congo Jane and Will Cudjoe, is undercut by another significant silence in the text. All of the plot lines of the story tracing Ursa's political (and, of course, personal) development converge at the moment when she acts to betray her father and insure his electoral defeat. Yet we do not see her handing over the documents to Beaufils, nor is the incident ever directly discussed. Marshall's refusal to focus on Ursa's act is unusual, since one of her characteristic stylistic traits is "the inexorable scrutiny of those crucial moments in people's lives that finally define their development" (S. Willis 63). But just as in her account of Jane and Will, revolutionary action is occluded in the text. Moreover, the three brief chapters after Ursa's action make the ending of the novel awkward and somewhat truncated. The chapters switch the focus first to Celestine and then to Astral, the women most completely co-opted emotionally and economically by the PM. In characteristic fashion, Celestine's concern is mainly for the PM, and Astral's primarily for herself.

Marshall's displacement of Ursa's most important political act in the novel in part represents a refusal to allow politics to dominate *Daughters*. She recognizes the importance of political commitment and action and makes them integral to her story, but she carefully constructs her novel so that politics never becomes the only focus. However, the occlusion of Ursa's transfer of the papers suggests not only the limitations of a solely political outlook and approach but also problems inherent in the act itself. Ursa relies on a quick intervention to destabilize the system and then an equally quick exit. She hands over the resort plans, stays just long enough to see the election results, and flies back to the United States early in the morning on the day after the balloting. The transaction functions as an exemplary example of the Outsider Narrative. The short-term gains from her act are clear—the PM and the corruption increasingly associated with him are out—but the long-term effects are more questionable.

The PM has been replaced by the young and idealistic Beaufils who, along with his wife, is dedicated to the good of the district of Morlands and to sweeping governmental reform. But the entire novel has emphasized the pervasive corruption of contemporary social and political systems in Triunion and beyond. Beaufils himself admits that the PM never had a chance to achieve the good that he desired for his country because of the ruling party's stranglehold on Triunion (*D* 361). To combat such deeply embedded structural obstacles, Ursa has passed power to yet another political couple, a formation that *Daughters* has already depicted as at best an unstable one. If Beaufils and his wife are able to bring about real political change, they will do so despite overwhelming odds. The question is whether Ursa's act has produced a substantive improvement, or whether her disruption has simply recast the ongoing cycle of corruption with a different set of characters. In any case, whatever the ultimate results of her intervention, she will not be there to experience them personally. She maintains the Outsider Narrative.

Ursa's triumph over her father and his political corruption resemble in disturbing ways his attempted betrayal of Morlands with the resort. In general, both avoid open disclosure and honest confrontation.[38] Each opts for silence and secrecy, which have been traditional methods of male political power. Ursa's act can also be read as a classic oedipal maneuver enacted in the political realm, a variation of the male plot, in which the daughter rather than the son establishes independence through the destruction of paternal power.[39] As such, it is an unusual deed; Lynda Boose points out that mythical accounts of daughters taking destructive action against fathers are extremely rare (Boose and Flowers 38).[40] Indeed, Ursa reverses several classic Greek tragic plots. In contrast to Iphigenia and Agamemnon, for example, here the daughter sacrifices the father for the common good.

More intriguing are Ursa's connections with Antigone. Confined within her family like Antigone, Ursa, unlike the Greek heroine, refuses to remain trapped there. Page duBois's brilliant revisionist treatment of Antigone, which returns her to the ancient Greek historical context, presents her as "bound up in the pollution of her family" (376).[41] Ursa, in contrast, opposes her familial pollution. DuBois explains Antigone as representing "aristocratic as opposed to democratic values" (382), while Ursa clearly chooses the democratic. In duBois's reading, Antigone stands for archaic maternal lineage along with aristocratic rule against the more democratic but paternal law of Creon's emerging city-state. Ursa, too, ultimately comes to represent the mother against the father. Finally neither she nor Antigone can tolerate the metaphorical killing of the mother that Irigaray associates with the founding of the state.

The problem remains that the action embodying Ursa's defiance of paternal power in many ways relies on classic tactics of male politics in order to challenge those politics. As critics have repeatedly emphasized, such binary reversals are problematic. Although they can alter the balance of power in the state and bring in different rulers, relying on the corrupt tactics of the past almost guarantees that the basic corruption will remain. The tactics of the PM, Oedipus, Agamemnon, and Creon are dubious bases for a political order with different values, particularly feminist ones. It is in part because of the connections of Ursa's delivery of the resort plans with traditionally male paradigms that Marshall does not emphasize the act itself. The silence surrounding the transfer of the papers suggests the need for women to find a way beyond such tactics.

From yet another perspective it can be argued that Ursa's intervention is actually an exemplary postmodern political act. Jean-François Lyotard writes of the "master-warrior-speaker" that "One should not attack him head-on but wage a guerrilla war of skirmishes and raids in a space and time other than those imposed for millenia [*sic*] by the masculine logos" ("One" 14). This technique is more obviously effective in the case of the speaker than with the master or warrior, and not surprisingly, it is in the arena of discourse that feminist theorists have particularly urged this kind of maneuver. Carol Cohn is typical in arguing that the goal should be

> to destabilize, delegitimize, and dismantle patriarchal discourses—to render their systems, methods, and presumptions unable to retain their dominance and power and thus to open spaces for other voices to be heard. Destabilizing and interrupting patriarchal discourse are seen as the prerequisites for establishing new paradigms and different theoretical tools and for creating systems of knowledge based on different values and interests. (155)

The continuing problem has been just exactly what happens after the destabilization. Elizabeth Ermath, like the majority of theorists,[42] emphasizes that feminist theory "does not seek to propose positive knowledge or to outline ideal states of affairs or to modify power structures in a particular, pre-determined direction." She describes the function of feminist theory as emphasizing "subversion and possibility, not alternative models." Since the goal is not "implementation," the "question of *what* new formation is modestly left to the processes of time" (6, 8). The consequences of this kind of approach for feminist activism in the state, however, are more questionable.

What these theoretical descriptions, along with Ursa's action, highlight is the important distinction between strategy and tactics. Strategy (from the Greek *strategos,* "general," itself derived from *stratos,* "army," and *agein,* "to lead") is long-term planning for and executing of large-scale operations. In contrast, tactics (from *tassein,* "to arrange") are short-term techniques to attain temporary positions. Thus, although Cohn calls her method "a *strategy*" (155), it can more accurately be termed a tactic. In addition, it is important to recognize that, as Carol Anne Douglas notes, the boundaries between strategy and goals sometimes can blur (*Love* 251).

Tactics can be useful in theoretical advances, particularly those involving discourse. Thus Lyotard connects the "immense impact" of the women's movement to the fact that "this movement solicits and destroys the (masculine) belief in meta-statements independent of ordinary statements" ("One" 15). But tactics have been of more dubious value in women's political actions. Atkinson emphasizes their "proper *supplemental* place" because of their limited potential for realizing long-range political goals (154). Unless carefully orchestrated in terms of such goals, tactics can become mere adventurism. Selective tactical interventions are in any case problematic because the marginality that they require in effect preserves the center. As the Editorial Collective of *Questions féministes* points out, "The underground where one may indeed fight is nonetheless not equivalent to freedom" (220). Finally, with tactics one can at least temporarily right wrongs, but one can seldom construct alternative systems.

From de Beauvoir on, feminist analyses and discussions of strategies and tactics have been rare. Douglas complains that radical and lesbian feminist writers have seldom dealt with these topics, and terms this omission "a failure of the movement" (283). She writes that the theorist who has given the most attention to strategy and tactics is Atkinson, who, along with the very few with a similar focus,[43] are no longer playing active roles in women's politics (239, 289). Douglas's criticism is equally valid for the other wings of the women's movement. Tactical discussions of specific issues abound, but too frequently "tactics cannot be directly linked with a particular long-term goal" (287). Although Douglas complains of the paucity of both tactical and strategic thinking, it is the lack of strategy that she finds especially dangerous. She goes so far as to write that this deficiency "probably has affected the level of activism" (4).

A continuing weakness of efforts to alter the relationship between women and the state has been a reliance on tactics without enough in the way of substantive strategy. On the activist side, Joyce Gelb and Marian Lief Palley, noting "an absence of overall 'strategizing' and planning within the movement," write that feminist groups largely "deemphasize long-range planning and program development" (36). M. E. Hawkesworth from a theoretical perspective points out the "dearth of discussion of the political institutions that would structure a just political order" (151). In part this tactical emphasis comes from a failure to agree on the parameters within which change should be effected. Silvia Federici comments that the women's movement "has continually shifted between a utopian dimension posing the need for a total change and a day to day practice that assumed the unchangeability of the institutional system" (339). Equally salient, however, are the nature of the power and the complexity of contemporary state systems that women face. Atkinson recognizes that tactics are the only alternative when the "strength of the opposition, in the given situation, is overwhelming, and cannot be attacked frontally." Thus she admits that "for the moment, 'tactics' *are* the strategy of the Oppressed" (154).[44] Since Atkinson wrote in 1974, not much has changed.

Feminist theorists often make a virtue of their strategic shortcomings by constructing a strong binary between strategy as a totalizing move and an ad hoc political approach that can respond to situations as they arise. For instance, Davina Cooper writes that those who reduce "all activism to strategy," and who thus "see every challenge, resistance or oppositional deployment of power as part of a coherent operation," run the risk of missing "a crucial element of both protest and change, . . . the intuitive, expressive, unprepared action" (140).[45] But strategy is supposed to be flexible and to be modified as situations develop. When General Dwight Eisenhower ordered the Allied troops onto the Normandy beaches, he did not provide them with blueprints dictating every lane they would traverse. But they did have the best maps available of their respective areas. And he—and they—certainly knew in what general direction they were headed. It is important to differentiate the need for some kind of functional long-term strategies from rigidly totalizing schemes. Cooper calls for feminists to deploy *both* strategic and intuitive political actions (139–41), but the movement's almost complete lack of larger strategies means that in practice ad hoc politics reign supreme.

Although *Daughters* raises the question of the long-term efficacy of Ursa's tactics by the occlusion of her action, it is important to note that Marshall does not simply condemn them. Tactics have been traditionally connected with guerilla warfare; Atkinson termed the two synonymous (154).[46] In the novel Mae explicitly compares her tactics to those of the Vietcong, hiding in the jungles, waiting for opportunities to attack, hitting with lightning speed, and then disappearing (*D* 296). But Mae's guerrilla tactics as she tries to regain strength after being forced out of City Hall as Sandy's community liaison serve a larger strategy, her Marshall Plan for the South Ward. Marshall thus represents the necessity for guerrilla tactics under certain conditions as well as the limitations of such maneuvers.

A classic outlet for the powerless, guerrilla tactics have long been a staple in confrontations between women and the state, particularly in the direct-action wing of the women's peace movement. Here the drama of such tactics that led to street theater being termed guerrilla theater—terrorism's status as "primarily theatre" (Wardlow 38) is also relevant in this connection—starkly illustrates their general limitations. Gwyn Kirk provides a colorful example:

> On April 1, 1983, a group of women in costume went over the fence at Greenham [Common] for a picnic on the base—they were dressed as teddy bears, pandas, a jester, a witch, and a hot-pink rabbit. Before being arrested they were escorted by the police and the soldiers, stiff-backed in their dark uniforms and camouflage jackets, theoretically in control. Beside them the women lolloped along, skipping and hopping, thoroughly enjoying themselves. Some people active in the labor movement deride this kind of action as whimsical, frivolous, indulgent, yet women undermined the authority of the military much more effectively than by shouting slogans. It was also great fun—a good example of politics that enlivens and feeds the participants, as it must if we are to keep at it and not burn out. ("Our Greenham Common: Feminism" 121)[47]

The language of Kirk's description supports the labor activists' criticisms of the action as "whimsical" ("a hot-pink rabbit"), "frivolous" ("lolloped along"), and "indulgent" ("thoroughly enjoying themselves"), while her defense of it in terms of its efficacy as opposed to "shouting slogans" and its "great fun" is relatively weak. The rabbit lollops while the cruise missiles sleep undisturbed, because the soldiers are not just *theoretically* in control.

Significantly, Adrienne Harris connects the political aesthetics and style of women's peace demonstrations with *écriture féminine* (106), once again suggesting the problems in infusing discursive tactics into political actions. She reflects the widespread tendency to confuse discursive change and political change. Finally, the connection of certain stereotypical feminine traits with guerilla tactics is also disturbing. Betty Reardon points out that "many of the negative 'feminine' characteristics are manifestations of the earliest type of guerilla warfare against an oppressor. Deception, obstructionism, recalcitrance, and unwelcome surprises are standard elements in nonformal warfare" (48). In this sense such tactics only reinforce the traditional connections of women and powerlessness. Using guerilla tactics, women will always remain within the confines of the Outsider Narrative.

Marshall's silence about the transfer of the resort plans, along with her somewhat truncated ending, insures that the emphasis in the novel falls on events that precede the act itself. Ursa's handing over the papers is the final result of an alliance between a mother and a daughter for political action. When Ursa returns to Triunion to aid Estelle in blocking the resort, the two finally begin to establish a "woman-to-woman relationship of reciprocity" such as Irigaray found crucial for freedom from paternal authority (*IR* 50). Ursa's position as daughter to her father has impeded political action on her part; as daughter to her mother she becomes free to act. Trapped in the patriarchal family, she is finally liberated by maternal ties.

Estelle, who has pushed to give her daughter exposure to the black heritage of the U.S. Civil Rights Movement, at the end of the novel moves to insure Ursa's access to the black heritage of the extended family. She has inculcated independence in Ursa as a child; she now takes care that strong female familial bonds will anchor that firmly established independence. Ignoring Celestine's personal hostility to her, Estelle has always encouraged the ties between Celestine and Ursa, which much more closely resemble a stereotypical mother-daughter relationship than Estelle and Ursa's do. At the end of *Daughters,* Estelle with similar generosity provides a second othermother for Ursa when she orders her daughter to visit Astral Ford, the PM's longtime mistress. As Astral and Ursa talk, Astral indirectly admits her maternal feelings for Ursa. Ursa in turn, "like a loving daughter," urges Astral to eat (*D* 405).

Occluding the act of delivering the papers and moving instead to Celestine and Astral at the end of the novel turn the textual focus toward personal aspects of the mother-daughter relationship rather than to its political ramifications.[48] Despite the primarily personal emphases of the final chapters, however, their maternal foci implicitly suggest some larger political directions. Irigaray sees the relationship between mothers and daughters as "a highly explosive nucleus": "Thinking it, and changing it, is equivalent to shaking the foundations of the patriarchal order" (*IR* 50).[49] Given the political results produced by Estelle and Ursa's working together, Marshall's emphasis at the end of the novel on Celestine and Astral as mothers suggests intriguing possibilities.

Irigaray writes that "If we are not to be accomplices in the murder of the mother [that in Irigaray's view precedes state formation,] we also need to assert that there is a genealogy of women." She points out that "Each of us has a female family tree: we have a mother, a maternal grandmother and great-grandmothers, we have daughters. Because we have been exiled into the house of our husbands, it is easy to forget the special quality of the female genealogy; we might even come to deny it." Irigaray urges women to "try to situate ourselves within that female genealogy so that we can win and hold on to our identity" (*SG* 19). Using broader African-based conceptions of the maternal role by othermothers and community othermothers, Marshall's depiction of Celestine and Astral in *Daughters* suggests some limitations in Irigaray's description of the female genealogy. Marshall thus expands the political possibilities for those whose identities have become firmly established in terms of such genealogies.

Behind othermothering and community othermothering are traditional patterns of the black African extended family, matrifocal and often matrilineal, which numerous critics have contrasted with the western patriarchal nuclear family.[50] Unlike the western valorization of individual autonomy and freedom from attachments, many African societies emphasized communal interdependence, believing that individual advancement was directly tied to the progress of everyone in the community.[51] Central to promoting community well-being has been the role of mothers, who were greatly esteemed in Africa.[52] Also highly valued were the patterns of cooperative child care that evolved.[53] The African practice of fostering children who were not orphans and whose parents also cared for them promoted community. When adapted to the conditions of slavery in the Americas, fostering emerged as othermothering (S. James 46).

The hybrid cultures of the Caribbean retained many of these African familial attitudes and practices.[54] Writing from this heritage, Marshall is well situated to work out some of their political implications. In the West Indies, where, as in many parts of Africa, the spheres of domestic and community life overlapped, women were central in society.[55] As in West Africa, conjugal ties did not necessarily function as women's primary or most emotionally intense relationships.[56] Constance Sutton and Susan Makiesky-Barrow note "the importance ascribed to the role of mother in contrast to the role of wife" (473).

African-based traditions, then, positioned the mother as a strong communal as well as individual presence in overlapping family and quasi-family networks. Such models could be particularly important in the redefinition of the patriarchal family that many feminists have long considered necessary for ending women's oppression. In any case, since western familial patterns are obviously changing whether or not feminist interventions occur, consideration of these alternatives could also be useful for anyone concerned with the state of the contemporary family. Marshall takes her place among many black women writers whose novels are rethinking and reconfiguring the nuclear family beyond the patriarchal domain (McDowell, "Reading" 85). As Estelle adds another othermother for Ursa, Marshall offers a powerful alternative to traditional western ideas about the nature of the family and women's roles within it.

Marshall presents motherhood, through both blood and "fictive kin" (Collins, *BFT* 120; see also Rapp 60–62), as one potential bond among women that offers a natural way for them to associate, surmounting some of the historical difficulties that women have faced in trying to forge ties with each other. Except for Estelle, all of the women around the PM are at some level competing with the others for his love and attention. Despite the substantial personal costs for her, Estelle's acceptance of sharing him presages her generosity in sharing her daughter, suggesting the importance of cooperation among women under patriarchal culture. *Daughters* also emphasizes the flexibility that such female ties can offer. Irigaray writes that "in our patriarchal culture the daughter is absolutely unable to control her relation to her mother" (*This Sex* 143), but Estelle's sending Ursa to visit Astral gives the daughter a primary role in evolving the relationship.

Equally important is the range of resources and role models to which othermothering allows daughters access. To Estelle, representing an uneasy synthesis between U.S. and West Indian cultures, and to Celestine, who stands for island tradition as well as the female familial line through her ties with the PM's mother, Ursa adds Astral, who offers a modern recension of the economic autonomy traditional among African and Afro-Caribbean women.[57] Thus for women's activity in the home, in politics, and in business, Ursa has role models. The three women can be seen as positive reinscriptions of three of the negative stereotypes that Collins includes among "controlling images" of black women: the Mammy (Celestine), the Matriarch (Estelle), and the Jezebel (Astral) (*BFT* 70–78).[58] The extent to which each parodies the applicable stereotype highlights the inadequacies of the negative images.

In addition to the personal benefits connected with othermothering, *Daughters* suggests some political possibilities of the practice. Barbara Christian writes that a question which African American women's novels of the late 1970s and early 1980s "leave unanswered is whether the bond between women might be so strong that it might transcend the racial and class divisions among women in America, and make possible a powerful women's community that might effect significant change" ("Trajectories" 247). Marshall, too, ultimately leaves this question unanswered. However, by ending her novel with Celestine and Astral, two women who are never shown independently intervening in politics, she highlights the importance of a woman's class along with her race and gender in determining her relationship to the state. Joyce Bennett Justus notes West Indian "solidarity among females regardless of social distinctions" (433), and Marshall draws on such traditions of solidarity when Estelle encourages Ursa's relationship with Celestine and sends Ursa to

Astral. Significantly, however, it is the woman from the United States and not either of the Caribbean women who moves toward solidarity, suggesting the transcultural potential of the West Indian women's traditions. The bonds that Estelle begins to forge transcend class through mothering[59] and leave open the political possibilities for such quasi-maternally based groups of women.

African American feminist theorists have explored a number of those possibilities. Collins sees black women's roles as othermothers as providing "a foundation for Black women's political activism" (*BFT* 129). When exemplary othermothers become community othermothers, they begin to function in the public as well as the private sphere (S. James 48); in a natural progression, community othermothering often leads to general community activism (Collins, *BFT* 131). Commenting on forms of black women's "politicized domesticity," Sara Evans notes that during the Civil Rights Movement in the South, "Black women known as 'the Mamas' were key leaders in every community" (65). Collins sees black women's experiences as both othermothers and community othermothers as fostering "a distinctive form of political activism based on negotiation and a higher degree of attention to context" (*BFT* 160). Along with Stanlie James, Collins emphasizes the new civic patterns that can emerge from the group-centered leadership and the ethic of care characteristic of community othermothers (James 50; *BFT* 131–32). Such approaches, which move maternal practice out into the community, offer vital alternatives to traditional western political and social formations. Thus James emphasizes African-based mothering forms as "an important Black feminist link to the development of new models for social transformation in the twenty-first century" (45). Obviously these theorists take othermothering far beyond anything that Marshall directly depicts in her novel. But it is significant that the personal network of mothers that begins to take shape at the end of *Daughters* carries the potential for developing in political directions.

Finally, it would be unfortunate to have worked through various problems in the ideologies of both the nuclear family and the heterosexual romance only to end up romanticizing either African cultural practices or maternal politics. Both present serious problems as well as exciting possibilities for women and the state. Despite African women's power and status within individual communities, men have long tended to dominate political life there, just as women still remain subordinate to men even in matrilineal societies. At the end of *Daughters* it is the PM, not the women, whom Ursa connects with African practices: "He was born on the wrong continent" (*D* 405).

Anna Wilson and Carrie Allen McCray also warn against romanticizing the contemporary black family. Wilson finds it "a nostalgic construction as much as it is a place of refuge; the reality is a site of exploitation as much as it is the locus for the preservation of culture" (86).[60] In today's black communities, the continuing breakdown of familial traditions has negatively impacted othermothering practices along with everything else. Finally, taking a familial model out of the black community, where centuries of tradition have supported and developed it and centuries of oppression have also shaped it, to deploy that model within very different cultural contexts would present formidable challenges.

The translation of maternal practices into the public realm also presents problems. Theorists have noted the traditional incompatibility of motherhood and action (Hirsch, *Mother/Daughter* 38). Kathy Ferguson points out that the inequality inherent in the relationship between mothers and children "makes it a poor model for larger relations of citizenship, which require equality among individuals and which are rooted in respect, not in love" (*FCB* 171).[61] Marshall in *Daughters* offers a possible answer to this objection by showing part of the novel's othermothering network as based on respect rather than love, reminiscent of the way in which *Bodily Harm* undercuts citizenship based on friendship. Celestine thoroughly dislikes Estelle, but her respect for the "*blanche neg*'" (97–99) is unmistakable. Obviously, the practice of community othermothering presupposes a different model of citizenship from Ferguson's, but just how the gap between it and current models could be bridged remains unclear.

Equally troubling is the tendency of maternal politics to remain localized. Mae, who is extremely successful in her role as a community othermother, is appointed to a position in City Hall, but the job is taken away from her after about a year and she returns to the Ward. Even in City Hall her job was that of community liaison, which highlights the difficulty for women of moving from local to more traditional forms of political power. Sandy calls Mae "the Coalition Lady" (*D* 280), and she is able to unite the South Ward to get him elected mayor. But the limits of her power—and of the kind of coalitions that she can create—are shown when at City Hall she is unable to forge larger coalitions that can adequately represent the interests of the Ward.

Another example of the limitations of maternally based initiatives in traditional politics is the case of the Mothers of the Plaza de Mayo in Argentina.[62] Ynestra King writes that although the Mothers have served as powerful witnesses against a corrupt regime, "they have never been able to move beyond their position as mothers and to take on real political authority" (293; cf. Dietz, "Citizenship" 33). As in the Argentine experience, African-based mothering practices too often position women in the social sphere, where their political activities have traditionally been confined, without adequate access to the realm of high politics. The challenge with such models is to insure their functioning beyond the social.

Chikwenye Okonjo Ogunyemi writes that the black woman writer, "conscious of black impotence in the context of white patriarchal culture, empowers the black man": "She believes in him; hence her books end in integrative images of the male and female worlds" (68–69). But Marshall refuses any such images. She ends *Daughters* with Ursa by herself, but with the prospect of new maternal bonds and support. Eugenia Collier describes Marshall's works as showing a "progression from the divided individual self to the self-made whole through merging with the community" ("Closing" 295).[63] In *Daughters,* for the first time in Marshall's novels, the community with which Ursa begins to merge is one that is constructed as much in terms of future opportunities as of past history—a fledgling community of women brought together through the expanded definitions of maternal relationship derived from African traditions.[64] For Marshall, the revolutionary couple remains the ultimate political goal. But another valid goal, in a sense *both* a tactic and a strategy, can offer its own rewards while potentially bridging the gap between the contemporary historical moment and a future where a reconstituted romance paradigm and a renewed politics can perhaps merge. That goal is creating the extended maternal relationships and seeking to realize the powerful political possibilities that Marshall only suggests in *Daughters.*

V

□□□□□□□□□□□□□□□□□□□□□□□□□□□□

Political and Sexual Liberations: Nadine Gordimer's *A Sport of Nature*

What is South Africa? A boiler into which thirteen million blacks are clubbed and penned in by two and a half million whites.

—Frantz Fanon, *Black Skin, White Masks*, 87

Look, young woman. If, for reasons that escape me, the process of government interests you, then all you've got to do is to play your cards right, and put yourself in a position where you have power. For a woman it's easy. You should marry a politician and run him. . . .

—Mr. Maynard to Martha Quest in Doris Lessing,
A Ripple from the Storm, 57

Let's leave definitiveness to the undecided; we don't need it. Our body, right here, right now, gives us a very different certainty. Truth is necessary for those who are so distanced from their body that they have forgotten it. But their "truth" immobilizes us, turns us into statues, if we can't loose its hold on us.

—Luce Irigaray, *This Sex Which Is Not One*, 214

And even when women have gained political influence or power, they have always—from Madame Pompadour to Golda Meir and Indira Gandhi—conducted their politics in the Procrustian bed of the male historical consciousness. . . .

—Günter Grass, *The Flounder*, 522–23

In an interview Donna Haraway commented: "Theoretical work in social movements is often done through figuration—through imagining powerful cultural figures." Such a figure, whether an imagined character or an actual person, exerts power as a "figure of possibility, a figure of criticism, a figure of contradictions." Haraway added that figuration as a theoretical mode "hasn't been worked out very well" (Darnovsky 67–68).[1] One of the reasons for this failure is that figuration has more often been deployed as a literary mode than an analytical one. As a successful theoretical figuration, Haraway's famous cyborg is a preeminent exception to the rule that figuration has functioned more effectively in fiction than in theory.

Hillela Capran, Nadine Gordimer's protagonist in *A Sport of Nature,* is one such powerful literary figuration. Hillela's cousin Sasha writes to his mother Pauline about South Africa—and, by extension, about black Africa in general: "*It will take another kind of being to stay on, here. A new white person. Not us*" (*SN* 218).[2] In Hillela, who continues living in Africa when Sasha and Pauline cannot, Gordimer is presumably producing this new revolutionary white subject for black Africa.

In her plot Gordimer also produces an exemplary Salvation Narrative of Politics. In marked contrast to the other novels in this study and to the overwhelming majority of contemporary novels about women and the state, *A Sport of Nature* traces a triumphant trajectory for Gordimer's new revolutionary subject. Indeed, the novel is a political Cinderella story of sorts.[3] Abandoned by her mother and ceded by her father to the care of relatives in South Africa, Hillela[4] rises from obscurity and survives tragedy to play an important role in African liberation politics. She moves from total political apathy as a girl and a young woman—an "ex go-go dancer" and a "little beach girl" (*SN* 135, 160, 252)—to become an accomplished political operative on three continents. Ultimately she marries a black African general who, after successively deposing both colonial and neocolonial rulers of his country, as president makes the nation a model for the entire continent.

Gordimer constructs Hillela as a revolutionary figure, powerful and energetic, with admirable ideals and sturdy independence of thought. An instinctive and inveterate transgressor in every area, she refuses almost all conventional intellectual categories and behavioral restrictions: "Categories were never relevant to her ordering of life" (*SN* 129).[5] Hillela scorns concerns of color in a country where color dictates every aspect of life, and she becomes the confidante, lover, adviser, and wife of black African male revolutionaries although she is a white Jewish woman. After her politicization, the highest ideals animate her conduct: "With her, it was already one world; what could be" (*SN* 242).

As prominent as the idealism in Hillela's character is her pragmatism. She possesses the traits of an adroit politician. Gordimer attributes Hillela's success primarily to instinct.[6] Never "one to make mistakes when following her instincts" (*SN* 227), in politics she adds calculation to the instincts that unerringly lead her to make "all the right connections" (*SN* 261).[7] A "past mistress of adaptation" (*SN* 360), she has the flexibility characteristic of most politicians who thrive. Unlike the women in *Daughters,* Hillela understands both strategy and tactics, and the difference between them. Although she occasionally "condone[s] means for ends" (*SN* 305; see also 254), she always maintains a clear overall strategy. In contrast to most of the women in *Bodily Harm,* violence does not deter her in pursuit of her political goals. Her view that force has to be met with force is expressed in a rigid binary: "You're a victim, or you fight and make victims" (*SN* 305).[8]

Hillela's status as a revolutionary political subject is connected with her position as a quintessential postmodern one.[9] Her mobile subjectivity is vintage postmodern. Dropping old identities and constructing new ones at will, she creates and re-creates herself. In the opening sentence of the novel, she changes her name on a train between Rhodesia and South Africa; after becoming involved with General Reuel, she gains an African name. Later she reconfigures her biography as she wishes (*SN* 199). For her everything is performative—"all her life [she] assumed instinctively from observance of those with whom she lived the appropriate attitude"—and the narrator[10] sums up her identity in that way: "What others perceive as character is often what has been practised long as necessity" (*SN* 222, 360). Hillela's infinite adaptability and her refusal of stasis connect her with the kind of nomadic figure frequently valorized by feminist theorists. This outsider figure has also become paradigmatic of postmodernism more generally. As Nira Yuval-Davis writes, "The exile, the person with fragmented identity, who belongs everywhere and nowhere, has become the symbol of the post-modern epoch" (409).

Hillela has other feminist connections. The majority of feminist theorists have also joined postmodernists in valorizing the political effects of fragmented subjectivity. Jane Flax is typical: "Only multiple and fluid subjects can develop a strong enough aversion to domination to struggle against its always present and endlessly seductive temptations" (*Disputed* 110). In addition, Hillela in various ways reflects all three of the prevailing narratives of feminist theory analyzed in chapter 2. An outsider who knows the value of coalitions and works in them constantly, after her first marriage she constructs her life as a version of the Salvation Narrative of Politics. She refuses to remain in the female social sphere, segregated from the realm of high politics. Although she does African relief work for a while, she ultimately leaves it behind, recognizing, as the General warns her, that politicians do not "come to power on soup powder" (*SN* 310).

Yet despite Hillela's political successes, her many positive qualities as a politician and a revolutionary, her admirable ideals and dedication, and her postmodern and feminist contemporaneity, she remains a disturbing character.[11] Haraway located the power of figurations in their reflecting possibilities, criticism, and contradictions (Darnovsky 67). Even with all of the compelling future possibilities and cogent criticisms of the present that Hillela embodies, she is supremely a character of contradictions. When beginning *Emma,* Jane Austen commented that she was creating a main character that no one except her would like (Austen-Leigh 157). Nadine Gordimer could have said much the same thing about Hillela.

Hillela's character and her actions support dual—and usually oppo-site—interpretations. She evokes oxymoronic descriptions; an acquain-tance describes her as "awful and rather marvelous" (*SN* 335). Pauline calls Hillela "a-moral," clarifying that she means "in the sense of the morality of this country" (*SN* 56). To be "a-moral" in terms of South African moral-ity is of course a positive trait. But Hillela is also beyond conventional morality in less admirable ways. Similarly, her motivations are seldom clear. She refuses an easy and comfortable marriage in the United States to par-ticipate personally in African liberation struggles. But at the time she aban-dons the projected marriage, she has established herself with General Reuel, whom she expects to become head of state and take her with him (see *SN* 321). Stephen Clingman points out that despite her transgressive behavior, she "always negotiates and comes to terms with the realities of power, both political and patriarchal" (*Novels* xx–xxi).[12]

"Moving on" is an expression often used to describe Hillela. The am-biguities of the phrase mirror her own ambiguities. At one level "mov-ing on" suggests the forward progression of the revolutionary, the determination and perseverance necessary. But underlying violence is re-flected by the Indo-European root of "move," "*mew," which means "to push away," from the Sanskrit "shoves." In addition, there are the sexual connotations of "moving on," which are reinforced by the similar con-notations of another phrase frequently used in connection with Hillela, "making out." Her ambiguities are highlighted by the uncomfortably large role sexuality plays in her political successes.

Hillela's story raises many questions about the cost of the success in the state that she achieves. Nomadic in her peregrinations, she lacks the consciousness of the *mestiza* because she takes only one side, abandoning all identity as an African white. Even her first husband, a committed African National Congress activist, is sometimes dismayed by her "lack of any identification with her own people" (*SN* 242). Nor does she show any loyalty whatsoever to other Jews (despite her choice of name)[13] or to other women. In "the momentum of moving on" (*SN* 307), she refuses history in an exemplary postmodern way. Abandoning the detritus of Africa's colonial past is one thing, but Hillela abandons personal as well as public history. As she rises, she turns her back entirely on close friends and relatives as well as on many other people who helped her. Hillela herself comments on "all the people I behaved so badly to" (*SN* 259; see also 311). Political gain comes at the cost of basic human feelings and human ties. In Hillela's case, postmodern fluidity often looks more like old-fashioned expediency.

In fact, the new revolutionary white subject resembles in disquieting ways the traditional male-identified colonial woman. Hillela constructs many new identities for herself, but she usually does so in basically reactionary ways. In such cases her method is always the same: through men. The narrator's question early in her career is valid for its trajectory as a whole: "*What credibility has she to show for herself, now, but the protection of yet another man?*" (*SN* 189). She uses men not only to gain political access, but also to determine who she will be at any given point. Throughout the novel Hillela molds her identity in accordance with the desires of the dominant man in her life at the time. For example, although she initially renames herself, it is Reuel who selects and bestows her African name, Chiemeka—significantly, a "female version" of his own name. Moreover, the couple's continued use of Hillela, the name she chose, as "the name of intimacy," with Chiemeka available "for official purposes," emphasizes the extent to which her public role is dependent on a man (*SN* 353).

As in most contemporary novels about women and the state, Hillela's initial relationships to the state are established through males. In contrast to other novels, however, they are for the most part maintained that way. Her Aunt Pauline sums it up: "Hillela's field was, surely, men" (*SN* 325; see also 204). Never without a "benefactor" for very long, Hillela cultivates a succession of "protectors" (*SN* 172, 187, 209). To please powerful men and to get what she wants, she excels at playing the roles of lover, daughter, or both. Hillela's relationship with Reuel is represented as an equal partnership, unlike those of Marshall's couples. She is described as "his peer," a "match for him" in every way, one who can "keep up with him" in the demands of his powerful position (*SN* 386–87). Ultimately, however, her power in the state is entirely derivative from and dependent on his. The revolutionary and postmodern subject paradoxically ends up wielding her power through marriage, the most traditional access to the state for women.

Hillela's dependence on men for her public roles does not derive from any lack of personal ability. Quick to learn, shrewd, determined, and energetic, she is a powerful political operative. Although her first husband's assassination offers her political credentials, "the qualification of tragedy," she rapidly establishes herself politically such that she "needed no proxy": "never mind 'Whaila Kgomani's widow', she had her life in her own hands" (*SN* 277, 253, 273). Nor is she unwilling to use women, helping herself to everything from their wardrobes to their husbands throughout the novel. Hillela relies on men for her relationships to the state simply because they can offer her the most political power. With her instinct "for calculation" and "for avoiding losers" (*SN* 277, 244), she recognizes that women have little to give in the public sphere.

An opportunist, an exploiter, a sycophant to the powerful, Hillela in certain ways reflects the worst traditional stereotypes of both the parasitic woman and the old-fashioned male politician. As an agile operator who shifts her identity at will to serve her own interests at any given time, she resembles the conventional politician saying one thing to one constituency and something else to the next, tailoring remarks to audiences. Long before postmodernism, the political hacks from Tammany Hall and Richard Daly's Chicago machine represented mobile and fluid subjectivity in the political realm.

With her disquieting resemblances to traditional stereotypes of the male politician, Hillela provides a monitory example to feminist theory of what has occurred historically when women have entered state politics. Again and again, studies have shown that the behavior of female politicians has been strikingly similar to that of their male peers. Vicky Randall writes that "women politicians do not behave very differently from men" (156; see also Verba 567). At every level the similarities persist, whether at the grass roots, where R. W. Connell points out the "broad *similarity* between women's and men's political attitudes, interests, and partisanship" ("The State" 518), or in national organizations representing women's interests in the United States, where Kay Lehman Schlozman notes that operations are similar to those of male groups (360; see also Randall 95). Scholars agree that in politics women tend to be slightly more liberal, to be more sensitive to issues of women's rights, and to be more opposed to violence than men.[14] But Robert Darcy, Susan Welch, and Janet Clark emphasize that "the differences are not very large in most instances" (154). In the specific case of U.S. party politics, M. Kent Jennings writes that the "vast interparty dissimilarities in ideology tend to swamp what modest differences are provided by gender" (239).

Obviously, what women in politics have been able to accomplish currently and in the past in terms of both political goals and political style has been limited by their status as a minority in the public realm and by their lack of experience and resources. Women have had to function in political systems whose rules and mores they had little if any role in establishing. Many feminist theorists have tended to work under the assumption that as women gain political power, they will be able to mold more humane and less adversarial state systems. But some scholars question whether even the current minimal liberal differences between male and female political views will persist as more women enter political elites. Darcy, Welch, and Clark point out that in the U.S. House of Representatives between 1972 and 1982, the voting gap between male and female members steadily decreased, with the decrease coming mainly because "women members became less liberal, relative to men, over time" (154).

None of these studies proves that the entrance of more women into politics will continue to replicate the status quo. But like Hillela's story, the results of these scholars suggest that some caution may be in order. Feminist theory has long been clear that the goal of feminism is to empower *all* women. In the political realm, however, the consequences of empowering nonfeminist or antifeminist women have consistently been negative for feminist goals. It may be time for the theory to face the ramifications of these experiences.

From the time that the unacceptably exclusionary effects of early second-wave feminist identity politics were acknowledged, feminist theorists have been concerned with substituting more flexible and open conceptions of "woman" into politics. In discussing coalitional politics Judith Butler correctly emphasizes that "the insistence upon the coherence and unity of the category of women has effectively refused the multiplicity of cultural, social, and political intersections in which the concrete array of 'women' are constructed" (*GT* 14). Yet Butler's point that some "political practices institute identities on a contingent basis in order to accomplish whatever aims are in view" (*GT* 16) exactly mirrors the conventional behavior of political hacks—and of Hillela.[15]

Butler's advocacy of fluid political identities represents the position of the overwhelming majority of current feminist theorists. But postmodern mobile subjectivities carry certain dangers if they are to move from feminist theory into political practice. Fluid subjective positions are finally a tactic, and as Marshall shows in *Daughters,* tactics without clear strategies can be at best pointless and at worst dangerous.

In Hillela's case, her strategy marks her regressiveness. Her saga is a political Cinderella story not so much because of her rise from apolitical obscurity to political power and prominence, but because it is romantic love that brings her into politics and remains her primary motivation in the public sphere. With her first husband Whaila, Hillela moves from political apathy into activism because she finds "a sign in her marriage, a sure and certain instruction to which one could attach oneself and feel the tug of history" (*SN* 232; see also 81). Despite this impetus, she admits that she never really understood the political ramifications of her life until Whaila was assassinated. After he is shot by agents of the South African government, she devotes her life to getting "rid of the people who came to the flat and shot Whaila" (*SN* 311). Throughout the entire novel her strategy is straightforward: "to free Whaila" (*SN* 289). As she educates herself in revolution after his death, she wastes no time in "the old theories of ends" (*SN* 254), because she has no need of them. Her own strategic goal is clear.

The extent to which Hillela's political quest has been at base a romantic one is shown by the closing words of *A Sport of Nature*. She and Reuel are honored guests at ceremonies marking the establishment of a new black state in the former South Africa. Amid singing and chanting, while cannons boom, a new flag rises and flares in the wind, which is described by the last two words of the novel as the flag of "Whaila's country." Critics have noted the phallicism of the utopian ending, with its cannons "ejaculat[ing]" (*SN* 396).[16] Such an ending is appropriate for the triumph of Hillela, whose strategic motivation has been romance and whose focus and methods have been male-centered.

❑   ❑   ❑

Hillela deals with the state through males and largely on male terms. But she does not always operate entirely by male values. In certain areas Hillela manages to produce elements of a revolutionary politics with feminist overtones. The intersections of her story with contemporary feminist theories are particularly telling since neither Hillela nor Gordimer herself is concerned with feminist politics.

Hillela often represents an early phase of feminist consciousness, characteristic of second-wave feminist theory in its beginnings. *A Sport of Nature* enthusiastically represents positions that feminist theorists initially supported, endorsements that current theory has subsequently qualified. Hillela thus provides an interesting measure of feminism's changing theoretical outlooks, while the reactionary ramifications of her behavior illustrate some of the reasons for the alterations.

A typical example is Hillela's transgressiveness. Initially second-wave feminists were enthusiastic about the political value of transgressive behavior.[17] Recent theorists have become substantially more wary, questioning whether transgression per se is necessarily progressive. Laurie Shrage points out that "not all nonconformist acts equally challenge conventional morality." Shrage writes: "For example, if a person wants to subvert the belief that eating cats and dogs is bad, it is not enough to simply engage in eating them" (196). Evaluating what she terms the "politics of transgression," Davina Cooper notes its limitation as "an oversimplified understanding of society and social change" and questions the underlying logic of such strategies—"that breaching norms eventually undermines them" (49). Diana Fuss agrees: "[E]very transgression, to establish itself as such, must simultaneously resecure that which it sought to eclipse" (*inside/out* 6). The ambiguities of Hillela's transgressive behavior underwrite the validity of such arguments. Sometimes it is politically charged, but often it is simply self-indulgent, directed toward her own immediate gratification and dangerous to others. Cooper's recommendation of "a more complex version of transgression, which goes beyond the violation of particular norms" (50), reflects structurally the path that much second-wave feminist theory has taken. The tendency has been not to jettison early tactics entirely but to call for more careful evaluation of the individual contexts in which a tactic initially favored can now be deployed.

Hillela's experiences overlap feminist theoretical concerns in two major areas, that of the family and of sex and the body. Both have been extremely controversial within feminism. Patricia Misciagno claims that "No other institution has caused such divisions within and between . . . feminists than has the family" (35), while Gayle Rubin describes "feminist thought about sex" as "profoundly polarized" ("Thinking" 303). In each of these areas Hillela's story highlights crucial difficulties that have created the feminist divisions.

Aside from the body, the metaphor most often used in connection with the patriarchal state is the family. Hillela never leaves men behind, but she consistently abandons and trashes the conventional nuclear family. She remains a familial outsider, disrupting the bonds and the bounds of every family that she joins. "[M]ade a sister" (*SN* 112) in Joe and Pauline's family in Johannesburg, she wreaks havoc there by sleeping with her cousin Sasha. In the Mézières family in Tanzania and then Ghana, the children claim her as a "sister" and a "cousin," the ambassador's wife considers her "a younger sister, a member of the family," and she approaches the husband and wife "almost as if" they were parents (*SN* 185, 192, 203). Hillela responds to this encompassing familial embrace by becoming the ambassador's mistress. After she is taken into the Burns family as their son Brad's future wife, the wedding is several times postponed for "family reasons" of the Burns clan (*SN* 303). Then Hillela herself delays it to go on an African mission, becomes Reuel's lover, and leaves Brad and all the Burnses behind. When Reuel dispatches her as an emissary to his rebel son, the narrator implies that Hillela sleeps with the son. Wherever Hillela goes, family ties are strained or dissolved.

The connections between the nuclear family and the state are complex, further complicated in the West and elsewhere by the connections of both institutions with the capitalist system.[18] A number of theorists have pointed out how the loyalties of the patriarchal nuclear family were deployed early in modern European history to strengthen allegiance to the centralized monarchical state.[19] Subsequently, as Shere Hite points out, "The family as an institution was overlooked when, two centuries or so ago, governments began to change over to a democratic system" (*Hite* 353)—an irony of sorts, since democracy originally arose in Athens when aristocratic political power, based on families, was broken. At present, with state institutions taking over many of the tasks traditionally performed by the family, the western nuclear family is in crisis. Exactly what the ramifications of the current weaknesses of the family are for the state remains unclear. However, the contemporary shift that some theorists see from family-based patriarchy to public patriarchy is particularly intriguing, since family patriarchies have historically been stronger systems than state ones.[20]

Feminist theorists evaluate the relationships between the nuclear family and the state negatively for women on empirical and ideological grounds. Private experiences of familial patriarchy buttress patriarchal state formations. Jean Bethke Elshtain writes that women's "long historic experiences in families dominated by men . . . continue to structure our response to politics and political relationships" (*PMPW* 127). Ideological replication from family to state is equally important. Lynda Boose and Betty Flowers describe the ideology on which the nuclear family is based as "closed, hierarchical, patronymic, and patriarchal," and note that reproducing this ideology in individual familial units serves to inculcate it structurally throughout the culture (4). Catharine MacKinnon agrees that the family models "authoritarian social relations" (*Toward* 48). Almost all feminist theorists concur that in order to evolve more humane and less authoritarian state institutions, new forms to replace the nuclear family are needed.[21] In *A Sport of Nature* Hillela provides two different models.

Gordimer successively separates Hillela from her mother, her father, and the families of the two aunts who take her in. Her experiences as, in Sasha's terms, "*more or less a lucky orphan*" (*SN* 367) leave her ignorant of both the positive and the negative powers of the ideology of the nuclear family. The narrator notes that Hillela has never known "the comfort and protection" offered by the place of the family "in a homogeneous society" (*SN* 303). Bereft of its benefits, she has also escaped its traps. By the end of the novel, when she deals with Reuel's family, although she herself has a daughter, "the abstract relations of her own childhood [left her] free of the patricidal and infanticidal loves between parents and children" (SN 332). Thus Hillela is ideally situated to experiment with familial forms.

A major feminist criticism of the nuclear family is its binding women within the private sphere, absorbing their time and energy so that public activities are not an option. *A Sport of Nature* depicts this deflection of female efforts from the public realm to the private when Hillela herself succumbs to conventional ideologies of the nuclear family during her marriage to Whaila. Her goal of "a big African family" (*SN* 243) combines traditional African valorizations of motherhood[22] with conventional western equations of wife with mother. Against Whaila's objections she desires a *"rainbow-coloured family,"* insisting that "An African wife isn't a wife if she doesn't produce children" (*SN* 269, 221). Assuming the traditional familial role of women as enablers of others, she proceeds "in animated confidence that she was escorting the first generation that would go home in freedom." In describing her motivation, Gordimer's language reflects the shift in Hillela's priorities from political to personal reproduction: "She would deliver what she had heard discussed there at [white South African] suburban tables, what had been aborted by hesitations and doubts . . ." (*SN* 243).

Thus the private ties of the nuclear family hinder Hillela's participation in politics. However, when Whaila is shot, Hillela learns that the public sphere prohibits the kind of private familial resolution for political conflict that she has envisioned. Familial love for individuals is not possible under the conditions dictated by African politics of the time: *"No rainbow-coloured family; that kind of love can't be got away with, it's cornered, it's easily done away with in two shots from a 9 mm. Parabellum pistol"* (*SN* 269). As an individualized solution to racism and African liberation, the rainbow family Hillela desires is self-centered and inadequate.

Nevertheless, while with Whaila, Hillela also begins to forge other bonds that ultimately become stronger for her than family connections. Through their relationship she learns the compelling importance of the struggle for black African freedom, and within that larger political context family ties are transmuted. Whaila becomes "lover and brother to her in the great family of a cause" (*SN* 245), as Hillela replicates in an acceptable public form the incest forbidden in the private family. With her dreams of a rainbow family destroyed, she moves to another level of abstraction, for which "the abstract relations of her own childhood" (*SN* 332) have uniquely prepared her. To the capacity for private abstraction learned in youth she adds the capacity for public abstraction that marks revolutionaries. After Whaila's death she refocuses her efforts in terms of freedom for the *"hungry crowds in the street,"* deciding that *"The only love that counts is owed to them" (SN* 269). Tragedy has taught her that in her historical moment political obligations are more binding and more important than family ties. By the time she reaches the United States, the public family has completely displaced the private one. She and Leonie Adlestrop have "no nuclear family but their distant ties, obligations, dependants held them fast" (*SN* 285).

Thus after her first husband's death Hillela substitutes political dedication—what Sasha terms *"the tremendous preoccupation that is liberation politics" (SN* 369)—for family ties. Her second marriage to Reuel also evades the nuclear family, although in a different way. The narrator describes Hillela's familial achievement positively. Once again she has refused to be co-opted by a family: "But Hillela has not been taken in by [Reuel's] African family; she has disposed it around her. Hers is the non-matrilineal centre that no one resents because no one has known it could exist. She has invented it. This is not the rainbow family" (*SN* 360). In her marriage to the General, Hillela's dreams of "the rainbow family," the multiracial nuclear family, have been supplanted by her own version of what feminist theorists term the "family of choice" or "social family."[23] Significantly, however, the choices involved seem to be primarily Hillela's. What connects the rainbow family and the new family is her centrality to and control of each form. In both cases her desires prevail. In terms of the private sphere, her role is preferable to that allotted to women in most nuclear families, but its political effects remain negligible.

Hillela's invention combines the household model of common residence with the familial model of kinship and conjugal association (Gonzalez 427).[24] It is neither entirely western nor entirely African but partakes of elements of both. For the traditional African polygamous unit that centers on women and children (Steady, *Black* 16–17), Hillela in part substitutes the western couple, where the male is central. Although the General has three wives, Hillela is the one who lives with him; as Kathrin Wagner points out, she assumes "a position, despite her youth and without reference to African traditions of precedence, as first among his wives" (93).[25] However, their relationship lacks the sexual exclusivity theoretically associated with western marriages, suggesting the African patterns of female sexual autonomy noted by Constance Sutton and Susan Makiesky-Barrow (472). Both Hillela and Reuel have various lovers.[26] With his second wife he continues to father children, whom Hillela takes charge of. Her appropriation of those children obviously reflects African patterns of communal child rearing. But Hillela seems to operate with a possessiveness and an exclusivity more characteristic of the western nuclear family than of African othermothering traditions. In certain ways she makes the children her own; to "the composure and good manners" of black children, they add "the precocity of white upper-class children" (*SN* 360).

Hillela's taking over the children reflects her more general pattern throughout the novel of displacing black African women. She marries two black African men and has affairs with others. At the end of the novel, her appearance in full African female attire at ceremonies celebrating South Africa's inauguration of black rule is a culminating public appropriation symbolic of her lifelong public and private appropriations from black African women. The narrator's admiring comment is that "there are not many whites who could carry it off" (*SN* 394). One could add that there are not many whites who would have attempted it in the first place. Hillela's African apparel indicates the importance of contextualizing Naomi Schor's suggestion that

> ultimately *female travesty,* in the sense of women dressing up as or impersonating other women, constitutes by far the most disruptive form of bisexuality: for, whereas there is a long, venerable tradition of naturalized intersexual travesty in fiction, drama, and opera, the exchange of *female* identities, the blurring of difference *within* difference remains a largely marginal and unfamiliar phenomenon. (370)

Without careful attention to contexts, such exchanges can remain simply colonial appropriations from the other.

Hillela's arrogation of the children reflects another of her important familial patterns: her lack of interest in conventional maternal relationships. Jane Gallop writes that for women, "the daughter's obligation to reproduce the mother, the mother's story—is a more difficult obstacle than even the Father's Law" (*Daughter's* 113). Hillela decisively rejects such reproduction. For example, she and her mother, Ruthie, share a powerful sexuality, but each deals with it differently. Reading her mother's letters to her lover, Hillela immediately responds to the descriptions of sexual passion, the "thirst of the skin" that she instinctively recognizes (*SN* 62, 340). But ultimately she tears up the letters and throws them away. As a young wife Ruthie falls prey to cheap glamour and "kitsch," abandoning her husband and child to join a Portuguese lover in Mozambique because she desires "passion and tragedy, not domesticity" (*SN* 59; see also 341). Hillela also forsakes the nuclear family and domesticity, but her motives are political, not personal. Significantly, the passion and tragedy she experiences in the process are genuine, not illusory like her mother's.

Louise Yelin has analyzed how Gordimer shows through Ruthie "the limits of a purely sexual politics," in order to stress a "political understanding of Hillela's sexuality" (201).[27] Ruthie is self-absorbed, defined totally in terms of the private sphere, while Hillela's commitment to African liberation connects her to others and to larger public concerns. When Hillela finally meets her mother, she has no interest in establishing any relationship. (The General, who expects her mother to live with them, protests: "We look after our elders" [*SN* 345].) Hillela's total lack of feeling for and identification with Ruthie emphasizes the differences between the two women. Haunani-Kay Trask has suggested that the return to the mother is usually connected with a return to the body (131); given Hillela's thoroughly embodied character throughout *A Sport of Nature,* in this sense she has no need for a maternal return.

Hillela loves her only daughter, Nomzano, but the distanced relationship maintained by the two is suggested by constant references to the daughter as "the namesake." At Nomo's birth Hillela explicitly disavows any desire for the daughter to replicate the mother and her story. Feeling "the reversal of parental feeling as it is supposed to be," she is proud "not to have reproduced herself" (*SN* 228). In context the reference is to the child's dark color, but clearly Hillela also does not want to reproduce the mentality and ideology of the white colonial; Yelin has traced how mothers in the novel come to symbolize colonial culture (198–99). In *Daughters* a distanced mother-daughter relationship produces political action. Ironically, Nomo, although named in honor of Winnie Mandela, replicates her mother's self-interest but not her political interests. By the time she is in primary school, she "already knew how to exploit being black" in predominantly white countries (*SN* 284), and she ultimately becomes an internationally famous fashion model.

Despite significant differences between the generations, certain disturbing reproductions of mothers and their stories remain in *A Sport of Nature.* When the narrator notes Ruthie's "useless beauty thrown away so cheap on the first man to take it up in a nightclub" (*SN* 347), the implied contrast is with Hillela, who learns to use her attractiveness to advance herself and her cause. But in both cases forms of explicit or implicit sexual barter are involved. Ruthie attempts to commodify her body for personal gain and fails; Hillela successfully commodifies her body by using it for both personal and political gain. Nomo provides a final recension of the story in terms of solely personal gain by professionalizing such commodification on the runway. Unlike Ursa and Estelle, the distanced relationship of Hillela and Nomo produces commerce, not politics.

Gordimer's depictions of Hillela and motherhood contest certain elements of traditional constructions of maternity criticized by feminist theorists, such as the "maternal sacrifice narrative" (E. Kaplan 36) and the repression of the figure of the mother who enjoys sexual pleasure (Marks and de Courtivron 36). But the direct impact of these elements on the state is minimal. Nor does Hillela's new familial form with its "non-matrilineal centre" (*SN* 360), promising as it sounds, in practice offer much toward renewing state institutions, constructed as it is around appropriations from other women. But *A Sport of Nature* does illustrate how the nuclear family obstructs women's participation in public life. Hillela has to refuse the personal history of the family in order to enter the public sphere.[28] Even in the West, the nuclear family has always been an ideal rather than a reality for the majority of the population, and Hillela's succumbing to it during her first marriage highlights the power of its force as a social fantasy. For those who desire women to play roles in the state, it remains a crucial force hindering full political access.

❑   ❑   ❑

Hillela's second major intersection with contemporary feminist theory is through her views on the body. This intersection, like that with the family, is complex. The novel emphasizes her trust in her body, especially her absolute confidence in knowledge gained through it. Sasha writes that she *"received everything through* [her] *skin, understood everything that way"* (*SN* 369). It is not simply the body itself but specifically her sexuality that Hillela trusts, although in the text Gordimer's emphasis repeatedly falls on the physical body.[29] The General believes that "she drew upon the surety of her sexuality as the bread of her being" (*SN* 330). Her concept of sexuality is a capacious one; Brad Burns notes that it "included her feeling for [her daughter]" (*SN* 290). However, in *A Sport of Nature* it is seen mainly through sexual liaisons.

Hillela's somatic attitudes reflect those of various early second-wave feminist theorists who sought through the female body alternatives to male knowledge and power. They drew on perceptions of what Alicia Ostriker terms "women's inclination to identify the self first of all with the body, and the body with reality" (120). The idea was that the female body could offer direct access to new options, in the political realm and elsewhere. Ann Rosalind Jones writes that from such perspectives Julia Kristeva, Luce Irigaray, and Hélène Cixous "oppose[d] women's bodily experience . . . to the phallic/symbolic patterns embedded in Western thought" ("Writing" 252). In the United States Adrienne Rich waxed

eloquent on the political and personal benefits that could accrue if
women began, "at last, to *think through the body*":

> The repossession by women of our bodies will bring far more essential
> change to human society than the seizing of the means of production by
> workers. . . . In such a world women will truly create new life, bringing
> forth not only children (if and as we choose) but the visions, and the
> thinking, necessary to sustain, console, and alter human existence—a new
> relationship to the universe. Sexuality, politics, intelligence, power, moth-
> erhood, work, community, intimacy will develop new meanings; thinking
> itself will be transformed. (*Of Woman* 284, 285–86)

It is precisely this kind of utopic vision of female bodily and sexual possibilities that Gordimer portrays through Hillela in *A Sport of Nature*.

The problems with Rich's utopic vision, and Gordimer's recension
of it, derive from a growing recognition on the part of feminist theorists of the constructed nature of the body itself. These theorists began
to emphasize the body as "a culturally mediated form" (Bordo, *Unbearable* 181), "structured, inscribed, constituted and given meaning *socially*
and *historically*" (Grosz, *Sexual* 111). Among the influences shaping the
body, feminist theorists followed Foucault in focusing on the central
role of discursive constructions. Silverman is typical: "not only is the
subject's relation to his or her body lived out through the mediation of
discourse, but that body is itself coerced and molded by both representation and signification" (146). Rosi Braidotti sums up the current consensus among feminist theorists:

> [The body] cannot be reduced to the biological, nor can it be confined to
> social conditioning. In a new form of "corporeal materialism," the body is
> seen as an inter-face, a threshold, a field of intersection of material and
> symbolic forces; it is a surface where multiple codes of power and knowl-
> edge are inscribed; it is a construction that transforms and capitalizes on
> energies of a heterogeneous and discontinuous nature. (*Patterns* 219)

Under such conditions the body can offer no access to unmediated truth
in politics or anywhere else. Although contemporary feminist theorists
continue to focus on embodiment for subversive purposes, the strategies
involved have increasingly become discursive ones, "elaborating alternative forms of knowledge and representation of the subject" (Braidotti,
Patterns 219), which usually have little direct or immediate influence on
the state.

Working within the parameters of a culturally and discursively mediated body, feminist political theorists have done important work in ex-

plicating the role of the body in traditional politics. A number of writers have pointed out the importance of concepts of citizenship as embodied, because traditional political theory assumes that the individual whom it invokes will have a male body.[30] Moreover, traditional political thought is hostile to the human body in a larger sense. Arguing that "from the very beginning of our civilization, even the most appealing formulations of freedom have been rooted in a freedom *from* the body and its demands," Wendy Brown has been one of the most significant figures in analyzing how "Western political man has regarded the body as a trap, a weapon, an instrument, a foundation, and a curse upon the mind, all more or less simultaneously" (*MP* 193, 180).

Brown traces how men have carried negative "valuations of the body into [their] construction of politics and institutionalized them there." She writes that "men's individual bodies, the realm of bodily maintenance, and the body politic—all are regarded as instruments or foundations at best, more often encumbrances, irritants, or threats to man and his political projects" (*MP* 180). In a politics so constituted, women can have no place. As Brown explains, "it should surprise no one that woman has been historically conceived as among the most inappropriate and subversive things one can introduce into politics: precisely because woman has been made to stand for body, sexuality, and life maintenance, she is dreaded in the political realm insofar as she is seen as contaminating politics with these banned goods" (*MP* 194–95). *A Sport of Nature* represents Hillela's importation of the "banned goods" of the body and sexuality into politics, but as means rather than as ends. Thus no substantive changes result in the configuration of the public sphere. Butler has urged feminists to think about the possibilities that "exist *by virtue of* the constructed nature of sex and gender" (*GT* 32). Butler of course is seeking to explore such possibilities in order to subvert current systems. Hillela, in contrast, systematically exploits the opportunities offered by traditional constructions of women and women's bodies.

A Sport of Nature does emphasize that Hillela's use of her sexuality alters as she matures. Gordimer metonymically represents the change during Hillela's first marriage as a move from sexual caresses to the handclasp of friendship. Whaila begins to trust her politically when he "in some inexplicable urge to honour the clasp of the hand in the way that his possession of her body could never do, in some certainty of trust that would transform both him and her and their relationship, told her the [Umkhonto military] plans in detail" (244). After his death, "*What was left behind was the handclasp,*" as she begins to interact with colleagues in that way, or with others in "comradely embrace," instead of sleeping with them (*SN* 250, 299; see also 261).

Yet Hillela never stops using her sexuality for political power. As the narrator explains, *"one who has been a beach girl never loses what she found durable in herself while making out."* After her marriage she still proffers sexual encouragement, but she no longer necessarily acts on it: *"[S]omething new has been learned, on the side, in the context of making out. One can offer, without giving. It's a form of power"* (*SN* 231). However, her sexuality continues to be central in her political triumphs: "Lust is the best aid raiser" (*SN* 284). Ultimately, the handclasp emerges as simply an additional tactic beyond her sexual repertoire, not a replacement for it.

For those who dislike current constructions of women, Hillela's use instead of critique of these constructions is disturbing. She reinforces, albeit for her own purposes, stereotypical equations of woman with body. It might be argued that her deployment of such constructs is so extreme that her excess reveals them for what they are. However, even aside from the serious problems with mimicry and parody as political tactics, particularly the many possibilities for misreading their reproduction of whatever they critique, in the novel Hillela's excessiveness does not seem to function satirically. Diane Elam has pointed out the connections of romance and postmodernism, and these associations are significant in *A Sport of Nature*. Hillela's sexuality is presented as romantic, not satiric, excess.

Hillela's conduct positions her in the midst of a long-running dispute about sex in feminist theory, a conflict that figured prominently in the "Sex Wars" covered in connection with *Bodily Harm*. Rubin describes two strains of feminist thought about sex, one that demands complete sexual freedom for women and opposes any restrictions at all, and another that views sexual liberation for women as "inherently a mere extension of male privilege" ("Thinking" 301; see also Philipson, "Beyond" 451–53). An early binary representing the first view as "pro-sex" and the second as "anti-sex" reflects the way that complexities of the debate quickly became obscured. Moreover, in different ways the AIDS epidemic prematurely narrowed the debates among heterosexual women on sexual practices and their meaning. The discussion was increasingly conducted primarily among lesbians, who in their turn often narrowed the focus to sadomasochistic practices. The result was continuing inadequate theorization by feminists of the significance of sexual liberation for women.

Throughout her work Gordimer has usually represented women's sexual activity as liberatory, emphasizing "the primal power of sexuality to redirect and transform lives" (Wagner 88). These views have been explained in both literary terms, specifically the influence of D. H. Lawrence's writings (Gordimer, *Writing* 2–3), and biographical ones.

Gordimer as a young woman found sexual exploration one way of rebelling against the stifling South African environment in which she grew up; Wagner writes that Gordimer has represented "her sexuality as a powerfully integrative force in her early years" (87; see also Gordimer, *Essential* 113). Her views of sexual liberation are thus tied to her generation, for many of whom the sexual revolution of the 1960s appeared an unalloyed good compared to the repression they experienced when young.

Hillela's actions reflect the liberatory view of sex, but in crucial ways the ambiguities in her sexual behavior illustrate the importance of the position of the other side in the debates, those who insisted that direct imitation of male behavior cannot ultimately liberate. This issue arises overtly in *A Sport of Nature* when a male character concedes that "Hillela's attitude to sex was like that of an honorary man" (*SN* 204). In context, Gordimer clearly intended the remark to be complimentary, and she expends a great deal of effort throughout the novel to encourage positive views of Hillela's sexuality. Along with the recurring comparisons of Hillela's and Ruthie's sexuality to Hillela's advantage and the metonymic substitution of the handclasp for sex, Gordimer continually emphasizes Hillela's sexuality as instinctual. An early associate's insistence that she was "innocent" is a similar textual defense (*SN* 175, 177; see also 56). In interviews Gordimer has defended Hillela by claiming that she had little choice initially but to bed-hop: "[A]ll she has are her good looks, her nice little body, and some intelligence" (Kenyon, *Women Writers Talk* 105). But readers never see Hillela relying on any intelligence until later in the novel, and even after she begins to develop her mind, she continues to rely on her physical charms as well. Hillela's success depends on traditional male constructions of woman as body, and in exploiting these, her sexual behavior replicates prevailing male practices.

Gordimer obviously intended for Hillela's attitudes toward the body to have particular revolutionary resonance given their South African context. Emphasizing that apartheid centers on the body and physical differences, Gordimer has suggested "a particular connection between sexuality, sensuality, and politics inside South Africa." In a nation where personal appearance dictates political status, the entire "legal structure is based on the physical, so that the body becomes something supremely important" (B & S 304). She writes similarly in *A Sport of Nature*: "*The laws that have determined the course of life for* [Hillela and Whaila] *are made of skin and hair, the relative thickness and thinness of lips and the relative height of the bridge of the nose*" (*SN* 206). Even within the South Africa context, however, the position is not convincing. The final irony of Gordimer's positive portrayal of Hillela's sexuality as liberatory is that in South

Africa, it is not the body itself but the body as constructed by the state that is central. Apartheid, a system based on minute somatic classifications and distinctions, depends on human constructions and interpretations of other human bodies.

❑   ❑   ❑

Gordimer's positive aspirations for her protagonist clearly extend beyond the South African confines of her story. Various comments of hers indicate that the focus on the body and sexuality in *A Sport of Nature* was meant to counter misconceptions about the kind of people who make the best political operatives. In an interview Gordimer discussed how those whom she and other "serious-minded people" dismissed as political "lightweights" actually achieved more than the putative "heavyweights." Speculating that "perhaps there are more ways of being effective than we would allow," Gordimer commented that in her experience, "the most unexpected people, who you would have never thought could have done anything, have . . . become effective in unconventional ways" (B & S 292; see also Kenyon, *Women Writers* 105). In another interview she focused specifically on sexuality in political contexts: "So many people . . . who have never known real political activists, imagine them as either monklike or nunlike. And I know that they're not like that at all. Having the revolutionary temperament, the daring, usually goes along with very sexually attractive personalities, strong sexuality in both men and women" (B & S 278). Gordimer has said that "the two greatest drives in people's lives, the two most important things, are sex and politics" (B & S 304). Her remarks on the temperament of "real political activists" combine these primary drives. Her point is not simply that politics involves sexuality, but that revolutionary power and sexual power tend to be integrally connected. To represent this relationship, in *A Sport of Nature* she opens up the political sphere to explore the role of a person with this combination of traits. And, in particular, the novel investigates what transpires when the figure with these traits happens to be a woman.

A Sport of Nature focuses on the major role that has historically symbolized the intersection of sex and politics in a woman: the courtesan. Gordimer has admitted her lifelong fascination with "women who have been the power behind the throne so to speak, the Madame de Pompadours and the Maintenons, all sorts of figures in history who seemed to have had a strong political influence." She has also noted the prevailing misrepresentation of these figures and the sexist reason for it: "But because they were women, they are just remembered as so-and-so's mistress" (B & S 292–93).[31] In *A Sport of Nature* the narrator comments at one point about women who have assignations with powerful political figures: "Such girls have no names" (*SN* 328). Gordimer gives a name to one such "girl" and in doing so rewrites the story of the courtesan.[32] Through Hillela, whom a friend calls "a natural mistress, not a wife" and gossips in Reuel's nation compare to Madame de Pompadour or Evita Perón (*SN* 205, 386), Gordimer makes the case for the public complexity of this figure. She does so primarily through literary means, in the language she uses and the way she constructs her narrative.

Nannerl O. Keohane has written that "no good models for depicting women in authority" exist (97). What is true for women in authority generally is particularly true for the courtesan and her unique kind of political power.[33] History records a number of famous courtesans, but not one of them has written her own story. At the same time, given the nature of courtesans' political activities, no outsider can adequately represent them. The historical and literary results were predictably scurrilous. In the absence of accurate information, fantasy and stereotypes substituted.

The genre that originally evolved to depict the courtesan and women like her was the secret history.[34] With sordid classical antecedents in Suetonius and especially Procopius, the French *chronique scandaleuse* and its English relations proliferated in Europe during the seventeenth and early eighteenth centuries. The historical validity of the kind of stories they retailed is reflected by the fact that these short-lived genres contributed little to the development of historiography, but played a significant role in the emergence of the novel.

Secret history as a genre tends to flourish at times when female access to political power generates widespread cultural anxieties. For example, Procopius capitalized on Byzantine fears of the emperor Justinian's wife, Theodora. The reappearance of the secret history in early modern England and France also reflected the unprecedented political power of individual women during the period. Three female sovereigns—Elizabeth, Mary, and Anne—occupied the English throne, while wives and courtesans from Queen Henrietta Maria and the mistresses of Charles II to Anne of Austria and Madame de Maintenon either directed affairs of state or wielded power over the kings who did. The deep and pervasive cultural concern over the actions of women rulers and regents, which in state business was at least at times a matter of public record, was exponentially greater in the case of mistresses, whose political influence was almost impossible to assess accurately. On both sides of the Channel the actual extent of the political power exercised by royal courtesans was the subject of unending public and private speculation. Anxieties about their state power underwrote the salaciousness that became the essence of journalistic and historical accounts of them. These depictions dictated the way such women have been represented ever since.

Amy Richlin writes of the "mapping of the morals of the body politic onto a woman's body" (74), but in the case of courtesans, what actually tended to be mapped onto women's bodies were private fears and concerns about public morals. Male fears of powerful women have long been documented. Suzanne Dixon speculates that in the political realm, "male fear of female domination" and "male contempt for men who have fallen victim to it" are connected with "the usual fear a dominant class retains of the suppressed group (totalitarian and monarchic governments usually block freedom of assembly; slave owners live in dread of uprisings; South Africans constantly fantasize about black revolution) reinforced by more fundamental feelings" (220, 213). These "more fundamental feelings" have been connected by numerous psychoanalytic theorists from Karen Horney to Dorothy Dinnerstein and Nancy Chodorow with the child's perception of an all-powerful mother. Only more recently have female fears of those who exercise power, whatever their sex, begun to be explored.[35] For both men and women, these deep-seated fears combined with the overt concern that any unofficial exercise of political power, whether by royal courtiers or by party machines, has always generated.

The figure of the courtesan exists at an intersection of the public and the private spheres, but because of the dearth of reliable information, no history written about such women by others can actually be personal history. And yet their narratives have traditionally been constructed entirely in personal terms, reducing their public political identities to private sexual ones. For example, those who have researched the lives of courtesans from Theodora to Pamela Harriman constantly emphasize that the talents and abilities of these women extended far beyond sexual prowess.[36] But texts inevitably reduce them to their sexual roles. The treatment of Harriman in the press after her death was typical, with the *Daily Mail* calling her "the world's expert on rich men's ceilings" and suggesting that historians who review the twentieth century "will find traces of Pamela Harriman's lipstick all over it" (S. B. Smith 445). With Harriman, as with her historical predecessors, one stereotype of female behavior—the tramp—was deployed to negatively reinforce a less threatening one, the domestic woman in the private sphere. As Russell Baker remarked of Harriman, "Ambition driven by grit, gall and sexual guile are still widely considered unseemly in a woman" (qted. in S. B. Smith 451). Feared as dangerous in political life, the courtesan has traditionally been reinscribed into the private realm as simply a whore. This construction of courtesans provides yet another example of the kinds of efforts that have been made to remove women from the public sphere and anchor them safely in the domain of the private.

Theorists have analyzed at length the difficulties of creating a narrative when dealing with postmodern concepts of identities that are fluid, split, and mobile. However, that is not the primary problem that Gordimer explores in *A Sport of Nature*, although it, along with more general questions about the viability of writing biography, is certainly involved. Hillela cannot be contained by traditional biographical and fictional structures because the information as well as the language and narrative forms necessary for adequate representation of this kind of woman does not exist.

Throughout *A Sport of Nature* Gordimer's style and narrative emphasize the dearth of accurate information about Hillela and women like her. The rhetoric of conjecture and the language of uncertainty repeatedly recur: "perhaps"; "probably"; "if"; "may have"; "could have"; "must have"; "apparently"; "maybe"; "surely"; "it is also possible"; "it seems unlikely"; "nobody seems to know." Convoluted constructions underscore the speculative nature of proffered interpretations: "This suggests that if it were true"; "She who people say was once Hillela" (*SN* 290, 25). Using reportorial techniques of attribution, the narrative painstakingly identifies its sources, from South African government surveillance reports to the reminiscences of former acquaintances and film footage from around the world. Often the care taken to emphasize the commitment to accuracy itself undermines the validity of the text. Unreliable sources are constantly quoted, and identified as such: "the persistent rumour"; "Malice has it"; "rivals and political enemies . . . said"; "hearsay" (*SN* 252, 184, 188, 324). The text flaunts its lack of knowledge. The story is full of gaps, which the narrative stresses. Sometimes different sources contradict each other; at other times there are no sources at all. The geography at points is as vague as the temporal progression. For example, the reader never learns exactly where or for how long Hillela lived in Eastern Europe. A number of critics have pointed out how the shifting narrative focalization undermines confidence in the authority of the text.[37]

Gordimer thus carefully structures *A Sport of Nature* so that the account continually undercuts its own truth claims. The result, as numerous critics have noted, is that the figure of Hillela is kept at a distance in the novel,[38] just as famous courtesans always have been in stories about them. Hillela is a fantasy figure because such women have always been fantasy figures, repositories of the fears and projections of others. Gordimer's concern is with the ways in which the fantasies have been constructed—and misconstrued.

Gordimer insists throughout *A Sport of Nature* that the political dimensions of the courtesan's story are central. The novel is a study in the construction of a woman's public identity.[39] In *Burger's Daughter* Rosa remarks: "There's nothing more private and personal than the life of a mistress, is there?" (304; see also Driver 185). But in the case of the courtesan, Rosa is wrong. Therefore, in *A Sport of Nature* emphasis repeatedly falls on the public nature of Hillela's role. While in Eastern Europe, for instance, she "disappears into what is known about the mission, in that country at that time. No history of her really can be personal history, then; its ends were all apparently outside herself" (*SN* 261). Gordimer explicitly refutes private constructions: "the President has seen her in a light other than that of perpetuator of a blood-line" (*SN* 359).

Gordimer's narrative reflects the discourses that have historically constructed the courtesan. Some of them are common to all public figures: "These generalities have gathered the velvet of the years, befitting the past of someone who has achieved a certain position" (*SN* 273). But in the case of powerful political women, and exponentially of course in the case of the courtesan, sexual stereotypes usually predominate. The narrative commentary in *A Sport of Nature* invokes such constructions. Sexual innuendo abounds, and personal interpretations of Hillela's behavior are stressed over political ones. Remarks repeatedly construe information about her negatively. The narrator seldom fails to suggest the worst, with remarks that are often snide or sardonic and sometimes openly hostile. Often when adequate information is not available, the narrator falls back on sexual stereotypes ("the little tramp on Tamarisk Beach" [*SN* 211]). Others speak similarly: "a little tart, like her mother"; a "clever cock-teaser"; a "bitch"; a "camp-follower"; a "pretty little floozy"; a "real poppet" (*SN* 114, 127, 150, 182).

These sexual stereotypes reflect how limited the political roles traditionally considered acceptable for women have been. Dixon writes:

> Most societies do have a legitimate public role for women, but it is usually one without the most prestigious kind of power and tends to be an extension of the society's private construction of the feminine—such as a benevolent super-mother, bestowing largesse and concern on subjects; a pious wife or daughter performing a sacral function; the lady of impeccable virtue, producing perfectly pedigreed heirs. (219)

Amy Richlin terms this safely domestic paragon the "first lady," and points out that from Livia and Julia Domna to Queen Victoria and Barbara Bush, this figure has been "the normative model of the ruling woman as perfect wife and mother" (65). For women active in the state who cannot or will not fit this model, the options are few and unsavory. Almost all of the alternative categories, such as the Roman *meretrix augusta* and the Chinese "usurping concubine" (Richlin 66, Dixon 214), involve sexual transgression.

The binary construction of political women—the pure "first lady" icon ensconced in the private world with occasional forays into the social sphere, set against the sexual woman actively exercising power in the public sphere—is one specific example of the larger cultural binary that separates "good girls" from "bad girls." (This second binary is of course itself a subset of the pervasive virgin/whore dichotomy that marks traditional thought about women.) The good girls adhere to patriarchal rules governing proper feminine conduct—or, from another perspective, good girls hoard their "sexual resources for later investment" (Rapp 55). The bad girls flout patriarchal rules, but the ultimate effect of their rebellion is unclear. Although Gallop notes that "to affirm one's identity as bad girl can be a first step in breaking out of obedient femininity," she questions whom the role really serves: "Does the bad girl break out of the strictures demanding woman's obedience or does she just titillate the patriarchs?" (*Around* 238, 230). Gallop details how the binary between good girls and bad girls has "historically set women against each other": "The split serves patriarchy not only by marginalizing disloyal women, not only by setting women nearer the center of power against those less domesticated, but by ensuring that the women closest to power renounce their selves in order to keep that proximity. One of the constants behind the good girl/bad girl dichotomy is that it is bad to have power" (*Around* 237–38).[40]

What Gallop describes as a "moralized split" runs through western culture and feminist theoretical interpretations of it. Versions of it are clear in the two feminist views of sex as well as in the binary between the mother and the sexual woman. Kate Ellis connects it to divisions in the nineteenth-century women's movement between radicals supporting women's sexual liberation and ur-cultural feminists demanding protection for women (439). Gallop sees the split in the pernicious divisions within feminism created by stigmatizing certain women as "not feminist (enough)" and others as "male-identified" (*Around* 238; *Feminist* 23). The division also surfaces in feminist disagreements over prostitution. Early theorists such as Ti-Grace Atkinson claimed prostitutes as "the only street fighters we've got" (124), while Carol Pateman is typical of later theorists in opposing prostitution as "part of the patriarchal structure of civil society."[41]

As Gordimer shows the sexual discourses that proliferate around Hillela in *A Sport of Nature*, she suggests the inadequacy not only of traditional language and narrative to represent the courtesan but also of traditional categories of women to contain her. Against the prevailing stereotype of the courtesan as simply a whore, Gordimer makes her case for Hillela. She challenges the reader with a woman of substantial abilities, who is comfortable exercising power in the public sphere and who also deploys her sexuality there. As Gordimer defends Hillela's sexual behavior as natural (for example, *SN* 172), the implication is that the designation of whore is simply a discursive mechanism evolved both to contain the sexual activity of women and to discourage them from entering the public sphere. Through Hillela, *A Sport of Nature* continually brings into question the categories of good girls and bad girls.

Gordimer's emphasis on the narrative problems in telling Hillela's story highlights the constructed nature of the courtesan's history. In texts, as in life, courtesans are made into objects for others. Hillela combines in contradictory ways the revolutionary and the reactionary. That it is finally impossible to categorize her either way is due in part to the discourse itself, which, encumbered with lacunae, contradictory accounts, vague or inaccurate language, and stereotypes, refuses the information necessary for interpretation.

❑   ❑   ❑

If Gordimer in *A Sport of Nature* has recognized and represented many of the difficulties in evaluating the courtesan, in writing the novel she has not evaded all of them herself. A major problem is generic, stemming from the hybridity that Bill Ashcroft has termed "the primary characteristic of all post-colonial texts" (185). Wagner calls the female *bildungsroman* Gordimer's "core genre" (89), and it functions as the core in *A Sport of Nature*. But the novel contains elements of a number of other genres, ranging from history to tragedy and the utopia. Above all, *A Sport of Nature* develops from its *bildungsroman* base as a hybrid of the two primary genres that traditionally have been employed to represent the courtesan: the picaresque and the romance.

The two genres pair poorly. Shelley Sunn Wong points out that "subjects are interpellated, or called into particular subject positions, by different generic formations" (53). The positions constructed for the protagonist of romance and the protagonist of the picaresque are in crucial ways diametrically opposed.[42] The picara is active and independent, an energetic transgressor of conventional mores in every area. The innocent heroine of romance is dependent and passive. Picaras are on their own in a world largely hostile; the romance evolves "under the sign of destiny and providence" (Jameson 142). The picaresque is quotidian, an ironic genre, while the romance is utopian and relies on idealization. Marriage is destabilizing in the picaresque and stabilizing in the romance. Even in such minor matters as the treatment of maternal figures the two genres diverge; the romance has been read as a quest for the mother, while in the picaresque maternal influence tends to be negative. The opposition of the two genres is clear from readings of the picaresque as "a critique of romance" that "deidealizes or delegitimates [romantic] plots and heroes" (Yelin 200; see also Guillén 74).

At the surface level of plot, *A Sport of Nature* is predominantly picaresque.[43] Hillela shares many characteristics with the picaresque protagonist: her marginality, her social mobility, her deceptiveness, her solipsism, her absence of conventional morality, her service to a succession of masters, and her position as a functional orphan. Like such protagonists, she is a protean figure. She also exhibits the oxymoronic "picaresque conjunction of innocence and transgression" (Yelin 199). The picara traditionally survives as either a confidence artist or a prostitute (Mancing 282); part of the moral ambiguity that Hillela derives from the genre comes from her connections with both figures. In addition, the picaresque protagonist shares many traits with the old-fashioned stereotypical politician.

Most accounts of courtesans have been written as picaresque narratives, while the rest usually take the form of the romance. Thus the preponderance of the picaresque in *A Sport of Nature* is appropriate enough. But from the beginning there were problems fitting female protagonists into the genre. As Giancarlo Maiorino notes of one of the earliest texts focused on a picara, "the picaresque shift of gender is not a pleasant one" ("Introduction" xix; see also Guillén 86). As a genre with a "homosocial economy" (N. Davis 138), the associations of the picaresque were overwhelmingly masculine. It was difficult to center on a woman without making her a bearer of masculine ideology. Gordimer's method for feminizing this predominantly masculine genre was to infuse her picaresque surface plot with powerful romance elements.[44] This literary solution undoubtedly reflected her own personal proclivities. Critics constantly quote Gordimer's early description of herself as "a romantic struggling with reality." But they seldom note the last part of her sentence: "[S]urely this very engagement implies innate romanticism?" ("A Writer" 28).[45] This "innate romanticism" occasionally creates difficulties in Gordimer's work. Although in most of her novels she has mixed and destabilized various genres with great success, the mutual destabilizations of the picaresque and the romance in *A Sport of Nature* proved an exception.[46]

The romance elements in the novel are generally not as prominent as the picaresque ones. Some of them, such as the descriptions of Hillela's lush physicality that are typical of a romance heroine, are mainly decorative. But problems arise because too often the romance elements provide the determining features of the narrative. Hillela's political strategy, for example, derives from romance,[47] and this motivation coexists awkwardly with the picaresque plot. Romance directs the ideology, particularly in the emphasis on sexuality as a political solution. Similar to the direct connections Gordimer seeks to establish between Hillela's personal sexuality and African liberation is Gordimer's characteristic use of interracial sex as a political signifier. Wagner points out that in *A Sport of Nature,* as in all of Gordimer's novels, interracial sex functions "as a form of redemption for the white colonial" (58).[48] Although in this instance Gordimer does undermine the "white bias" that Anne Cranny-Francis has noted as characteristic of romance (188),[49] the problematic romantic insistence on individual love as an effective substitute for political action remains. The romanticization of black life and especially of black males throughout Gordimer's work,[50] so prominent in *A Sport of Nature,* reflects the same kind of ideological simplification.

The novel's utopian ending also comes straight out of romance. In this case romance dictates the gap in the text characteristic of contemporary women's political novels, because the happy ending of romance requires the elision of history. Readers see the ceremonies marking the liberation of black South Africa, but they are given no information at all about how it was actually accomplished (an occlusion reminiscent of the gap in the works of many feminist theorists between the present and the rich political futures they envision). Again and again in *A Sport of Nature,* the romance bears the ideology while the picaresque carries the action. The resulting rifts between plot and theme generate many of Hillela's ambiguities.

Ironically, the main problem in *A Sport of Nature* that derives from grafting together the picaresque and the romance arises not from their many contrary characteristics but from one crucial element that they share. Economic issues are key in both genres. Cranny-Francis writes that the desire encoded by the romance is "not sexual, but economic," with the economic motives "displaced into gender terms" to make women's romantic quests more palatable to readers (186, 184).[51] Economic struggle is also central to the picaresque, which is particularly marked by economic exploitation (Mancing 276).[52] Francisco J. Sánchez and Nicholas Spadaccini identify "the sexual body, the institution of marriage, the corruption of that institution, and the broader phenomena of economic pragmatism" as "related elements of the same discourse" in picaresque narrative (297). Adventure in the picaresque and emotion in the romance function to mystify the economic elements that are determinative in both. In *A Sport of Nature,* joining the two genres intensifies the economic element. Thus Gordimer's desire to portray Hillela and her sexuality as progressive political forces is continually subverted by the economic elements common to both picaresque and romance, which enhance opportunistic and exploitative aspects of her character.

Finally, Hillela remains an anomaly, a singular case. Throughout the novel Gordimer emphasizes her status as an exceptional individual, the *lusus naturae* of the title. By the end of the novel, as the narrator notes in connection with Hillela's second marriage, she has become a symbolic figure (*SN* 386).[53] In both political and literary terms she symbolizes the complete transformation, the quasi-organic mutation that *A Sport of Nature* posits as necessary for whites who want to participate in black-ruled African states. But Gordimer's figuration of this human mutation, compelling in so many ways, is finally unconvincing.

Foucault describes power as "only a certain type of relation between individuals" (*Politics* 83). The power that Gordimer's figuration represents is suspect because of the kind of relations between individuals it requires. On the one hand, Hillela's relationships demand a substantial sacrifice of basic humanity, as shown in her indifference to her ties and obligations to those closest to her, who love her and help her. In contrast to this complete rejection of the past are her other relationships that fail to break enough with traditional patterns, such as her replication of patriarchal roles for women as defined by their bodies and as secondary to men in the state. Thus Gordimer's utopian depiction of Hillela's sexuality as a new form of revolutionary salvation ultimately fails because it reinforces too many negative stereotypes of women's character and behavior. A *lusus naturae* represents some kind of radical break with previous forms. In Hillela's case the breaks with past patterns are either not complete enough or overly complete, in the sense that too many positive human elements disappear. As a fictional figuration of a revolutionary woman, she remains inadequate.

Significantly, even as an exception the example of Hillela reinforces certain basic premises in feminist theory about women and the state. She shows how the current model of the nuclear family limits women's access to the public sphere and also reflects the need for redefinition of traditional maternal roles to give women state access. The resignification of her public role as a courtesan into a private one, along with related questions about the larger conventional classifications of good and bad girls, illustrates how, as Butler emphasizes, "identity categories tend to be instruments of regulatory regimes" ("Imitation" 13), dangerous to women in the state as well as in the private and social spheres.

In producing her figuration Gordimer is also able to raise significant questions about the relationships between women and the state. She critiques current constructions of political activists and political efficacy. If Hillela's sexuality remains unconvincing as a revolutionary force, Gordimer's insistence that politics involves personal sexuality is a reminder of the human complexities of the state that theory is ill-equipped to handle. Brilliant in analyzing the ramifications of the abstract male body of the citizen, feminist theory has been less interested in the complex roles played by the bodies of individual women in the state, such as the courtesan. Gordimer also raises questions about the costs for women of success in state politics. What Hillela sacrifices for a black-ruled South Africa renders the costs of revolution in personal terms in a way that theory necessarily elides. Are women willing to make radical personal sacrifices in order to effect revolutionary change? Hillela also raises questions about the extent to which female success in the state is worthwhile for women without feminism. Just what do her political achievements actually mean for other women?

In the end, not much. Because of Hillela's status as an exception, her viability as a general political model is limited. The limitations are highlighted by the way her anomalousness is measured in the novel. Not only is the prevailing standard male desire, but the evaluation is done in terms of her *difference* from other women. The narrator asserts: "In fact, no man wanted Hillela to be like any other woman, would allow her to be even if it had been possible for her, herself" (*SN* 359–60; see also 204, 384–85, 387). The mutation remains strictly a solo act, with the word "allow" revealing the male control that dictates the terms of the performance.

Because of the focus on Hillela, other women in *A Sport of Nature* who more realistically represent contemporary women's relationships to the state, ranging from the nameless black African freedom fighters described only in terms of their breasts and feet (*SN* 285–86) to Christa Zeederburg, the dedicated Afrikaner revolutionary in exile, receive scant attention. Still others concerned with the state, such as Leonie Adlestrop and Pauline, become in effect political caricatures. Pauline, constructed as Hillela's opposite in every way, from her unkempt hair to her operation on principles rather than instinct, has the misfortune to be the major beneficiary in the novel of Gordimer's conflicted relationship with South African liberalism.[54] Thus her activism is trivialized, her intentions mocked, and her smallest hypocrisies analyzed and ridiculed in ways that Hillela's glaring inconsistencies never are. At the same time, the focus on her in terms of Sasha's ongoing oedipal antagonisms also slights her substantial political efforts by structuring so much of her story in private terms.

Wagner connects Gordimer's treatment of liberals in the novel with her romanticism: "It is a rampant romanticism which lies at the root of Gordimer's often dismissive treatment of even the best efforts of well-meaning 'liberals' to make a difference" (40). However, it is not just the liberals in *A Sport of Nature* who suffer from Gordimer's romanticism, but all the women in the novel. Romance allows only one Cinderella; the rest of the mortal women in the fairy tale are portrayed negatively. In many ways the most pernicious effect of the romance elements that shape Hillela's story is their marginalization of the political activities of other women in the text, whose experiences with the state parallel those of contemporary women readers far more closely than Hillela's Cinderella story ever does.

VI

□□□□□□□□□□□□□□□□□□□□□□□□□□□□

Mothers and Capitalists in International Politics: Margaret Drabble's *The Gates of Ivory*

Khieu Samphan, member of the Khmer Rouge:
  I dream of a perfect society.
  We would erase everything. We would empty out the cities.
  We would start the world over again. . . .
  It requires patience. The seasons are long
  In History.

—Hélène Cixous, *The Terrible but Unfinished Story*
of Norodom Sihanouk, King of Cambodia, 36

One of these mornings, when you reach the bottom of your cup, coffee or tea, it could be either, you will look and there will be a severed finger, bloodless, anonymous, a little signal of death sent to you from the foreign country where they grow such things.

—Margaret Atwood, "True Romances," 44

After victory parades, heroes dead or alive are honored. Days of national mourning are always a big hit. No danger that the dead will protest. And what do the mothers say?

—Günter Grass, *The Flounder, 522*

Hou Youn, member of the Khmer Rouge:
  Pol Pot remains unimaginable.

—Cixous, *Sihanouk, 173*

In Margaret Drabble's *The Gates of Ivory,* the prevailing view of late twentieth-century political life is represented by a production of *Coriolanus* by Aaron Headleand, a stepson of the novel's central female character. Aaron's production rewrites Shakespeare to offer "a vision of a world of arbitrary, bloody power, of power for its own sake." Politics is a brutal male domain under the "rule of the old men," a realm of violence and illusion. Coriolanus himself, reduced to a "warrior barbarian," is killed early in the play (*GI* 179). In this world in which "the Old Fox is King," only the titular hero's "flashing carapace" remains as an icon with which Menenius and the invisible handful who rule the state manipulate supporters and enemies alike (*GI* 179, 180).

Juxtaposed with this stark western vision of political power reconstructed from the ruins of Roman and Shakespearean grandeur and ruthlessness are the politics of Pol Pot and contemporary Kampuchea. Another invisible, unreadable old man, like Shakespeare's Menenius a "villain-hero" (*GI* 179), Pol Pot is portrayed as an absence, a void in the text. So is his "small, expendable country," which is described as a "hole in the map of the world," "an empty space," a "vacuum" (*GI* 66, 269). In London both the Vietnamese Embassy and the Foreign Office insist that Kampuchea does not exist: "It has not existed, for Britain, for many years" (*GI* 66). Drabble plays on this official nonexistence to produce a space in her novel that the western characters' imaginations fill through their quests both personal and political.

Appropriately enough, no one in the novel ever confronts Pol Pot or actual Kampuchean politics. Whether in Aaron's *Coriolanus* or the new Cambodia, actual state power in *The Gates of Ivory* is represented as hidden through disguise and deferral, its workings never confronted or understood by any of the characters. Simultaneously, the tangible results of this power, the "hundred miles of mass graves" stretching from Phnom Penh (*GI* 358), mock and frustrate those women and men in the novel who are driven to seek political origins and causes, to understand the international politics of the late twentieth century.

The relationships of women to these politics is one of Drabble's major concerns in *The Gates of Ivory.* To represent women's political roles, Drabble invokes three powerful stereotypes traditionally used to explain the role of women, and particularly their absence, in the public sphere. She focuses on women's positions as mothers, their limitations because of the female body, and their predominantly private sensibilities, their tendency to focus on local and personal concerns. The power of any stereotype, and its danger, derives from the partial and limited truths that it incorporates; any dismantling requires confrontation with those truths as well as straightforward critique. The comprehensiveness of Drabble's analysis in *The Gates of Ivory* comes from her willingness to confront these stereo-types directly. Thus she represents women's own complicity with the stereotypes while also depicting that complicity as in part a choice. One implication is that beyond complicity may lie unexplored political pos-sibilities for women. Drabble also opens out and expands the conven-tional stereotype of women as apolitical, in the process undercutting the gendered associations of the stereotype itself. While discussing the Bloomsbury group in an interview, Drabble once commented on their belief "in casting off sexual stereotypes." She went on to say that she felt "we shouldn't think too much in terms of stereotypes—either the newly forged ones or the old ones—that we ought to question them all the time" (Satz 192). This is precisely her procedure throughout *The Gates of Ivory*, as she raises questions about conventional stereotypes of women's unfitness for or disinterest in high politics.

As in all of the novels in this study, the woman protagonist comes in contact with state power through her relationship with a man. Liz Headland's friend Stephen Cox, a novelist ostensibly writing a play about Pol Pot, has gone to Kampuchea to satisfy his curiosity about the politics of the Khmer Rouge. Several years later, Liz receives a package containing papers in Stephen's handwriting, along with a human finger bone and other assorted materials. Ultimately, she feels compelled to go to Kampuchea herself to try to discover what has happened to him.

Despite considerable surface realism, Drabble's work has always been postmodern in its self-reflexiveness and limited closures.[1] In *The Gates of Ivory*, parody, the quintessential postmodern mode, literally becomes re-alism because, as Stephen reflects, "We live in the age of parody" (40). Thus Liz's journey is a comic parody of Stephen's tragic quest, which, from the time that he leaves London on an Air France jet piloted by Commandant Parodi, is itself paradoxically figured as a parody. The *Odyssey*'s description of the gates of horn and ivory (XIX.560–65) pro-vides the epigraph for *The Gates of Ivory*, and Roberta Rubenstein points out how Drabble parodies the Homeric poem and many of its modern versions in the novel ("Fragmented" 145). Also important for *The Gates of Ivory* is Virgil's more famous description of the gates at the end of Book VI (893–96) in the *Aeneid*. There, for reasons that have puzzled critics for over two millennia, Aeneas and the Sibyl depart from the lower world through the ivory gate, the portal of false dreams.[2] In addition to parodying the *Odyssey*, both Stephen's and Liz's journeys parody Aeneas's descent to the underworld.

Aeneas in his journey finds both his father Anchises and a vision of the future greatness of the Roman state. In contrast to the *Aeneid*, *The Gates of Ivory* offers no illustrious political futures and very few fathers.[3]

Rejecting earlier Freudian readings of Volumnia as "mother-villain" (*GI* 179), Aaron's *Coriolanus* decenters maternal power and concerns, but Drabble does not. *The Gates of Ivory* offers numerous mothers, villainous and otherwise. However, in contrast with most contemporary women novelists and almost all feminist critics since the late 1970s, Drabble's emphasis in the novel usually falls on the mothers of sons rather than of daughters.[4] A remark she gives to Sally Headleand, Liz's daughter, shows Drabble's amused consciousness of her deviation (not to mention High Modernist regression) from reigning literary norms. Sally complains that her mother "just wasn't up to date. Nobody seems to have told her that mother-daughter relationships are all the rage. Mothers and sons are out" (*GI* 261). But for Drabble in *The Gates of Ivory,* the concerns of state politics often lead back to mothers and sons. When Stephen fantasizes about interviewing Pol Pot, he begins with military and political matters: "*Combien d'hommes avez-vous sous votre commandant?*" But one of his final questions is "*Est-ce que vous aimiez votre mère, est-ce qu'elle vous aimait?*" (*GI* 353). The relationship between mothers and sons is one of several major sites through which Drabble represents women and the state.

One of the most important of these relationships is that of Savet Akrun, a Kampuchean refugee in Camp Site Ten[5] on the Thai-Kampuchean border, and her missing son Mitra. Last seen when Khmer Rouge soldiers overtook their traveling group of families, Mitra, like Pol Pot, is invoked throughout the novel as an absence. Conflicting accounts of his potential whereabouts are periodically inserted. Finally, in the closing paragraph of the novel, Mitra suddenly appears, striding through the forest:

> He will not present himself at Site Ten, he will not reach the family embrace. He will not step back through the gates of horn. He will march on, armed, blooded, bloodied, a rusty Chinese rifle at his back. Many have died and many more will die in their attempt to maim and capture him. He grows and grows, he multiplies. Terribly, he smiles. He is legion. He has not been told that he is living at the end of history. He does not care whether his mother lives or dies. He marches on. He is multitudes. (*GI* 462)

The conclusion is a powerful one, in stark contrast to the "feminine" endings that critics have associated with Drabble.[6] It is particularly chilling in view of Suzanne Mayer's observation that in each of Drabble's works, the closing line offers "clues to her view of her own characters and can often be used as a gauge of their future prospects" (86).

Depicted as an automaton, a "war machine" like Aaron's Coriolanus (*GI* 179), and like him the puppet of old men like Pol Pot, Mitra is a nightmare vision of politics reduced to raw force. Drabble's description highlights the violence of state power. Masculine terms predominate, from the phallic rifle to the reference to Mitra as "legion." Reflecting numerical strength through Roman military might, "Legion" was also the name given by the man possessed by multiple demons who was cured by Jesus (Mark 5:1–20; Luke 8:26–39). The demoniac's dwelling among the tombs mirrors Mitra's situation, while the conflation of Roman, biblical, and contemporary references emphasizes the diachronic nature of the problem. Mitra cannot "step back through the gates of horn," through which true dreams issue, because the violent public sphere in which he functions denies the validity of the domestic world of everyday concerns. Thus, the representation excludes women because they are irrelevant in the worlds forged by such power, particularly in their familial roles. Mitra, who no longer cares about his mother, is separated from "the family embrace." Since he himself "multiplies," metaphorically denying or appropriating female reproductive capacities, there is no need for women where he is. Nor is there any reason for women to want to be there.

Drabble's novel thus ends with a powerful image reflecting the stereotypical binary between the peaceful, loving, nurturing female and the violent, callous, militaristic male. This essentialist dualism has been reinforced throughout *The Gates of Ivory*, as violence is repeatedly connected with a denial of the maternal and familial. Typical is Savet Akrun's view of her second son Kem as a "child of violence," and her belief that his rage is "natural" because he has "no home, no country, no language" (*GI* 201). All the connections that Kem lacks carry maternal connotations: the mother tongue, the mother country, the mother's sphere. In the novel international politics, too, demand repression of the family. "Under Pol Pot, Sihanouk lost five children and fourteen grandchildren," one character muses. He then adds: "Sihanouk is willing to deal with the Khmer Rouge" (*GI* 71).[7]

In terms of the state, the natural feminist theoretical corollary to this kind of fictional representation would seem to be something like the "feminist maternal politics of peace" proposed by Sara Ruddick and developed—and sometimes severely criticized—by others concerned with merging feminist approaches with peace studies and activism.[8] Emphasizing the "peacefulness latent in maternal practice," which she claims as "a 'natural resource' for peace politics," Ruddick calls for "a new political identity: the feminist, maternal peacemaker who draws upon the history and traditions of women to create a human-respecting politics of peace" (*Maternal* 137, 157, 245). This formulation has retained substantial appeal despite the many formidable objections that have been raised against it.[9] Some critics have condemned Ruddick's biological essentialism (Grant

71). Others criticize her failure to take historical and cultural contexts into account. As Wendy Brown points out, the figure of the mother "varies tremendously by culture and class . . . and may be more singularly identified by the common devaluation of her work than by her particular bearing in the world; she is everywhere oppressed, but she is not everywhere more protective, empathic, nurturant, pacifistic, and communal in orientation than her male counterpart" (*MP* 186).[10]

Ruddick's ideas have also been attacked for their reinscription of patriarchal ideology, particularly in idealizing motherhood and understating maternal aggression and ambivalence. Still others have emphasized the support that women throughout history have given to warfare. Noting "the instinctive erasure of women's presence in war," Miriam Cooke has pointed out "the distortions that have always been necessary to construct the age-old story of war as men's business" (178). Although as Ruddick indicates, historically women have dominated pacifist movements ("Preservative" 232), from classical times other women have also encouraged and participated in wars. From the Spartan mothers who challenged their sons to come back with their shields or on them to the U.S. mothers who fought in the Persian Gulf, mothers are deeply implicated in martial practices. Indeed, Elshtain devotes a section in *Women and War* to tracing structural parallels between the "Good Soldier" and the "Good Mother" (221–25).[11] Today the "story of war as men's business" is becoming more and more difficult to construct, as women all over the world bear arms in both liberation struggles and national armies. The complexity of the relationship between women and war, and the strong cultural pressure to maintain the traditional gendering of martial activities as male, emerged clearly in controversies among both feminists and nonfeminists over the participation of women, and particularly of mothers, in the Gulf War.[12]

Ruddick herself concedes that maternal peacefulness is a "myth" ("From Maternal" 143; see also *Maternal* 219–20). But she argues that it is "an empowering myth" ("From Maternal" 148). In view of the long-term, ongoing feminist project of demystifying and demythologizing motherhood, it is somewhat ironic that a number of theorists and activists have agreed with her. Along with Nancy Chodorow's treatment of mothering, Ruddick's peaceful mother has continued to resist historical contextualization to triumph as a feminist myth. In both cases the theories have endured because they account for some common cultural formations while simultaneously offering broad reassurances by obscuring less pleasant psychological as well as social realities. As Roland Barthes notes of all myths, both theoretical accounts distort by abolishing the "simplicity of human acts" and rendering instead the "complexity of essences" (143). Moreover, in both cases the "essentially polemical purpose" that Pierre Macherey connects with all myths is clear (23).

Drabble herself is personally enthusiastic about motherhood. She has described it as "permanently good" and "the greatest joy in the word," admitting that she views "motherhood in such positive terms that [she feels] almost embarrassed to state it" (Cooper-Clark 28).[13] Motherhood is generally portrayed positively in her novels, too, especially the early ones; Elaine Showalter has called Drabble "the novelist of maternity" (*Literature* 305).[14] But *The Gates of Ivory* offers a more nuanced and critical portrayal of motherhood, particularly of the problems it can create for women in their roles as state citizens. For example, although the impact of Drabble's ending derives in part from the mythic dichotomies it reflects, the bulk of her text undercuts them. Most of Drabble's representations of women and the state emphasize the gap between theory and practice in any maternal peace politics. Although denial of the familial and the maternal is often implicated in violence, the novel brings into question any political solution based on putative domestic and maternal virtues transferred to the state. Like some of Ruddick's critics, who emphasize that "the force of what women as nurturers do on the interpersonal level . . . is painfully problematic in the global arena" (Forcey, "Feminist" 366), Drabble focuses on political limitations in traditional maternal roles and attitudes.[15]

The dominant maternal image throughout *The Gates of Ivory* is a prize-winning photograph of Savet Akrun. With the caption "Where is my son?" supplied by a European relief agency, the complexity of the actual woman has been reduced to an "icon" (*GI* 22, 136), a mother commodified on a poster for charitable appeals. Liz wonders whether Mme. Akrun posed "as an emblematic figure for her nation" (*GI* 23). However, Mme. Akrun, educated in Paris (ironically, the source of the Pol Pot group's communism[16]), wears "a slightly Westernized sarong" in the famous photograph (*GI* 22). Once again, the reality of a contemporary Kampuchean recedes in the text, leaving only what the western imagination simultaneously desires and constructs. In addition, the image raises questions about the claims that have been made for the political power wielded by women through symbolic forms. In this connection Rosemary Ridd notes particularly "women's capacity to embody the culture and essence of their people" (5).[17] The photograph and the stories behind it indicate the sentimentalizing and essentializing tendencies of such symbolic political gestures.

Like the European characters, Mme. Akrun lives in a parody, for the refugee camp is described as "a parody of the town, a parody of the village" (*GI* 337). Her motherhood, too, carries parodic overtones. A maternal icon commodified for western consumption, her famous photograph ultimately becomes in the text only an ironic simulacrum. Having spent years obsessively grieving for her older son, she becomes reconciled to his disappearance after her second son Kem, a delinquent who has joined the resistance fighters in Kampuchea, returns seriously wounded. Maimed, barred from the world of violence gendered male in the novel ("He is no use to the guerrillas or to the bandits now"), he cannot leave his mother's little hut, "his bamboo prison." Kem's personality is transformed. Adjectivally feminized, the former rebel becomes "humble," "grateful," "sweet of nature," "safe," and "good." Infantilization follows feminization: "He is her darling, her favourite, her little one." Drabble draws on all the stereotypes of castrating mothers in the passage to show that once Kem is emasculated, mutilated, and passive, he becomes Mme. Akrun's ideal child.[18] He displaces all thoughts of Mitra: "She is reborn as Mother. Her family is complete once more. She is happy" (*GI* 340).

But of course Mme. Akrun's family is *not* complete. Mitra still stalks the jungles, although his mother remains unaware and unconcerned. Like Candide, she literally cultivates her garden in the refugee camp (*GI* 337). But Mme. Akrun should be worrying about Mitra, and not only because she is his mother. Drabble shows that what the mother has viewed as her own personal quest, a search for a lost son, is in addition a serious political threat. No politics will be safe for women—or for anyone—until what Mitra represents has been understood, confronted, and destroyed.

Through Mme. Akrun, Drabble represents maternal thinking as a potentially dangerous barrier between women and the state. Consumed with family concerns, Mme. Akrun cares for little beyond them. Her maternal role, satisfied through any son available, blinds her to larger state issues; she seeks no role in politics. "The nation dies," she explains to Liz. "It is sad, but what can one do?" (*GI* 335). In part a laudable refusal of the destructive elements of nationalism, her attitude is at the same time a refusal of civic responsibility. Luce Irigaray shows the consequences of this kind of maternal mentality: "[A]s long as women are concerned about their wombs, . . . that will be their (only) concern. The social structure, political and religious authority, symbolic exchanges—in short, all serious spiritual things remain in the hands of men" (*Je* 134). Thus Mme. Akrun's reductive maternity helps to insure male political control.

Feminist theorists have been clear on the problems of obsessive mothering for both mother and child. They have also recognized, as Lynne Segal notes, that the "weight of responsibility for one's own children can mean a contraction of social vision."[19] However, Segal is typical in describing the results of this contracted vision mainly in local terms, as "an envy and resentment of the welfare of others" (6). Drabble, in contrast, depicts the larger political dangers of the obliviousness to state concerns in constricted maternal vision. While feminist theorists emphasize some of the difficulties in integrating altruistic maternal attitudes and practices with state power structures, Drabble's novel suggests that limitations in the attitudes themselves resist such integration.

Irigaray, like most feminist theorists, emphasizes that it is "the patriarchal world that has confined women to motherhood" (*Je* 134). Drabble in *The Gates of Ivory* instead highlights the element of choice in maternal practice. Unlike her iconic status on the relief organization's poster, Mme. Akrun's exclusively maternal focus is shown as not entirely externally imposed. Even a parody allows some free play beyond the original. Drabble depicts Mme. Akrun as trapped in a discourse that she, too, has been complicitous in constructing. When Stephen meets her, he tries to get her to discuss her own experiences, but she can speak of herself only in terms of her son Mitra. The "ritual narrative" that she herself has crafted dictates that she "cannot move over the borders of her tale" (*GI* 152). Nor does she show any desire to move beyond it.

Drabble shows that the stereotype of the overprotective mother that Mme. Akrun embodies has never been her only option. Mme. Akrun is a person of consequence in her community, an educated woman in a society that traditionally has placed a high value on learning. Josephine Reynell points out that the importance of education as an institution in Khmer culture is shown by their continuing efforts to maintain schools in the refugee camps (164). A teacher in the Centre for Adult Education, Mme. Akrun also serves on the Khmer Women's Association Literacy Committee.[20] With teacher shortages a major problem in the camps (Reynell 167), her role gives her substantial status.

Mme. Akrun is described as "a respectable matron, honoured amongst her fellows" (*GI* 337). "Matron," with its Latin root *mater*, obviously highlights the maternal role in a woman of distinguished position. But the word can also mean a supervisor in an institution, such as a school, a hospital, or a prison. In Mme. Akrun's case, the schoolmistress merges with the prison officer, as she restricts not only her son Kem, described as "waiting in his bamboo prison" (*GI* 340), but also herself. Like many traditional mothers, and like many theorists of maternal peace politics, she limits herself in part by consistently overrating her own maternal power. She believes that because she bore Mitra, she can bring him back into her world (*GI* 132). Similarly, she blames only herself for Kem's wounded pain (*GI* 339). In so doing she fails to confront or even consider the political forces, national and international, that have forged her sons' destinies. *The Gates of Ivory* is a novel about displaced people, both literal and metaphorical, eastern and western: political refugees, aid workers, journalists, and prosperous Europeans alienated from themselves. Initially displaced from the state by political upheaval, Mme. Akrun further displaces herself from it by her exclusively matrifocal vision.

❑   ❑   ❑

Drabble develops Mme. Akrun through the traditional stereotype of woman as too mired in maternal and familial concerns to enter the public realm. She draws on a related stereotype as she represents not just the social constructions of motherhood but the female body itself as disqualifying women from public action. Just after the onset of an unexpected menstrual period, Liz meets with various Thai officials to discuss Stephen's disappearance:

> She is worrying not about death but about leakage. She continues to worry about it, as she passed from department to department. . . . She cannot take in what is said to her, she cannot follow her interpreter. She is bleeding. She is treated with courtesy, with delicacy, but this she does not even notice. The entire male world of communism, Marxist-Leninism, inflation, American imperialism, rice production, exchange mechanisms, statistics, hostages, the CIA, the SAS and the KGB, the Chinese, the KPNLF, Sihanouk, and Hun Sen, war, death, and Ho's marble mausoleum dissolve and fade before the bleeding root of her body, impaled on its grey-white stump. Woman-being, woman-life, possess her entirely. Shames and humiliations, triumphs and glories, birth and blood. Let armies fight and die, let people starve. She hopes that the seat of her skirt will not be stained when she rises. (*GI* 379)

A number of feminist theorists have analyzed how various taboos surrounding menstruation have damaged women psychologically, as women internalize religious and cultural ideas of pollution and defilement. Haunani-Kay Trask is among those who have also connected negative male interpretations of menstruation with women's exclusion from social and political authority (24).[21] Liz's attitudes in the passage read like a parody of sexist rationalizations of women's incapacity for government. Between her elation that she can still menstruate without hormone replacements and her incessant concern over spotting, Liz's focus on her body, like Mme. Akrun's focus on her son, blocks out state and political concerns entirely. The ludicrousness of her narrowed priorities is emphasized by the overwriting in the passage ("the entire male world," "triumphs and glories," "let people starve"). The extent of Liz's overreaction to her body as female is suggested when, falling ill on her trip, she diagnoses her condition as toxic shock syndrome, a diagnosis on which serious doubt is later cast. Drabble's stereotypes represent the female body in its actual and potential maternity as creating a mind-set that makes women uninterested in and incapable of effective political participation.

Drabble offers two other critiques of this kind of attitude in the novel, showing integration of the female body and the state through characteristic parody in the West and tragedy in the East. In England the parody is provided by Polly Piper, who, after devoting herself to Wittgenstein at Cambridge, takes a position writing copy for an ad agency and shows "a marked flare for selling women's products" (Drabble, *Radiant* 153). Her employment history spans a Civil Service job dealing with women's prisons, an executive position with a company producing both ladies' underwear and romantic fiction, and finally, at its apex, "a career in sanitary protection." ("It's always been my passion," she explains [*GI* 155].) Polly's position on body politics basically reverses Liz's. While Liz mindlessly separates the female body and politics, Polly with a different kind of mindlessness joins them. When first introduced as a character in *The Radiant Way*, Polly had become so enthusiastic about proposals to exempt sanitary napkins from the value-added tax that she was considering a campaign for Parliament based on the issue (154). By the time of *The Gates of Ivory*, she has enlarged her campaign goals to include the tampon, which she considers "the liberator of womankind" (*GI* 155). After Polly is made a baroness, Alix speculates that in the House of Lords the formidable Polly "will lecture the old boys on VAT on sanitary wear and other women's issues and it will do them a power of good" (*GI* 432).[22]

Laudable as far as it goes, Polly's approach imposes unnecessary limits on what "women's issues" actually are, as the unfortunate pun suggests. Much more than tampons is required for women's access to high politics. Focusing an oppositional discourse primarily in terms of the female body ignores structural constraints on women's political participation. In an interview Drabble commented that in *The Radiant Way*, she suggested in Polly "a dynamic woman who is going to do extremely well in the man's world" (Kenyon, *Women Writers* 37). The parodic treatment of her in *The Gates of Ivory* indicates one of the reasons for her advancement. Although Polly's intent is to widen the political sphere to include women, the limits of her own particular feminist approach make her easily marginalized and contained.

In contrast, the tragic potential of "women's issues" for the state is shown by the impact of politics on Kampuchean women in the novel. Characters discuss the many women who ceased menstruating during the dispersions under Pol Pot, and stories are told of the refugees who stopped menstruating prematurely or never started at all. Shaped by national and international politics, the female body inevitably is marked by the public realm in ways that a politics narrowly focused on the body too often evades. Patricia Mann writes that "when feminists seek to reappropriate either the maternal body or the sexual body of women, they become enmeshed in binary gender narratives which are no longer adequate to women's and men's dynamically evolving notions of parental and sexual agency." Mann's call for "an embodied metaphor of struggle that does not embroil us in previous kinship narratives and social identities" (161) is particularly salient in the context of women's relationship to the state.

Woman as mother and as body and therefore unfit for the public realm has been a political stereotype since Aristotle. For him, as Susan Moller Okin points out, woman's function was limited to breeder of citizens and household guardian (90). But if *The Gates of Ivory* represents women's complicity in these stereotypes, it also exposes other dynamics that have fueled these exclusions. Behind the figures of the mother and the female body lurk male fears.

Jean Bethke Elshtain provides useful historical context for Drabble's stereotypes by detailing the motivations that led Aristotle to relegate women to the private sphere. She points out "the widespread fear of the 'private' power of women that permeated Athenian society, particularly fear of the mother":

> This fear compelled the man to leave home, not simply by removing himself physically but by fending off "home" emotionally, even politically. . . .
> It is as if the Athenian male were torn between two powerful fields of force: Mother and Market, household and *polis,* private and public, and chose to take his chances outside, to make his mark in public action, frequently warfare . . ., rather than to confront what John Knox would later term "the monstrous regiment of women." (*PMPW* 51)

Elshtain indicates that women's public speech was silenced partly "because that which defines them and to which they are inescapably linked—sexuality, natality, the human body . . .—was omitted from political speech." This omission she connects with the role politics plays as "in part an elaborate defense against the tug of the private, against the lure of the familial, against evocations of female power" (*PMPW* 15–16).[23] In *The Gates of Ivory* Mitra, who escapes into warfare from his mother and her "bamboo prison" (*GI* 340), is one example of the kind of political dynamic that Elshtain delineates. Stephen Cox, who represents the theory behind Mitra's practice, is another.

Stephen's mother is another of the many oppressive maternal figures who dominate *The Gates of Ivory*. Insisting on "the family as sanctuary," she seeks to trap her four sons "in their boyish juvenile world of mother-dependent greed and fear" (*GI* 104). Stephen, luckier than Mitra, escapes her by going to the university and becoming an intellectual. In the process he also becomes a "dangerous creature, a dreamer of ideological dreams" (*GI* 82). He embraces a revolutionary theoretical politics, which becomes his version of the Salvation Narrative of Politics. Its ruthlessness is highlighted by the connections drawn between Stephen and *Macbeth* in *The Gates of Ivory* (50, 136, 353, 417). Stephen believes that what the human race, mired in pettiness and acquisitiveness, needs to make it capable of better things is "a Big Idea. A *really* Big Idea." Eschewing the "slow march of bloodless reform," he seeks a "cataclysm," "a deep, violent, volcanic shift" to purge and purify human nature and change the way things are (*GI* 83). Both his self-consciously naive politics and his loss of faith in them lead to his fascination with Pol Pot and his trip to Kampuchea.

Appropriately for a person with his "primal hopes and interests" (*GI* 275), Stephen tends to think in binary terms. He instinctively structures his life through binaries: "He is evading the choice between Konstantin and Miss Porntip, between the light and the dark" (*GI* 108). For the "simplicity" that he admits he seeks (*GI* 105), such Manichean thinking is of course ideal. In the political world, however, it can be dangerous, as is "simplicity" as a goal. Here Foucault's emphasis on the ubiquity of power at every level is useful in highlighting the inevitable play of conflict, however the political realm may be demarcated. The rigid binaries that construct and maintain ideological purity crumble in the pragmatic space of everyday politics, necessarily constructed through constant compromise if they are not to be totalitarian.

The kind of rigid binary thinking represented by Stephen, the same kind of thinking that originally excluded women from the political world, is shown in the novel to be dangerous because it refuses to take account of the human complexity of politics. As Joan Scott points out, "political movements develop tactically and not logically, improvising appeals, incorporating and adapting various ideas to their particular cause. By conceiving of such movements as mélanges of interpretations and programs (instead of as coherently unified systems of thought) we come closer not only to how they operated but to the web of relationships within which they developed" (61–62). It is this "web of relationships," what Scott describes as "the fluidity and complexity of human interactions" (66), that Stephen denies and refuses to face.

Lonely in his life and in his death, a man with only two good friends, Stephen obsessively follows his chimerical politics not just to escape from his mother but to escape from other people generally. Only as he lies dying does he begin to understand that the abstraction of his politics has actually disguised deep personal antipathy. He recognizes that "he did not love the people," indeed that "he feared and hated the people" (*GI* 357). Chandra Mohanty has connected the abstraction of this kind of thinking with dominion and colonialism ("Introduction" 16), while Ruddick describes it as "central to militarist thinking" (*Maternal* 97; cf. Segal 197). In *A Natural Curiosity,* the predecessor to *The Gates of Ivory,* Stephen's original interest in Pol Pot was explained as deriving from his belief that the Kampuchean "represented the apotheosis of the demented intellectual" (172). By the end of *The Gates of Ivory,* Stephen recognizes that in a far lesser but still dangerous way he, too, has been a "demented intellectual," as his ideas have distorted his politics.

The conflict between the self and the other that many see as central to relationships between mothers and daughters is in certain ways even more apropos for mothers and sons, where the otherness is marked by gender. Despite all the connections Drabble establishes in *The Gates of Ivory* between mothers and their sons' behavior in and out of politics, she insists that no simple corollary is possible. It is Alex the social worker, not Liz the psychoanalyst, who originally connects Paul Whitmore's serial murders with his mother's failure to love him. Even Alex is forced finally to admit that "the explanation was inadequate, if factually true" (*GI* 197). Because of Drabble's refusal of any simple equations, in *The Gates of Ivory* the failure to recognize and respect the other as an individual that marks poor relationships between mothers and sons comes to represent the refusal to see human beings as separate individuals that characterizes militaristic and totalitarian politics.

Against the kind of abstract, absolutist, and global thinking represented by Stephen, Drabble again draws on stereotypes to depict the women of her novel as focused on the everyday, the local, and the particular. Along with Mme. Akrun, stereotypically grounded in the family, and Liz, stereotypically grounded in the body, the women characters stereotypically personalize experience. Liz's interest is caught by the newspaper clipping about Mme. Akrun since it is a "human interest story, not a hard-news story" (*GI* 23). Stephen's friend Hattie Osborne, coming across the letters "HO" in his papers, is sure that they are her initials, until she finally realizes that they refer to Ho Chi Minh (*GI* 49). Because the private sphere consumes their attention in *The Gates of Ivory,* Drabble's women shut out public concerns. Far from the world of Pol Pot, "social engineering" devolves into questions of who can converse comfortably and politely with whom (*GI* 111). John Stuart Mill wrote that

"A woman seldom runs wild after an abstraction" (Rossi, *Feminist* 221). Drabble's women in *The Gates of Ivory* never do.

Drabble shows that the personalized and localized mind-sets of her female characters, centering on the self and often failing to advance very far beyond, derive at least partly from a failure to confront the deep differences among human beings that make state politics necessary. At the same time, however, this kind of thinking does not accommodate the deadly binaries and abstractions of Stephen's approaches. Meeting Mme. Akrun, Stephen has no interest at all in the human being before him. Abstracting the scrawny, aging Kampuchean woman with receding gums and blackened teeth into a symbol, he recasts her as a work of art: "the icon of sorrow, the maimed Pietà, the mother of absences, Mater Dolorosa" (*GI* 151). Liz's visit is also unsatisfactory because of her preconceptions of Mme. Akrun. But Liz at least can see the discrepancies between her ideas and the actual human being she confronts, and she recognizes the inadequacies of her constructions.

The political importance of Liz's kind of thinking as antithetical to Stephen's is shown when Stephen, fatally ill in Kampuchea, recognizes that Liz "could have saved him": "She would have forced particularity upon him" (*GI* 363). The very female stereotypes that Drabble has invoked and critiqued—woman as body, woman as maternal and familial—echo in Stephen's thoughts about Liz as savior. She is "solid, fleshly," and "an embodied woman"; she has "husbands, children" (*GI* 364). Liz's "particularity" is her submersion in the everyday: the personal, the local, and the temporary. Drabble shows this perspective as a crucial defense against the rigid binaries and cold abstraction that mark Stephen's theoretical and Mitra's militarized politics, but she simultaneously reveals its limits. In the face of actual Kampucheans, Liz finds herself reduced merely to presence. "Perhaps it is enough that she sits here," she thinks as she fails to find anything significant to say to Mme. Akrun (*GI* 336). Later, failing similarly to understand and respond to Chet's story of his ordeal, she wonders: "Is it enough, to listen and to believe?" (*GI* 404). The particularity of most of the women in the novel reduces their direct relationships to the state to those of witnesses or victims. If in *The Gates of Ivory* women represent the particularized excess that forces the deconstruction of the discursive bases of dangerous politics, Pol Pot and Mitra become the savage excess that destroys civil society and that remains impervious to the few interventions attempted by women in the novel.

In *The Gates of Ivory* the gap between women and the state ultimately figures the relation of the West as a whole to international politics. Just as Drabble draws on stereotypes of poor mother-son relationships to represent the inhumanity of totalitarian politics, and uses the stereotype of women's bodies making them unfit for the *polis* to suggest male fears, she takes the stereotypical connection of women with the particular and reinscribes it on western culture as a whole. In the space of international politics constructed by the novel, all of the western characters, not just the women, are reduced to witnesses or victims. The prototype is Stephen, who is feminized first as "a witness and an observer" (*GI* 416) and then dies as a victim. Western impotence despite goodwill and the best intentions is also highlighted by the relief workers, who labor faithfully to repair the human ravages of high politics but can in no way influence the course of state policies. (Significantly, even the motivations of the aid workers are in most cases linked to private, particularly filial, concerns: "exorcising ghosts, repaying debts, settling old accounts" [*GI* 127; see also 189–90].) Stephen, who has sought to revitalize his political faith by witnessing Kampuchea, briefly bridges the two worlds of East and West by his death. But the connection turns out to be illusory. At the end of the novel, all concern for Stephen rapidly evaporates during the party following his memorial service. The depiction of the guests' absorption in their own affairs shows Drabble at her literary best in a brilliant tour-de-force in the comedy of manners. However, like western society itself in *The Gates of Ivory*, the comedy of manners sustains its effects by careful omissions and rigid refusals to confront deeper issues. At the party Kampuchea is reduced to a topic for social conversation and localized to a Vietnamese resettlement project in Northam (*GI* 453).

The long party sequence is a powerful summation of the contrasts that Drabble has developed throughout the novel between "Good Time" and "Bad Time," particularized in "all the Good Times of the West" and "the Bad Time of Cambodia" (*GI* 3). Through onomatopoeia, alliteration, and consonance, she represents those in the West as incapable of bridging the gap between the superficial sociability and acquisitiveness of their private lives ("chitter chatter petty mutter petty bitty bitch bunch bite and suck" [*GI* 82]) and the brutal world of international politics ("the sound of spade on skull" [*GI* 132, 366; cf. 78]). The structure of the novel, with its movements back and forth between eastern and western settings and its concomitant changes in narrative focalization and time, highlights the ultimate failures of connection and coherence. No conjunctions are possible, even at the most basic level of violence. The gap between Paul Whitmore, the local London serial killer, and Pol Pot, the national architect of genocide, remains too great, despite their homonymous first names. Significantly, even Whitmore's brutality as, in Stephen's words, "a private killer, not an official one" (*GI* 13),[24] evades satisfactory explanation throughout the trilogy of novels that *The Gates of Ivory* closes.

In Drabble's version of the Outsider Narrative in *The Gates of Ivory,* the women characters position themselves as political outsiders because of excessive focus on maternity, the female body, and the particular. Outsiderhood provides neither protection for ideological purity nor any other political benefit in the novel. It merely signifies impotence. Drabble adds a new strand to the Outsider Narrative when she represents not only women but western culture generally as having no substantive impact on international politics. At the same time, she also reverses the Outsider Narrative by questioning whether that pervasive alienation matters at all. Ubiquitous personal and private foci are not the only forces blocking western access, gendered female in the novel, to the domain of traditional high politics, symbolized by Kampuchea as an absence in the text.

In addition to the everyday world of the West, where Liz's particularity can deconstruct the binaries of Stephen's theoretical politics even as it limits her own political viability, one other world is vividly represented in *The Gates of Ivory.* This is the world under construction by international corporate capitalism, where money and greed are relentlessly forging a more global culture. The new rules of this world produce new rulers. In Korea, Rambo "is king," while Stephen wonders whether there is "a country in the world where Coca-Cola is not king?" (*GI* 163, 123). In Drabble's novel transnational economic ties make nationalisms and the politics that created and are created by them increasingly irrelevant. Indeed, traditional politics of all kinds seem insignificant, parodies of substantive power in postindustrial capitalist civilization. Alix and Brian Bowen, putative Socialists, strongly disapprove of capitalism, but they enjoy its luxuries and "cannot help profiting" from it (*GI* 450). Those characters who espouse visionary revolutionary politics end up dead (Stephen) or remain absences (Pol Pot) in the novel.

Significantly, in *The Gates of Ivory* the world of rampant capitalism—unadulterated, unapologetic, and unstoppable—is represented by a woman. The irrepressible Porntip Pramualratana, called Miss Porntip and nicknamed "O," is Drabble's supreme parodic creation in a novel built on multileveled parody. Miss Porntip is constructed from competing stereotypes, a barrage of contradictory discourses, every one of which she energetically destabilizes. At some level parody usually legitimates even as it undermines. By pitting parody against parody, drawing on certain elements of a stereotype while contradicting others through competing stereotypes, Drabble uses parody against itself to press the limits of the technique. Typical is her self-reflexive parody as the English characters first encounter Miss Porntip in Stephen's papers. They quickly dismiss her as "a bad joke": "Had Stephen not realized that foreigners were no longer funny, that racial stereotypes were out? If Stephen's novel features a Miss Porntip, then perhaps it is just as well that it has been mislaid" (*GI* 270). In the process of deploying competing parodic discourses, Drabble produces the most energetic, capable, and strong-minded female character in the novel.

Stereotypes of Asian women have long been staples in western male fantasies, and for the last decade Thai women have played a major role. Baudrillard's fulsome descriptions are representative. He terms Thai women "the fulfillment of Western man's dreams." Describing their physiques as "privileged to be the currently fashionable form of ethnic beauty," he calls them "so beautiful that they have become the hostesses of the Western world" (*Cool* 168).[25] In *The Gates of Ivory* Miss Porntip's beauty is depicted in these terms. She is petite, gorgeous, sensual, and pleasing to men. Having reproduced stereotypes to portray Miss Porntip's appearance, however, Drabble then proceeds to parody other Asian stereotypes. The sexism and racism of views such as Baudrillard's are made overt in his essay through simile, when he associates the sexuality of Thai women with the eroticism of the Arabian Nights and the Nubian slaves of imperial Rome (*Cool* 168). It is this kind of racism and sexism that Drabble mercilessly parodies in her portrayal of Miss Porntip's singular personality.

Despite her stunning sensuality, Miss Porntip is no geisha girl. She lacks entirely the passivity and muteness of the stereotype. Insofar as she exhibits the "unlimited desire" that Edward Said has connected with the stereotypical Oriental (*Orientalism* 188), it turns out to be a desire for money and profit. Only in business is she "insatiable" (*GI* 79). There the hyperfeminine Miss Porntip shows the cold, calculating, rapacious drive of the stereotypical successful capitalist. Just as she defies male stereotypes of the Asian woman, she similarly demolishes feminist stereotypes of nonwestern women. Feminist work has tended to focus on these women as either "underdeveloped versions" of western women (Jagose 15) or else as "victims of multinational capital" (Mohanty, "Introduction" 29).[26] Nonwestern women are usually portrayed as suffering from "double colonization," being "colonized by a traditional patriarchy as well as by metropolitan imperialist interests" (Harlow 33). In contrast, Miss Porntip, with her far-flung business investments and holdings, bows to neither native male nor western corporation. She herself is the imperialist, and "Her empire is vast" (*GI* 79).

Miss Porntip reverses the standard economic binary between the rich West and the poor third world on which Drabble plays throughout the novel. She dismisses Britain as industrially "senile" (*GI* 61) and extols the PacRim future. Although postcolonial studies initially tracked unidirectional cultural flows from a "homogenizing West" (Grewal and Kaplan 12), recent theorists have pointed out that such models grossly oversimplify the intricate and diverse patterns of exchange that are emerging.[27] Inderpal Grewal and Caren Kaplan write that any analysis of center-periphery relations that deals with "the direction of influence, technology, and knowledge as one-way is not only ethno- or Eurocentric, . . . but inaccurate" (12). Miss Porntip exemplifies the selective accommodation of the periphery to the center. Her rise has coincided with the American military buildup in Thailand, which shaped her entrepreneurial and consumerist attitudes. However, she is never reduced to alienated imitation. She prefers the healthy Thai diet to western "rubbish food" (*GI* 100). Although she approves of Coca-Cola in theory, in practice she contemptuously declines drinking it (*GI* 100, 122–23). Like Thailand itself, which was never formally colonized despite British and French efforts, Miss Porntip resists imperialism in certain ways. Conrad, for example, she detests as a "racist sexist swine" (*GI* 100).

With Miss Porntip's vigorous capitalism go the political views that support it. Liz's everyday particularities implicitly deconstruct the binaries of Stephen's theoretical politics, but Miss Porntip directly attacks them by simple reversal. Parodic excess marks her insistence that communism and socialism are dead and her explication of her version of freedom and democracy:

> "Socialism finished, simplicity finished, poverty finished, USSR and China and Vietnam all finished. Liberty, is all. Growth, is all. Dollars, is all. . . . Equality and fraternity is poverty and sickness. Is men working like beast, like buffalo. Is men killing one another like beast, like worse beast. Is no good. . . . Is finished. Is new world now." (*GI* 106)

Miss Porntip can recognize the totalitarian and militaristic tendencies of Stephen's thought. But the desire for simplicity that she dismisses in his beliefs reemerges in her own metonymy and overstatement, where they are no less dangerous than in his.[28]

Drabble narratively organizes these various parodic strands into an ostensibly triumphant feminization of the classic rags-to-riches capitalist story. The daughter of a poor farming family in the hills of northeast

Thailand, Miss Porntip builds her business empire through a succession of traditional female occupations and the successful commodification of herself. She moves from her aunt's coffee shop to a massage parlor, then to a parlor of her own, and finally to numerous titles in beauty contests.[29] She self-consciously textualizes her achievements as female. Proudly she claims a part in rewriting the single story available for women in Thailand, "Village Maiden to Beauty Queen," into a "new history," a "new story," a "New Plot." What she offers instead, according to her, is the "success story of the woman, the independence of the woman" (*GI* 79).

In certain ways Miss Porntip does represent unusual female independence within the context of *The Gates of Ivory*. Refusing romantic paradigms, she judges men by how "useful" they are (*GI* 61). Motherhood and the body in no way limit her. She handles both, as she handles everything, by either commodification or consumption. She describes her gorgeous jewels as her "children," her beauty as her "capital" and an "asset," and even her bottom as yet another "great asset" (*GI* 101, 59, 80). Miss Porntip is the only woman in the novel to vigorously assert an ideological position.[30] She is also the only woman who deals effectively with the state, albeit indirectly. For example, her powerful connections enable Liz to make the official arrangements necessary to continue the search for Stephen. When Liz is ready to travel, "Miss Porntip works wonders. Doors open for her, men in uniform leap to attention, documents write themselves for her in magic ink" (*GI* 375).

Drabble portrays economic power for women favorably throughout the novel and suggests its positive political impact. She herself is no Marxist; in an interview in 1987, she rather defensively claimed that "my books occupy a sort of bourgeois middle ground, but then so do I, and I'm not ashamed of it" (Clifford 19).[31] In *The Gates of Ivory* she depicts female economic power as yet another protection against the dangers of theoretical revolutionary politics. Stephen admires Liz as "the apotheosis of the bourgeoisie" (*GI* 215). Part of her "particularity" that he feels could have saved him involves her economic position: "She had bank accounts, investments, employees, employment. She was plugged into Reality and Property" (*GI* 364). At another level, Drabble through Miss Porntip suggests that power in the economic sphere may be one way for women to gain at least some access to political power in an era when international capitalism is supplementing traditional nationalistic politics. But Drabble is also careful to show the limits of this kind of power. Significantly, the access that Miss Porntip's economic power allows is only to government *products*—visas, official documents—which have predominantly private rather than public purviews. Female power in the economic sphere does not offer full political access. Even with

Miss Porntip, the sphere of high politics is still represented as deferred for women.

Ultimately, *The Gates of Ivory* calls into question just how original Miss Porntip's much vaunted "New Plot" for women actually is. Reversing roles, she has simply inserted herself into a traditional, not to say hackneyed, male plot. She is in most ways a socialist and radical feminist nightmare of what the triumph of "power feminism" and other mutations of liberal feminism would entail. Moreover, although her rewriting of the single Thai story beyond Beauty Queen may seem to offer new alternatives, they are structurally the same options that have traditionally been available to Thai women. Miss Porntip actually expands rather than extends the older narrative. Anthropologists have long noted the "unusually high public profile of women" in Thailand (Eberhardt 3), particularly their longstanding and large-scale involvement in economic activities.[32] Thai women's traditional social roles include a range of economic responsibilities. In rural areas women in trade outnumber men two to one, while urban women are prominent in various entrepreneurial endeavors (Phongpaichit 3). Despite their predominance in the economic sphere, however, women have almost never assumed political or bureaucratic roles in the nation. The Thai state is dominated by men. In her own context, then, Miss Porntip represents simply local practice exponentially magnified rather than a significant new direction for women. Like the western women in the novel, although not for the same reasons or to the same extent, her access to the state is limited.

In any case, literary parameters limit Miss Porntip's potential as a viable model. Constructed through many competing discourses, all of them manipulated parodically, she remains finally beyond realistic conventions. The discourse of AIDS, for example, which permeates the milieu through which Miss Porntip has risen, is never invoked. Nor are there any references to the state policies that have allowed her to flourish, such as the measures adopted and the practices condoned by an "authoritarian government seeking a balance of payments surplus and a tourist trade at any price to its own people" (Turim 82).[33] Miss Porntip's own exploitation of others as a successful capitalist, and particularly her exploitation of other women (*GI* 79), is not criticized. Drabble has to occlude such realistic considerations in order to maintain Miss Porntip as a predominantly comic character. These limitations insure her parodic success, even as they curtail her realism.

Thus at a certain level the English who misread Miss Porntip originally as "a fiction" and "a figment of the imagination" are correct (*GI* 270). When Stephen meets her, he initially considers her an "apparition" and then a "dream" (*GI* 41, 43). For the rest of the novel she is tied to elements of the feminine supernatural. Described as "hallucinatory" (*GI* 51), as a character she is constructed on the generic border where realism and fantasy merge. Stephen tells her that she is "Cleopatra and Circe" (*GI* 121). She is portrayed as both "the New Woman of the East," joining indigenous practice and international capitalism, and a sorceress, a "sweet succubus" who "weaves her spells and mixes her potions" (*GI* 78–79). Significantly, she cannot enter England. Liz's ex-husband Charles, who has been fascinated by her in Bangkok, recognizes that she will not come to Stephen's funeral, because "she would not convince, in [Liz's house in] St John's Wood" (*GI* 448).

Miss Porntip cannot convince in part because she remains too excessive a creation of the western imagination, too much an exotic Other to function in metropolitan reality. But the unbelievable excess represented by Miss Porntip derives from the realistic as well as the fantastic register, from the successful businesswoman as well as the chimerical sorceress. Few Englishwomen in Liz's world could actually wield economic and political power comparable to Miss Porntip's. "The time of the economic power of the women" (*GI* 59), which she proudly proclaims, has yet to arrive for them. Only through parody can Drabble produce a strong and dynamic woman capable of operating consistently and effectively beyond the private sphere. If Miss Porntip's shortcomings as a representative of international capitalism are too clearly portrayed to allow a reading of her as a satisfactory political alternative for western women, she nevertheless represents an option that they have not even begun to explore adequately.

Seventy years ago, the persona in Virginia Woolf's *A Room of One's Own* explained that news of a legacy from her aunt arrived around the time that legislation giving women the vote passed. "Of the two—the vote and the money—the money, I own, seemed infinitely the more important," she remarks (37). Woolf goes on in her essay to show exactly why economic power was so crucial for a woman. What was true in 1929 is even more true today, with the growing global ascendancy of capitalism. Yet how women should operate politically in the context of an apparently triumphant capitalism is a question that few feminist theorists have wanted to confront in specific terms. Some are beginning to comment on the increasing displacement of political processes by economic ones. For example, Anna Yeatman writes that the state is functioning "more and more like a market player" (*Postmodern* 111). Anne Phillips sees democracy itself as "being redefined in consumerist terms": "In the current reassertions of the market over planning, governments increasingly appeal to the elusive sovereignty of the consumer as more democratic and enabling than the process of political decision-making"

(*Engendering* 50–51). The dissolution of Eastern European communism, on which *The Gates of Ivory* ironically plays, most dramatically brought such developments to the fore, but they had been clear earlier in other places, if much less striking.

The basic problem is that these relatively recent developments have received minimal analysis in feminist terms. From the beginning, the strong socialist and radical feminist slants characteristic of feminist theory led to the blanket hostility to capitalism in any form that continues unabated. Theorists have compellingly shown women's weak positions in markets and the persistent segregation of the market by gender.[34] Aihwa Ong assembles a number of Asian examples to illustrate that under capitalism, "industrial labor relations articulating with local norms often elaborate and reinvent principles of male and racial superiority" (289). But at this point condemnatory analyses of the many shortcomings of the market, at which feminist theory has traditionally excelled, are no longer enough. At a time when a democrat of the caliber of Vaclav Havel can write that a market economy is the "only one that reflects the nature of life itself" and that as such it "best corresponds to human nature" (62, 65), there is every reason for feminists to question the value systems invoked. (In this particular case, protest against yet another substitution of predominantly male traits for general human ones is also obviously in order.) Mathew Horsman and Andrew Marshall's claim that "capitalism has become a game that it is virtually impossible not to play" (xiii) may well be an overstatement, but it is a useful indicator of the prevailing climate of opinion. To evolve feminist theories of the state at this time requires consideration of the terms on which feminists will or will not enter the capitalistic "game."

Although brief, a fascinating footnote by Wendy Brown offers a rare feminist attempt at a more balanced assessment. Brown writes that "the market may be least imprinted by gender relations, i.e., despite the fact that women are everywhere economically ghettoized and disadvantaged, it may be one of the most gender-neutral spheres of activity." She emphasizes the competitive ethos of the market and its domination by men as powerful negative factors. Nevertheless, Brown goes on to assert: "[A]s the recent enormous female incursion into this realm has made so evident, its highly alienated aspect combined with its highly concrete nature renders it less 'gendered' than, for example, politics or personal life. The economic realm is less about sensibility and involves less of human interiors than these other realms, precisely because it is alienated and concrete." Ultimately, Brown concludes that sexism is "most contingent and least permeating in the economic realm" (*MP* 18, n. 4).[35] Feminist theory needs to explore the ramifications of these kinds of insights. Similarly, in the realm of state politics, Horsman and Marshall note that states have so far had little success in regulating or restraining the global economy (213). They nevertheless suggest that under current economic conditions, "the nation-state has a reasonable claim to being the only sponsor of equity over efficiency" (235). Feminist critics and theorists need to test such contentions, to see whether advancing such claims could be advantageous for women.

It has long been clear that power for women in the economic realm has serious limitations. For example, Hilary Lips notes a 1988 study concluding that women did not attain "higher public status in societies in which they controlled the means of production." Lips writes that apparently "control over the distribution of resources, rather than over their production, is the crucial aspect of power relations between the sexes" (108). But if focusing only on economic claims for women is insufficient, it is equally insufficient to ignore them. Whether the emerging economic order is to be challenged or appropriated by women, it is necessary for them to understand it. Although Miss Porntip is clearly not enough, she is in some ways better than nothing. Whether those ways are ultimately viable for women needs to be reevaluated by feminist theory in light of the continuing changes in the global status of capitalism.

In *The Gates of Ivory* the gap between the state—the "rule of the old men," the space of Pol Pot and of Mitra—and women remains unbridgeable. Women's ties to the private sphere, while narrowing their own political vision, can deconstruct the theory that supports such politics. But the space between the theoretician and the ruler, and the theoretician and the fanatic with a gun who protects such a ruler, is inaccessible to women. That space, represented in the novel by the absent Kampuchea, remains a male preserve.

It is not only Miss Porntip who exceeds literary boundaries in *The Gates of Ivory*. Drabble opens the novel by writing: "This is a novel—if novel it be" (3). Throughout the work she brings into question the adequacy of the traditional novel to deal with the kind of material she attempts to incorporate. In connection with Pol Pot, Stephen and his friends discuss "whether one could use monsters in fiction" (*GI* 365). The answer offered by *The Gates of Ivory* seems to be negative, since neither Stephen, who turns from the novel to drama for this particular subject, nor Drabble herself succeeds in representing the elusive Khmer leader.

In a long self-reflexive passage (*GI* 137–38), Drabble evaluates various formal options and problems presented for her subject by the form of the novel. Dismissing two possible stories, the successful searches for Mitra and Stephen, she insists that in both the "mismatch between narrative and subject is too great." She questions why she should "impose the story line of individual fate upon a story which is at least in part to do with numbers?" The individual—the personal, the particular, and the local that are the bedrock of the traditional novel—becomes in the context of the Kampuchean tragedy entirely insufficient: "Why pause here? Why discriminate?" Most of all, such personalizing becomes immoral: "A queasiness, a moral scruple overcomes the writer at the prospect of selecting individuals from the mass of history, from the human soup." The immersion in the particular that separates women, along with the contemporary western culture that they come to represent in *The Gates of Ivory,* from international politics, in the formal realm prevents the traditional novel from satisfactorily encompassing such subjects. The horrors of Pol Pot resist novelistic representation.

In a sense Kampuchea functions as a separate order of discourse that *The Gates of Ivory* cannot intersect. However, discussion in such terms simply exposes the inadequacy of critical language such as "order of discourse" in the face of between one and two million Kampuchean dead under Pol Pot.[36] Drabble herself highlights the insufficiency of any kind of language to convey the meaning of historical atrocity as Liz recoils from the compilations in Stephen's "Atrocity Stories" (*GI* 142): "'*Between* 12 and 32 million killed' is a phrase that cannot exist. '*Between* 20 and 80 million'? I mean, are you *serious?* Do you call this *language?* What kind of history, what kind of mathematics is this, what has happened to those spare tens of millions?" (*GI* 140–41).

For this kind of subject matter, Drabble questions whether the writer should try to find "the most disjunctive, the most disruptive" of forms, a form without "a grain of comfort or repose" (*GI* 138). In *The Gates of Ivory* Drabble repudiates many of her earlier approaches toward the novel as a genre, particularly the commitment she had long shown to the traditional novel.[37] Earlier in her career she expressed objections to using "extracts from diaries and things like that" in structuring novels (Firchow 117). However, in *The Gates of Ivory* she deploys such material sporadically throughout the narrative. Disrupting fiction with fact, she inserts the historical numbers and "Atrocity Stories" (*GI* 142) from Stephen's papers into her text and also appends a bibliography at the end of the novel.

This significant alteration in structural approach suggests that Drabble believed—or feared—that the fictional elements of the novel alone would be insufficient to convey the magnitude of the Cambodian tragedy. She therefore brings in external historical and bibliographical supports to reinforce her own story. One of the resulting formal dangers is, as Gérard Genette notes, that discourse inserted into story will predominate (141), often in effect becoming detachable. This potential Drabble basically admits when amid the "Atrocity Stories" she reverts to parenthetical parabasis: "(You may skip them, if you wish)" (*GI* 142). Overall, despite her desire to disrupt novelistic form, she is unable to do so to any great extent. The very narrative devices she originally connects with the stories she does *not* want to write—"a certain amount of trickiness, a certain deployment of not-quite-acceptable coincidences, a certain ruthless tidying up of the random movements of people and peoples" (138)—reappear in *The Gates of Ivory*. And if Mitra's failure to return denies closure to one possible prodigal son plot line, another prodigal son, Konstantin Vassiliou, does return at the end of the novel.

Appropriately enough for this novel, Konstantin returns to his mother rather than, as in the biblical prototype, to his father. Drabble's determination to undermine the limitations of the traditional novel, and therefore perhaps surmount them, is nowhere better shown than in her refusal at the end of *The Gates of Ivory* to represent Konstantin and Rose Vassiliou at Liz's party. She excludes them because they "belong to a different world and a different density." Drabble explains: "They have wandered into this story from the old-fashioned, Freudian, psychological novel, and they cannot mix and mingle with the guests of Liz Headleand" (*GI* 461). Having called into question the capacity of the traditional novel to represent certain kinds of state politics, Drabble refuses in at least one small way to succumb to what the "old-fashioned, Freudian, psychological novel" can accomplish.

In an interview Drabble remarked that the function of the novel is "to explore new territory" (B. Milton 59). She herself has always been ambitious in doing so. It is a critical commonplace that over the course of her career she has continually broadened her scope, moving steadily away from individual and private concerns toward public ones.[38] In 1984 she admitted to an interviewer that she wanted to write "a kind of big England novel" (Satz 195), a desire reflected in *The Radiant Way* (1987) and continued in *A Natural Curiosity* (1989).[39] *The Gates of Ivory* in 1991, the final novel in this trilogy, remains the high-water mark so far in Drabble's progression toward larger issues. The writer often considered to be the "chronicler of contemporary Britain, the novelist people will turn to a hundred years from now to find out how things were" (P. Rose 109),[40] takes on international themes.

Suzanne H. Mayer has connected Drabble's expansion of scope in her novels to her focus on women, suggesting that "this enlarged scope is to divert attention from the lack of answers women find, or from the author's faith in providing them" (88). Similarly, Brenda Murphy has found parallels between Drabble's artistic development and that of the women's movement, postulating a progression in both from "simple identification of self as opposed to one's prescribed societal role, through the confidence bred of individuation, to a movement beyond the self and an embracing of wider social concerns" (39–40). This analogy somewhat oversimplifies the history of second-wave activism by rendering it in terms of progression, instead of simultaneity with emphases differing over time. The women's movement is still concerned with freeing individual women from social constraints, while from the beginning it had an encompassing social agenda. However, the movement's virtual abandonment of the group consciousness-raising techniques of its early period and its lessening concern with individualistic goals do in a rough way reflect Drabble's turn away from the personal and domestic subject matter of her early novels (too often termed "women's novels"[41]) to broad social panoramas in her later ones.

At this point *The Gates of Ivory* demarcates certain formal limits of possibility for Drabble's explorations of women and their roles in larger political contexts. The satisfactory solutions that evaded her in the domestic realm prove even less available in a wider milieu. Like the Women's Movement itself, the novelist ends up unable to find a place of substantive power for women in the world of national and international politics. At the time that she was presumably working on *The Radiant Way*, Drabble told an interviewer that she was seeking a new method of relating the novel to history and "revitalizing things that have dropped out of the novel" (Berkley 60). Although blocked in certain ways in *The Gates of Ivory*, Drabble shows her ambition and her determination by refusing to allow Rose Vassiliou and her son into the conclusion of her novel.

A very minor character in *The Gates of Ivory*, Rose is also the female protagonist of *The Needle's Eye* (1972), generally considered Drabble's "watershed novel" (E. C. Rose, *Critical* 4).[42] Drabble herself admitted that "I only began to be aware that I could actually write a novel and include some of the things I deeply cared about when I reached *The Needle's Eye*" (B. Milton 60). The critical consensus is that *The Needle's Eye* marks a crucial shift from primarily private subjects in her first five novels to wider public concerns.[43] The novel also represents a change in her representations of women. Showalter writes that before the character of Rose, Drabble's heroines find "a kind of peace in the acknowledgment of, and submission to, female limitation" (*Literature* 305). Rose is everything that most of the major female characters in *The Gates of Ivory* are not. She is a devoted mother who returns to her marriage because of her children. She is also an heiress who refuses the goods of consumer society and gives her money away. Finally, she is a dedicated worker for the Africa Council in London. The inability of this kind of character to function actively at the end of *The Gates of Ivory* measures the distance between even the most committed political woman and the brutal world of contemporary international politics.

At the same time, Drabble's refusal to return to her own novelistic past is a measure of the importance that she sees her contemporary subject matter as having for the novel's future and our own. The silence of Rose Vassiliou and her son at the end of the novel—"We cannot overhear their conversation" (462)—reflects the obstacles faced by the woman novelist and the woman political activist who are committed to dealing with the male stranglehold on the world of international politics.

Thus in *The Gates of* Ivory, the Outsider Narrative, which the novels of Atwood, Marshall, and Gordimer seriously question as a political strategy for women, expands to become all-inclusive. Applying this narrative to the West as a whole as well as to women, Drabble emphasizes the total loss of political efficacy. The Coalition Narrative, which fares poorly in all of the novels except Gordimer's fantasy, has no place in Drabble's work, except occasionally for humanitarian purposes. Opportunities for coalitions to shape political events are minimal under such conditions. Finally, the Salvation Narrative of Politics, which the other novelists have shown as an overreading that everyday life does not sustain, receives a devastating critique from Drabble. Stephen, who has espoused one form of this narrative, ultimately understands its dangers when he travels to Kampuchea, where Pol Pot literally inscribed such a narrative on an entire people in blood.

These theoretical narratives are obviously not invalidated simply because contemporary women novelists ignore, critique, or attack them. The novelistic and theoretical political narratives serve very different purposes. But as feminists develop theories of the state, the novelists' narratives provide useful reminders of various factors that theorists must account for, ranging from state violence to the role of familial elements in the state, and from questions of deficiencies in feminist strategy to the valorization of the discursive in current state theory. Is Foucauldian local resistance, for example, the only viable alternative for women at this point, or is it simply another form of the excessive romanticization of the individual ubiquitous at the end of the twentieth century? In the realm of the state, feminist theorists admit that both disruption and reform are necessary. But most of their attention has centered on methods of disruption. Given the fact that, as Zillah R. Eisenstein points out, "many women are still forced to turn to the liberal reforms that can affect their lives in dealing with their everyday problems" (*Radical* 197), what kind of reforms can be useful for the present and also contribute to the long-term changes that feminisms ultimately desire? How can we tell which reforms simply further the status quo and which move us toward a different political future?

At one point in *The Gates of Ivory,* Liz and her friend Simon are looking at some Cambodian stamps from the package of Stephen's things sent to her. Liz is bewildered to see a commemorative stamp of a "slightly oriental Prince Charles and Princess Di," along with one of a Madonna and child by Correggio. Liz is puzzled. "Why on earth Correggio?" she asks.

"It was his anniversary," Simon answers. "1984, the 450th anniversary of his death. Lots of countries did commemorative stamps."

Liz's confusion mounts. "I thought the country had been reduced to mud and rubble. I thought people were starving. . . . And you tell me they go on producing stamps to commemorate European artists who painted Christian religious motifs 450 years ago?"

"People will produce stamps through anything," Simon replies.

The passage reveals a great deal about neocolonialism, commercialism, and the limits of nationalism in a global age. However, its impact also depends on the emphasis on the continuities of everyday life despite state politics. Indeed, Simon proceeds to question whether the Khmer Rouge had produced any stamps at all. His justification for their probable failure to do so is that the Khmer Rouge "were very extreme." "Most people," he explains, "keep the postal services going" (*GI* 116).

The novel as a genre generally represents life at the level of the recipients of mail. For both historical and formal reasons, the novel has had minimal success in representing the structural concerns of politics at which theory excels. Stephen White notes that an "intense concern for the unique life history of each *individual* is largely out of place in the world of politics" (105). From the beginning, that concern has been the province of novelists. It is the perspective shaped by that concern that comprises the unique contribution that novelists can offer to the ongoing feminist theoretical debates about the state. Martha Nussbaum reminds us that "a story of class action, without the stories of individuals, would not show us the point and meaning of class actions, which is always the amelioration of individual lives" (71). If those lives are necessarily abstracted in theorists, it is nonetheless important that such lives remain the ultimate test of any theory. Atwood, Marshall, Gordimer, and Drabble provide representations of such lives that help to shape the kind of questions that contemporary women seeking better lives for themselves and others in the twenty-first century will need to answer about feminist politics and the state.

Notes

Preface: Hobbes's Fish

1. On Hobbes, see Okin 197–99; Elshtain, *PMPW* 108–115; Pateman, *SC* 43–50. In *Compassionate,* Jones subtitles one section "*Leviathan* as Phallic Mother" (86–92; see also 42–71). Clegg contrasts Hobbes's view of power with that of Machiavelli (3–7, 20–38), including a useful summary table (34).

2. Examples of similar descriptions include Franzway, Court, and Connell 33; Pringle and Watson, "Fathers" 229; Reinelt 87.

3. For example, J. Allen 30; T. Mitchell 77; Pringle and Watson, "Women's" 63.

4. An exception would be the openings of *Bodily Harm* and *Daughters,* where the protagonists do consciously try to avoid politics, but in both novels the tactic is portrayed as a mistake.

5. Among many examples are Dietz, "Context" and "Citizenship"; Mouffe, "Feminism"; Young, "Polity"; K. B. Jones, "Citizenship."

6. See Brown, *SI* 49; Young's treatment of the city is a related example (*Justice* 226–56).

7. For example, D. Cooper 65, 100; Fuss, *inside/out* 5; Irigaray, *This Sex* 166; Gilbert 21.

8. Power as depicted by the novelists is reminiscent of West's description of patriarchal power as "experienced by modern women as intensely nondiscursive, as utterly unimaginative, as profoundly negating, and, in short, as frighteningly and pervasively *violent*" (261).

9. Cf. Silverblatt: "Social forms do not, as in neo-evolutionary jargon, reproduce themselves; they are remade and unmade by the human beings who live them" (154; see also 155).

10. Similarly, Virginia Woolf writes that the characters in *Antigone* "suggest too much; when the curtain falls we sympathize, it may be noted, even with Creon himself" (*Three* 170, n. 39).

11. Brown emphasizes that "Not maleness but institutionalized ideals of manhood are the problem" (*MP* 187).

12. Flax also writes that in *Leviathan,* "Hobbes is clearly puzzled about how to fit the family into his state of nature. There are only a few fragments

about the family, in which he offers an almost radical feminist account" ("Mother-Daughter" 29–30).

I: Introduction:
Women and Fictions of the State

1. Critical commentary on feminist speculative fiction has similarly pro-liferated. Among many useful treatments are Cranny-Francis 29–142; Hogeland 106–28; Lefanu; Barr; Rosinsky; Andermahr; Neely; Har-away 178–80, 186; and particularly Russ, "Recent," and selected essays in Le Guin.

2. See Lauret; Greene; Zimmerman, *SS* 64–65, 111, 170–71, 207–9, 211–12; Rosenfelt; Y. Klein; Langer; Payant 209–16; A. Wilson 87–89; Palmer 73, 88, 95–96. Lauret divides 1970s feminist writing into two phases and does the same for novels of the 1980s (86–88). Most critics see the early 1980s as a transitional period. Rosenfelt places the break between feminist and postfeminist fiction in 1985 (269, 272), although that date seems some-what late. By 1984 Langer was already entitling an article "Whatever Happened to Feminist Fiction?" Zimmerman's configuration of lesbian fiction in the 1980s has a break in 1982, with a brief political phase, be-fore a return to less political topics beginning in the later 1980s (*SS* 172, 207–232).

3. Rosenfelt notes that when she gave an MLA paper on the topic, Cora Kaplan commented that she was talking not about *postfeminist* texts but *postmodernist* ones (290, n. 24). She explains that she uses "postfeminist" in order "to connote not the death of feminism but its uneven incorpora-tion and revision inside the social and cultural texts of a more conserva-tive era," emphasizing that the term "acknowledges the existence of a world and a discourse that have been fundamentally altered by feminism" (269). Although for convenience I follow Rosenfelt and Greene in terming the novels from 1980 on "postfeminist," the term is for many rea-sons a problematical one. (See, for example, Greene's useful observations [198].) In my view the best comment on it remains Fraser's: "[I]t will not be time to speak of postfeminism until we can legitimately speak of post-patriarchy" ("The Uses" 191).

4. On feminism during the 1980s, see F. Davis 471–90; Ryan 137, 139; N. Whittier 118, 137, 197, 226, 256; Greene 196; Minkoff 480; Lauret 64–67; Connell, *Gender* 273; Costain and Costain 211, n. 11.

5. Lauret disagrees with this negative assessment of the writing, seeking to "problematise the whole notion of bad writing" (7). Her *Liberating Lit-erature* analyzes the role of feminist fiction in second-wave American feminism, as does Hogeland's treatment of the consciousness-raising novel. For other treatments of the role of fiction, see Greene 1–27, 32–33, 50–57; J. Arnold et al., "Lesbians" 28–30; Payant 26–27, 33; J. Frye, *Living* 199.

6. Critics of the feminist theory-practice split are legion; de Lauretis points out that debates on it spanned the 1970s ("Upping" 264; see also 269, n. 8), and they have continued unabated since then. A number of African American feminist critics and radical feminists have been particularly critical of theorists (e.g., hooks, *Yearning* 23–31; Christian, "Race"; B. Smith, "Truth" 105–6; Barry, "Deconstructing"; Douglas, "I'll Take"). Beyond the United States, see H. Eisenstein, "Femocrats" 102–3, and *Gender Shock* 97; Weir 96.

7. Among many examples, see Kristeva in Marks and de Courtivron 137; Riley 111–13; Alcoff 426–28; Moi 13; B. Martin, "Feminism" 14. K. E. Ferguson treats the problem in "Interpretation." From a crowded field I singled out Butler to quote in part because in many ways her own feminist politics have been exemplary. In another essay she herself questions the consequences of using "a false ontology of women as a universal in order to advance a feminist political program" ("Gender" 325; see also *GT* 4). Pringle and Watson alter the terms of the argument somewhat by emphasizing the "discursive marginality" that women share, "along with continuing inequalities at every level" ("Women's" 68). On strategic essentialism, see Spivak, "French" 73. Sommer writes that "Spivak's work is associated with this idea, although Scholes suggests that John Locke came upon it some time ago." Sommer also notes that "Fuss anticipates Spivak's position" (105, n. 7).

8. Thompson writes: "In language as in culture more generally, strategies of subversion 'have a good chance of being *also* strategies of condescension reserved for those who are sufficiently assured of their position in the objective hierarchies to be able to negate them without appearing to ignore them or to be incapable of satisfying their demands'" (52, with internal quotation from Pierre Bourdieu).

9. De Lauretis herself does so (*Technologies* 36), as does Snitow ("Gender" 30).

10. A number of critics point out, however, that imagining alternative systems, whether they are feasible or not, has its own role in political theory (K. Ferguson, *FCB* 155; Meese 85; W. Brown, *MP* 191–92; and for a more general discussion, Elshtain, *PMPW* 168–69). On the other hand, Foucault makes the case that "to imagine another system is to extend our participation in the present system" (*Language* 230).

11. For example, Elshtain, *PMPW* 202; MacKinnon, *Toward* 157; H. Eisenstein, *Gender* 22; Pringle and Watson, "Women's" 54–55; Moore 185; J. Allen 21; Connell, *Gender* 126, and "The State" 508; and W. Brown, who terms it "an admittedly ambiguous lack" (*SI* 167). Even MacKinnon, whose work constructs one of the few such theories, entitles her major study of the subject "*Toward* a Feminist Theory of the State" (emphasis added). Australian feminists are the major theorists who have worked with the state, in contrast to British and American neglect of it (Reinelt 102, n. 6; Weir 94).

12. Weiss notes as an exception to the prevailing lack of scholarly attention to the state the decade from the late 1970s into the 1980s, with the BSBI ("Bringing the State Back In") movement, but argues that interest has again subsided (1–2, 209; see also W. Brown, *SI* 15–16, 18; Magnusson 70–71; Mooers and Sears 52–53). Others argue for a continuing scholarly concern with the state; see, for example, Moore in the case of social anthropology (134), and Bonefield, who connects the resurgence of interest to "the conservative shift to power in the main capitalist countries" (96).

13. Franzway, Court, and Connell point out that "the bulk of feminist writing about the state has taken the form of *policy studies*" (12).

14. My summary of these debates follows Silverblatt 140–53; see also Randall 197–98, Moore 183–84, Burstyn 51–59.

15. Darcy, Welch, and Clark 152; Chapman 3; Carroll and Zerilli 61.

16. Diamond and Quinby xvi; Randall 58; Phillips, *Engendering* 99; Segal 210.

17. Gelb and Palley point out that the easiest route to success for emergent groups is "single issue reformist politics that does not threaten displacement of existing power configurations" (9; see also Gelb, "Social" 274).

18. Verba 568; Rosenfelt and Stacey 350; Lauret 53, 64–65; Katzenstein, "Comparing." Kay Boals explains that women have a relatively small stake in politics-as-usual because "mainstream politics is biased in favor of political participation by those who are generally satisfied with the status quo, and it tends to discourage the expression of alienation" (169).

19. Phillips, *Engendering* 85, 61; Katzenstein, "Comparing."

20. Gelb, "Social"; Ferree, "Equality"; Pringle and Watson, "Women's" 58–59.

21. Freeman treats second-wave feminism's organizations and structures in *Politics,* "From Seed," and *Women* 543–46; see also F. Davis, S. Evans, and P. Martin. Among critics who agree with Freeman on problems with organizational structurelessness are Ryan (58, 94); Phillips (*Engendering* 120–46); Vickers (51–52); J. Evans (105–6); Reinelt (91–92); Hansen and Philipson (7); Acker (140–41); and Delmar (26). Others are more positive. Kirk finds "no simple correspondence between formal organization and effectiveness" ("Our Greenham Common: Not Just" 268), and K. E. Ferguson notes that "We do not have blueprints for large, nonhierarchal organizations, but we have numerous indications that such organizations are possible" (*FCB* 207). Douglas connects some feminist organizing principles with anarchist ideas (*Love* 30–31; 289). Significantly, B. Barnett points out that "the emphases on participatory democracy . . . that have been viewed as distinctive characteristics of White women's organizing in the late 1960s and 1970s can be found in Black women's political activism and organizing several decades earlier" (202–3; see also Minkoff 478).

22. Numerous critics have noted the inadequacies of the various taxonomies of feminism (e.g., Gatens, "Power" 120; Palmer 59; Ryan 87; Haraway 155–56; the most extended treatment is that of K. King). In terms of precise historical accuracy, they are correct. Nevertheless, I have retained the

conventional tripartite division into liberal feminism, socialist (and Marxist) feminism, and radical feminism because, although admittedly a blunt instrument, the triple division works well enough within the literary contexts of this study in designating the general type and methods of state intervention desired. Discussions of the classifications are legion; Firestone offered one of the earliest (38–45), and a good recent one is in Sturgeon (170–78). For treatments of the turn from radical to cultural feminism, see particularly Echols, *Daring,* along with Bell and Klein, an important collection concerned to separate radical feminism from cultural feminism and to combat charges of essentialism. Within Bell and Klein, Richardson (146–47) and Lienert (155–58, 162) in particular contest Echols's genealogies. Finally, what N. Whittier writes of the category of radical feminism is true of almost every feminist classification: Each "is more usefully understood as an identity that is constructed by activists, and is subject to debate and redefinition, than as a historically constant ideology" (5).

23. Bunch, "Reform"; Fuss, *inside/out* 5. See also Fraser and Bartky 4; Ferree and Martin 6; D. Cooper 65, 100; Echols, "Nothing" 466; Gelb, "Feminist" 130; Phelan 166–70; S. Watson, *Playing* 11; and especially Spalter-Roth and Schreiber.

24. This charge would be leveled again and again; twenty years after Kollias, W. Brown noted "the steady slide of political into therapeutic discourse" (*SI* 75). See also Echols, *Daring* 264, 283–84; Vickers 50–51; Hogeland xvi, 26–31; Phillips, *Engendering* 116–17; Fuss, *Essentially* 101–2; Lauret 61–64; Ryan 137; Hawkesworth 164–65.

25. Reinelt 84–85; Ryan 87, 89; N. Whittier 197; Spalter-Roth and Schreiber105; cf. Freeman, *Politics* 51.

26. Although academic feminists are not a large group, neither are feminist political activists. Donahue writes that "The most recent, comprehensive quantitative study of voluntary activists in the United States of all ages . . . finds that women's rights related political activity is just 1% of women's issue based activism" (77). Mansbridge reports that in telephone interviews, one-quarter to one-third of U.S. women considered themselves feminists, with little variance in terms of race or class (27). Mueller cites opinion polls revealing "higher support for feminist issues among women of color than white women" ("Organizational" 266), while Z. Eisenstein in her 1994 study offers figures: "85 percent of black women say they see a need for a strong women's movement (compared with 64 percent of white women)" (*Color* 213; see also Ryan 125; E. Klein, "Diffusion" 27–28).

27. The literature on feminist analyses of liberalism is huge. Jaggar's section on liberalism offers an overview; among other examples are Okin 197–230; MacKinnon, *Toward* 157–70; Z. Eisenstein, *Radical;* Phelan 3–18; Phillips, *Feminism* 1–23; Dietz, "Context"; Connell, "The State" 510–14, 533, 535–36; Chapman 143–48; Elshtain, *Meditations* 55–70; L. S. Brown 63–105.

28. See also Baym 105; Reinelt 102. Z. Eisenstein names Betty Friedan as the only significant liberal theorist of the second wave (*Radical* 197), while L. S. Brown adds Janet Radcliffe Richards (80).

29. See Rowland and Klein 9, 13–14. L. S. Brown notes that contemporary anarchist-feminists also do not produce theory (114).

30. See Sturgeon 172; Weir 93–94; Hansen and Philipson 27, 29. Hansen and Philipson notes that "the core of people drawn to socialist feminism have had a predisposition to theoretical work": "unlike radical feminists, key theorists in the movement have tended to be academics rather than poets or cultural intellectuals" (27).

31. See Marx and Engels 82; Jaggar 61–62; O'Brien 180; Janeway 190. Jessop writes of the need to "exorcise the spectre haunting Marxist state theory—the prospect of a general theory of the state" (211).

32. On the evolution of socialist-feminist activism, see Hansen and Philipson 8–12, 25–30. Weir notes the "sparse number of accounts documenting socialist feminism as an organized political practice" (93).

33. Hansen and Philipson emphasize the importance of the academy "in preserving radical traditions, particularly in the absence of a vital movement": "In a time of political retrenchment, university intellectuals have major responsibility for nurturing the flame of socialist feminism and passing on its history, with the goal of insuring its future" (29).

34. For example, admitting that oppositional voices have to enter the public realm to be heard, K. E. Ferguson writes that "Feminism cannot simply turn its back on the existing public world because that world does not oblige by leaving us alone" (*FCB* 180; see also 208). In addition, see Bunch, "Reform" 195; O'Brien 203–4; Benhabib, "Feminism" 30; Segal 205; de Lauretis, *Technologies* 84; Young, "Ideal" 315–17.

35. Misciagno writes that "the structural underpinnings for a widespread acceptance of radical feminism [do] not exist" (42), while Darcy et al. agree that although there is support for greater equality for women, "support does not exist for erasing the basic institutions of our society, whether it be the family or our system of indirect democracy" (156). Rosenfelt and Stacey admit that "social democracy and even old-fashioned liberalism" are "perhaps the best we can hope for in the foreseeable future as a soil for regenerating more utopian visions" (342–43). See also Gelb and Palley 8–9, 199; O'Barr 49; and Douglas, *Love* 19.

36. See, for examples, K. E. Ferguson, *FCB* 193; Misciagno 37; Cornell, "What" 82–83; Ryan 61, 155, 161. Ryan writes that from the beginning, "it was mainly radical feminists . . . who freely used ideological designations to label, and thus discredit, other feminists" (157), although Hansen and Philipson note the use of such tactics by socialist feminists (28). Among activists, by the late 1970s Ryan notes that "intolerance and dogmatism within the movement had played itself out" (70).

37. A notable exception is McDowell, who writes: "[E]ven though the proposition of a fruitful relationship between political activism and the

academy is an interesting (and necessary) one, I doubt its feasibility. I am not sure that either in theory or in practice black feminist criticism will be able to alter significantly circumstances that have led to the oppression of black women" (*Changing* 10).

38. As in other countries, H. Eisenstein notes the "gap in perceptions, vocabulary, and assumptions" between femocrats and feminist academics in Australia (*Gender* 32). See also Pringle and Watson, "Fathers" 234.

39. Sturgeon points out that although not all socialist feminists are poststructuralists, "socialist feminism, with its emphasis on the social construction of gender and the necessity to see multiple systems of domination in operation, provided the foundation for a turn to poststructuralism" (172; see also Lienert 167).

40. It should be noted that despite these and other similar assertions about the state, Foucault was perfectly capable of occasionally contradicting himself: "[M]aybe, after all, the State is no more than a composite reality and a mythical abstraction whose importance is a lot more limited than many of us think" ("Governmentality" 20).

41. Cf. Cixous's description of writing as "*the very possibility of change,* the space that can serve as a springboard for subversive thought, the precursory movement of a transformation of social and cultural structures" (Marks and de Courtivron 249).

42. See, among many examples, Ebert 26–28, 38; Fraser and Bartky 4; D. Cooper 73; Grant 159, 181; W. Brown, *MP* 127, 191–92, 197; Hawkesworth 145–48; West 264–76.

43. Examples include E. Abel, "Race" 184, 199; Doane, "Commentary" 76; Flax, "Postmodernism" 632; A. Harris 94–95; Sprengnether 8, 10; Plaza 77, 85–87; Waugh 39. See also D. Meyers, and Fraser, "The Uses" 183–85.

44. Elshtain also discusses how psychoanalytic theory "resolves politics into psychological categories" (100) in her chapter "Freud and the Therapeutic Society" in *Meditations* (85–102). There she comments that "any theory that casts a relentlessly suspicious spotlight on action may diminish possibilities for individual and shared commitment by turning the self inward rather than pushing the self into the world" (95). See also Delphy on the Anglo-American appropriation of "French Feminism" to legitimate the introduction of essentialism and particularly psychoanalysis into feminism.

45. See also Mooers and Sears 62–63.

46. S. Hall, "Local" 25–27, "Old" 45. Cf. Appiah's chapter on "Altered States" (158–72), in which he discusses the difficulties of state formation in Africa but admits that "despite all their limitations, African states persist, and, so it seems to me, in Ghana, as in a number of other places, the decline has been halted" (169).

47. See also Hawley x–xi; Horsman and Marshall 235; Wallerstein 99.

48. In addition to those quoted in this paragraph, see Randall 196; Sassoon 28; Borchost and Siim 151, 154; Burstyn 68; Connell, "The State" 531, 535; Kristeva, *Nations* 50; Adcock 210.

49. For discussion of the rise of the novel, see Watt; McKeon; Hunter; Todd; Richetti; Spencer; L. Davis; and Langbauer 1–5, 12–30.

50. Kenyon writes that women writers "have revitalised the realistic novel" (*Women Novelists* 6). Much has been written on women writers' use of realism; DeKoven and M. Hite (*Other*) offer particularly useful perspectives, as does Greene (3–6, 21–22, 84–85) and also Lauret (3–5, 83–84, 91–95).

51. Jehlen; Armstrong; J. Mitchell, *WLR* 287–94; van Boheemen 4–5, 30–31. Yelin points out that "colonial and post-colonial women's writing makes us see the female consciousness that occupies the foreground of English or European novels as the consciousness of white, middle-class females and as a product of a specific colonial (racial) and patriarchal (sexual) ensemble in which the consciousness of white women and the power of white men are dependent on the exploitation of women and men of color" (192).

52. Some of the best work, such as that of Ballaster and D. Ross, has been done in terms of the novel's connections with romance; see also Todd and Spencer.

53. Cf. Douglas: "To ignore those who are not already radicalized is to be doomed to defeat" (*Love* 270).

54. See also Okin 319 and Lienert 168.

55. Friedan based her classic work on the "strange discrepancy between the reality of our lives as women and the image to which we were trying to conform, the image that I came to call the feminine mystique" (11). See also de Lauretis, *Alice* 15; Cornell, "What" 76–77, 86–87, 98.

56. In addition to the writers listed in note 5, see especially J. Frye 18–31, 190–98, and also Belsey 51; Langer 36; Spivak, "Three Feminist" 31; Lewis 26; K. B. Jones, *Compassionate* 223.

57. See, among many examples, comments by Greene 22; DuPlessis 20–21; M. Hite, *Other* 167; Robinson 17; de Lauretis, *Feminist* 11.

58. Some would consider Marshall an exception to this claim. Pettis writes that her recent study was motivated by "Marshall's status in American literature," particularly the fact that "significant numbers of Americans knowledgeable about literature remain ignorant" of her. Pettis hoped "to increase her much-deserved visibility to a multicultural audience" (*Toward* 5–6; see also Trescott C2). My view is that if Marshall is not already in the informal canon, she soon will be.

59. Two useful treatments, however, are Felski and also Hein and Korsmeyer's collection.

60. In addition, because of my own background this study tilts toward U.S. feminism, although I have tried to include information about other countries.

61. At the same time, however, Morgan also admitted that "Class oppression is alive and well within the movement," and pointed out specific steps that were being taken to institute change (*Sisterhood* xxxi).

62. Echols discusses how the "bourgeois" charges against feminists made by male radicals encouraged women's liberationists to distance themselves from liberal feminists and NOW ("Nothing" 461–62). See also F. Davis 79. In the 1990s Mohanty blamed the media for "falsely homogeneous representation of the movement" ("Introduction" 7).

63. Delphy is discussing leftist women's attacks on "bourgeois women" (*Close* 119–37; see also MacKinnon, *Toward* 47–50). MacKinnon and also Russo argue in similar terms that attacks on white women "at some level [reflect] a fundamental denial of women's oppression *as women* (that is, on the basis of gender)" (Russo 303). MacKinnon writes: "Unlike other women, the white woman who is not poor or working class or lesbian or Jewish or disabled or old or young *does not share her oppression with any man*" ("From Practice" 54). See also M. Frye, *Willful* 168, n. 17; Baym 114; Benhabib, "Feminism" 30. Finally, Rapp offers a salutary reminder of the ambiguities of the term "middle class" itself (63).

64. See also J. Mitchell, "Reflections" 47. Heilbrun speculates that "Perhaps privilege allows the adoption of radical, deeply disturbing ideas, particularly regarding gender?" ("Fighting" 39).

65. Bookman and Morgen 8; see also K. B. Jones, "Citizenship" 805. However, Chapman notes: "Cross-national study has shown that the relationship between socio-economic status (ses) and grass-roots political participation is modified in favour of low-ses individuals when the institutional context includes redistributive institutions. . . ." But she emphasizes that political participation increases only in the case of men: "the existence of redistributive institutions is actually found to increase the *gender* gap" (7).

66. J. Mitchell, too, writes that "It is never extreme deprivation that produces the revolutionary" (*WE* 21).

67. Randall also points out that British historians may have underrated working-class women's participation in feminist activism (215; see also Greene 49).

68. See also Lorde and Star, "Interview" 69. That the Combahee River Collective's critique of mainstream feminism in terms of identity cuts both ways is ironic.

69. Marshall describes herself as "part of the whole ferment of that period," explaining that the Civil Rights Movement "was something that I came to in a very natural way, because . . . there was always this talk of politics when I was growing up" (Bröck 204; see also A. Elam 104; Marshall, "From the Poets" 25, and "Shaping" 101–2.)

70. See Irvine, *Collecting* 10–11. In 1995 alone, the Atwood Society *Newsletter* noted her participation in efforts to save governmental funding for Toronto's Harbourfront, her sponsorship of an organization to establish a memorial to Canadian antifascist fighters in the Spanish Civil War, and her signature on an open letter from twenty-six writers urging western governments to pressure Beijing to release Chinese dissident Wei Jingsheng (*AtN* 16 [Spring/Summer 1996]: 9, 10, 13).

71. Creighton portrays Drabble as "moved occasionally, but reluctantly, to political activism," and mentions her joining a demonstration opposing the Rhodesian settlement in 1971 and the protest outside the House of Commons in June 1981 by the World Disarmament Campaign (*Drabble* 20).

72. Drabble noted, however, that she regretted that the Labour Party manifesto on which she was commenting did not contain more about "the redistribution of wealth" ("Minority" 10).

73. Marshall connects this political element with her immigrant mother and the other Bajan women who gathered in the kitchen to talk when she was growing up: "The political perspective that was so much a part of the way they thought and saw the world became my way of looking at the world" (Baer 24). See also G & S 297; Seaman 411; Marshall, "Shaping" 103.

74. For example, B & S 282; Atwood, "ATLANTIS" 208; Seaman 411; Cooper-Clark 21.

75. Drabble comments that "The truth is more important than ideology" (Cooper-Clark 21).

76. B & S 83, 210, 282, 299, 311; see also Gordimer, *Writing* 130.

77. See also Ingersoll 5, 27,118; Atwood, "ATLANTIS 210; Jamkhandi 5–6.

78. Marshall, whose feminism has seldom been criticized in print, has been accused of homophobia and strongly defended against that charge. See Kubitschek 52–53; Spillers, "*Chosen*" 172–74, and "Black" 267, 288, n. 1; DeLamotte, *Places* 67–69, 178, n. 19. Marshall's own response is in Pettis, "*MELUS*" 125–26.

79. Other examples of narrow definitions can be found in Gerrard, who describes the feminist novel as one "whose ideological line is so undigested that it makes its fiction into a hasty scaffolding" (2), and Ogunyemi, who terms it "a form of protest literature" that is "unapologetically propagandist or strident or both" (64). Gerrard points out that the feminist label is "now used to describe a *bad* feminist book": "[W]e tend to erase 'feminist' from the most successful feminist novels" (106, see also 107–8, 169). Shulman's article on the topic is especially good. See also Payant 5, 106–7, 216–17.

80. See also Draine 374; Ingersoll 162.

81. Meese has a good discussion of feminist prescriptive criticism (140–42), which she describes as "An idea presented before its time." She finds resistance to it "somewhat ironic since prescriptive criticism merely makes explicit a feminist version of the prescription implicit in most critical discourse" (141).

82. In the interview Drabble went on to say: "My mother was a feminist in her day and still is. In fact she is rather more outspoken about some of it than I am" (Lauritzen 255). Problems that Drabble has admitted with her mother may be relevant in this connection; see Hardin 278; Rozencwajg 339–40; B. Milton 55–56; Creighton, *Drabble* 20–21, and "Sisterly" 16.

83. Many have analyzed Gordimer's hostility to feminism. Wagner is particularly good on Gordimer's "reductive view" of it (77; see 71–90, 248, n. 25). See also Lockett 12–13; Lazar 213–16; and Driver 183–85, 195–200.

84. Gordimer indicated that she recognized feminists would disagree with her (B & S 168).

85. Greene's series of careful differentiations reflects the current consensus: "Feminist fiction is not the same as 'women's fiction' or fiction by women: not all women writers are 'women's writers,' and not all women's writers are feminist writers, since to write about 'women's issues' is not necessarily to address them from a feminist perspective" (2). See also E. Rose, "Sexual" 86–87; Hogeland xiv–xvii. Cf. Braidotti, *Nomadic* 163–65; Gordon, "What's New" 30; Grant 124; Delmar 11, 13, 23.

86. In the same interview Drabble also said that she was tired of being asked to review books by other women (Gussow 41).

87. Having been frequently criticized for the putative limitations of her early "women's" novels, when Drabble began writing novels with a broader scope, she was then criticized for being excessively topical, journalistic, and sociological. (See, for example, Packer xvi.)

88. Nate in *Life Before Man* might be considered an exception to this generalization, but because two of the three central characters are women, the narrative point of view is still predominantly female.

89. Wagner points out that "the female *Bildungsroman* is, after all, her core genre" (89); see also S. Roberts 177.

90. See also G & S 291; and Dance 17, where Marshall says: "That's my ideal audience, although I invite and welcome *everyone* to read the work."

91. Bröck 194, 195; Pettis, "*MELUS*" 129.

92. See also Pettis, "*MELUS*" 129; Baer 24–25; A. Elam 105.

93. This comment on the need for a blueprint is ironic in view of Drabble's remark quoted above (p. 52; see also p. 59), in which she objects to "the way feminists think I ought to be writing a blueprint for everybody's life" (Hannay 148).

II: Three Political Narratives

1. Mooers and Sears locate the "separation of the economic from the political under capitalism" as "one of the key sources of the ideological mystification of capitalist social relations" (57); see also Ackelsberg, "Communities" 300. Piven discusses the welfare state and reconfigurations of the economic sphere in the United States (279–81). On configurations of "civil society," see Mooers and Sears 56–57, 61, 63–67; W. Brown, *SI* 17, 139, 180–84; Pateman, *SC* 11–12; Yuval-Davis and Anthias 5–6, 10–11; Connell, "The State" 511. Phillips warns of "the division that is growing between up those who emphasize civil society as the focus for democratic development and those who stress the state" (*Engendering* 117). However, J. James points out that it is "not

always feasible to maintain a sharp division between the state and civil society" (6).

2. But see W. Brown, *MP* 18, n. 4.

3. See also Smith-Rosenberg 103–4; Laclau and Mouffe 162–63, 179–80; Saxonhouse 8; McClure 347; K. E. Ferguson, *FCB* 7.

4. T. Mitchell and also Fraser ("Talking" 166–70) offer useful commentary on changing configurations of the various spheres.

5. That sexist separation of spheres is not limited to male theorists is shown by Arendt's efforts to limit the social sphere to the private realm.

6. See also Bourque and Grossholtz; cf. Kerber, "Separate" 30.

7. Dinnerstein's and Chodorow's were among the earliest second-wave discussions of the origins of male fears of women; to suggest the range of subsequent treatments, examples are Hawkesworth 99–105; Elshtain, *PMPW* 142–43, 286–97; Janeway 294–95; Hartsock, *Money* 237–45; Cornell, "What" 87–90; A. Rich, "Compulsory" 187.

8. Mueller points out that in the United States, "Almost every woman who achieved office prior to 1970 was appointed to fill a vacancy caused by the death of her husband or someone else" ("Collective" 100–101). But by 1987 Darcy et al. noted that the percentage of congressional widows was continuing to drop (79). See also Chapman 40.

9. On the Nairobi conference, see also Johnson-Odim 317; Hull 3; F. Davis 486–89; Gilliam 234, n. 13.

10. Echols, "Nothing" 463–66; Swerdlow 228, 231–35; Y. King 282, 295–97; Costain and Costain 208; Felski 171–72; Douglas, *Love* 288.

11. Costain and Costain; Freeman, "Whom"; F. Davis 184–204; Minkoff 480; Ryan 2; Gelb, "Feminist" 131; Gelb and Palley 216. Cf. Borchost and Siim on feminists and the state in Denmark (151–54).

12. However, Carroll and Zerilli point that despite feminist theoretical negativity toward mainstream politics, "many empirical feminist political scientists have suggested that women must enter the formal political arena in order to achieve equality" (61).

13. For an example of opposing views, see Dahlerup 122–23.

14. Sawer 124; Lebsock 36; E. Klein, "Diffusion" 30.

15. Franzway et al. also cite evidence from a 1981 study that compared "measures of the status of women . . . with measures of the strength of state structure and the scope of state action." These factors "tend to be positively correlated across a sample of 36 countries. That is, by and large, the stronger the state the better the position of women. (Analysis shows this is not an artifact of levels of economic development)" (29).

16. Sassoon 26, 30; Borchost and Siim 148; W. Brown, *SI* 168; Z. Eisenstein, *Color* 8.

17. See also Benjamin on feminists' reactions to otherness. Obviously men, too, often see otherness as threatening. However, the characteristic male response to otherness is attack; women, in contrast, tend to try to retreat or placate.

18. Cf. Meese's description of "the difficult, utopic dream of nonoppositional difference" as the desire of feminism (86).

19. Fox-Genovese contends that "middle-class feminism has come to rely more and more heavily on the rhetoric of sisterhood precisely as the social and economic prospects for an inclusive feminism have been diminishing, for even the advancement of individual women profits from the illusion of a general female solidarity" (*Feminism* 22).

20. For example, Gunew; Braidotti (*Nomadic*); Davies (*Black* 1–37, 44–47, 132–35, 147–51); Anzaldúa; Grewal (234, 251); and Minkoff (490).

21. Cf. Foucault: "After all, is it not one of the fundamental traits of our society that destiny takes the form of the relation to power, of the struggle along with or against it? The most intense point of lives, the one where their energy is concentrated, is precisely there where they clash with power, struggle with it, endeavour to utilise its forces or to escape its traps" ("The Life" 80).

22. See also hooks, "Choosing," and Modleski, *Feminism* 22, 33–34. Finke raises related issues.

23. Probyn points out that "the metaphor of the nomad unfortunately recalls some of the more unsalubrious aspects of tourism. The nomad or the tourist is posed as unthreatening, merely passing through; however, his person has questionable effects" (184). See also Davies, *Black* 23–26.

24. Fraser points out that "Even the lone exile is a member of the community of the imagination and thus is also a situated critic" ("False" 65). See also Bordo, "Feminism" 142–45.

25. F. Davis emphasizes, however, that the percentages of women elected to Congress, state legislatures, and governorships remain small (186–87).

26. See also Lynn 404; Lips 188–90; Piven 282. F. Davis covers the "gender gap" in detail (415–32).

27. See H. Eisenstein, "Femocrats"; Yeatman, *Bureaucrats;* Pringle and Watson, "Women's" 59–61; Whittier 481.

28. Phillips writes that "In 1985, Norway took the world record": "Women made up 34.4 per cent of the Storting (the national assembly), held eight out of eighteen cabinet posts, contributed 40.5 per cent of the membership of county councils and contributed 31.1 per cent of the membership of municipal councils" (*Engendering* 83). However, Hernes points out that "It is the powerful organizations and institutions rather than voters and political parties that have become the central gatekeepers in the Scandinavian state system, and these have not been as willing as political parties to recruit women or take up women's issues" (75–76). She also warns that Scandinavia has not so far provided "clear evidence of what women's entry into the public realm and their increasing political participation will bring in terms of political change" (89). Similarly, Chapman's analysis highlights Norwegian problems as well as triumphs (4, 241–57). See also Pringle and Watson, "Women's" 61–62; Adams 423; E. Ross 411.

29. For representative examples, see Clingman, *Novels* 217–18, 222; Wagner 5–32, 106; Yelin 207, n. 9; Temple-Thurston 179; G & S 283, 297–98; Pettis, *Toward* 29, 32–33; Pannill 63–64; Ingersoll, xi–xiii, 40–41, 80–81; J. Foster 153; Yglesias 7.

30. For example, Creighton, *Drabble* 17–18; Greene 18; Packer xi.

31. It should be noted that Dean's "reflective solidarity" was evolved in part to get beyond what she sees as "the tactical solidarity of coalition politics" (27)—but almost all theorists of coalition seek more than simply tactical alliances. Most emphasize the function of coalitions in facilitating a full airing of differences among participating groups. For typical examples of positive comments on coalitions, see Mouffe, "Feminism" 378–79; Haraway 155–57, 245, n. 7; K. E. Ferguson, *FCB* 241–43; Fraser and Nicholson 34–35; Grewal 234, 243–44. Collins terms coalitions "essential" for African American women (*BFT* 33; see also 36), while Minkoff writes that "Case studies suggest that women of color have a more established, historical commitment to a collectivist perspective" (482; see also Steady, "Women"). But J. James warns that "Multiracial alliances in the United States are fairly difficult to sustain; racial antagonisms and distrust fray, if not splinter, coalition politics" (155; see also 106–21, 154–67, 234–38).

32. On Reagon's essay, see K. King 93–99; Mohanty, "Feminist" 84–87; Phelan 168–69. Another good treatment of the difficulties in coalitions is G. Arnold. See also Duggan and Hunter 70–71; Douglas, *Love* 232, 266–70, 290–92; Z. Eisenstein, *Color* 220–21; Lorde, *Sister* 142; E. Klein, "Diffusion" 32; Connell, *Gender* 284–85.

33. Laclau and Mouffe emphasize "the constitutive character of social division and antagonism" (193). However, Dean points out that Mouffe "neglects the way a 'constitutive outside' can be understood as already part of and within each citizen" (43). Cf. Sedgwick 59, 61–62.

34. For commentators on this history, see notes 21 and 22 in chapter 1, along with Mueller, "Organizational" 266, and Donahue 73. Lauret's survey focuses specifically on Women's Liberation (52–73).

35. Gelb and Palley 3; Gelb, "Social" 285, 274.

36. In addition to those quoted in this paragraph, see K. B. Jones, *Compassionate* 10; Doane 76; Segal 128; Hassan.

37. See also Modleski, *Feminism* 15–17.

38. For example, Deleuze and Guattari; Jameson 221; Welchman 173; and Flax, *Disputed* 102. Cf. Waugh's comment that "the 'schizophrenia' of the postmodern text, a condition identified as the splitting of thought and feeling, is simply a *fin-de-siècle* caricature of the western tradition of Cartesian dualism in its liberal-humanist version (defining of the 'self' in terms of a transcendent rationality which necessitates splitting off what is considered to be the 'emotional' on to what is considered to be the feminine)" (31; see also 210).

39. For example, Ackelsberg, "'Sisters,'" and M. Friedman.

40. Cf. Ethel Klein's claim that the rise of any political consciousness "begins with affiliation, a recognition of group membership and shared interests," with the first stage being "a feeling of belonging to one's group" (*Gender* 3, 98). See also Lips 183–88.

41. On the political novel, in addition to Howe see Boyers (who updates Howe's description of the form [8–9]); S. Harris's collection, particularly her introduction (vii–xxiii); Sulieman, *Authoritarian;* Morson 81; Greene 23–24.

42. Ryan writes that "a multi-group movement supports the activation of large numbers of people, but, in so doing, runs the risk of displacing ideological commitment." She points out that this danger undercuts coalitional possibilities but also shows the importance of "ideological dialogue between groups supporting the same goal": "[W]hile a shared goal may bring people together, an essential part of the mobilization process is a unifying ideology that keeps them together" (156; see also G. Arnold 287).

43. Hartsock, "Staying" 117; B. Watson 113; Newton, "History" 101; Bystydzienski 3; J. Miller 241. See also Ridd; Reinelt 98–99; Phillips, *Engendering* 102; W. Brown, *MP* 207–9; and Hartsock's chapter "An Alternative Tradition: Women on Power" in *Money* (210–30). Singer surveys and critiques the feminist conceptualizations of power offered by Janeway, Gilligan, Hartsock, and French. Finally, Steady points out differences between western and African conceptions of power (*Black* 30).

44. See Bookman and Morgen 9–10; Cohen et al. 3–6; Borchost and Siim 149; Segal 217–18; Lebsock 35–36, 57. S. Harris's collection discusses women novelists' redefinitions of the political.

45. See also Verba 570; Christiansen-Ruffman 389; J. Evans 108; Phillips, *Engendering* 102–04.

46. Treatments of the relationship between the personal and the political are legion, but selected examples include Grant 33–39, 158–60, 181–82; Phillips, *Engendering* 93–119; hooks, *Talking* 105–111; K. E. Ferguson, *FCB* 200–201, 254–55, n.109; Coward, "Female" 32–35; Phelan 47–52; Scott 20–27; de Lauretis, *Feminist* 9; Butler, "Lesbian S & M" 171; Young, "Impartiality" 74.

47. An example is statements like "The woman-only meeting is a fundamental challenge to the structure of power" (M. Frye, *Politics* 104).

48. See O'Driscoll; B. Rich 548–49; Zimmerman, *SS* 61–62 and "What" 218.

49. McDowell writes that the "family romance is de-romanticized" in black women writers (*Changing* 78), although see A. Wilson 76, 87, and hooks, *Killing* 71. Siebers claims that "the new model of community is based on the romantic couple" (9). See also Hirsch, *Mother/Daughter* 11. Cf. Barrett, "Words" 204.

III: Fantasies of Power:
Margaret Atwood's *Bodily Harm*

1. On Rennie's name, see Carrington, "Another" 49. For various religious associations in the novel, see D. Jones; Kirtz 118, 125–26; Goodwin 114.

Significantly, given the important role that pornography plays in the novel, Stewart points out that "the structure of conversion . . . characterizes the narrative of pornography in all its discourses" (258).

2. In a conversation with Irvine, Atwood said that the action in *Bodily Harm* "takes place in a few hours" (*Collecting* 95), about the right length for a consciousness-raising session. E. T. Hansen has noted that parts of the text ("passages that undermine to some extent the conventional authority of the narrator by defying the spatio-temporal 'consensus' on which such authority relies") use the consciousness-raising model. She also draws on Bartky's phenomenology arguments, but in a different way than my argument does; Hansen connects Bartky's points with problems in Lora's role at the end of the novel (7, 11, 20–21).

3. Atwood in one interview commented that she left the ending deliberately unclear about Rennie's escape from prison because "I like the reader to participate in writing the book" (Ingersoll 227; see also Castro 221). However, in another interview she indicated that Rennie does escape. She said that she did not make *Bodily Harm* "nearly as frightening as the actual thing. If I had chosen Latin America rather than the Caribbean as the setting, my heroine would not have gotten out alive" (Harpur D1). On the ending of the novel, see A. Davidson 4–9; E. T. Hansen 17–21; Carrington, "Another" 56–62; Finn 64–66; Irvine, *Collecting* 89–91; Rosenberg 133; Epstein 89–90; Bouson 130–31; Brydon 183; Lucking 90–92. S. Wilson writes that in addition to the two alternative conclusions suggested by the text, Atwood's manuscript drafts of the novel include two additional "resolved endings" (*MAF* 228). The number of potential endings extant suggests Atwood's problems in writing the conclusion. Patton also works with the epigraphs and revisions in the *Bodily Harm* manuscripts (164–70).

4. Bartky points out that feminist consciousness may be divided, with awareness not only of personal victimization but also of personal privilege, revealing "the extent to which [the individual is] implicated in the victimization of others" (16).

5. Although Patton is quoted here, other critics do exactly the same thing. For example, Irvine, *Collecting* 102; Kirtz 118; Rubenstein, *Boundaries* 106, and "Pandora's Box" 261, 268; Adachi F17.

6. See Sargent's collection, which reprints Hartmann's famous essay and responses to it. Among numerous other discussions are MacKinnon's extended analysis in *Toward* (1–80); Hartsock, *Money* 145–54; Scott 34–37; Connell, *Gender* 41–47, 292; and Grant's brief overview (153–55).

7. Brownmiller writes that feminists began to politicize rape in 1971 (390).

8. S. Wilson writes that many critics see 1981, the year Atwood published *True Stories* as well as *Bodily Harm,* as a crucial turning point toward political commitment in Atwood's work, although Wilson herself disagrees (*MAF* 209; see also Wilson's "Camera" 43). Cf. Rosenberg 62, 133.

9. L. Henderson writes that it is unclear why the Porn Wars emerged at this particular time; she quotes Alice Echols's explanation in terms of a reac-

tion to the sexual revolution of the 1960s, which increased women's sexual vulnerabilities along with their sexual opportunities (Henderson 173; see also Echols, *Daring* 288–90). In addition to the large-scale "wars," the local repercussions were turbulent (Freccero 311). The papers from the Barnard conference are in Vance; see also Snitow et al., *Powers,* and Ellis 432–33, who writes that her essay as a whole represents the conference organizers' views (436). K. King warns that "the scope of the so-called 'Sex Debates' . . . currently is too narrowly drawn around the April 1982 Barnard conference and its synecdochic expansion, the academy," emphasizing that the conference "and its products identify only one range of activity and activism" (140; cf. Gallop, *Feminist* 76). In retrospect, Mann sees the Porn Wars as forecasting "a disconcerting broadening of feminist concerns" (62). But Kaminer points out one lesson from the antipornography movement's ascendancy: "As a form of terrorism, sexual violence works" (202). Among the many commentators on the Sex Wars, Duggan and Hunter offer a particularly useful chronology of events from 1966 to 1994 and coverage of subsequent "Sex Panics"; B. Rich covers the 1980s.

10. Factual information in the rest of this paragraph is from Duggan and Hunter 16, 25–26, and Itzin 5.

11. MacKinnon quotes Dworkin's restatement: "Pornography is the theory, pornography is the practice" ("From Practice" 53). MacKinnon herself, who would carry the campaign against pornography into the 1990s, wrote that "Pornography is masturbation material. It is used as sex. It therefore is sex" (*Only Words* 17). Significantly, Brownmiller at one point in *Against Our Will* actually raises the question of whether one of her analogies is extreme (395).

12. Ironically, MacKinnon herself points out that "sometimes you become what you're fighting" (*Feminism* 91). Many feminists have written in response to MacKinnon; in addition to W. Brown, one of the best analyses is by Butler in *Excitable* (63–69, 82–95).

13. Writing that "the academic market is hot for pornography," Wicke accuses this academic work of creating "a metapornography" (79, 62, 67).

14. See also Day 89, 93; Segal 107–8; Kittay 109; Gubar 737.

15. For example, Lucking 78; Ingersoll 64; Carrington, "Margaret Atwood" 32–33; Hulbert 41. Cf. Kirtz.

16. Atwood said that in *Bodily Harm* she "was writing a spy story from the point of view of one of the ignorant peripherally involved women" (qted. in Howells 106). On Atwood's generic manipulations, see especially Rao's first chapter, and for *Bodily Harm* see also Epstein; Patton 162–64, 169–70; Lucking 76–77, 92.

17. Carrington writes that "the two most striking ingredients of Atwood's fiction are satire and romance" ("Margaret Atwood" 28), but actually the romance in her work is almost always satirized. In an interview Atwood herself claimed that her writing is "closer to caricature than to satire—distortion rather than scathing attack" (Ingersoll 54–55). However, "caricature" suggests

a comic lightness that belies the seriousness of Atwood's best work. Lorraine M. York explains some of the excessive hostility directed against Atwood in terms of "the intersection of Atwood's feminism and her position as satirist": "I theorize that satire is *the* no-woman's land of literary modes because, as Atwood herself has pointed out, women have been socialized to believe that 'if you can't say something nice, don't say anything at all'" (*AtN* 17 [Fall/Winter 1996]: 2).

18.   Among analyses of the novel's narrative structure are E. T. Hansen; Carrington, "Another" 48–52; Epstein 84–85; Rao 109; and Lynch. Irvine in *Collecting* interprets the entire novel as structured by Rennie's consciousness during her surgery: "Rennie never leaves the hospital room" (96).

19.   Rennie's initial perception that the prisoners are female suggests her myopic tendency to relate everything to herself. Cf. Carrington, "Another" 55.

20.   The internal quotation is from Fernbach 31.

21.   W. Brown analyzes the ramifications of Machiavelli's "literal collapse of the distinction between war and politics" (*MP* 116).

22.   Redner points out that the state's monopoly on violence, the second part of Weber's definition, is "frequently treated as the only one by commentators" (640). However, Connell notes limitations to this putative monopoly, pointing out that violence against wives and against gays has been widely viewed as "socially legitimated use of force" (520; see also D. Cooper 76, n. 6).

23.   Franzway et al. term the state itself "the major institution of violence" (53).

24.   Foucault's exclusion of violence from power relations is somewhat ironic, given one of his comments suggesting that Arendt's distinction of domination from power is "something of a verbal one" (*Foucault Reader* 378). On force as an articulation of power, see also Wartenberg 93–96.

25.   For example, Mooers and Sears criticize theorists of radical democracy for their lack of attention to state violence: "[T]hey either abstract from entirely or reduce to near invisibility the special coercive aspects of state power" (53; see also 57).

26.   J. Mitchell writes that "historically it has been woman's lesser capacity for violence as well as for work, that has determined her subordination. In most societies woman has not only been less able than man to perform arduous kinds of work, she has also been less able to fight. Man not only has the strength to assert himself against nature, but also against his fellows" (*WE* 103). Baym comments that "Women certainly do violence, but they usually aren't very good at it" (105).

27.   Appropriately enough for the days of Shulamith Firestone and the early trust in technology, Gearhart settled on ovular merging, "the mating of two eggs," as a promising possibility (282). See also Atkinson 54–55, and Douglas, *Love* 245, on such proposals. Differing feminist viewpoints on violence are also discussed by Douglas in *Love* (278–83).

28.   Most critics, taking off from the novel's epigraph from John Berger's *Ways of Seeing,* emphasize the importance of seeing in the novel. Good exam-

ples are Irvine, who works with invisibility, "the politics of voyeurism" (56), and distorted perceptions throughout *Collecting,* and S. Wilson, who focuses on Atwood's use of camera images ("Turning"; "Camera"). Patton asserts that "sight itself is a political act" (154). However, Rao argues that *Bodily Harm* actually "undermines the belief in the reliability of the eye" (104). Noting Atwood's general tendency to undercut "the privilege of the visual over the other senses," she writes that "The texts in fact favour a tactile modality of perception rather than sight" (xxi). The repeated images of hands throughout the novel, which most critics also emphasize (typical are Carrington, "Another" 52–54, and Kirtz 118–21), support Rao's contentions.

29. For example, see O'Brien, W. Brown, *MP* 96, and on torture, Foucault, *DP,* Part I (1–69), and Theweleit 300–301.

30. For instance, "Since Rennie's invaded cells, organs, and senses also represent cancer of the earth and a colonized Mother Nature . . ., her healing prefigures the possibility of the earth's healing" (S. Wilson, *MAF* 227). Or, "The body politic is the form writ large of the individual body, in this instance the female body; bodily harm and exploitation in one domain are correspondingly registered in the other" (Rubenstein, *Boundaries* 101).

31. Cf. the African proverb quoted by Marshall to an interviewer: "It's woman's power on which a society ultimately depends" (Dance, "Interview" 19).

32. Significantly, A. Rich describes "the maintenance of a mother-son relationship between women and men" as "one form of false consciousness that serves compulsory heterosexuality" ("Compulsory" 191).

33. Fanon's work offers good examples of this kind of celebration. At the individual level he presents violence as "a cleansing force," which restores hope and self-respect and invests characters "with positive and creative qualities." The native's violence that wipes out other tribes—historically, in too many cases, genocide—is recoded by him as a unifier of the nation (*Wretched* 93–94). Chow notes that "the desire for revenge—to do to the enemy *exactly* what the enemy did to him, so that colonizer and colonized would meet eye to eye—is the fantasy of envy and violence that has been running throughout masculinist anti-imperialist discourse since Fanon" (40).

34. See Foucault on the emergence of the idea that "villainy is yet another mode of privilege" in "the birth of a literature of crime" (*DP* 68–69).

35. Irigaray, who also writes that "Woman has functioned most often by far as what is at stake in a transaction, usually rivalrous, between two men," suggests that the pornographic scene is yet another place where a woman serves as the mediation between men (*This Sex* 157, 199; see also 31–32).

36. Cf. Heilbrun's comment that "Lord Peter Wimsay once said that nine-tenths of the law of chivalry was a desire to have all the fun" (*Writing* 20). See also Snitow, "Mass Market," for connections between romance novels and pornography.

37. For example, Ackelsberg, "'Sisters'"; M. Friedman; K. B. Jones, "Citizenship" 807. Other theorists have contested such moves; Young, for example, writes that "Insofar as feminist groups have been impelled by a desire for closeness and mutual identification, . . . our political effectiveness may have been limited" ("The Ideal" 301).

38. For specific cases see Chaudhuri and Strobel, whose collection documents women's resistance along with their complicity.

39. Similar racial splits marked the antirape movement (see A. Davis, *Women* 172–201; Omolade 255; Johnson-Odim 323).

40. See also *BFT* 169–70; Forna; B. Martin, "Sexual" 106–7; Gallop, *Around* 70.

41. On Rennie as putative author of *Bodily Harm,* see S. Wilson, *MAF* 206, and McCombs, "Atwood's" 85. Howells points out that although Rennie cannot write her assigned article on pornography from a woman's point of view, Atwood does it for her (119). On Rennie and language, see Rainwater 23–24.

42. Faludi critiques the "trend stories" of the 1980s as serving political agendas by substituting moralism for social or political analysis (79–82, 160).

43. An excellent treatment is Hutcheon's seventh chapter (138–59).

44. Atwood wrote part of *Bodily Harm* while visiting the Caribbean (Irvine, *Collecting* 102). In an interview she said that although she had been collecting "scenes and images," *Bodily Harm* "didn't fall into place until I met somebody on a beach in the West Indies who told me the whole story of her life—none of which got into the book—but that story just made a few things fall into place" (Ingersoll 164). In another interview she indicated that that she condensed three islands into two (Castro 222). Rao (110, n. 40) and Irvine (*Collecting* 27) write that St. Lucia and St. Vincent are the islands on which the novel is modeled; Goodwin says only St. Vincent (113).

45. Kolodny points out that the police pornography collection reflects sequences in *This is Not a Love Story,* the well-known Canadian Film Board documentary in which Atwood reads a poem (96–97).

46. Drabble speaks similarly; see Kenyon, *Women Writers* 34.

47. For example, Kollias 133; Freeman, *Politics* 86; Federici 339.

48. See, for example, M. Meyers; J. James 80–82; Fanon, *Wretched* 77.

49. Cf. Butler, *Excitable* 5–6.

50. See also Piercy, "Margaret" 65–66.

IV: The Romance of Politics:
Paule Marshall's *Daughters*

1. This theme, Marshall asserted, "informs the novel at its deepest level" (Dance, "Interview" 20); see also Seaman 410, Russell 16, G & S 288, 298. The best analysis of *Daughters* is in DeLamotte's *Places* (120–64), which I wish had been available before this chapter was written. De-

Lamotte analyzes the various discourses represented in the novel; she interprets Marshall's couples and the ending much more positively than I do, and also gives a different explanation for the text's silence about delivering the papers.

2. In the same interview, when asked what *Daughters* was about, Marshall laughingly replied: "Like most of my novels, *Daughters* is about people, politics, culture, history, race, racism, morality, marriage, children, friendship, love, sex, the triumph and sometimes defeat of the human spirit, as well as a few other things I threw in for good measure" (Dance 2). She immediately qualified the remark by saying that the story is mainly about a family, a marriage, and a daughter. Despite this personal focus, "politics" does appear second in her original list, right after the obviously primary "people."

3. Marshall uses the same five nouns to describe Jane and Will in an interview about the novel (Dance, "Interview" 6).

4. See also Macherey 85–87; cf. Foucault, *History* 27.

5. Pettis writes that "In part, *Daughters* itself, in the form of a novel about male and female cooperative political venture, becomes that proposed investigation" (*Toward* 68).

6. On this pattern, see Gilkes 73–74, but see also Joseph and Lewis 109–112, who write that during the Civil Rights Movement, "it was a conscious and willing decision on the part of women as well as men to send the men forth" (110).

7. See Tilly and Gurin 28; Mueller, "Collective" 98.

8. On othermothering and community othermothering, see S. James, "Mothering"; McAdoo; Collins, *BFT* 119–23, and "Meaning" 4–7; Mann 169; Troester 13–14. On Marshall's use of them, see DeLamotte, *Places* 162–63, and Denniston 160–61, 164. Denniston points out that "Miz-Mack," the PM's mother, also functions as a community othermother (160).

9. Appiah describes this class as a "kleptocracy" (150).

10. See DeLamotte, *Places* 124, 157. An interesting analogy in terms of African American women writers is suggested by F. Foster, who emphasizes these writers' historical roles as mediators between men and women, blacks and whites, northerners and southerners, and adults and children ("Between" 57).

11. The term "romance" here and in the remainder of this discussion relies on the general and popular sense of the word rather than its more strictly literary definitions. Although Stacey and Pearce correctly emphasize the "multiple discourses of romantic love" throughout history in different cultures (27; see also Jackson 58), the concern here is primarily with current western representations as well as practices of romance, ranging from courtship and marriage to Harlequin books. In this connection Modleski's reminder that "romances are the property of us all—and not of just white Anglo-Saxon and American women either" and her insistence that

"the popularity of romances is a *cross*-cultural phenomenon" are important (*Feminism* 43; see also the figures for sales of romance novels given in Krentz 11). For contemporary theories of romance, see Stacey and Pearce 24–37.

12. Kathleen Gilles Seidel, a writer of romance novels, pushes the regression even farther back than Light, writing that romance novels offer fantasies about "a return to childhood" (Krentz 163).

13. See Collins, *BFT* 49; A. Davis, *Women* 15–19, 23; and A. Davis, "Reflections" 7–8, 14–15, which is almost certainly "the Angela Davis article" mentioned by Ursa in *Daughters* (12; see also Russell 16). Kerber notes that "the nuances of relationships between slave men and women are debated by historians" ("Separate" 26).

14. Gordimer in *A Sport of Nature* includes women fighters in African liberation armies (285–86, 287).

15. Moore 148–49, 171–73; A. Ferguson, *Sexual* 170–80; Pierson 222–25; French 458; MacKinnon, *Toward* 10–11; Connell, "The State" 535.

16. Accad 238; Moore 173–78; Grewal and Kaplan 25; Tohidi 251–53, 260; M. Cooke. See also Gilliam; Peake; Maitse 438; Anthias 159–60; Enloe 22; Harlow 39, 37. Randall notes that historically, revolutions that attack the patriarchal family have supported it once their regimes are established (197).

17. Pointing out that romantic love "has somewhat disappeared from the discursive arena" (10), Pearce and Stacey offered their 1995 collection as an attempt to fill this gap. Their review of the current status of romance describes it as "a category 'in crisis'" (24; see also 14).

18. Snitow's essay appeared in the 1983 collection she edited. In 1995 Jackson still found romantic love "somewhat neglected by feminists," despite their attention to "its fictional representation" (49). She writes that earlier feminist theorists "underestimated how deeply rooted" romantic desires were in women's psyches (56). See also B. Rich 544–48.

19. Examples are Radway's *Reading* (the methodology of which is critiqued in Modleski's *Feminism* [41–45]); Modleski's *Loving* and "Disappearing"; Radford's *Progress;* Snitow's "Mass Market"; Light's "'Returning"; Rabine's "Romance"; and Assiter. Krentz's collection offers valuable assessments of the genre by romance writers themselves.

20. N. Frye notes romance's "curiously proletarian status as a form generally disapproved of, in most ages, by the guardians of taste and learning, except when they use it for their own purposes. The close connection of the romantic and the popular runs all through literature" (23).

21. See also de Beauvoir, *Second* 774; Greer 146; Langford 263; Cancian 253; Modleski, *Loving* 46–47. Light, too, points out how the romance offers and uses "unequal heterosexuality as a dream of equality" (22). Wade-Gayles discusses black women and the negative aspects of romantic love (*No* 206–7). Zimmerman covers problems resulting from lesbian writers' deployment of romantic love conventions (*SS* 78–79).

22. See also de Beauvoir, *Second* 742–43; Ebert 9; Jackson 54. Snitow writes similarly of "a protective male who will somehow make reparation to the woman he loves for her powerlessness" ("Mass Market" 261).

23. In this connection one of Atkinson's comments provides a telling gloss on Estelle's adamant refusal to leave the PM, and particularly on her vociferous denials that she has wasted her life, despite her admission that in staying with him she has become "a stranger to [her]self" (*D* 223). Atkinson writes: "The combination of his power, her self-hatred, and the hope for a life that is self-justifying—the goal of all living creatures—results in a yearning for her stolen life—her Self—that is the delusion and poignancy of love" (62). Also relevant is D. C. Jack's 1991 study that "found heterosexual coupledom to be a major cause of depression in women, as in order to maintain relationships with men, they sacrificed their own needs, repressed their resultant anger and ended up losing a sense of self" (Langford 253).

24. Ironically, Viney was actually lucky that her mistreatment was only verbal; see J. James on police brutality toward black women (30–31). This passage is one of several analyzed by DeLamotte, who identifies *Invisible Man* as a subtext for *Daughters* (*Places* 123, 121). I would add that the central "invisible man" in the novel is the PM, who remains an enigma in many ways, both present to all the women in his life and simultaneously absent to each of them, since none of them can entirely know him.

25. Radway actually describes romance fiction as "*compensatory literature*" (95). See also Millett 51, 49; Firestone 132, 138–39; Rowland 82; Cranny-Francis 183; Cancian 257, 261; Ebert 9–10.

26. Estelle, too, writes to her parents after years in Triunion: "I've really come to see things here and in the States in pretty much the same light. There's the same work to be done. I drive past Armory Hill, the big slum we have here, and I could be driving through all the Harlems in the States" (*D* 224). Cf. J. Williams 53.

27. DeLamotte, who evaluates doubleness in *Daughters* more positively than I do (see *Places* 129–31, 138, 143, 159–60), provides a useful extended footnote tracing ramifications of this concept (168–69, n. 7). A theme of her study is the "importance for narrative art" of the "mode of superimposition [Marshall] has developed" (1; see also 3–9). A. Elam describes this technique in Marshall as "very cinematic" (102).

28. Hogeland writes that "The most frequent images used to describe feminist consciousness were images of duality and splitness" (31). Snitow, too, emphasizes "doubleness" as "a word that crops up everywhere in feminist discussion," interpreting it as a "reminder of the unresolved tension on which feminism continues to be built" ("Gender" 19).

29. A. Rich, "Compulsory" 197; N. Miller, *Subject* 44; Showalter, "Women's" 33, and see also "Feminist" 266; Meese 146; S. Smith, *Poetics* 51; A. Ferguson, *Sexual* 77 and "On Conceiving" 163–65; Neely 94.

30. Coser points out that Justin Beaufils's "name signals his role as a good and just son of the island as well as his membership in the 'minority' group of

French creoles, traditionally poor and alienated from power decisions" (see also DeLamotte, *Places* 145–46), while his wife from Spanish Bay represents "another minority group" on the island (72–73).

31.   See also Millett 45–49; Modleski, *Feminism* 13; Moore 136; Ackelsberg, "'Sisters'" 347; Misciagno 33, 35; Jaggar 336; E. Willis 99; de Beauvoir, "Interview" 146; Boose and Flowers 3–4; Flax, "Family" 250, 253; Franzway et al. 37. However, as Lauret emphasizes, "Critiques of the family as a restrictive and oppressive institution [have] a rather different resonance in the Black community: in a hostile world the family was often a stronghold for support" (69).

32.   The comment of their college friends on Viney and Ursa—"If you see one, you know you *gots* to see the other" (*D* 66)—is faintly reminiscent of the comments on Congo Jane's and Will Cudjoe's inseparability.

33.   Michie mentions only "circumventing" the mother (15).

34.   Hirsch offers a third analysis of maternity in connection with Clytemnestra, Antigone, and Iphigenia (*Mother/Daughter* 30–39), while Hartsock also interprets political ramifications of the *Oresteia* (*Money* 190–94). See also *KR* 151–52 and French 50. Cf. Jardine, "Pre-Texts" 221–22, and "Death" 130.

35.   Examples include Collins, *BFT* 115–37, "Meaning," and "Shifting"; Joseph; and Joseph and Lewis 75–126. For a literary perspective, see Troester; Wade-Gayles, "Truths"; de Weever 133–65; Dance, "Black"; Washington; Hirsch, "Maternal"; Adams 418. Most critics include "reverence for the mother as a characteristic feature of black women's literature" (Register 277); E. Ross writes that the work of black women writers of fiction, nonfiction, and academic studies "places the mother at the center, honors her work and care in a way that the dominant culture does not, and portrays directly the mother's subjectivity" (402). However, Hirsch notes "the disturbing disjunction between the celebration of mothers in the essays of black women writers and the much more ambivalent portrayals in their novels" ("Maternal" 417). Hirsch includes Marshall among those whom she believes write from the position of daughter rather than mother (416).

36.   De Weever finds "very little bonding between mother and daughter" in black women novelists, commenting that the mothers "do not really mother daughters but challenge them" (16, 173).

37.   See also Joseph and Lewis 79–81. Cf. on literary criticism, Rushing, "Images of Black Women" 410.

38.   Exceptions to this generalization include Ursa's desire to talk with her father about the resort (thwarted by his evasion of serious conversation with her) and his voluntarily showing the resort plans to Estelle. Ultimately, however, neither the PM nor Ursa is willing to force the issue with the other.

39.   Marshall in an interview underplays the destructive aspects of Ursa's act, pointing out that it "is designed, not to defeat the PM, but rather

to restore him to his original commitment and values" (Dance, "Interview" 20; see also A. Elam 103). But the novel itself undercuts this positive spin. The parallel would be bombing a country into oblivion in order to save it; the PM's career by this time represents values so incompatible with his original ones that the only way he can be saved is to destroy that career. Whether or not he joins Beaufils's party as adviser and honorary head (significantly for his feminization throughout the novel, these two positions are frequently associated with women), the base of his political power as an individual has been completely destroyed. Although Estelle obviously intends to persuade him to join with Beaufils, her past inability to influence him does not augur well for the attempt. DeLamotte, although describing the action as "an almost patricidal gesture," analyzes it as a "rescue" of the PM (*Places* 138; see also 139–40). But "rescue" seems somewhat euphemistic for an act that destroys a person as he has existed and insures that he can never function in that way again. See also Denniston, *Fiction* 164; Pettis, *Towards* 70.

40. Duncan also writes that the "evil, murderous usurper daughter" is a figure missing from literature and myth (131).

41. On the Antigone story, see also Elshtain, "Antigone's"; Hartouni; Dietz, "Citizenship" 26–30; Hirsch, *Mother/Daughter* 32–34; Kerber, *No* 299–302; K. B. Jones, *Compassionate* 158–59.

42. Typical examples are O'Brien 209–210; Haraway 173; and Reardon 84, 92. See also K. E. Ferguson, *FCB* x.

43. Douglas also mentions Rita Mae Brown (*Love* 289).

44. De Certeau agrees, writing that "The space of a tactic is the space of the other" and "a tactic is an art of the weak" (37; see his discussion, 34–39).

45. Cf. Yuval-Davis 422, and B. Martin, "Foucault" 10.

46. Wardlow defines guerrilla actions narrowly in military terms in *Political* (46), but the extension of the meaning to include political connotations is generally accepted. On terrorism and force, see Wartenberg 95–96. See also Janeway 227–33; Reagon 366.

47. See also Y. King 282–83, and Swerdlow 231.

48. Even at the personal level Collins points out how mothering relationships "can serve as a private sphere in which cultures of resistance and everyday forms of resistance are learned" (*BFT* 51).

49. Cf. S. Hite: "The relationship most essential to disrupt, in order for patriarchy to work, is the relationship between mother and daughter" ("Bringing" 60).

50. For example, Ladner 273, 282; Brooks-Higgenbotham 126; Busia 9–10; Steady, *Black* 17; Gonzalez 423–25; S. James 46–47; Collins, *BFT* 119–23. Maraire calls the extended family "Africa's most powerful resource" (31). On families in Africa, see also Courville, and on the matrifocal family, see Raymond Smith 39–57; Momsen 1; Sutton and Makiesky-Barrow 487.

51.   S. James 46; Sutton and Makiesky-Barrow 495–96; Collins, *BFT* 105–106; Washington 159.

52.   Omolade 248–49; Brooks-Higgenbotham 126; Wilentz xxxi–xxxii; Steady, *Black* 29; Rushing, "Images of Women" 18–19. Rushing quotes the Yoruba proverb that "Mother is gold" (19).

53.   Collins, *BFT* 120–21; Steady, *Black* 29, 33; Denniston xx.

54.   Wilentz writes that the Caribbean areas "allowed for the survival of African cultural traditions" during the time of slavery in ways that U.S. slavery did not (106; see also 100).

55.   Sudarkasa 53; G. Wilson 305; Justus 433, 447; Sutton and Makiesky-Barrow 472–73.

56.   Ladner 286; Steady, *Black* 33; Sutton and Makiesky-Barrow 486; Justus 448.

57.   On African and Afro-Caribbean female economic autonomy, see Ladner 286; Brooks-Higginbotham 126; Steady, *Black* 15; Collins, *BFT* 49; Sutton and Makiesky-Barrow 473, 482, 491; Cudjoe 16, 63; Moses 499ff. Momsen writes that "Today the Caribbean region has one of the highest levels of female economic activity rates" in the developing world (3).

58.   Collins's fourth and final image is the Welfare Mother. Through Marshall's ironic reinscriptions, Astral and Ursa's refusals of parodies of this role can be seen in the parallel episodes of their abortions. The Welfare Mother image is also invoked by Viney in discussing her difficulties with the police captain (*D* 330).

59.   DeLamotte writes that Ursa's visit to Astral "subvert[s] the class hierarchy, by insinuating into it the complexities of the mother-daughter hierarchy, the only relationship Ursa and Astral could establish in which Ursa would be cast as the subordinate" (*Places* 150). See also Denniston 164.

60.   See also McCray 70, and on patriarchal elements in the black family, hooks, *Killing* 62–76.

61.   See also Dietz, "Citizenship"; Elshtain, *Women* 240; K. B. Jones, *Compassionate* 150–52.

62.   On the Mothers, see Elshtain, "The Mothers"; Agosín 470–72, 475–76; Harlow 243–48; Ridd 5; Bunch, "A Global" 183; Snitow, "Gender" 21; Tronto 5–6.

63.   DeLamotte points out that most treatments of Marshall's work emphasize in different ways the shifting connections between personal and community histories ("Women" 241, n. 2).

64.   DuPlessis identifies "reparenting in invented families" as one of the narrative strategies through which twentieth-century women writers undermine the romance plot (xi). On Marshall's concept of community, E. Collier points out that her representations move out "from the Barbadian community in Brooklyn to Africa and all the places where a stolen people were taken and where they carved for themselves new worlds" ("Closing" 314). What Collier delineates in terms of race is reinscribed in *Daughters* with the addition of gender. On community in Marshall, see also Pettis, *Toward* 36–38.

V: Political and Sexual Liberations:
Nadine Gordimer's *A Sport of Nature*

1. On figuration, see also Braidotti, *Nomadic* 1–5, 75–76, 102, 113–14, 165, 275–76.

2. K. Wagner points out that the necessity "for such a new individual is articulated from [Gordimer's] earliest novels onward" (40). She adds: "The core theme which connects the [first] ten novels is indeed the search which runs through all of them for a way to achieve integration with an Africa that has appeared to allow its white children only the mutually untenable options of either internal or external exile . . ." (140). See also Gordimer, *Essential* 31–37 and 308. On *A Sport of Nature* in this connection, see Wagner 93.

3. Cf. *SN* 186; see also D. Johnson 9, K. Parker 218.

4. Throughout *A Sport of Nature* Hillela is referred to by her first name. Before she marries and takes her husband's surname, her last name is mentioned only once, as is her father's (*SN* 20, 47). Winnett writes that Hillela's "last name is as irrelevant as Rosa Burger's was decisive" (149).

5. Significantly, the one time that Hillela thinks in terms of categories, she fails. She wants her and Whaila's children to be "Our colour. A category that doesn't exist: she would invent it" (*SN* 208). Her hopes of a "rainbow family" of course die with Whaila's assassination.

6. B. King describes her as "a white woman living through her senses, like an animal" (11). Clingman, too, notes her "animal-like self-fulfilling presence" ("*SN* & B" 179).

7. By the time Hillela reaches the United States, Gordimer merges instinct and calculation in describing her "instinct for calculation" (*SN* 277).

8. One of her colleagues claims that had things "turned out differently, she was the type to become a terrorist, a hijacker. A Leila Khalid" (*SN* 254).

9. Just how certain characteristics of the two categories overlap deserves detailed consideration in a more general context than a single novel can provide.

10. When this chapter refers to "*the* narrator," the term is used simply for convenience. *A Sport of Nature* offers no single unified narrative consciousness. Peck points out that "Much of the narration is in shifting third-person voices" (163), while Macaskill emphasizes that "It is not always possible unequivocally to locate an origin for various passages" (68). Critics differ over the exact number of narrative positions represented; see Yelin 196, Weinhouse 93, Temple-Thurston 176, Smyer 83, B. Cooper 84–86, Snitow, "A New" 732.

11. The extent of critical uneasiness with Hillela as a protagonist is shown by attempts to decenter her from the novel by suggesting that her cousin Sasha is the real hero (Thurman 89; Clingman, "*SN* & B" 179–80; Newman 102; see also Peck 158). But even without Gordimer's comment that

"titles are very important—the whole story must be in the title" (Gray, "Landmark" 82), the overwhelming textual emphasis on Hillela clearly shows that *A Sport of Nature* is her novel.

12. See also Clingman, "*SN* & B" 187–88; Peck 161.

13. Gordimer noted in a 1987 interview that "oddly enough, Hillela is the first Jewish hero or heroine I've ever had in my nine novels" (B & S 297). Most critics agree with Ettin that "Gordimer's connection with her Jewish family roots does not bear very rich literary fruit" (30). Wade writes that any analysis "of the Jewish theme in Nadine Gordimer's writing, especially her novels, is an exploration of the absent, the unwritten, the repressed": "Unlike her great American contemporaries, she seems unable to make conscious use of either Jewish identity or her relative closeness to the immigrant experience to obtain for her, a insider, the luxury of an outsider's objectivity and critical perspective on her society" (155, 169). Wade also notes the significance of Gordimer's "elementary" mistakes about Jewish life and ceremony in *A Sport of Nature*: "A factual error in a Gordimer text is a matter of extreme rarity; her precision about such matters is legendary in the world of writers, obsessional" (167, 166). An exception to the critical consensus is Peck, who writes that "Gordimer's considerable emphasis on Hillela's Jewish background" provides "a dual evocation of the wandering Jew and the Holocaust survivors" (162). See also Clingman, "*SN* & B" 182. Gordimer's own assessment is that Hillela's "Jewishness doesn't really play much part in her life" (B & S 297; see also *SN* 9, 87, 123, 308).

14. Verba 567; Jennings 238.

15. Although Butler notes that coalitions do not require "an internally multiplicitous self that offers its complexity at once" (*GT* 16), neither did old-fashioned politics.

16. For example, Ettin 70; D. Johnson 9. On the ending generally, see also Winnett 152; Clingman, "*SN* & B" 188; Yelin 203.

17. D. Cooper also notes the "current fetishization" of transgression "within progressive lesbian and gay circles" (48–49). Although Cooper's primary focus is on lesbian and gay uses of the strategy, her arguments are equally relevant to feminism.

18. Critics emphasize the "contradictory relationship of capitalism to the family" (D'Emilio 108), with Z. Eisenstein speaking for many who find the traditional family "anachronistic for the advanced capitalist economy" ("The State" 55). See also Millett 45–46; Firestone 18–20; Fanon, *Black* 141–43, 148–49; hooks, *Killing* 72–73; Thorne 20, 23; Steady, *Black* 51; Fineman 226–36; J. Collier, Rosaldo, and Yanagisako 31, 40–46; Dietz, "Citizenship" 19–20; Gordon, "Family" 274–75; Connell, "The State" 515.

19. For example, Randall 197; Boose and Flowers 4; K. B. Jones, *Compassionate* 40–42; Franzway et al. 35. See also Rubin, "Traffic" 106–7, on marriage systems and state-making.

20. A. Ferguson, *Sexual* 248, 161–62; Connell, "The State" 528. See also Norton 261; Moore 147.

21. With the growing instability of the western family, contemporary conservatives also agree that reconceptualization of the nuclear family is necessary, although their model is the mythic U.S. family of the 1950s. (O'Brien points out that "The history of political conservatism . . . is tuned to a continuing coda of despair for the fate of the family" [94].) An exception to feminist calls for replacing the nuclear family is Elshtain, who writes that "What we call human capacities could not exist outside a familial mode . . ." (*PMPW* 326–27).

22. Steady, *Black* 29; Brooks-Higginbotham 126; Rushing 18–19; Ladner 279; Omolade, "Black" 248–49.

23. See A. Ferguson, *Sexual* 92, and "On Conceiving" 175; Weston.

24. Gonzalez points out the mistaken tendency to identify the family with the household (421, 423, 425). On distinctions between them, see Rapp.

25. B. Cooper notes that *A Sport of Nature* offers "one of the least critical portraits of polygamy yet painted by a woman writer of Africa" (82). But the portrait is positive only from Hillela's perspective, not from that of the General's other wives. Their reactions to Hillela suggest her intrusiveness. The first wife dislikes Hillela's behavior when she visits, "the ease with which the white woman made herself at home where she should have been ill at ease in strange surroundings, feeling the reserve of a way of life that doesn't belong to white people." Although the second wife grudgingly respects Hillela, she views her as a "usurper, a foreigner" (*SN* 358, 359). A number of critics have pointed out problems in Gordimer's treatment of black women. Bazin's article is the most substantial analysis of the later novels. See also Bröck-Sallah 76–78; Wagner 77–79; Ravell-Pinto 130–31. Newman does note that *A Sport of Nature* "provides a welcome corrective to literary and political readings of Empire which concentrate exclusively on the male hero," drawing on Susan M. Greenstein's point that "the white woman has always tended to be marginalized in the literature of imperialism" (93–94). However, correcting one marginalization and in the process creating another make for questionable advances.

26. Wagner suggests that their mutually accepted infidelity "derives perhaps more immediately from Gordimer's romanticisation of European, and in particular French, sexual culture than from any grasp of the real tensions which may beset polygamous relationships in a non-ideal and often westernised African context" (93). Gordimer does mock other European misunderstandings of polygamy when Marie-Claude says of Hillela, "To be one wife among several, the way the Africans do it—that's to be a mistress, isn't it?" (*SN* 205).

27. Yelin notes some of the contrasts between Hillela and her mother, but her argument does not require much detail. Gordimer has expended considerable effort to construct the two as opposites in various ways.

For example, Ruthie is described as "childish" and "self-absorbed" (*SN* 341); Hillela's level of self-absorption is high, but even as a young girl she is never childish. Ruthie fails to understand men and is fooled by a number of them, while Hillela, who "by some instinct understood the male, loved men" (*SN* 179), is fooled only once, when very young. Unlike Ruthie, who "was somehow never able to be aware of anything outside her own skin," Hillela, because of her belief that "only sexual love . . . was to be trusted," uses her skin to connect with others (*SN* 59, 290; see also 341). Fletcher also discusses the relationship between the two (54–55).

28.   J. Cooke writes that Hillela's presence at the celebration of black rule in South Africa, and the absence of all members of Pauline's family, suggest "that getting out of the family is a necessary condition to participation in the new South African world" (29; see also Wagner 146–47). On families in Gordimer's fiction generally, see Cooke's essay; B. King 15–16; Clingman, "*SN & B*" 183.

29.   Winnett notes that *A Sport of Nature* "registers human bodies minutely: breasts, penises, hands, facial lines, toes, and hair" (151). Every critic who writes on the novel discusses Hillela and the body. Fletcher's exploration of how "the truth of the body becomes an ideology in itself" (60) is one of the longer treatments, drawing interesting connections between Hillela and Cixous (54–55, 59–61), although Clingman is also useful (*Novels* xiv-xxii, "*SN & B*" 178–89).

30.   For example, among numerous theorists, Pateman's *SC* and Z. Eisenstein's *Female* and also *Color* are book-length treatments. See also K. B. Jones, "Citizenship" 794–95; Butler, *GT* 128–34; and Gatens, "Power" 124–35.

31.   See also B & S 278. Gordimer in another interview spoke of discussing with friends "the fact that the power behind the throne . . . has always been known as someone's mistress." When the group tried to think of analogous male situations, Gordimer says that she "popped up with Sartre and Simone de Beauvoir, but it wasn't acceptable as they're too equal" (Kenyon, *Women Writers* 105).

32.   In an interview Gordimer remarked that she saw "a relationship between Hillela and the true courtesan. They were always politically powerful; and their field was always men" (B & S 278; cf. *SN* 325 and also 204).

33.   For analysis of the kind of power wielded by courtesans, see Dixon 210–12; Wartenberg 104–112; French 125.

34.   On secret history, see R. Mayer 94–112; Richetti 119–67.

35.   Discussions of women's problems with power include Singer; Messenger 320–22; J. B. Miller 247–48; Grant 119, 140–41; W. Brown, *MP* 207–9; Gordon, "What's" 23–24.

36.   See P. Allen on Theodora, and S. B. Smith on Harriman.

37.   Yelin writes that without any "master narrative that takes precedence over the others," Gordimer "undermines not only the authority and authenticity of any particular account but also narrative authority and the nar-

rative ideology of authenticity in general" (196). See also Peck 163; B. Cooper 85; Yelin 197.

38. For example, Peck 162–64; D. Johnson 9; Smyer 82; Snitow, "A New" 732; Craig 411; Fletcher 57–58; Wagner 146–47; Weinhouse 95–96.

39. Gordimer in one interview called the novel "a case history" (B & S 268).

40. See also Philipson, and Cornell, "What" 77, 83. On how traditional patterns of "idealization and demonization" of women vindicate the positions of men, see Hawkesworth 67–68.

41. Pateman writes: "When women's bodies are on sale as commodities in the capitalist market, . . . the law of male sex-right is publicly affirmed, and men gain public acknowledgment as women's sexual masters" (*SC* 201, 208). See also Collins, *BFT* 175–76; Shrage; Pateman, "Defending"; Barry, "Pornography" 453–54; F. Davis 326–28; L. S. Brown 88–90. Kaminer does note "a general feminist consensus that condemns arresting prostitutes while their customers go free" (188).

42. Characteristics of the picaresque in this paragraph are taken from the following: Maiorino, "Renaissance Marginalities" xiv, xxii; Guillén 79–81, 95; Mancing 276, 281; E. Friedman, 190; Sánchez and Spadaccini 292–93, 296, 298; Yelin 199, 200; Brink 262; Freibert 26–27. Characteristics of the romance are from Radway 97, 124, 151; DuPlessis 5; Light 25, n. 4; Jackson 53; Zimmerman, *SS* 78; Modleski, "Harlequin" 437; Snitow, "Mass Market" 261; Baruch 2; Stacey and Pearce 29; J. Mitchell, *WLR* 104; M. Roberts 227–28.

43. The best treatment of the picaresque in *A Sport of Nature* is by Yelin, who focuses on Gordimer's dismantling of *Kim,* "Kipling's imperial picaresque," and on her grafting of "the picaresque narrative of Hillela onto the more conventional story of her cousin Sasha" (195, 192). Yelin also notes: "Ironically, as an English-speaking Jew in South Africa, [Gordimer] writes from a position like that of the authors of the classic Spanish picaresque, many of whom . . . are thought to have been *conversos* who never fully assimilated into sixteenth-century Spanish society" (207, n. 9). See also Brink.

44. Gordimer has insisted that in *A Sport of Nature* she "wasn't trying to create a modern Moll Flanders" (Kenyon, *Women Writers* 105)—a remark that perhaps reflects some anxiety that she might have done so. See also Sampson; Brink.

45. The initial clause of Gordimer's remark has led to considerable critical commentary on the dialectic between romance and realism in her work. Among many examples are Lomberg; Clingman, *Novels* 219–22; Smyer 72; Wagner 39–40.

46. However, Yelin notes certain generic manipulations that do work effectively in *A Sport of Nature:* "Gordimer destabilizes the generic distinctions between the domestic novel in which women, as/and consciousness, and the family romance occupy center stage, the adventure novel dominated by men of action, and the political or philosophical novel, which encompasses consciousness and action alike" (201–2).

47.   Yelin reads the romance as connected with private life in *A Sport of Nature* (193); my view is that the romance is integrally connected to Hillela's public role.

48.   See also Wagner 59, 90–96, 142–48; Bazin 42; Driver 186–89. Bröck-Sallah notes that in the context of apartheid, selecting "sexuality as the privileged site for the construction of partnership . . . is a very challenging strategy," but that the construction is executed "in completely patriarchal terms" (73). Collins's remark on "the seeming naiveté many white women have concerning interracial relationships with Black men" (*BFT* 190) is relevant to Gordimer's portrayals.

49.   Stacey and Pearce also note that "white agendas have dominated discussions of love and romance" (22). Simmonds finds no "academic text on love that incorporates interracial relationships in theories of romantic love" (211). The essays in Pearce and Stacey by Simmonds, K. Perry, and (charles) analyze interracial romance (171–222).

50.   On this romanticization, see Ettin 71; Wagner 57, 105, 123–24, 153–62; Driver 200. Ravell-Pinto offers a counterview (132–33). See also Gordimer, *Writing* 131, and her comments on whites writing about blacks in *Essential* 279.

51.   On the economic base of romantic love as an institution, see also Millett 51; Firestone 132, 138–39; DuPlessis 2; Chodorow 74; Rowland 82; Ebert 9–10; Cancian 253, 261.

52.   See also Mancing 282–83; Guillén 77–80; Maiorino, "Renaissance" xxii; Cruz 249–52, 264, 267; Brink 262, 264.

53.   Almost all critics comment on Hillela's status as an unrealistic figure. She is like a "mirage," "something between a fata morgana and a character" (Thurman 89); she is "a matrix of various narrative potentialities" (Smyer 84); her life is like those of "mythic heroes" (D. Johnson 9); she is a "free and untrammelled fantasy figure" (B. Cooper 83); her function is that of "a transcendent archetype" (Clingman, "*SN & B*" 185; see also 183–84, and *Novel* xviii); she is "a visionary, symbolic figure" (Visel 39). See also Weinhouse 94–95 and Yelin 194–95.

54.   Wagner places Pauline in the second of three distinct groups of liberals in Gordimer's fiction, a group "made up of those who attempt to involve themselves directly in some sort of anti-apartheid activism." She writes: "It is this class which Gordimer herself perhaps knows best, towards which she feels most ambivalent, and which at times becomes the target of her sharpest irony" (16). Gordimer commented in an interview that she had "great sympathy for characters like Pauline" (Kenyon, *Women Writers* 106), but this sympathy is not apparent in *A Sport of Nature*. On Pauline and liberalism, see also Thurman 88; B. Cooper 69–71; Peck 155–57; Craig 411; Weinhouse 95–96; K. Parker 218; Yeatman, *Bureaucrats* 157. On Gordimer and liberalism generally, see Clingman, *Novels* 57–63, 144–47; Wagner 13–28, 140–41; Rowland Smith 14–16; Peck 155–57. Cf. Engle 107. Comments on liberalism by

Gordimer are in B & S 56, 93–94, 101–102, 193–94, 213, 291–92, and Sampson.

VI: Mothers and Capitalists in International Politics: Margaret Drabble's *The Gates of Ivory*

1. Harper discusses Drabble as realist, modernist, and postmodernist, while Rubenstein analyzes Drabble's movements from realism to postmodernism in "Fragmented."

2. Reflections of Virgilian descriptions in Book VI include *GI* 3–4, 243, 400.

3. The fathers who do appear in the novel, such as Charles Headleand, are generally not shown in their paternal roles.

4. Segal notes that "mothers and daughters became the other principal preoccupation of feminists in the late seventies, alongside rape and male violence" (136; see also Palmer 112, E. Ross 401, n. 15)—although Joseph in 1984 pointed out the "critical dearth of resources on [Black] mother and daughter relationships" (17). In contrast to proliferating studies of (at least white) mother-daughter relationships, Forcey writes that few studies of the mother-son relationship from the mother's perspective exist (*Mothers* 29; see also C. Klein). Forcey also comments that conventional as well as "revised feminist interpretations of the responsibility of mothers for the well-being of sons [are] personally and politically damaging for both women and men" (*Mothers* 14). In *The Radiant Way*, the first novel of the trilogy that *The Gates of Ivory* concludes, Drabble focuses on mother-daughter relationships; see Rubenstein, "Sexuality."

5. Among border camps currently designated by numbers, only Site 2 and Site 8 exist (Mysliwiec 98–99). Drabble obviously combined them to produce her fictional Site Ten.

6. The lines on Mitra have some of the attributes that critics have connected with "feminine" endings in Drabble's works, such as ambiguity and avoidance of closure. But the conclusion of *The Gates of Ivory* is definitely *not* life-affirming and survival-oriented, attributes that have also been termed "feminine" in this connection. (See, e.g., Irvine, "No" 74, 78, 80, 84). The accuracy and usefulness of the gendering of these critical descriptions is questionable. What Drabble herself said about the end of *The Radiant Way*—"the end is only a mood isn't it" (Kenyon 33)—is true for most of her novels. The description of Mitra does provide the "concluding two-faced symbol which looks backward over the novel, reflecting all the symbols and themes of the work, and also looks forward, prophesying a future" that N. Stovel has noted as characteristic of Drabble's endings ("Feminine" 87–88). It is also a telling reversal of the "particularly maternal denials of endings" that Irvine sees in some of Drabble's early novels ("No" 76). Other critics who have discussed Drabble's endings include E. C. Rose, "Feminine"; Pickering 482–83; Campbell 33.

7. Of course, as A. Barnett points out, Sihanouk's "vision was always unrelentingly self-serving." Describing Sihanouk as a "creature of colonialism," Barnett also notes that "A French fascist admiral had placed him on the throne when he was eighteen years old and by no means in line to be king" (122–23).

8. An excellent collection on the subject is Harris and King. See also the collections edited by Ridd and Callaway, and by Cooper, Munich, and Squier. Among more negative treatments are Elshtain's *Women and War*, Elshtain and Tobias's edited collection, and Segal (162–203); see also Richards. Fairly balanced appraisals are offered by Forcey, "Feminist," and Pierson. On women's antimilitarist movements, see also Sturgeon 69–75, Enloe 11–13. Harlow discusses maternal activism and its representations (225–33).

9. Among many who discuss problems in Ruddick are Dietz, "Citizenship," and "Context" 10–13, 15; Boling 608–10; Wartenberg 193–201; Grimshaw 227–53; Mouffe, "Feminism" 373–77; Grant 70–71.

10. Mohanty writes: "That women mother in a variety of societies is not as significant as the value attached to mothering in these societies. The distinction between the act of mothering and the status attached to it is a very important one . . ." ("Under" 60).

11. Segal notes that soldiers' lives are marked by "subservience, obedience, and passive dependence," characteristics traditionally considered feminine (187).

12. Mann offers a useful analysis of women's roles in the Gulf (163–72).

13. In another interview Drabble said that she believes that "the mother-child relationship is great salvation and is an image of unselfish love." She added that she feels "a great confidence in the family situation that comes through whether I want it to or not" (Preussner 569). At another time she admitted that her husband's view was that she has "far too rosy a view of parent/child relationships and the normal family" (Hannay 145). See also Satz 187–88; Atwood, "Margaret Atwood Talks" 126, 130; Creighton, *Drabble* 24–25; Rayson 43–44.

14. S. Mayer contends, however, that after *The Needle's Eye*, the "novelist of maternity is done" (85). On mothers in Drabble's fiction generally, see G. Whittier and Rayson. Drabble herself commented in an interview: "Some women novelists very much dislike the way I write about maternity, and say I only praise what is socially acceptable" (Hannay 145). In addition, if motherhood per se in Drabble's novels is generally portrayed positively, mothers as individuals are not. In another interview she admitted that she had not been "very good at . . . creating 'good' mothers": "I'd written books and books before someone pointed out that I was perpetually producing these 'bad' mothers" (B. Milton 55). She later commented more specifically that her mothers "of the old generation tend not to be terribly good mothers," although the "daughters get on with them all right"; she also agreed with the interviewer that she did not depict "devouring mothers" (Preussner 569).

15. Significantly, Ruddick herself describes the "task of extending the perspective of care from intimate to public" as "morally and conceptually difficult" ("Rationality" 250).

16. See Kiernan, xvi; cf. *GI* 368.

17. See also Moghadam 18; Reynell 133.

18. Cf. A. Rich: "The mother's passion for the son is an accused passion: accused of weakening, of binding, of castrating" (*What* 146).

19. See also Tronto 161; J. Mitchell, *WE* 162.

20. Drabble's historical accuracy is notable here. Reynell writes that adult literacy education in the Cambodian Refugee Camps is organized by the Khmer Women's Association, which "caters mainly to women" (168).

21. See also Trask 21–25; A. Rich, *Of Woman* 103–7, 117; Grosz, *Volatile* 202–7; cf. *GI* 156. Writing about "the extreme ugliness of most of the words and phrases that describe the female condition," Drabble herself commented: "What have women been up to, all these centuries, guiltily accepting their own uncleanliness . . ." ("The fiendish" 45; see also Drabble, "Mimesis" 9, and Packer 14, # 69).

22. Hattie speculates that perhaps Polly "has been offered the post of shadow minister for Women by the lads of Walworth" (*GI* 416).

23. Writing similarly of male fears of "the sexual and reproductive powers of women" that are projected "outward into social forms, by imbedding the need to defend themselves against women in institutions and activities, including those called 'political,'" Elshtain inserts a parenthetical warning: "To argue this is *not* to state that politics is only a reaction formation or serves only defensive purposes" (*PMPW* 142–43).

24. On Whitmore and his relationship with his mother, see Rubenstein, "Severed."

25. Ong writes that the practices of transnational corporations "also promoted a sexual image of Third World women workers" (292).

26. Brewer writes that "race in the context of the globalization of capitalism makes gender the center of the new working class" (18). Ong agrees that "transnational capitalism ha[s] produced, along with microchips, discourses that naturalize the subordination of women in industrial enterprises" (291). See also Haraway 166–72; Mohanty, "Introduction" 28–31, and "Under" 57–64.

27. Said is an example of the earlier approaches (*Culture* 292), while Hannerz in "Creolisation" (554–56) and "Notes" (69–73) represents more recent views. Drabble briefly discusses her views of England's relationship with the nonwestern world in her interview with Hannay (134–35).

28. However, Miss Porntip's constant measurement of life in financial terms does make overt some of the economic realities that Drabble fails to emphasize in connection with other characters. One small example is the travel expenses of Stephen, Liz, and Charles, who hop jets with abandon as they journey between England and various parts of Southeast Asia, expenses that are never mentioned in the novel.

29.   Drabble's historical accuracy in constructing Miss Porntip's life is impressive, including the poverty of her region, the U.S. Air Force's construction of roads and bases there, her four years of education, the role of her aunt in her life, and the importance of beauty contests as escape routes from poverty. These and other salient details are drawn from Phongpaichit (30, 32, 37, 45, 49, 51, 55, 64, 68), who is listed in the bibliography appended to *The Gates of Ivory*. Ong notes that U.S. firms in Southeast Asia encouraged beauty competitions as an extracurricular activity for their women workers (292). Finally, Miss Porntip's connections with prostitution are also realistic. Rosca writes that 2 million prostitutes—10 percent of those in the world—live in Thailand, with 800,000 of these women younger than sixteen (17).

30.   Miss Porntip's "plans to launch a new Asian mini-tampon" (*GI* 79) place her in implied contrast with Polly.

31.   Cf. Creighton, *Drabble* 109–10.

32.   On the economic and political status of Thai women, see Eberhardt 3–5, 50, 73; Phongpaichit 2–6, 21, 75; Potter 5, 15, 18–19.

33.   See also Rosca.

34.   For example, Piven 277; Kerber, "Separate" 28; Marks and de Courtivron 217.

35.   Brown adds that "Understanding sexism as most contingent and least permeating in the economic realm illuminates why a) liberal feminism, by its nature preoccupied with economic discrimination, has such a thin conception of sexism and b) Marxist-feminism, by its nature searching for economic accounts of sexism, founders in this endeavor" (*MP* 18, n. 4).

36.   The estimate is Mysliwiec's (2–3). Kiernan believes that a million and a half (more than one-fifth of Kampuchea's population) perished (v). Robert Jackson, who provided the preface for Mysliwiec's book, blames the Khmer Rouge for over a million deaths (iii; see also ix). Mysliwiec also points out that U.S. bombings between 1969 and 1973 killed over a million Cambodians (2).

37.   Typical was her admission of her "awful leaning toward the conventional novel" in her interview with Firchow (112). Harper's essay analyzes this position (148–52).

38.   See, for example, the articles by Cunningham, N. Stovel ("From Wordsworth"), B. Stovel, and Fox-Genovese. Drabble herself mentions the shift from private to public in her interviews with Gussow (41), Satz (189–91), and Poland (162–63). Critics who discuss Drabble's development in other terms include Bromberg, Pickering, Murphy, and Rubenstein ("Fragmented").

39.   See also Atwood, "Margaret Atwood Talks" 73; Clifford 19; Hannay 133; Cooper-Clark 23–24.

40.   Cf. Crieghton's description of Drabble as "a central chronicler of contemporary urban middle-class life" (*Drabble* 14).

41. For example, Satz 189; Poland 282; E. C. Rose, "Introduction" 1–4; Creighton, *Drabble* 37.
42. When asked in a 1978 interview which of her novels she was "most fond of," Drabble replied: "I think probably *The Needle's Eye*" (B. Milton 60).
43. For example, N. Stovel, "From Wordsworth" 134–35, 137; B. Stovel 56–57; Murphy 39; Pickering 476, 479; Bromberg 188. An exception is S. Mayer, who considers Drabble's first six novels as a unit focusing on maternity (76).

Works Cited

Abel, Elizabeth. "Race, Class, and Psychoanalysis? Opening Questions." Hirsch and Keller 184–204.

Abel, Katy. "Andrea Dworkin: 'What Is Intercourse?'" *Frontline Feminism 1975–1995: Essays from Sojourner's First 20 Years.* Ed. Karen Kahn. San Francisco: Aunt Lute Books, 1995. 345–50.

Accad, Evelyne. "Sexuality and Sexual Politics: Conflicts and Contradictions for Contemporary Women in the Middle East." Mohanty et al. 237–50.

Ackelsberg, Martha A. "Communities, Resistance, and Women's Activism: Some Implications for a Democratic Polity." Bookman and Morgen 297–313.

Ackelsberg, Martha A. "'Sisters' or 'Comrades'? The Politics of Friends and Families." Diamond 339–56.

Acker, Joan. "Feminist Goals and Organizing Processes." Ferree and Martin 137–44.

Adachi, Ken. "Atwood on *Bodily Harm:* 'It Isn't Autobiographical.'" *Toronto Star* 27 September 1981: F17.

Adams, Alice. "Maternal Bonds: Recent Literature on Mothering." *Signs* 20 (1995): 414–27.

Adcock, Cynthia. "Fear of 'Other': The Common Root of Sexism and Militarism." McAllister 209–19.

Agosín, Marjorie. "Amidst the Smoke We Remember: Mothers of the Plaza de Mayo." Bell and Klein 470–78.

Alcoff, Linda. "Cultural Feminism Versus Post-Structuralism: The Identity Crisis in Feminist Theory." *Signs* 13 (1988): 405–36.

Allen, Judith. "Does Feminism Need a Theory of 'The State'?" S. Watson 21–37.

Allen, Pauline. "Contemporary Portrayals of the Byzantine Empress Theodora (A.D. 527–548)." Garlick, Dixon, and Allen 93–103.

Althusser, Louis. *Lenin and Philosophy and Other Essays.* Trans. Ben Brewster. New York: Monthly Review Press, 1971.

Amiel, Barbara. "Life after Surviving." *Maclean's* 92 (15 October 1979): 66–67.

Andermahr, Sonya. "The Politics of Separatism and Lesbian Utopian Fiction." Munt 133–52.

Anderson, Benedict. *Imagined Communities: Reflections on the Origin and Spread of Nationalism.* 1983. New York: Verso, 1991.

Anthias, Floya. "Women and Nationalism in Cyprus." *Woman—Nation—State.* Eds. Nira Yuval-Davis and Floya Anthias. London: Macmillan, 1989. 150–67.

Anzaldúa, Gloria. "La Conciencia de la Mestiza: Towards a New Consciousness." *Making Face, Making Soul: Haciendo Caras.* Ed. Anzaldúa. San Francisco: Aunt Lute Books, 1990. 377–89.

Appiah, Kwame Anthony. *In My Father's House: Africa in the Philosophy of Culture.* New York: Oxford University Press, 1992.

Arendt, Hannah. *The Human Condition.* Chicago: University of Chicago Press, 1958.

Arendt, Hannah. *On Violence.* New York: Harcourt, 1970.

Arens, W., and Ivan Karp. "Introduction." *Creativity of Power: Cosmology and Action in African Societies.* Eds. W. Arens and Ivan Karp. Washington: Smithsonian Institution Press, 1989.

Armstrong, Nancy. *Desire and Domestic Fiction.* New York: Oxford University Press, 1987.

Arnold, Gretchen. "Dilemmas of Feminist Coalitions: Collective Identity and Strategic Effectiveness in the Battered Women's Movement." Ferree and Martin 276–90.

Arnold, June, et al. "Lesbians & Literature." *Sinister Wisdom* 1.2 (1976): 20–33.

Ascher, Carol. "Compromised Lives." *Women's Review of Books* 9.2 (November 1991): 7.

Ashcroft, Bill, Gareth Griffiths, and Helen Tiffin. *The Empire Writes Back: Theory and Practice in Post-Colonial Literatures.* London: Routledge, 1989.

Assiter, Alison. "Romance Fiction: Porn for Women?" Day and Bloom 101–9.

Atkinson, Ti-Grace. *Amazon Odyssey.* New York: Links Books, 1974.

Atwood, Margaret. "An ATLANTIS Interview with Margaret Atwood." *Atlantis* 5 (1980): 202–11.

Atwood, Margaret. *Bodily Harm.* New York: Simon and Schuster, 1982.

Atwood, Margaret. "If You Can't Say Something Nice, Don't Say Anything At All." *Language in Her Eye: Views on Writing and Gender by Canadian Women Writing in English.* Eds. Libby Scheier, Sarah Sheard, and Eleanor Wachtel. Toronto: Coach House Press, 1990. 15–25.

Atwood, Margaret. "Introduction." Plimpton xi–xviii.

Atwood, Margaret. "Margaret Atwood Talks to Margaret Drabble." *Chatelaine* 60 (April 1987): 73, 124, 126, 130.

Atwood, Margaret. *Second Words: Selected Critical Prose.* 1982. Boston: Beacon Press, 1984.

Atwood, Margaret. *Surfacing.* New York: Simon and Schuster, 1972.

Atwood, Margaret. "True Romances." *True Stories: Poems.* New York: Simon and Schuster, 1981. 40–44.

Atwood, Margaret. "Women's Novels." *Good Bones and Simple Murders.* New York: Doubleday, 1994. 25–30.

Atwood, Margaret, and Students. "A Conversation." VanSpanckeren and Castro 233–43.

Austen-Leigh, James Edward. *Memoir of Jane Austen.* Oxford: Clarendon Press, 1926.

Awkward, Michael. *Inspiriting Influences: Tradition, Revision, and Afro-American Women's Novels.* New York: Columbia University Press, 1989.

Backhouse, Constance, and David H. Flaherty. *Challenging Times: The Women's Movement in Canada and the United States.* Montreal: McGill-Queen's University Press, 1992.

Baer, Sylvia. "Holding onto the Vision." *Women's Review of Books* 8.10–11 (July 1991): 24–25.

Ballaster, Ros. *Seductive Forms: Women's Amatory Fiction from 1684 to 1740.* Oxford: Clarendon Press, 1992.

Barnett, Anthony. "'Cambodia Will Never Disappear.'" *New Left Review* 194 (1990): 101–25.

Barnett, Bernice McNair. "Black Women's Collectivist Movement Organizations: Their Struggles during the 'Doldrums.'" Ferree and Martin 199–219.

Barr, Marleen S. *Feminist Fabulation: Space/Postmodern Fiction.* Iowa City: University of Iowa Press, 1992.

Barrett, Michèle. "Feminism and the Definition of Cultural Politics." Brunt and Rowan 37–58.

Barrett, Michèle. "Max Raphael and the Question of Aesthetics." *New Left Review* 161 (1987): 78–97.

Barrett, Michèle. "Words and Things Materialism and Method in Contemporary Feminist Analysis." Barrett and Phillips 201–19.

Barrett, Michèle, and Anne Phillips, eds. *Destabilizing Theory: Contemporary Feminist Debates.* Stanford, CA: Stanford University Press, 1992.

Barry, Kathleen. "Pornography and the Global Sexual Exploitation of Women." Bell and Klein 448–55.

Barry, Kathleen. "Deconstructing Deconstructionism (or, Whatever Happened to Feminist Studies?)" Bell and Klein 188–92.

Barthes, Roland. *Mythologies.* 1957. Trans. Annette Lavers. 1972. New York: Hill and Wang, 1986.

Bartkowski, Frances. "Epistemic Drift in Foucault." Diamond and Quinby 43–58.

Bartky, Sandra Lee. *Femininity and Domination: Studies in the Phenomenology of Oppression.* New York: Routledge, 1990.

Baruch, Elaine Hoffman. *Women, Love, and Power: Literary and Psychoanalytic Perspectives.* New York: New York University Press, 1991.

Bassin, Donna, Margaret Honey, and Meryle Mahrer Kaplan, eds. *Representations of Motherhood.* New Haven, CT: Yale University Press, 1994.

Baudrillard, Jean. *America.* Trans. Chris Turner. London: Verso, 1988.

Baudillard, Jean. *Cool Memories.* Trans. Chris Turner. London: Verso, 1990.

Baym, Nina. "The Agony of Feminism: Why Feminist Theory is Necessary After All." Eddins 101–17.

Bazin, Nancy Topping. "Sex, Politics, and Silent Black Women: Nadine Gordimer's *Occasion for Loving, A Sport of Nature,* and *My Son's Story.*" Fletcher 30–61.

Bazin, Nancy Topping, and Marilyn Dallman Seymour. *Conversations with Nadine Gordimer.* Jackson: University Press of Mississippi, 1990.

Behn, Aphra. *Oroonoko, or The Royal Slave.* 1688. New York: Norton, 1973.

Bell, Diane, and Renate Klein, eds. *Radically Speaking: Feminism Reclaimed.* Melbourne: Spinifex Press, 1996.

Bell, Roseann P., Bettye J. Parker, and Beverly Guy-Sheftall, eds. *Sturdy Black Bridges: Visions of Black Women in Literature.* Garden City, NY: Anchor Press, 1979.

Belsey, Catherine. "Constructing the Subject: Deconstructing the Text." Newton and Rosenfelt 45–64.

Benhabib, Seyla. "Feminism and Postmodernism: An Uneasy Alliance." Benhabib et al. 17–34.

Benhabib, Seyla. "On Contemporary Feminist Theory." *Dissent* 36 (1989): 366–70.

Benhabib, Seyla, Judith Butler, Drucilla Cornell, and Nancy Fraser. *Feminist Contentions: A Philosophical Exchange.* New York: Routledge, 1995.

Benjamin, Jessica. "The Shadow of the Other (Subject): Intersubjectivity and Feminist Theory." *Constellations* 1.2 (1994): 231–54.

Berkley, Miriam. "PW Interviews Margaret Drabble." *Publishers Weekly* 31 May 1985: 59–60.

Beverley, John, and Marc Zimmerman. *Literature and Politics in the Central American Revolutions.* Austin: University of Texas Press, 1990.

Black, Naomi. "Ripples in the Second Wave: Comparing the Contemporary Women's Movement in Canada and the United States." Backhouse and Flaherty 94–109.

Boals, Kay. "Review Essay: Political Science." *Signs* 1 (1975): 161–74.

Boling, Patricia. "The Democratic Potential of Mothering." *Political Theory* 19 (1991): 606–25.

Bonefield, Werner. "Reformulation of State Theory." *Capital & Class* 33 (1987): 96–127.

Bookman, Ann, and Sandra Morgen. *Women and the Politics of Empowerment.* Philadelphia: Temple University Press, 1988.

Boose, Lynda E., and Betty S. Flowers, eds. *Daughters and Fathers.* Baltimore: Johns Hopkins University Press, 1989.

Borchost, Anette, and Birte Siim. "Women and the Advanced Welfare State—A New Kind of Patriarchal Power?" Sassoon 128–57.

Bordo, Susan. "Feminism, Postmodernism, and Gender-Scepticism." Nicholson, *Feminism* 133–56.

Bordo, Susan. *Unbearable Weight: Feminism, Western Culture, and the Body.* Berkeley: University of California Press, 1993.

Boris, Eileen. "The Reconstruction of Mothering." *Women's Review of Books* 12.12 (September 1995): 20.

Bourque, Susan C., and Jean Grossholtz. "Politics an Unnatural Practice: Political Science Looks at Female Participation." *Politics and Society* 4 (1974): 225–66.

Bouson, J. Brooks. *Brutal Choreographies: Oppositional Strategies and Narrative Design in the Novels of Margaret Atwood.* Amherst: University of Massachusetts Press, 1993.

Bowen, Angela. "Enabling a Visible Black Lesbian Presence in Academia: A Radically Reasonable Request." Bell and Klein 62–66.

Boyers, Robert. *Atrocity and Amnesia: The Political Novel Since 1945.* New York: Oxford University Press, 1985.

Braidotti, Rosi. *Nomadic Subjects: Embodiment and Sexual Difference in Contemporary Feminist Theory.* New York: Columbia University Press, 1994.

Braidotti, Rosi. *Patterns of Dissonance.* Trans. Elizabeth Guild. New York: Routledge, 1991.

Brennan, Timothy. "The National Longing for Form." *Nation and Narration.* Ed. Homi K. Bhabha. London: Routledge, 1990. 44–70.

Brewer, Rose M. "Theorizing Race, Class and Gender: The New Scholarship of Black Feminist Intellectuals and Black Women's Labor." James and Busia 13–30.

Brink, André. "Mutants of the Picaresque: *Moll Flanders* and *A Sport of Nature.*" *Journal of Literary Studies* (Pretoria, South Africa) (1990): 261–74.

Bröck, Sabine. "'Talk as a Form of Action': An Interview with Paule Marshall, September 1982." *History and Tradition in Afro-American Culture.* Ed. Günter H. Lenz. New York: Campus Verlag, 1984. 194–206.

Bröck-Sallah, Sabine. "Plots to a Happy Ending: Re-Reading Closure." Parker and Meese 59–81.

Bromberg, Pamela S. "The Development of Narrative Technique in Margaret Drabble's Novels." *Journal of Narrative Technique* 16 (1986): 179–91.

Brooks-Higginbotham, Evelyn. "The Problem of Race in Women's History." Weed 122–33.

Brown, Beverley, and Parveen Adams. "The Feminine Body and Feminist Politics." *m/f* 3 (1979): 35–50.

Brown, L. Susan. *The Politics of Individualism.* Montreal: Black Rose Books, 1993.

Brown, Wendy. *Manhood and Politics: A Feminist Reading in Political Theory.* Totowa, NJ: Rowman & Littlefield, 1988.

Brown, Wendy. *States of Injury: Power and Freedom in Late Modernity.* Princeton, NJ: Princeton University Press, 1995.

Brownmiller, Susan. *Against Our Will: Men, Women and Rape.* New York: Simon and Schuster, 1975.

Brunt, Rosalind, and Caroline Rowan. *Feminism, Culture and Politics.* London: Lawrence and Wishart, 1982.

Brydon, Diana. "Caribbean Revolution & Literary Convention." *Canadian Literature* 95 (1982): 181–85.

Bunch, Charlotte. "A Global Perspective on Feminist Ethics and Diversity." Cole and Coultrap-McQuin 176–85.

Bunch, Charlotte. "The Reform Tool Kit." Bunch et al. 189–201.

Bunch, Charlotte, et al. *Building Feminist Theory.* New York: Longman, 1981.

Burstyn, Varda. "Masculine Dominance and the State." *Socialist Register* (1983): 45–89.

Busia, Abena P. B. "Words Whispered over Voids: A Context for Black Women's Rebellious Voices in the Novel of the African Diaspora." *Black Feminist Criticism and Critical Theory. Studies in Black American Literature.* Vol. 3. Eds. Joe Weixlmann and Houston A. Baker, Jr. Greenwood, FL: Penkevill, 1988. 1–41.

Butler, Judith. "Contingent Foundations: Feminism and the Question of 'Postmodernism.'" Butler and Scott 3–21.

Butler, Judith. *Excitable Speech: A Politics of the Performative.* New York: Routledge, 1997.

Butler, Judith. *Gender Trouble: Feminism and the Subversion of Identity.* New York: Routledge, 1990.

Butler, Judith. "Gender Trouble, Feminist Theory, and Psychoanalytic Discourse." Nicholson, *Feminism* 324–40.

Butler, Judith. "Imitation and Gender Insubordination." Fuss 13–31.

Butler, Judith, and Joan W. Scott, eds. *Feminists Theorize the Political.* New York: Routledge, 1992.

Butler, Judy. "Lesbian S & M: The Politics of Dis-Illusion." Linden et al. 169–75.

Bystydzienski, Jill M., ed. *Women Transforming Politics: Worldwide Strategies for Empowerment.* Bloomington: Indiana University Press, 1992.

Campbell, Jane. "Becoming Terrestrial: The Short Stories of Margaret Drabble." *Critique* 25 (1983): 25–44.

Cancian, Francesca M. "Gender Politics: Love and Power in the Private and Public Spheres." Rossi, *Gender* 253–64.

Carrington, Ildikó de Papp. "Another Symbolic Descent." *Essays on Canadian Writing* 26 (Summer 1983): 45–63.

Carrington, Ildikó de Papp. "Margaret Atwood." *Canadian Writers and Their Works.* Fiction Series, Vol. 9. Eds. Robert Lecker, Jack David, Ellen Quigley. Toronto: ECW Press, 1987. 23–116.

Carroll, Susan J., and Linda M. G. Zerilli. "Feminist Challenges to Political Science." *Political Science: The State of the Discipline II.* Ed. Ada W. Finifter. Washington: American Political Science Association, 1993. 56–76.

Carroll, William K., ed. *Organizing Dissent: Contemporary Social Movements in Theory and Practice.* Toronto: Garamond Press, 1992.

Carter, Angela. *The Sadeian Woman and the Ideology of Pornography.* New York: Pantheon, 1979.

Castro, Jan Garden. "An Interview with Margaret Atwood: 20 April 1983." VanSpanckeren and Castro 215–32.

Cavin, Susan. *Lesbian Origins.* San Francisco: ism Press, 1985.

Chapman, Jenny. *Politics, Feminism, and the Reformation of Gender.* London: Routledge, 1993.

(charles), Helen. "(Not) Compromising: Inter-Skin Colour Relations." Pearce and Stacey 197–209.

Chaudhuri, Nupur, and Margaret Strobel, eds. *Western Women and Imperialism: Complicity and Resistance.* Bloomington: Indiana University Press, 1992.

Chodorow, Nancy J. *Feminism and Psychoanalytic Theory.* New Haven, CT: Yale University Press, 1989.

Chow, Rey. *Writing Diaspora: Tactics of Intervention in Contemporary Cultural Studies.* Bloomington: Indiana University Press, 1993.

Christian, Barbara. *Black Women Novelists: The Development of a Tradition, 1892–1976.* Westport, CT: Greenwood Press, 1980.

Christian, Barbara. "The Race for Theory." *Cultural Critique* 6 (Spring 1987): 57–63.

Christian, Barbara. "Trajectories of Self-Definition: Placing Contemporary Afro-American Women's Fiction." Pryse and Spillers 233–48.

Christiansen-Ruffman, Linda. "Women's Conceptions of the Political: Three Canadian Women's Organizations." Ferree and Martin 372–93.

Cixous, Hélène. *The Terrible but Unfinished Story of Norodom Sihanouk, King of Cambodia.* Trans. Juliet Flower MacCannell, Judith Pike, and Lollie Groth. Lincoln: University of Nebraska Press, 1994.

Clegg, Stewart R. *Frameworks of Power.* London: Sage, 1989.

Clifford, Judy. "A Substance of Entertainment." *London Times* 27 April 1987: 19.

Clingman, Stephen. "*A Sport of Nature* and the Boundaries of Fiction." B. King 173–90.

Clingman, Stephen. *The Novels of Nadine Gordimer: History from the Inside.* 1986. 2nd ed. Amherst: University of Massachusetts Press, 1992.

Cohen, Cathy J., Kathleen B. Jones, and Joan C. Tronto, eds. *Women Transforming Politics: An Alternative Reader.* New York: New York University Press, 1997.

Cohn, Carol. "Emasculating America's Linguistic Deterrent." Harris and King 153–70.

Cole, Eve Browning, and Susan Coultrap-McQuin, eds. *Explorations in Feminist Ethics: Theory and Practice.* Bloomington: Indiana University Press, 1992.

Collier, Eugenia. "The Closing of the Circle: Movement from Division to Wholeness in Paule Marshall's Fiction." M. Evans 295–315.

Collier, Jane, Michelle Z. Rosaldo, and Sylvia Yanagisako. "Is There a Family? New Anthropological Views." Thorne, *Rethinking* 31–48.

Collins, Patricia Hill. *Black Feminist Thought: Knowledge, Consciousness, and the Politics of Empowerment.* 1990. New York: Routledge, 1991.

Collins, Patricia Hill. "The Meaning of Motherhood in Black Culture and Black Mother/Daughter Relationships." *Sage* 4.2 (1987): 3–10.

Collins, Patricia Hill. "Shifting the Center: Race, Class, and Feminist Theorizing About Motherhood." Glenn, Chang, and Forcey 45–65.

Combahee River Collective. "The Combahee River Collective Statement." B. Smith, *Home Girls* 272–82.

Connell, R. W. *Gender and Power: Society, the Person, and Sexual Politics.* Stanford, CA: Stanford University Press, 1987.

Connell, R. W. "The State, Gender, and Sexual Politics: Theory and Appraisal." *Theory and Society* 19 (1990): 507–44.

Cooke, John. "'Nobody's Children': Families in Gordmer's Later Novels." B. King 21–32.

Cooke, Miriam. "WO-man, Retelling the War Myth." Cooke and Woollacott 177–204.

Cooke, Miriam, and Angela Woollacott, eds. *Gendering War Talk*. Princeton, NJ: Princeton University Press, 1993.

Cooper, Brenda. "New Criteria for an 'Abnormal Mutation'? An Evaluation of Gordimer's *A Sport of Nature*." *Rendering Things Visible: Essays on South African Literary Criticism*. Ed. Martin Trump. Athens: Ohio University Press, 1990. 68–93.

Cooper, Davina. *Power in Struggle: Feminism, Sexuality and the State*. New York: New York University Press, 1995.

Cooper, Helen M., Adrienne Auslander Munich, and Susan Merrill Squier, eds. *Arms and the Woman: War, Gender, and Literary Representation*. Chapel Hill: University of North Carolina Press, 1989.

Cooper-Clark, Diana. "Margaret Drabble: Cautious Feminist." E. C. Rose, *Critical* 19–30.

Copi, Irving M. *Introduction to Logic*. 5th ed. New York: Macmillan, 1978.

Cornell, Drucilla. "What Is Ethical Feminism?" Benhabib et al. 75–106.

Cornell, Drucilla L. "Gender, Sex, and Equivalent Rights." Butler and Scott 280–96.

Coser, Stelamaris. *Bridging the Americas: The Literature of Paule Marshall, Toni Morrison, and Gayl Jones*. Philadelphia: Temple University Press, 1995.

Costain, Anne N. *Inviting Women's Rebellion: A Political Process Interpretation of the Women's Movement*. Baltimore: Johns Hopkins University Press, 1992.

Costain, Anne N., and W. Douglas Costain. "Strategy and Tactics of the Women's Movement in the United States: The Role of Political Parties." Katzenstein and Mueller 196–214.

Courville, Cindy. "Re-examining Patriarchy as a Mode of Production: The Case of Zimbabwe." James and Busia 31–43.

Coward, Rosalind. "Are Women's Novels Feminist Novels?" Showalter, *New* 225–39.

Coward, Rosalind. "Female Desire and Sexual Identity." Díaz-Diocaretz and Zavala 25–36.

Coward, Rosalind. "Sexual Politics and Psychoanalysis: Some Notes on their Relation." Brunt and Rowan 171–86.

Craig, Patricia. "The Wayward Girl's New Departure." *Times Literary Supplement* 17 April 1987: 411.

Cranny-Francis, Anne. *Feminist Fiction: Feminist Uses of Generic Fiction*. New York: St. Martin's Press, 1990.

Creighton, Joanne V. "An Interview with Margaret Drabble." Schmidt 18–31.

Creighton, Joanne V. *Margaret Drabble*. New York: Methuen, 1985.

Creighton, Joanne V. "Sisterly Symbiosis: Margaret Drabble's *The Waterfall* and A. S. Byatt's *The Game*." *Mosaic* 20 (1987): 15–29.

Crews, Frederick. *The Critics Bear It Away: American Fiction and the Academy*. New York: Random House, 1992.

Cruz, Anne J. "Sonnes of the Rogue: Picaresque Relations in England and Spain." Maiorino 248–72.

Cudjoe, Selwyn R., ed. *Caribbean Women Writers*. Wellesley, MA: Calaloux, 1990.

Cunningham, Gail. "Patchwork and Patterns: The Condition of England in Margaret Drabble's Later Novels." *The British and Irish Novel Since 1960*. Ed. James Acheson. New York: St. Martin's Press, 1991. 126–41.

Dahlerup, Drude. "Confusing Concepts—Confusing Reality: A Theoretical Discussion of the Patriarchal State." Sassoon 93–127.

Dance, Daryl C. "Black Eve or Madonna? A Study of the Antithetical Views of the Mother in Black American Literature." Bell, Parker, and Guy-Sheftall 123–32.

Dance, Daryl Cumber. "An Interview with Paule Marshall." *The Southern Review* 28 (Winter 1992): 1–20.

Darcy, R[obert], Susan Welch, and Janet Clark. *Women, Elections, and Representation*. New York: Longman, 1987.

Darnovsky, Marcy. "Overhauling the Meaning Machines: An Interview with Donna Haraway." *Socialist Review* 21.2 (1991): 65–84.

Davidson, Arnold E. "The Poetics of Pain in Margaret Atwood's *Bodily Harm*." *American Review of Canadian Studies* 18 (1988): 1–10.

Davidson, Arnold E., and Cathy N. Davidson, eds. *The Art of Margaret Atwood: Essays in Criticism*. Toronto: Anansi, 1981.

Davies, Carol Boyce. *Black Women, Writing and Identity: Migrations of the Subject*. London: Routledge, 1994.

Davies, Carole Boyce, ed. *Moving Beyond Boundaries. Volume 2: Black Women's Diasporas*. London: Pluto Press, 1995.

Davis, Angela. "Reflections on the Black Woman's Role in the Community of Slaves." *Black Scholar* 3.4 (December 1971): 2–15.

Davis, Angela Y. *Women, Race & Class*. 1981. New York: Vintage, 1983.

Davis, Flora. *Moving the Mountain: The Women's Movement in America Since 1960*. New York: Simon and Schuster, 1991.

Davis, Lennard J. *Factual Fictions: The Origins of the English Novel*. New York: Columbia University Press, 1983.

Davis, Nina Cox. "Breaking the Barriers: The Birth of López de Ubeda's *Pícara Justina*." Maiorino 137–58.

Day, Gary. "Looking at Women: Notes Toward a Theory of Porn." Day and Bloom 83–100.

Day, Gary, and Clive Bloom, eds. *Perspectives on Pornography: Sexuality in Film and Literature*. London: Macmillan, 1988.

Dean, Jodi. *Solidarity of Strangers: Feminism after Identity Politics*. Berkeley: University of California Press, 1996.

de Beauvoir, Simone. Interview with Alice Schwarzer [1972]. Marks and de Courtivron 142–50.

de Beauvoir, Simone. *The Second Sex*. Trans. and ed. H. M. Parshley. 1952. New York: Vintage, 1974.

de Certeau, Michel. *The Practice of Everyday Life*. Trans. Steven F. Rendall. Berkeley: University of California Press, 1984.

de Groot, Joanna, and Mary Maynard. "Facing the 1990s: Problems and Possibilities for Women's Studies." *Women's Studies in the 1990s: Doing Things Differently?* Eds. Joanna de Groot and Mary Maynard. London: Macmillan, 1993. 149–78.

DeKoven, Marianne. "Male Signature, Female Aesthetic: The Gender Politics of Experimental Writing." *Breaking the Sequence: Women's Experimental Fiction.* Eds. Ellen G. Friedman and Miriam Fuchs. Princeton, NJ: Princeton University Press, 1989. 72–81.

DeLamotte, Eugenia. *Places of Silence, Journeys of Freedom: The Fiction of Paule Marshall.* Philadelphia: University of Pennsylvania Press, 1998.

DeLamotte, Eugenia. "Women, Silence, and History in *The Chosen Place, The Timeless People.*" *Callaloo* 16 (1993): 227–42.

de Lauretis, Teresa. *Alice Doesn't: Feminism, Semiotic, Cinema.* Bloomington: Indiana University Press, 1984.

de Lauretis, Teresa. *Technologies of Gender: Essays on Theory, Film, and Fiction.* Bloomington: Indiana University Press, 1987.

de Lauretis, Teresa. "Upping the Anti (sic) in Feminist Theory." Hirsch and Keller 255–70.

de Lauretis, Teresa, ed. *Feminist Studies/Critical Studies.* Bloomington: Indiana University Press, 1986.

Deleuze, Gilles, and Félix Guattari. *Anti-Oedipus: Capitalism and Schizophrenia.* Trans. Robert Hurley, Mark Seem, and Helen R. Lane. 1972. Minneapolis: University of Minnesota Press, 1994.

Delmar, Rosalind. "What Is Feminism?" Mitchell and Oakley 8–33.

Delphy, Christine. *Close to Home: A Materialist Analysis of Women's Oppression.* Trans. Diane Leonard. London: Hutchinson, 1984.

Delphy, Christine. "French Feminism." Bell and Klein 383–92.

D'Emilio, John. "Capitalism and Gay Identity." Snitow et al. 100–13.

Denniston, Dorothy Hamer. *The Fiction of Paule Marshall: Reconstructions of History, Culture, and Gender.* Knoxville: University of Tennessee Press, 1995.

de Weever, Jacqueline. *Mythmaking and Metaphor in Black Women's Fiction.* New York: St. Martin's Press, 1992.

Diamond, Irene, ed. *Families, Politics, and Public Policy: A Feminist Dialogue on Women and the State.* New York: Longman, 1983.

Diamond, Irene, and Lee Quinby, eds. *Feminism and Foucault: Reflections on Resistance.* Boston: Northeastern University Press, 1988.

Díaz-Diocaretz, Myriam, and Iris M. Zavala, eds. *Women, Feminist Identity, and Society in the 1980's: Selected Papers.* Philadelphia: John Benjamins, 1985.

Dietz, Mary G. "Citizenship with a Feminist Face: The Problem with Maternal Thinking." *Political Theory* 13 (1985): 19–37.

Dietz, Mary G. "Context Is All: Feminism and Theories of Citizenship." *Daedalus* 116.4 (Fall 1987): 1–24.

di Leonardo, Micaela. "Morals, Mothers, and Militarism: Antimilitarism and Feminist Theory." *Feminist Studies* 11 (1985): 599–617.

di Leonardo, Micaela, ed. *Gender at the Crossroads of Knowledge: Feminist Anthropology in the Postmodern Era.* Berkeley: University of California Press, 1991.

Dinnerstein, Dorothy. *The Mermaid and the Minotaur: Sexual Arrangements and Human Malaise.* 1976. New York: Harper, 1991.

Dixon, Suzanne. "Conclusion—The Enduring Theme: Domineering Dowagers and Scheming Concubines." Garlick, Dixon, and Allen 209–25.

Doane, Mary Ann. "Commentary: Post-Utopian Difference." Weed 70–78.

Donahue, Jesse. "Movement Scholarship and Feminism in the 1980s." *Women & Politics* 16.2 (1996): 61–80.

Douglas, Carol Anne. "I'll Take the Low Road: A Look at Contemporary Feminist Theory." Bell and Klein 417–20.

Douglas, Carol Anne. *Love and Politics: Radical Feminist and Lesbian Theories.* San Francisco: ism Press, 1990.

Doyle, Laura. *Bordering on the Body: The Racial Matrix of Modern Fiction and Culture.* New York: Oxford University Press, 1994.

Drabble, Margaret. "Fairy-Tales." *The Listener* 4 April 1968: 441.

Drabble, Margaret. "The Fiendish Curse." *More Words.* London: BBC, 1977. 45–46.

Drabble, Margaret. *The Gates of Ivory.* 1991. New York: Penguin, 1993.

Drabble, Margaret. "Mimesis: The Representation of Reality in the Post-War British Novel." *Mosaic* 20 (1987): 1–14.

Drabble, Margaret. "Minority View." *London Times* 5 June 1970: 10.

Drabble, Margaret. *A Natural Curiosity.* 1989. New York: Penguin, 1990.

Drabble, Margaret. *The Radiant Way.* 1987. London: Penguin, 1988.

Drabble, Margaret. "Rape and Reason." *The Observer* 10 December 1978: 9.

Drabble, Margaret. "A Woman Writer." *On Gender and Writing.* Ed. Michelene Wandor. London: Pandora Press, 1983. 156–59.

Drabble, Margaret. "Women and Literature." *Contemporary Women in Life and Literature: Lecture-Essays from the 1979 Women's Conference. Angelica et Americana* 13. Copenhagen: Department of English, University of Copenhagen, 1981. 13–30.

Draine, Betsy. "An Interview with Margaret Atwood." *Interviews with Contemporary Writers.* Ed. L. S. Dembo. 2nd ser. Madison: University of Wisconsin Press, 1983. 366–81.

Driver, Dorothy. "Nadine Gordimer: The Politicisation of Women." Rowland Smith 180–204.

duBois, Page. "Antigone and the Feminist Critic." *Genre* 19 (1986): 371–83.

Duggan, Lisa, and Nan D. Hunter. *Sex Wars: Sexual Dissent and Political Culture.* New York: Routledge, 1995.

Duncan, Erika. "Mothers and Daughters." Miner and Longino 131–40.

DuPlessis, Rachel Blau. *Writing beyond the Ending: Narrative Strategies of Twentieth-Century Women Writers.* Bloomington: Indiana University Press, 1985.

Dworkin, Andrea. *Pornography: Men Possessing Women.* 1979. New York: Perigee, 1981.

Eberhardt, Nancy, ed. *Gender, Power, and the Construction of the Moral Order: Studies from the Thai Periphery.* Madison, WI: Center for Southeast Asian Studies, 1988.

Ebert, Teresa L. *Ludic Feminism and After: Postmodernism, Desire, and Labor in Late Capitalism.* Ann Arbor: University of Michigan Press, 1996.

Echols, Alice. *Daring to be BAD: Radical Feminism in America 1967–1975.* Minneapolis: University of Minnesota Press, 1989.

Echols, Alice. "Nothing Distant about It: Women's Liberation and Sixties Radicalism." Cohen, Jones, and Tronto 456–76.

Eddins, Dwight, ed. *The Emperor Redressed: Critiquing Critical Theory.* Tuscaloosa: University of Alabama Press, 1995.

Editorial Collective, *Questions féministes.* "Variations on Common Themes." Marks and de Courtivron 212–30.

Eisenstein, Hester. "Femocrats, Official Feminism and the Uses of Power." S. Watson 87–103.

Eisenstein, Hester. *Gender Shock: Practicing Feminism on Two Continents.* Boston: Beacon Press, 1991.

Eisenstein, Hester, and Alice Jardine, eds. *The Future of Difference.* 1980. New Brunswick, NJ: Rutgers University Press, 1988.

Eisenstein, Zillah R. *The Color of Gender: Reimaging Democracy.* Berkeley: University of California Press, 1994.

Eisenstein, Zillah R. *The Female Body and the Law.* Berkeley: University of California Press, 1988.

Eisenstein, Zillah R. *The Radical Future of Liberal Feminism.* 1981. Boston: Northeastern University Press, 1993.

Eisenstein, Zillah. "The State, the Patriarchal Family, and Working Mothers." Diamond 41–58.

Elam, Angela. "To Be in the World: An Interview with Paule Marshall." *New Letters* 62.4 (1996): 96–105.

Elam, Diane. *Romancing the Postmodern.* London: Routledge, 1992.

Ellis, Kate. "I'm Black and Blue from the Rolling Stones and I'm Not Sure How I Feel about It: Pornography and the Feminist Imagination." Hansen and Philipson 431–50.

Elshtain, Jean Bethke. "Antigone's Daughters: Reflections on Female Identity and the State." Diamond 300–11.

Elshtain, Jean Bethke. "Feminist Discourse and Its Discontents: Language, Power, and Meaning." *Signs* 7 (1982): 603–21.

Elshtain, Jean Bethke. *Meditations on Modern Political Thought: Masculine/Feminine Themes from Luther to Arendt.* 1986. University Park: Pennsylvania State University Press, 1992.

Elshtain, Jean Bethke. "The Mothers of the Disappeared: Passion and Protest in Maternal Action." Bassin, Honey, and Kaplan 75–91.

Elshtain, Jean Bethke. *Public Man, Private Woman: Women in Social and Political Thought.* Princeton, NJ: Princeton University Press, 1981.

Elshtain, Jean Bethke. *Women and War.* New York: Basic Books, 1987.

Elshtain, Jean Bethke, and Sheila Tobias, eds. *Women, Militarism, and War: Essays in History, Politics, and Social Theory.* Savage, MD: Rowman & Littlefield, 1990.

Engle, Lars. "The Political Uncanny: The Novels of Nadine Gordimer." *Yale Journal of Criticism* 2 (1989): 101–27.

Enloe, Cynthia. *The Morning After: Sexual Politics at the End of the Cold War.* Berkeley: University of California Press, 1993.

Epstein, Grace A. "*Bodily Harm:* Female Containment and Abuse in the Romance Narrative." *Genders* 16 (1993): 80–93.

Ermath, Elizabeth Deeds. "Feminist Theory as a Practice." Parker and Meese 3–17.

Ettin, Andrew Vogel. *Betrayals of the Body Politic: The Literary Commitments of Nadine Gordimer.* Charlottesville: University Press of Virginia, 1993.

Evans, Judith, et al., eds. *Feminism and Political Theory.* London: Sage, 1986.

Evans, Mari, ed. *Black Women Writers (1950–1980): A Critical Evaluation.* Garden City, NY: Anchor Press/Doubleday, 1984.

Evans, Sara M. "The Women's Movement in the United States in the 1960s." Backhouse and Flaherty 61–71.

Fabian, Johannes. "Of Dogs Alive, Birds Dead, and Time to Tell a Story." *Chronotypes: The Construction of Time.* Eds. John Bender and David E. Wellbery. Stanford, CA: Stanford University Press, 1991. 185–204.

Falk, Candace. *Love, Anarchy, and Emma Goldman.* 1984. rev. ed. New Brunswick, NJ: Rutgers University Press, 1990.

Faludi, Susan. *Backlash: The Undeclared War Against American Women.* New York: Crown, 1991.

Fanon, Frantz. *Black Skin, White Masks.* 1952. Trans. Charles Lam Markmann. New York: Grove Press, 1968.

Fanon, Frantz. *The Wretched of the Earth.* 1961. Trans. Constance Farrington. New York: Grove Weidenfeld, 1963.

Federici, Silvia. "Putting Feminism Back on Its Feet." Sayres et al. 338–46.

Felski, Rita. *Beyond Feminist Aesthetics: Feminist Literature and Social Change.* Cambridge, MA: Harvard University Press, 1989.

Ferguson, Ann. "On Conceiving Motherhood and Sexuality: A Feminist Materialist Approach." Trebilcot 153–82.

Ferguson, Ann. *Sexual Democracy: Women, Oppression, and Revolution.* Boulder, CO: Westview Press, 1991.

Ferguson, Kathy E. *The Feminist Case Against Bureaucracy.* Philadelphia: Temple University Press, 1984.

Ferguson, Kathy E. "Interpretation and Genealogy in Feminism." *Signs* 16 (1991): 322–39.

Fernbach, David. *The Spiral Path: A Gay Contribution to Human Survival.* London: Gay Men's Press, 1981.

Ferree, Myra Marx. "Equality and Autonomy: Feminist Politics in the United States and West Germany." Katzenstein and Mueller 172–95.

Ferree, Myra Marx, and Patricia Yancey Martin, eds. *Feminist Organizations: Harvest of the New Women's Movement.* Philadelphia: Temple University Press, 1995.

Fineman, Martha Albertson. *The Neutered Mother, the Sexual Family, and Other Twentieth Century Tragedies.* New York: Routledge, 1995.

Finke, Laurie. "The Rhetoric of Marginality: Why I Do Feminist Theory." *Tulsa Studies in Women's Literature* 5 (1986): 251–72.

Finn, Geraldine. "Feminism and Fiction: In Praise of *Praxis,* Beyond *Bodily Harm.*" *Socialist Studies/Etudes Socialistes* (1983): 51–78.

Firchow, Peter, ed. "Margaret Drabble." *The Writer's Place: Interviews on the Literary Situation in Contemporary Britain.* Minneapolis: University of Minnesota Press, 1974. 102–21.

Firestone, Shulamith. *The Dialectic of Sex: The Case for Feminist Revolution*. New York: Quill, 1970.

Flax, Jane. *Disputed Subjects: Essays on Psychoanalysis, Politics and Philosophy*. New York: Routledge, 1993.

Flax, Jane. "The Family in Contemporary Feminist Thought: A Critical Review." *The Family in Political Thought*. Ed. Jean Bethke Elshtain. Amherst: University of Massachusetts Press, 1982.

Flax, Jane. "Mother–Daughter Relationships: Psychodynamics, Politics, and Philosophy." Eisenstein and Jardine 20–40.

Flax, Jane. "Postmodernism and Gender Relations in Feminist Theory." *Signs* 12 (1987): 621–43.

Fletcher, Pauline. "Beyond Ideology: Nadine Gordimer and the Sense of the Body." Fletcher 46–61.

Fletcher, Pauline, ed. *Black/White Writing: Essays on South African Literature*. Lewisburg, PA: Bucknell University Press, 1993.

Forcey, Linda Rennie. "Feminist Perspectives on Mothering and Peace." Glenn, Chang, and Forcey 355–75.

Forcey, Linda Rennie. *Mothers of Sons: Toward an Understanding of Responsibility*. New York: Praeger, 1987.

Forna, Aminatta. "Pornography and Racism: Sexualizing Oppression and Inciting Hatred." Itzin 102–12.

Forster, E. M. *Aspects of the Novel*. 1927. New York: Harcourt, 1954.

Foster, Frances. "Between the Sides: Afro-American Women Writers as Mediators." *Nineteenth-Century Studies* 3 (1989): 53–64.

Foster, John Wilson. "The Poetry of Margaret Atwood." McCombs, *Critical* 153–67.

Foucault, Michel. "Afterword: The Subject and Power." *Michel Foucault: Beyond Structuralism and Hermeneutics*. Eds. Hubert L. Dreyfus and Paul Rabinow. 2nd ed. Chicago: University of Chicago Press, 1982. 208–26.

Foucault, Michel. *Discipline and Punish: The Birth of the Prison*. Trans. Alan Sheridan. 1975. New York: Vintage, 1979.

Foucault, Michel. *The Foucault Reader*. Ed. Paul Rabinow. New York: Pantheon, 1984.

Foucault, Michel. "Governmentality." *Ideology and Consciousness* 6 (1979): 5–21.

Foucault, Michel. *The History of Sexuality: An Introduction*. Trans. Robert Hurley. Vol. 1. 1976. New York: Vintage, 1990.

Foucault, Michel. *Language, Counter-Memory, Practice: Selected Essays and Interviews*. Ed. Donald F. Bouchard. Trans. Donald F. Bouchard and Sherry Simon. 1977. Ithaca, NY: Cornell University Press, 1988.

Foucault, Michel. "The Life of Infamous Men." *Michel Foucault: Power, Truth, Strategy*. Eds. Meaghan Morris and Paul Patton. Sydney: Feral Publications, 1979. 76–91.

Foucault, Michel. *Politics, Philosophy, Culture: Interviews and Other Writings, 1977–1984*. Trans. Alan Sheridan et al. New York: Routledge, 1988.

Foucault, Michel. *Power/Knowledge: Selected Interviews and Other Writings, 1972–1977*. Ed. Colin Gordon. New York: Pantheon, 1980.

Fox-Genovese, Elizabeth. "The Ambiguities of Female Identity: A Reading of the Novels of Margaret Drabble." *Partisan Review* 46 (1979): 234–48.

Fox-Genovese, Elizabeth. *Feminism Without Illusions: A Critique of Individualism.* Chapel Hill: University of North Carolina Press, 1991.

Frady, Marshall. "Profiles: Jesse Jackson—Part I." *New Yorker* 3 February 1992: 36–69.

Franzway, Suzanne, Dianne Court, and R. W. Connell. *Staking a Claim: Feminism, Bureaucracy, and the State.* Boston: Allen & Unwin, 1989.

Fraser, Nancy. "False Antitheses: A Response to Seyla Benhabib and Judith Butler." Benhabib et al. 59–74.

Fraser, Nancy. "Introduction: Revaluing French Feminism." Fraser and Bartky 1–24.

Fraser, Nancy. "Talking about Needs: Interpretive Contests as Political Conflicts in Welfare-State Societies." Sunstein 159–81.

Fraser, Nancy. "The Uses and Abuses of French Discourse Theories for Feminist Politics." Fraser and Bartky 177–94.

Fraser, Nancy, and Sandra Lee Bartky. *Revaluing French Feminism: Critical Essays on Difference, Agency, and Culture.* Bloomington: Indiana University Press, 1992.

Fraser, Nancy, and Linda J. Nicholson. "Social Criticism without Philosophy: An Encounter between Feminism and Postmodernism." Nicholson, *Feminism* 19–38.

Freccero, Carla. "Notes of a Post-Sex Wars Theorizer." Hirsch and Keller 305–25.

Freeman, Jo. "From Seed to Harvest: Transformations of Feminist Organizations and Scholarship." Ferree and Martin 397–408.

Freeman, Jo. *The Politics of Women's Liberation.* New York: David McKay, 1975.

Freeman, Jo. "Whom You Know Versus Whom You Represent: Feminist Influence in the Democratic and Republican Parties." Katzenstein and Mueller 215–44.

Freeman, Jo, ed. *Women: A Feminist Perspective.* 1975. 3rd ed. Palo Alto, CA: Mayfield, 1984.

French, Marilyn. *Beyond Power: On Women, Men, and Morals.* 1985. New York: Ballantine, 1986.

Freibert, Lucy M. "The Artist as Picaro: The Revelation of Margaret Atwood's 'Lady Oracle.'" *Canadian Literature* 92 (Spring 1982): 23–33.

Friedan, Betty. *The Feminine Mystique.* 1963. New York: Laurel, 1984.

Friedman, Edward H. "Trials of Discourse: Narrative Space in Quevado's *Buscón.*" Maiorino 183–225.

Friedman, Marilyn. "Feminism and Modern Friendship: Dislocating the Community." Sunstein 143–58.

Frye, Joanne S. *Living Stories, Telling Lives: Women and the Novel in Contemporary Experience.* Ann Arbor: University of Michigan Press, 1986.

Frye, Marilyn. *The Politics of Reality: Essays in Feminist Theory.* Trumansburg, NY: Crossing Press, 1983.

Frye, Marilyn. *Willful Virgin: Essays in Feminism 1976–1992.* Freedom, CA: Crossing Press, 1992.

Frye, Northrop. *The Secular Scripture: A Study of the Structure of Romance.* Cambridge, MA: Harvard University Press, 1976.

Fuss, Diana. *Essentially Speaking: Feminism, Nature & Difference.* New York: Routledge, 1989.

Fuss, Diana, ed. *inside/out: Lesbian Theories, Gay Theories.* New York: Routledge, 1991.

Gallop, Jane. *Around 1981: Academic Feminist Literary Theory.* New York: Routledge, 1992.

Gallop, Jane. *The Daughter's Seduction: Feminism and Psychoanalysis.* 1982. Ithaca, NY: Cornell University Press, 1983.

Gallop, Jane. *Feminist Accused of Sexual Harassment.* Durham, NC: Duke University Press, 1997.

Gallop, Jane, Marianne Hirsch, and Nancy K. Miller. "Criticizing Feminist Criticism." Hirsch and Keller 349–69.

Garlick, Barbara, Suzanne Dixon, and Pauline Allen. *Stereotypes of Women in Power.* New York: Greenwood Press, 1992.

Gatens, Moira. "Power, Bodies and Difference." Barrett and Phillips 120–37.

Gates, Henry Louis, Jr. "Criticism in the Jungle." *Black Literature and Literary Theory.* Ed. Gates. New York: Methuen, 1984. 1–24.

Gates, Henry Louis, Jr., ed. *Reading Black, Reading Feminist: A Critical Anthology.* New York: Meridian, 1990.

Gearhart, Sally Miller. "The Future—If There Is One—Is Female." McAllister 266–84.

Gelb, Joyce. "Feminist Organization Success and the Politics of Engagement." Ferree and Martin 128–34.

Gelb, Joyce. "Social Movement 'Success': A Comparative Analysis of Feminism in the United States and the United Kingdom." Katzenstein and Mueller 267–89.

Gelb, Joyce, and Marian Lief Palley. *Women and Public Policies.* 1982. rev. ed. Princeton, NJ: Princeton University Press, 1987.

Genette, Gérard. *Figures of Literary Discourse.* Trans. Alan Sheridan. New York: Columbia University Press, 1982.

Gerrard, Nicci. *Into the Mainstream.* London: Pandora, 1989.

Gibson, Pamela Church, and Roma Gibson. *Dirty Looks: Women, Pornography, Power.* London: British Film Institute, 1993.

Gilbert, Kate. "Fastening the Bonds of Womanhood." *Women's Review of Books* 13.9 (June 1996): 21.

Gilkes, Cheryl Townsend. "Building in Many Places: Multiple Commitments and Ideologies in Black Women's Community Work." Bookman and Morgen 53–76.

Gilliam, Angela. "Women's Equality and National Liberation." Mohanty et al. 215–36.

Gilligan, Carol. *In a Different Voice: Psychological Theory and Women's Development.* Cambridge, MA: Harvard University Press, 1982.

Gindin, James. "Drabble, Margaret." *Contemporary Novelists.* 4th ed. Ed. D. L. Kirkpatrick. New York: St. Martin's Press, 1986. 247–49.

Glenn, Evelyn Nakano, Grace Chang, and Linda Rennie Forcey, eds. *Mothering: Ideology, Experience, and Agency.* New York: Routledge, 1994.

Gonzalez, Nancie Solien. "Household and Family in the Caribbean: Some Definitions and Concepts." Steady, *Black* 421–29.

Goodwin, Ken. "Revolution as Bodily Fiction—Thea Astley and Margaret Atwood." *Antipodes* (Winter 1990): 109–15.

Gordimer, Nadine. *Burger's Daughter.* 1979. Harmondsworth, UK: Penguin, 1984.

Gordimer, Nadine. *The Essential Gesture: Writing, Politics and Places.* Ed. Stephen Clingman. 1988. London: Penguin, 1989.

Gordimer, Nadine. *A Sport of Nature.* 1987. London: Penguin, 1988.

Gordimer, Nadine. "A Writer in South Africa." *London Magazine* 5.2 (1965): 21–28.

Gordimer, Nadine. *Writing and Being.* Cambridge, MA: Harvard University Press, 1995.

Gordon, Linda. "Family Violence, Feminism, and Social Control." Thorne, *Rethinking* 262–86.

Gordon, Linda. "What's New In Women's History." de Lauretis, *Feminist* 20–30.

Grace, Sherrill E., and Lorraine Weir, eds. *Margaret Atwood: Language, Text, and System.* Vancouver: University of British Columbia Press, 1983.

Graff, Gerald. "The Pseudo-Politics of Interpretation." *The Politics of Interpretation.* Ed. W. J. T. Mitchell. Chicago: University of Chicago Press, 1983. 145–58.

Gramsci, Antonio. *An Antonio Gramsci Reader: Selected Writings, 1916–1935.* Ed. David Forgacs. New York: Shocken, 1988.

Grant, Judith. *Fundamental Feminisms: Contesting the Core Concepts of Feminist Theory.* New York: Routledge, 1993.

Grass, Günter. *The Flounder.* Trans. Ralph Manheim. 1978. San Diego: Harcourt, 1989.

Graulich, Melody, and Lisa Sisco. "Meditations on Language and the Self: A Conversation with Paule Marshall." *National Women's Studies Association Journal* 4 (1992): 282–302.

Gray, Stephen. "Landmark in Fiction." *Contrast* 8.2 (1973): 78–83.

Greene, Gayle. *Changing the Story: Feminist Fiction and the Tradition.* Bloomington: Indiana University Press, 1991.

Greenstein, Susan M. "Miranda's Story: Nadine Gordimer and the Literature of Empire." *Novel* (1985): 227–42.

Greer, Germaine. *The Female Eunuch.* 1970. New York: Bantam, 1972.

Grewal, Inderpal. "Autobiographic Subjects and Diasporic Locations: *Meatless Days* and *Borderlands.*" Grewal and Kaplan 231–54.

Grewal, Inderpal, and Caren Kaplan, eds. *Scattered Hegemonies: Postmodernity and Transnational Feminist Practices.* Minneapolis: University of Minnesota Press, 1994.

Griffin, Susan. *Pornography and Silence: Culture's Revenge Against Nature.* 1981. New York: Harper, 1982.

Grimshaw, Jean. *Philosophy and Feminist Thinking.* Minneapolis: University of Minnesota Press, 1986.

Grosz, Elizabeth. *Sexual Subversions.* Sydney: Allen & Unwin, 1989.

Grosz, Elizabeth. *Volatile Bodies: Toward a Corporeal Feminism.* Bloomington: Indiana University Press, 1994.

Gubar, Susan. "Representing Pornography: Feminism, Criticism, and Depictions of Female Violation." *Critical Inquiry* 13 (1987): 712–41.

Guillén, Claudio. "Toward a Definition of the Picaresque." *Literature as System: Essays Toward the Theory of Literary History.* Princeton, NJ: Princeton University Press, 1971. 71–106.

Gunew, Sneja. "Migrant Women Writers: Who's on Whose Margins?" *Gender, Politics, and Fiction.* Ed. Carole Ferrier. 1985. St. Lucia: University of Queensland Press, 1986. 163–78.

Gussow, Mel. "Margaret Drabble: A Double Life." *New York Times Book Review* 9 October 1977: 7, 40–41.

Habermas, Jürgen. *Theory and Practice.* Trans. John Viertel. Boston: Beacon Press, 1974.

Hall, John A., and G. John Ikenberry. *The State.* Minneapolis: University of Minnesota Press, 1989.

Hall, Stuart. "The Local and the Global: Globalization and Ethnicity." A. King 19–40.

Hall, Stuart. "Old and New Identities, Old and New Ethnicities." A. King 41–68.

Hannay, John. "Margaret Drabble: An Interview." *Twentieth-Century Literature* 33 (1987): 129–49.

Hannerz, Ulf. "Notes on the Global Ecumene." *Public Culture* 1.2 (1989): 66–75.

Hannerz, Ulf. "The World in Creolisation." *Africa* 57 (1987): 546–59.

Hansen, Elaine Tuttle. "Fiction and (Post) Feminism in Atwood's *Bodily Harm.*" *Novel* 19 (1985): 5–21.

Hansen, Karen V., and Ilene J. Philipson. *Women, Class, and the Feminist Imagination: A Socialist-Feminist Reader.* Philadelphia: Temple University Press, 1990.

Haraway, Donna J. *Simians, Cyborgs, and Women: The Reinvention of Nature.* New York: Routledge, 1991.

Hardin, Nancy S. "An Interview with Margaret Drabble." *Contemporary Literature* 14.3 (1973): 273–95.

Harlow, Barbara. *Barred: Women, Writing, and Political Detention.* Hanover, NH: Wesleyan University Press, 1992.

Harper, Michael F. "Margaret Drabble and the Resurrection of the English Novel." E. C. Rose, *Critical* 52–73.

Harpur, Tom. "Atwood's Priority: How Do We Stop War?" *Toronto Star* 5 October 1981: D1, D3.

Harris, Adrienne. "Bringing Artemis to Life: A Plea for Militance and Aggression in Feminist Peace Politics." Harris and King 93–113.

Harris, Adrienne, and Ynestra King, eds. *Rocking the Ship of State: Toward a Feminist Peace Politics.* Boulder, CO: Westview Press, 1989.

Harris, Sharon M., ed. *Redefining the Political Novel: American Women Writers, 1797–1901.* Knoxville: University of Tennessee Press, 1995.

Hartmann, Heidi. "The Unhappy Marriage of Marxism and Feminism: Towards a More Progressive Union." Sargent 1–41.

Hartouni, Valerie A. "Antigone's Dilemma: A Problem in Political Membership." *Hypatia* 1.1 (1986): 3–20.

Hartsock, Nancy C. M. *Money, Sex, and Power: Toward a Feminist Historical Materialism.* 1983. Boston: Northeastern University Press, 1985.

Hartsock, Nancy. "Postmodernism and Political Change: Issues for Feminist Theory." *Cultural Critique* 14 (Winter 1989–90): 15–33.

Hartsock, Nancy. "Staying Alive." *Building Feminist Theory.* Bunch et al. 111–22.

Hassan, Ihab. "Quest for the Subject: The Self in Literature." *Contemporary Literature* 29 (1988): 420–37.

Havel, Vaclav. *Summer Meditations.* Trans. Paul Wilson. New York: Knopf, 1992.

Hawkesworth, M. E. *Beyond Oppression: Feminist Theory and Political Strategy.* New York: Continuum, 1990.

Hawley, John C. *Writing the Nation: Self and Country in the Post-Colonial Imagination.* Atlanta: Rodopi, 1996.

Heilbrun, Carolyn G. "Fighting for Feminism." *Women's Review of Books* 13.10–11 (1996): 39.

Heilbrun, Carolyn G. *Writing a Woman's Life.* New York: Ballantine, 1988.

Hein, Hilde, and Carolyn Korsmeyer, eds. *Aesthetics in Feminist Perspective.* Bloomington: Indiana University Press, 1993.

Henderson, Lisa. "Lesbian Pornography: Cultural Transgression and Sexual Demystification." Munt 173–91.

Henderson, Mae Gwendolyn. "Speaking in Tongues: Dialogics, Dialectics, and the Black Woman's Literary Tradition." Wall 16–37.

Hernes, Helga Maria. "Women and the Welfare State: The Transition from Private to Public Dependence." Sassoon 72–92.

Hewitt, Nancy A. "Compounding Differences." *Feminist Studies* 18 (1992): 313–26.

Hirsch, Marianne. "Maternal Narratives: 'Cold Enough to Stop the Blood.'" Gates, *Reading* 415–30.

Hirsch, Marianne. *The Mother/Daughter Plot: Narrative, Psychoanalysis, Feminism.* Bloomington: Indiana University Press, 1989.

Hirsch, Marianne, and Evelyn Fox Keller, eds. *Conflicts in Feminism.* New York: Routledge, 1990.

Hite, Molly. *The Other Side of the Story: Structures and Strategies of Contemporary Feminist Narrative.* 1989. Ithaca, NY: Cornell University Press, 1992.

Hite, Shere. "Bringing Democracy Home." *Ms.* 5 (March/April 1995): 54–61.

Hite, Shere. *The Hite Report on the Family.* New York: Grove Press, 1994.

Hobbes, Thomas. *Leviathan.* Ed. Richard Tuck. 1991. Cambridge: Cambridge University Press, 1992.

Hogeland, Lisa Maria. *Feminism and Its Fictions: The Consciousness-Raising Novel and the Women's Liberation Movement.* Philadelphia: University of Pennsylvania Press, 1998.

hooks, bell. *Ain't I a Woman: Black Women and Feminism.* Boston: South End Press, 1981.

hooks, bell. "Choosing the Margin as a Space of Radical Otherness." *Framework* 36 (1989): 15–23.

hooks, bell. *Killing Rage: Ending Racism*. 1995. New York: Holt, 1996.

hooks, bell. *Sisters of the Yam: Black Women and Self-Recovery*. Boston: South End Press, 1993.

hooks, bell. *Talking Back: Thinking Feminist, Thinking Black*. Boston: South End Press, 1989.

hooks, bell. *Yearning: Race, Gender, and Cultural Politics*. Boston: South End Press, 1990.

Horney, Karen. *Feminine Psychology*. Ed. Harold Kelman. 1967. New York: Norton, 1973.

Horsman, Mathew, and Andrew Marshall. *After the Nation-State: Citizens, Tribalism, and the New World Disorder*. London: HarperCollins, 1994.

Howe, Irving. *Politics and the Novel*. New York: Horizon Press, 1957.

Howells, Coral Ann. *Margaret Atwood*. London: Macmillan, 1996.

Hulbert, Ann. "Femininity and Its Discontents." *New Republic* 20 & 27 September 1982: 40–42.

Hull, Gloria T. "The Black Woman Writer and the Diaspora." *Black Scholar* 17.1 (March/April 1986): 2–4.

Hunter, J. Paul. *Before Novels: The Cultural Contexts of Eighteenth-Century English Fiction*. New York: Norton, 1990.

Hutcheon, Linda. *The Canadian Postmodern: A Study of Contemporary English-Canadian Fiction*. New York: Oxford University Press, 1988.

Ingersoll, Earl G., ed. *Margaret Atwood: Conversations*. Princeton, NJ: Ontario Review Press, 1990.

Ireland, Mardy S. *Reconceiving Women: Separating Motherhood from Female Identity*. New York: Guilford Press, 1993.

Irigaray, Luce. *The Irigaray Reader*. Ed. Margaret Whitford. Oxford: Blackwell, 1991.

Irigaray, Luce. *Je, Tu, Nous: Toward a Culture of Difference*. Trans. Alison Martin. 1990. New York: Routledge, 1993.

Irigaray, Luce. *Sexes and Genealogies*. Trans. Gillian C. Gill. New York: Columbia University Press, 1993.

Irigaray, Luce. *This Sex Which Is Not One*. 1977. Trans. Catherine Porter with Carolyn Burke. Ithaca, NY: Cornell University Press, 1985.

Irvine, Lorna. *Collecting Clues: Margaret Atwood's Bodily Harm*. Toronto: ECW Press, 1993.

Irvine, Lorna. "No Sense of an Ending: Drabble's Continuous Fictions." E. C. Rose, *Critical* 73–86.

Itzin, Catherine, ed. *Pornography: Women, Violence and Civil Liberties*. 1992. Oxford: Oxford University Press, 1993.

Jackson, Stevi. "Women and Heterosexual Love: Complicity, Resistance, and Change." Pearce and Stacey 49–62.

Jacobus, Mary. *Reading Women: Essays in Feminist Criticism*. New York: Columbia University Press, 1986.

Jaggar, Alison M. *Feminist Politics and Human Nature*. Totowa, NJ: Rowman and Littlefield, 1983.

Jagose, Annamarie. *Lesbian Utopics.* New York: Routledge, 1994.

James, Joy. *Resisting State Violence: Radicalism, Gender, and Race in U.S. Culture.* Minneapolis: University of Minnesota Press, 1996.

James, Stanlie M. "Mothering: A Possible Black Feminist Link to Social Transformation?" James and Busia 44–54.

James, Stanlie M., and Abena P. A. Busia, eds. *Theorizing Black Feminisms: The Visionary Pragmatism of Black Women.* 1993. London: Routledge, 1994.

Jameson, Fredric. *The Political Unconscious: Narrative as a Socially Symbolic Act.* 1981. London: Methuen, 1986.

Jamkhandi, Sudhakar R. "An Interview with Margaret Atwood." *Commonwealth Novel in English* 2.1 (1983): 1–6.

Janeway, Elizabeth. *Powers of the Weak.* New York: Morrow, 1980.

Jardine, Alice. "Death Sentences:* Writing Couples and Ideology." *Poetics Today* 6.1–2 (1985): 119–31.

Jardine, Alice. "Pre-Texts for the Transatlantic Feminist." *Yale French Studies* 62 (1981): 220–36.

Jeffreys, Sheila. "Return to Gender: Post-modernism and Lesbianandgay Theory." Bell and Klein 359–74.

Jehlen, Myra. "Archimedes and the Paradox of Feminist Criticism." Keohane et al. 189–215.

Jennings, M. Kent. "Women in Party Politics." Tilly and Gurin 221–48.

Jessop, Bob. *The Capitalist State: Marxist Theories and Methods.* New York: New York University Press, 1982.

Johnson, Diane. "Living Legends." *New York Review of Books* 16 July 1987: 8–9.

Johnson, Samuel. *The Rambler.* Eds. W. J. Bate and Albrecht B. Strauss. *The Yale Edition of the Works of Samuel Johnson.* Vol. 3. 1969. New Haven, CT: Yale University Press, 1979.

Johnson, Samuel. *Poems.* Ed. E. L. McAdam, Jr., with George Milne. *The Yale Edition of the Works of Samuel Johnson.* Vol. 6. New Haven, CT: Yale University Press, 1964.

Johnson-Odim, Cheryl. "Common Themes, Different Contexts: Third World Women and Feminism." Mohanty et al. 314–27.

Jones, Ann Rosalind. "Mills & Boon Meets Feminism." Radford 195–218.

Jones, Ann Rosalind. "Writing the Body: Toward an Understanding of *L'écriture Féminine.*" *Feminist Studies* 7 (1981): 247–63.

Jones, Dorothy. "'Waiting for the Rescue': A Discussion of Margaret Atwood's *Bodily Harm.*" *Kunapipi* 6.3 (1984): 86–100.

Jones, Kathleen B. "Citizenship in a Woman-Friendly Polity." *Signs* 15 (1990): 781–812.

Jones, Kathleen B. *Compassionate Authority: Democracy and the Representation of Women.* New York: Routledge, 1993.

Joseph, Gloria I. "Black Mothers and Daughters: Traditional and New Populations." *Sage* 1.2 (Fall 1984): 17–21.

Joseph, Gloria I., and Jill Lewis. *Common Differences: Conflicts in Black and White Feminist Perspectives.* Garden City, NY: Anchor Press/Doubleday, 1981.

Justus, Joyce Bennett. "Women's Role in West Indian Society." Steady, *Black* 431–50.

Kaite, Berkeley. *Pornography and Difference.* Bloomington: Indiana University Press, 1995.

Kaminer, Wendy. *A Fearful Freedom: Women's Flight from Equality.* Reading, MA: Addison-Wesley, 1990.

Kaplan, Caren. "Deterritorializations: The Rewriting of Home and Exile in Western Feminist Discourse." *Cultural Critique* 6 (1987): 187–98.

Kaplan, Caren. "The Politics of Location as Transnational Feminist Critical Practice." Grewal and Kaplan 137–52.

Kaplan, Cora. *Sea Changes: Essays on Culture and Feminism.* London: Verso, 1986.

Kaplan, E. Ann. *Motherhood and Representation: The Mother in Popular Culture and Melodrama.* London: Routledge, 1992.

Kappeler, Susanne. *The Pornography of Representation.* Minneapolis: University of Minnesota Press, 1986.

Katzenstein, Mary Fainsod. "Comparing the Feminist Movement of the United States and Western Europe: An Overview." Katzenstein and Mueller 3–20.

Katzenstein, Mary Fainsod, and Carol McClurg Mueller, eds. *The Women's Movements of the United States and Western Europe.* Philadelphia: Temple University Press, 1987.

Keller, Evelyn Fox, and Helene Moglen. "Competition: A Problem for Academic Women." Miner and Longino 21–37.

Kelly, Joan. "The Doubled Vision of Feminist Theory." *Women, History and Theory: The Essays of Joan Kelly.* Chicago: University of Chicago Press, 1984. 51–64.

Kenyon, Olga. *Women Novelists Today: A Survey of English Writing in the Seventies and Eighties.* New York: St. Martin's Press, 1988.

Kenyon, Olga, ed. *Women Writers Talk.* New York: Carroll & Graf, 1989.

Keohane, Nannerl O. "Speaking from Silence: Women and the Science of Politics." *A Feminist Perspective in the Academy: The Difference It Makes.* Eds. Elizabeth Langland and Walter Gove. Chicago: University of Chicago Press, 1981. 86–100.

Keohane, Nannerl O., Michelle Z. Rosaldo, and Barbara C. Gelpi, eds. *Feminist Theory: A Critique of Ideology.* Chicago: University of Chicago Press, 1982.

Kerber, Linda K. *No Constitutional Right to be Ladies: Women and the Obligations of Citizenship.* New York: Hill and Wang, 1998.

Kerber, Linda K. "Separate Spheres, Female Worlds, Woman's Place: The Rhetoric of Women's History." *Journal of American History* 75.1 (1988): 9–39.

Kiernan, Ben. *How Pol Pot Came to Power.* London: Verso, 1985.

King, Anthony D., ed. *Culture, Globalization and the World-System: Contemporary Conditions for the Representation of Identity.* Binghamton, NY: Department of Art and Art History, SUNY-Binghamton, 1991.

King, Bruce, ed. *The Later Fiction of Nadine Gordimer.* New York: St. Martin's Press, 1993.

King, Katie. *Theory in Its Feminist Travels.* Bloomington: Indiana University Press, 1994.

King, Ynestra. "Afterword: If I Can't Dance in Your Revolution, I'm Not Coming." Harris and King 281–98.

Kirk, Gwyn. "Our Greenham Common: Feminism and Nonviolence." Harris and King 115–30.

Kirk, Gwyn. "Our Greenham Common: Not Just a Place But a Movement." Harris and King 263–80.

Kirtz, Mary K. "The Thematic Imperative: Didactic Characterization in *Bodily Harm*." Mendez-Egle 116–30.

Kittay, Eva Feder. "Womb Envy: An Explanatory Concept." Trebilcot 94–128.

Klein, Carole. *Mothers and Sons.* Boston: Houghton Mifflin, 1984.

Klein, Ethel. "The Diffusion of Consciousness in the United States and Western Europe." Katzenstein and Mueller 23–43.

Klein, Ethel. *Gender Politics: From Consciousness to Mass Politics.* Cambridge, MA: Harvard University Press, 1984.

Klein, Yvonne M. "Myth and Community in Recent Lesbian Autobiographical Fiction." *Lesbian Texts and Contexts: Radical Revisions.* Eds. Karla Jay and Joanne Glasgow. New York: New York University Press, 1990. 330–38.

Kollias, Karen. "Class Realities: Create a New Power Base." Bunch et al. 125–38.

Kolodny, Annette. "Margaret Atwood and the Politics of Narrative." *Studies on Canadian Literature: Introductory and Critical Essays.* Ed. Arnold E. Davidson. New York: Modern Language Association, 1990. 90–109.

Krentz, Jayne Ann, ed. *Dangerous Men and Adventurous Women: Romance Writers on the Appeal of the Romance.* Philadelphia: University of Pennsylvania Press, 1992.

Kristeva, Julia. *The Kristeva Reader.* Ed. Toril Moi. Oxford: Blackwell, 1986.

Kristeva, Julia. *Nations without Nationalism.* New York: Columbia University Press, 1993.

Kubitschek, Missy Dean. "Paule Marshall's Women on Quest." *Black American Literature Forum* 21 (1987): 43–60.

Kulkarni, Harihar. "Paule Marshall: A Bibliography." *Callaloo* 16 (1993): 243–67.

Laclau, Ernesto, and Chantal Mouffe. *Hegemony and Socialist Strategy: Towards a Radical Democratic Politics.* 1985. London: Verso, 1994.

Ladner, Joyce A. "Racism and Tradition: Black Womanhood in Historical Perspective." Steady, *Black* 269–88.

Langbauer, Laurie. *Women and Romance: The Consolations of Gender in the English Novel.* Ithaca, NY: Cornell University Press, 1990.

Langer, Elinor. "Whatever Happened to Feminist Fiction?" *New York Times Book Review* 4 March 1984: 1, 35–36.

Langford, Wendy. "'Snuglet Puglet Loves to Snuggle with Snuglet Piglet': Alter Personalities in Heterosexual Love Relationships." Pearce and Stacey 251–64.

Lauret, Maria. *Liberating Literature: Feminist Fiction in America.* London: Routledge, 1994.

Lauritzen, Monica. "The Contemporary Moment: An Interview with Margaret Drabble." *Papers on Language and Literature.* Göteborg, Sweden: Gothenburg Studies in English, 1985. 245–55.

Lazar, Karen. "Feminism as 'Piffling'? Ambiguities in Nadine Gordimer's Short Stories." B. King 213–27.

Lebsock, Suzanne. "Women and American Politics, 1880–1920." Tilly and Gurin 35–62.

Lederer, Laura, ed. *Take Back the Night: Women on Pornography*. New York: Morrow, 1980.

Lefanu, Sarah. *Feminism and Science Fiction*. Bloomington: Indiana University Press, 1989.

Le Franc, Bolivar. "An Interest in Guilt: Margaret Drabble." *Books and Bookmen* 14 (September 1969): 20–21.

Le Guin, Ursula K. *Dancing at the Edge of the World*. 1989. New York: Harper, 1990.

Lessing, Doris. *A Ripple from the Storm*. London: Michael Joseph, 1958.

Lévi-Strauss, Claude. *The Savage Mind*. Trans. George Weidenfeld. 1962. Chicago: University of Chicago Press, 1966.

Lewis, Reina. "The Death of the Author and the Resurrection of the Dyke." Munt 17–32.

Lienert, Tania. "On Who Is Calling Radical Feminists 'Cultural Feminists' and Other Historical Sleights of Hand." Bell and Klein 155–68.

Light, Alison. "'Returning to Manderley'—Romance Fiction, Female Sexuality, and Class." *Feminist Review* 16 (April 1984): 7–25.

Linden, Robin Ruth, Darlene R. Pagano, Diana E. H. Russell, and Susan Leigh Star, eds. *Against Sadomasochism: A Radical Feminist Analysis*. San Francisco: Frog in the Well, 1982.

Lips, Hilary M. *Women, Men, and Power*. Mountain View, CA: Mayfield, 1991.

Lockett, Cecily. "Feminism(s) and Writing in English in South Africa." *Current Writing: Text and Reception in Southern Africa* 2 (1990): 1–21.

Lockridge, Kenneth A. *On the Sources of Patriarchal Rage*. New York: New York University Press, 1992.

Lomberg, Alan. "Withering into the Truth: The Romantic Realism of Nadine Gordimer." Rowland Smith 31–45.

Lorde, Audre, and Susan Leigh Star. "Interview with Audre Lorde." Linden et al. 66–71.

Lorde, Audre. *Sister Outsider*. 1984. Freedom, CA: Crossing Press, 1986.

Lucking, David. "In Pursuit of the Faceless Stranger: Depths and Surfaces in Margaret Atwood's *Bodily Harm*." *Studies in Canadian Literature* 15 (1990): 76–93.

Lynch, Denise E. "Personalist Plot in *Bodily Harm*." *Studies in the Humanities* 15.1 (1988): 45–57.

Lynn, Naomi B. "Women and Politics: The Real Majority." Freeman, *Women* 402–22.

Lyotard, Jean-François. "One of the Things at Stake in Women's Struggles." *Sub-Stance* 20 (1978): 9–17.

Macaskill, Brian. "Placing Spaces: Style and Ideology in Gordimer's Later Fiction." B. King 59–73.

Macherey, Pierre. *A Theory of Literary Production.* Trans. Geoffrey Wall. Boston: Routledge, 1978.

Machiavelli, Niccolò. *The Prince and the Discourses.* New York: Modern Library, 1950.

MacKinnon, Catharine A. *Feminism Unmodified: Discourses on Life and Law.* Cambridge, MA: Harvard University Press, 1987.

MacKinnon, Catharine A. "From Practice to Theory, or What Is a White Woman Anyway?" Bell and Klein 45–54.

MacKinnon, Catharine A. *Only Words.* Cambridge, MA: Harvard University Press, 1993.

MacKinnon, Catharine A. *Toward a Feminist Theory of the State.* Cambridge, MA: Harvard University Press, 1989.

Magnusson, Warren. "Decentering the State, or Looking for Politics." W. Carroll 69–80.

Maiorino, Giancarlo, ed. *The Picaresque: Tradition and Displacement.* Minneapolis: University of Minnesota Press, 1996.

Maitse, Teboho. "The Past Is the Present: Thoughts from the New South Africa." Bell and Klein 436–40.

Malraux, André. *Man's Hope.* Trans. Stuart Gilbert and Alastair MacDonald. 1938. New York: Modern Library, 1941.

Mancing, Howard. "The Protean Picaresque." Maiorino 273–91.

Mann, Patricia S. *Micro-Politics: Agency in a Postfeminist Era.* Minneapolis: University of Minnesota Press, 1994.

Mansbridge, Jane. "What Is the Feminist Movement?" Ferree and Martin 27–34.

Maraire, J. Nozipo. *ZenZele: A Letter for My Daughter.* New York: Delta, 1996.

Marcus, Jane. "Storming the Toolshed." Keohane et al. 217–35.

Marks, Elaine, and Isabelle de Courtivron, eds. *New French Feminisms.* New York: Schocken, 1981.

Marshall, Paule. *Daughters.* New York: Atheneum, 1991.

Marshall, Paule. "From the Poets in the Kitchen." *Callaloo* 6.2 (1983): 22–30.

Marshall, Paule. "Shaping the World of My Art." *New Letters* 40 (October 1973): 97–112.

Martin, Biddy. "Feminism, Criticism, and Foucault." Diamond and Quinby 3–19.

Martin, Biddy. "Sexual Practice and Changing Lesbian Identities." Barrett and Phillips 93–119.

Martin, Biddy, and Chandra Talpade Mohanty. "Feminist Politics: What's Home Got to Do with It?" de Lauretis, *Feminist* 191–212.

Martin, Patricia Yancey. "Rethinking Feminist Organizations." *Gender & Society* 4 (1990): 182–206.

Marx, Karl, and Friedrich Engels. *The Communist Manifesto.* 1848, trans. 1888. London: Penguin, 1985.

Mayer, Robert. *History and the Early English Novel: Matters of Fact from Bacon to Defoe.* Cambridge: Cambridge University Press, 1997.

Mayer, Suzanne H. "Margaret Drabble's Short Stories: Worksheets for her Novels." Schmidt 75–90.

McAdoo, Harriette Pipes. "Black Mothers and the Extended Family Support Network." Rodgers-Rose 125–44.

McAllister, Pam, ed. *Reweaving the Web of Life: Feminism and Nonviolence.* Philadelphia: New Society, 1982.

McClure, Kirstie. "The Issue of Foundations: Scientized Politics, Politicized Science, and Feminist Critical Practice." Butler and Scott 341–68.

McCombs, Judith. "Atwood's Fictive Portraits of the Artist: From Victim to Surfacer, from Oracle to Birth." *Women's Studies* 12 (1986): 69–88.

McCombs, Judith, ed. *Critical Essays on Margaret Atwood.* Boston: G.K. Hall, 1988.

McCombs, Judith, and Carole L. Palmer. *Margaret Atwood: A Reference Guide.* Boston: G.K. Hall, 1991.

McCray, Carrie Allen. "The Black Woman and Family Roles." Rodgers-Rose 67–78.

McDowell, Deborah E. *"The Changing Same": Black Women's Literature, Criticism, and Theory.* Bloomington: Indiana University Press, 1995.

McDowell, Deborah E. "Reading Family Matters." Wall 75–97.

McKeon, Michael. *The Origins of the English Novel, 1600–1740.* Baltimore: Johns Hopkins University Press, 1987.

Meese, Elizabeth A. *Crossing the Double-Cross: The Practice of Feminist Criticism.* Chapel Hill: University of North Carolina Press, 1986.

Mendez-Egle, Beatrice, ed. *Margaret Atwood: Reflection and Reality.* Edinburg, TX: Pan American University, 1987.

Messenger, Ruth. "Women in Power and Politics." Eisenstein and Jardine 318–26.

Meyers, Diana T. "The Subversion of Women's Agency in Psychoanalytic Feminism: Chodorow, Flax, Kristeva." Fraser and Bartky 136–61.

Meyers, Marian. *News Coverage of Violence Against Women.* Thousand Oaks, CA: Sage, 1997.

Michie, Helena. "Not One of the Family: The Repression of the Other Woman in Feminist Theory." *Discontented Discourses: Feminism / Textual Intervention / Psychoanalysis.* Eds. Marleen S. Barr and Richard Feldstein. Urbana: University of Illinois Press, 1989. 15–28.

Miller, Jean Baker. "Women and Power." *Rethinking Power.* Ed. Thomas E. Wartenberg. Albany, NY: SUNY Press, 1992. 240–48.

Miller, Nancy K. *Subject to Change: Reading Feminist Writing.* New York: Columbia University Press, 1988.

Millett, Kate. *Sexual Politics.* 1969. New York: Ballantine, 1989.

Milton, Barbara. "Margaret Drabble: The Art of Fiction LXX." *Paris Review* 20 (Fall-Winter 1978): 39–65.

Milton, Edith. "Home at Last." *Women's Review of Books* 13.4 (January 1996): 8.

Miner, Valerie, and Helen E. Longino. *Competition: A Feminist Taboo?* New York: Feminist Press, 1987.

Minkoff, Debra C. "Organizational Mobilizations, Institutional Access, and Institutional Change." Cohen, Jones, and Tronto 477–96.

Misciagno, Patricia S. *Rethinking Feminist Identification: The Case for De Facto Feminism.* Westport, CT: Praeger, 1997.

Mitchell, Juliet. "Reflections on Twenty Years of Feminism." Mitchell and Oakley 34–62.

Mitchell, Juliet. *Woman's Estate*. New York: Pantheon, 1971.

Mitchell, Juliet. *Women: The Longest Revolution*. 1966. New York: Pantheon, 1984.

Mitchell, Juliet, and Ann Oakley, eds. *What Is Feminism?* Oxford: Blackwell, 1986.

Mitchell, Timothy. "The Limits of the State: Beyond Statist Approaches and Their Critics." *American Political Science Review* 85 (1991): 77–96.

Modleski, Tania. "The Disappearing Act: A Study of Harlequin Romances." *Signs* 5 (1980): 435–48.

Modleski, Tania. "Feminism and the Power of Interpretation: Some Critical Readings." de Lauretis, *Feminist* 121–38.

Modleski, Tania. *Feminism Without Women: Culture and Criticism in a "Postfeminist" Age*. New York: Routledge, 1991.

Modleski, Tania. *Loving with a Vengeance: Mass-Produced Fantasies for Women*. 1982. New York: Methuen, 1984.

Moghadam, Valentine M., ed. *Identity Politics and Women: Cultural Reassertions and Feminism in International Perspective*. Boulder, CO: Westview Press, 1994.

Mohanty, Chandra Talpade. "Feminist Encounters: Locating the Politics of Experience." Barrett and Phillips 74–92.

Mohanty, Chandra Talpade. "Introduction: Cartographies of Struggle: Third World Women and the Politics of Feminism." Mohanty et al. 1–47.

Mohanty, Chandra Talpade. "Under Western Eyes: Feminist Scholarship and Colonial Discourses." Mohanty et al. 51–80.

Mohanty, Chandra Talpade, Anne Russo, and Lourdes Torres, eds. *Third World Women and the Politics of Feminism*. Bloomington: Indiana University Press, 1991.

Moi, Toril. *Sexual/Textual Politics: Feminist Literary Theory*. London: Routledge, 1985.

Momsen, Janet, ed. *Women and Change in the Caribbean: A Pan-Caribbean Perspective*. Bloomington: Indiana University Press, 1993.

Mooers, Colin, and Alan Sears. "The 'New Social Movements' and the Withering Away of State Theory." W. Carroll 52–68.

Moore, Henrietta L. *Feminism and Anthropology*. Minneapolis: University of Minnesota Press, 1988.

Morgan, Robin, ed. *Sisterhood is Powerful: An Anthology of Writings from the Women's Liberation Movement*. New York: Vintage, 1970.

Morgan, Robin. "Theory and Practice: Pornography and Rape." Lederer 134–40.

Morson, Gary Saul. "Time and the Intelligentsia: A Patchwork in Nine Parts, with Loopholes." Eddins 81–100.

Moses, Yolanda T. "Female Status, the Family, and Male Dominance in a West Indian Community." Steady 499–513.

Mouffe, Chantal. "Feminism, Citizenship and Radical Democratic Politics." Butler and Scott 369–84.

Mouffe, Chantal. "Hegemony and New Political Subjects: Toward a New Concept of Democracy." Trans. Stanley Gray. *Marxism and the Interpretation of*

Culture. Eds. Cary Nelson and Lawrence Grossberg. Urbana: University of Illinois Press, 1988. 89–104.

Mueller, Carol. "The Organizational Basis of Conflict in Contemporary Feminism." Ferree and Martin 263–75.

Mueller, Carol McClung. "Collective Consciousness, Identity Transformation, and the Rise of Women in Public Office in the United States." Katzenstein and Mueller 89–108.

Munt, Sally, ed. *New Lesbian Criticism: Literary and Cultural Readings.* New York: Columbia University Press, 1992.

Murphy, Brenda. "Woman, Will, and Survival: the Figure in Margaret Drabble's Carpet." *South Atlantic Quarterly* 82 (Winter 1983): 38–50.

Mysliwiec, Eva. *Punishing the Poor: The International Isolation of Kampuchea.* Oxford: Oxfam, 1988.

Neely, Carol Thomas. "Woman/Utopia/Fetish: Disavowal and Satisfied Desire in Margaret Cavendish's *New Blazing World* and Gloria Anzaldúa's *Borderlands/La Frontera.*" Siebers 58–95.

Newman, Judie. *Nadine Gordimer.* London: Routledge, 1988.

Newton, Judith. "History as Usual?: Feminism and the 'New Historicism.'" *Cultural Critique* 9 (1988): 87–121.

Newton, Judith, and Deborah Rosenfelt, eds. *Feminist Criticism and Social Change: Sex, Class, and Race in Literature and Culture.* New York: Methuen, 1985.

Nicholson, Linda. "Introduction." Benhabib et al. 1–16.

Nicholson, Linda J., ed. *Feminism/Postmodernism.* New York: Routledge, 1990.

Norton, Theodore Mills. "Contemporary Critical Theory and the Family: Private World and Public Crisis." *The Family in Political Thought.* Ed. Jean Bethke Elshtain. Amherst: University of Massachusetts Press, 1982. 254–68.

Nussbaum, Martha C. *Poetic Justice: The Literary Imagination and Public Life.* Boston: Beacon Press, 1995.

O'Barr, Jean Fox. *Feminism in Action.* Chapel Hill: University of North Carolina Press, 1994.

O'Brien, Mary. *The Politics of Reproduction.* 1981. Boston: Routledge, 1983.

O'Driscoll, Sally. "Outlaw Readings: Beyond Queer Theory." *Signs* 21 (1996): 30–51.

Ogundipe-Leslie, 'Molara. "'Re-creating Ourselves All Over the World': A Conversation with Paule Marshall." C. B. Davies, *Moving* 19–26.

Ogunyemi, Chikwenye Okonjo. "Womanism: The Dynamics of the Contemporary Black Female Novel in English." *Signs* 11 (1985): 63–80.

Okin, Susan Moller. *Women in Western Political Thought.* 1979. Princeton, NJ: Princeton University Press, 1992.

Omolade, Barbara. "Black Women and Feminism." Eisenstein and Jardine 247–57.

Ong, Aihwa. "The Gender and Labor Politics of Postmodernity." *Annual Review of Anthropology* 20 (1991): 279–309.

Ostriker, Alicia Suskin. *Stealing the Language: The Emergence of Women's Poetry in America.* Boston: Beacon Press, 1986.

Packer, Joan Garrett. *Margaret Drabble: An Annotated Bibliography.* New York: Garland, 1988.

Palmer, Paulina. *Contemporary Women's Fiction: Narrative Practice and Feminist Theory.* Jackson: University Press of Mississippi, 1989.

Pannill, Linda. "From the 'Wordshop': The Fiction of Paule Marshall." *MELUS* 12.2 (1985): 63–73.

Parker, Alice A., and Elizabeth A. Meese, eds. *Feminist Critical Negotiations.* Philadelphia: John Benjamins, 1992.

Parker, Kenneth. "Imagined Revolution: Nadine's Gordimer's *A Sport of Nature.*" *Women and Writing in South Africa.* Ed. Cherry Clayton. Marshalltown, South Africa: Heinemann, 1989. 209–23.

Parry, Benita. "Problems in Current Theories of Colonial Discourse." *Oxford Literary Review* 9.1–2 (1987): 27–58.

Pateman, Carole. "Defending Prostitution: Charges against Ericsson." Sunstein 201–6.

Pateman, Carole. *The Sexual Contract.* 1988. Stanford, CA: Stanford University Press, 1992.

Patton, Marilyn. "Tourists and Terrorists: The Creation of *Bodily Harm.*" *Papers on Language and Literature* 28 (1992): 150–73.

Payant, Katherine B. *Becoming and Bonding: Contemporary Feminism and Popular Fiction by American Women Writers.* Westport, CT: Greenwood Press, 1993.

Peake, Linda. "The Development and Role of Women's Political Organizations in Guyana." Momsen 109–31.

Pearce, Lynne, and Jackie Stacey. *Romance Revisited.* New York: New York University Press, 1995.

Pearlman, Mickey, ed. *Mother Puzzles: Daughters and Mothers in Contemporary American Literature.* New York: Greenwood Press, 1989.

Peck, Richard. "What's a Poor White to Do? White South African Options in *A Sport of Nature.*" Rowland Smith 153–67.

Perry, Kathryn. "The Heart of Whiteness: White Subjectivity and Interracial Relationships." Pearce and Stacey 171–78.

Perry, Ruth, and Martine Watson Brownley, eds. *Mothering the Mind: Twelve Studies of Writers and Their Silent Partners.* New York: Holmes and Meier, 1984.

Pettis, Joyce. "A *MELUS* Interview: Paule Marshall." *MELUS* 17 (Winter 1991–1992): 117–29.

Pettis, Joyce. *Toward Wholeness in Paule Marshall's Fiction.* Charlottesville: University Press of Virginia, 1995.

Phelan, Shane. *Identity Politics: Lesbian Feminism and the Limits of Community.* Philadelphia: Temple University Press, 1989.

Philipson, Ilene J. "Beyond the Virgin and the Whore." Hansen and Philipson 451–59.

Phillips, Anne. *Engendering Democracy.* University Park: Pennsylvania State University Press, 1991.

Phillips, Anne, ed. *Feminism and Equality.* New York: New York University Press, 1987.

Phongpaichit, Pasuk. *From Peasant Girls to Bangkok Masseuses.* 1982. Geneva: International Labour Office, 1988.

Pickering, Jean. "Margaret Drabble's Sense of the Middle Problem." *Twentieth-Century Literature* 30 (1984): 475–83.

Piercy, Marge. "Margaret Atwood: Beyond Victimhood." McCombs, *Critical* 53–66.

Piercy, Marge. *Woman on the Edge of Time.* 1976. New York: Fawcett, 1983.

Pierson, Ruth Roach. "'Did Your Mother Wear Army Boots?' Feminist Theory and Women's Relation to War, Peace and Revolution." *Images of Women in Peace and War: Cross-Cultural and Historical Perspectives.* Ed. Sharon Macdonald, Pat Holden, and Shirley Ardener. London: Macmillan, 1987. 205–27.

Piven, Frances Fox. "Women and the State: Ideology, Power, and the Welfare State." Rossi, *Gender* 265–87.

Plaza, Monique. "The Mother/The Same: Hatred of the Mother in Psychoanalysis." *Feminist Issues* 2.1 (1982): 75–99.

Plimpton, George, ed. *Women Writers at Work: The Paris Review Interviews.* New York: Penguin, 1989.

Poland, Nancy. "Margaret Drabble: 'There Must Be a Lot of People Like Me.'" *Midwest Quarterly* 16 (April 1975): 255–67.

Potter, Sulamith Heins. *Family Life in a Northern Thai Village: A Study in the Structural Significance of Women.* Berkeley: University of California Press, 1977.

Preussner, Dee. "Talking with Margaret Drabble." *Modern Fiction Studies* 25 (1979–80): 563–77.

Pringle, Rosemary, and Sophie Watson. "Fathers, Brothers, Mates: The Fraternal State in Australia." S. Watson 229–43.

Pringle, Rosemary, and Sophie Watson. "'Women's Interests' and the Post-Structuralist State." Barrett and Phillips 53–75.

Probyn, Elspeth. "Travels in the Postmodern: Making Sense of the Local." Nicholson, *Feminism* 176–89.

Pryse, Marjorie and Hortense J. Spillers, eds. *Conjuring: Black Women, Fiction, and Literary Tradition.* Bloomington: Indiana University Press, 1985.

Rabine, Leslie W. "Romance in the Age of Electronics: Harlequin Enterprises." Newton and Rosenfelt 249–67.

Rabine, Leslie Wahl. "A Feminist Politics of Non-Identity." *Feminist Studies* 14 (1988): 11–31.

Radford, Jean, ed. *The Progress of Romance: The Politics of Popular Fiction.* London: Routledge, 1986.

Radford-Hill, Sheila. "Considering Feminism as a Model for Social Change." de Lauretis, *Feminist* 157–72.

Radway, Janice A. *Reading the Romance.* 1984. Chapel Hill: University of North Carolina Press, 1991.

Rainwater, Mary Catherine. "The Sense of the Flesh in Four Novels by Margaret Atwood." Mendez-Egle 14–28.

Randall, Vicky. *Women and Politics: An International Perspective.* 2nd ed. London: Macmillan, 1987.

Rao, Eleonora. *Strategies for Identity: The Fiction of Margaret Atwood.* New York: Peter Lang, 1993.

Rapp, Rayna. "Family and Class in Contemporary America: Notes toward an Understanding of Ideology." Thorne, *Rethinking* 49–70.

Rapping, Elayne. "A Novelist's Career." *Women's Review of Books* 7 (February 1990): 13.

Ravell-Pinto, Thelma M. "Women's Writing and the Politics of South Africa: The Ambiguous Role of Nadine Gordimer." C. B. Davies, *Moving* 125–36.

Rayson, Ann. "Motherhood in the Novels of Margaret Drabble." *Frontiers* 3.2 (1978): 43–46.

Reagon, Bernice Johnson. "Coalition Politics: Turning the Century." B. Smith, *Home Girls* 356–68.

Reardon, Betty A. *Sexism and the War System.* New York: Teachers College Press, 1985.

Redner, Harry. "Beyond Marx-Weber: A Diversified and International Approach to the State." *Political Studies* 38 (1990): 638–53.

Reed, Walter L. *An Exemplary History of the Novel: The Quixotic Versus the Picaresque.* Chicago: University of Chicago Press, 1981.

Register, Cheri. "Literary Criticism." *Signs* 6 (1980): 268–282.

Reinelt, Claire. "Moving onto the Terrain of the State: The Battered Women's Movement and the Politics of Engagement." Ferree and Martin 84–104.

Remnick, David. "Letter from Chechnya: In Stalin's Wake." *New Yorker* 24 July 1995. 46–62.

Reynell, Josephine. *Political Pawns: Refugees on the Thai-Kampuchean Border.* Oxford: Refugee Studies Programme, 1989.

Rich, Adrienne. "Adrienne Rich on Privilege, Power, and Tokenism." *Ms.* 8 (September 1979): 42–44.

Rich, Adrienne. "Compulsory Heterosexuality and Lesbian Existence." Snitow et al. 177–205.

Rich, Adrienne. *Diving into the Wreck: Poems 1971–1972.* New York: Norton, 1973.

Rich, Adrienne. "Notes Toward a Politics of Location." Díaz-Diocaretz and Zavala 7–22.

Rich, Adrienne. *Of Woman Born: Motherhood as Experience and Institution.* 1976. New York: Norton, 1995.

Rich, Adrienne. *What Is Found There: Notebooks on Poetry and Politics.* New York: Norton, 1993.

Rich, Adrienne. "When We Dead Awaken: Writing as Re-Vision." *College English* 34.1 (October 1972): 18–30.

Rich, B. Ruby. "Feminism and Sexuality in the 1980s." *Feminist Studies* 12 (1986): 525–61.

Richards, Janet Radcliffe. "Why the Pursuit of Peace Is No Part of Feminism." Elshtain and Tobias 211–25.

Richardson, Diane. "'Misguided, Dangerous and Wrong': On the Maligning of Radical Feminism." Bell and Klein 143–54.

Richetti, John. *Popular Fiction Before Richardson.* 1969. Oxford: Clarendon, 1992.

Richlin, Amy. "Julia's Joke, Galla Placidia, and the Roman Use of Women as Political Icons." Garlick, Dixon, and Allen 65–91.

Ridd, Rosemary. "Powers of the Powerless." Ridd and Callaway 1–24.

Ridd, Rosemary, and Helen Callaway, eds. *Caught Up in Conflict: Women's Responses to Political Strife.* London: Macmillan, 1986.

Riley, Denise. *"Am I That Name?": Feminism and the Category of "Women" in History.* Minneapolis: University of Minnesota Press, 1985.

Roberts, Michele. "Write, She Said." Radford 221–35.

Roberts, Sheila. "Nadine Gordimer's 'Family of Women.'" Rowland Smith 167–79.

Robinson, Sally. *Engendering the Subject: Gender and Self-Representation in Contemporary Women's Fiction.* Albany, NY: SUNY Press, 1991.

Rodgers-Rose, La Frances. *The Black Woman.* Beverly Hills, CA: Sage, 1980.

Rosca, Ninotchka. "Participant Observer." *Women's Review of Books* 12.6 (1995): 17.

Rose, Ellen Cronan, ed. *Critical Essays on Margaret Drabble.* Boston: G.K. Hall, 1985.

Rose, Ellen Cronan. "Feminine Endings—and Beginnings: Margaret Drabble's *The Waterfall.*" *Contemporary Literature* 21 (1980): 81–99.

Rose, Ellen Cronan. "The Sexual Politics of Narration: Margaret Drabble's Feminist Fiction." *Studies in the Novel* 20 (1988): 86–99.

Rose, Phyllis. "Margaret Drabble." *Writing of Women: Essays in a Renaissance.* Middletown, CT: Wesleyan University Press, 1985. 109–14.

Rosenberg, Jerome H. *Margaret Atwood.* Boston: Twayne, 1984.

Rosenfelt, Deborah Silverton. "Feminism, 'Postfeminism,' and Contemporary Women's Fiction." *Tradition and the Talents of Women.* Ed. Florence Howe. Urbana: University of Illinois Press, 1991. 268–91.

Rosenfelt, Deborah, and Judith Stacey. "Second Thoughts on the Second Wave." *Feminist Studies* 13 (1987): 341–62.

Rosinsky, Natalie M. *Feminist Futures: Contemporary Women's Speculative Fiction.* Ann Arbor: UMI Research Press, 1984.

Ross, Deborah. *The Excellence of Falsehood: Romance, Realism, and Women's Contribution to the Novel.* Lexington: University Press of Kentucky, 1991.

Ross, Ellen. "New Thoughts on 'the Oldest Vocation': Mothers and Motherhood in Recent Feminist Scholarship." *Signs* 20 (1995): 397–413.

Rossi, Alice S., ed. *The Feminist Papers: From Adams to de Beauvoir.* 1973. New York: Bantam, 1981.

Rossi, Alice S., ed. *Gender and the Life Course.* New York: Aldine, 1985.

Rowland, Robyn. "Politics of Intimacy: Heterosexuality, Love and Power." Bell and Klein 77–86.

Rowland, Robyn, and Renate Klein. "Radical Feminism: History, Politics, Action." Bell and Klein 9–36.

Rozencwajg, Iris. "Interview with Margaret Drabble." *Women's Studies* 6 (1979): 335–47.

Rubenstein, Roberta. *Boundaries of the Self: Gender, Culture, Fiction.* Urbana: University of Illinois Press, 1987.

Rubenstein, Roberta. "Fragmented Bodies/Selves/Narratives: Margaret Drabble's Postmodern Turn." *Contemporary Literature* 35 (1994): 136–55.

Rubenstein, Roberta. "Pandora's Box and Female Survival: Margaret Atwood's *Bodily Harm.*" McCombs, *Critical* 259–75.

Rubenstein, Roberta. "Severed Heads, Primal Crimes, Narrative Revisions: Margaret Drabble's *A Natural Curiosity.*" *Critique* 33 (1992): 95–105.

Rubenstein, Roberta. "Sexuality and Intertextuality: Margaret Drabble's *The Radiant Way.*" *Comparative Literature* 30 (1989): 95–112.

Rubin, Gayle. "Thinking Sex: Notes for a Radical Theory of the Politics of Sexuality." Vance 267–319.

Rubin, Gayle. "The Traffic in Women: Notes on the 'Political Economy' of Sex." Hansen and Philipson 74–113.

Ruddick, Sara. "From Maternal Thinking to Peace Politics." Cole and Coultrap-McQuin 141–55.

Ruddick, Sara. *Maternal Thinking: Toward a Politics of Peace.* Boston: Beacon Press, 1989.

Ruddick, Sara. "Preservative Love and Military Destruction: Some Reflections on Mothering and Peace." Trebilcot 231–62.

Ruddick, Sara. "The Rationality of Care." Elshtain and Tobias 229–54.

Rushing, Andrea B. "Images of Women in Modern African Poetry: An Overview." Bell, Parker, and Guy-Sheftall 18–24.

Rushing, Andrea Benton. "Images of Black Women in Afro-American Poetry." Steady, *Black* 403–16.

Russ, Joanna. *The Female Man.* New York: Bantam, 1975.

Russ, Joanna. "Recent Feminist Utopias." *Future Females: A Critical Anthology.* Ed. Marleen S. Barr. Bowling Green, OH: Bowling Green State University Popular Press, 1981.

Russell, Sandi. "Interview with Paule Marshall." *Wasafiri* 8 (1988): 14–16.

Russo, Ann. "We Cannot Live Without Our Lives: White Women, Antiracism, and Feminism." Mohanty et al. 297–313.

Ryan, Barbara. *Feminism and the Women's Movement: Dynamics of Change in Social Movement, Ideology and Activism.* New York: Routledge, 1992.

Sage, Lorna. *Women in the House of Fiction: Post-War Women Novelists.* London: Macmillan, 1992.

Said, Edward W. *Orientalism.* 1978. New York: Vintage, 1979.

Said, Edward W. *Culture and Imperialism.* 1993. New York: Vintage, 1994.

Sampson, Anthony. "In Search of a Way to Live." *Sunday Star* [Johannesburg] 5 April 1987: 17.

Sánchez, Francisco J., and Nicholas Spadaccini. "Revisiting the Picaresque in Postmodern Times." Maiorino 292–307.

Sanday, Peggy Reeves. *Female Power and Male Dominance: On the Origins of Sexual Inequality.* Cambridge: Cambridge University Press, 1981.

Sargent, Lydia, ed. *Women and Revolution: A Discussion of the Unhappy Marriage of Marxism and Feminism.* Boston: South End Press, 1981.

Sassoon, Anne Showstack, ed. *Women and the State: The Shifting Boundaries of Public and Private.* London: Unwin, 1987.

Satz, Martha. "'Less of a Woman As One Gets Older': An Interview with Margaret Drabble." *Southwest Review* 70 (1985): 187–97.

Sawer, Marian. "Gender, Metaphor and the State." *Feminist Review* 52 (1996): 118–34.

Saxonhouse, Arlene W. "Introduction—Public and Private: The Paradigm's Power." Garlick, Dixon, and Allen 1–9.

Sayres, Sohnya, Anders Stephanson, Stanley Aronowitz, and Fredric Jameson, eds. *The 60s Without Apology.* Minneapolis: University of Minnesota Press, 1984.

Scarry, Elaine. *The Body in Pain: The Making and Unmaking of the World.* New York: Oxford University Press, 1985.

Schlozman, Kay Lehman. "Representing Women in Washington: Sisterhood and Pressure Politics." Tilly and Gurin 339–82.

Schmidt, Dorey, ed. *Margaret Drabble: Golden Realms.* Edinburg, TX: Pan American University, 1982.

Schor, Naomi. "Female Fetishism: The Case of George Sand." *The Female Body in Western Culture: Contemporary Perspectives.* Ed. Susan Rubin Sulieman. Cambridge, MA : Harvard University Press, 1986. 363–72.

Scott, Joan Wallach. *Gender and the Politics of History.* New York: Columbia University Press, 1988.

Seaman, Donna. "The *BOOKLIST* Interview: Paule Marshall." 88 (15 October 1991): 410–11.

Sedgwick, Eve Kosofsky. *Epistemology of the Closet.* Berkeley: University of California Press, 1990.

Segal, Lynne. *Is the Future Female? Troubled Thoughts on Contemporary Feminism.* London: Virago, 1987.

Shils, Edward. *The Virtue of Civility: Selected Essays on Liberalism, Tradition, and Civil Society.* Ed. Steven Grosby. Indianapolis: Liberty Fund, 1997.

Showalter, Elaine. "Feminist Criticism in the Wilderness." Showalter, *New* 243–70.

Showalter, Elaine. *A Literature of Their Own: British Women Novelists from Brontë to Lessing.* Princeton, NJ: Princeton University Press, 1977.

Showalter, Elaine. "Women's Time, Women's Space: Writing the History of Feminist Criticism." *Feminist Issues in Literary Scholarship.* Ed. Shari Benstock. Bloomington: Indiana University Press, 1987. 30–44.

Showalter, Elaine, ed. *The New Feminist Criticism: Essays on Women, Literature, and Theory.* New York: Pantheon, 1985.

Shrage, Laurie. "Should Feminists Oppose Prostitution?" Sunstein 185–99.

Shulman, Alix Kates. "The 'Taint' of Feminist Fiction." *Ms.* (November/December 1991): 72–75.

Siebers, Tobin, ed. *Heterotopia: Postmodern Utopia and the Body Politic.* Ann Arbor: University of Michigan Press, 1994.

Siltanen, Janet, and Michelle Stanworth, eds. *Women and the Public Sphere: A Critique of Sociology and Politics.* New York: St. Martin's Press, 1984.

Silverblatt, Irene. "Interpreting Women in States: New Feminist Ethnohistories." di Leonardo, *Gender* 140–71.

Silverman, Kaja. *The Acoustic Mirror: The Female Voice in Psychoanalysis and Cinema.* Bloomington: Indiana University Press, 1988.

Simmonds, Felly Nkweto. "Love in Black and White." Pearce and Stacey 210–22.

Singer, Linda. "Value, Power and Gender: Do We Need a Different Voice?" *Power, Gender, Values.* Ed. Judith Genova. Edmunton, Alberta: Academic Printing, 1987.

Smith, Barbara, ed. *Home Girls: A Black Feminist Anthology.* New York: Kitchen Table Press, 1983.

Smith, Barbara. "The Truth that Never Hurts: Black Lesbians in Fiction in the 1980s." Mohanty et al. 101–29.

Smith, Raymond. *The Matrifocal Family: Power, Pluralism, and Politics.* New York: Routledge, 1996.

Smith, Rowland, ed. *Critical Essays on Nadine Gordimer.* Boston: Hall, 1990.

Smith, Sally Bedell. *Reflected Glory: The Life of Pamela Churchill Harriman.* 1996. New York: Touchstone, 1997.

Smith, Sidonie. *A Poetics of Women's Autobiography: Marginality and the Fictions of Self-Representation.* Bloomington: Indiana University Press, 1987.

Smith-Rosenberg, Carroll. "The Body Politic." Weed 101–21.

Smyer, Richard. "*A Sport of Nature:* Gordimer's Work in Progress." *Journal of Commonwealth Literature* 27.1 (1992): 71–86.

Snitow, Ann. "A Gender Diary." Hirsch and Keller 9–43.

Snitow, Ann. "Mass Market Romance: Pornography for Women Is Different." Snitow et al. 245–63.

Snitow, Ann. "A New Old-Fashioned Girl." *Nation* 30 May 1987: 731–33.

Snitow, Ann, Christine Stansell, and Sharon Thompson, eds. *Powers of Desire: The Politics of Sexuality.* New York: Monthly Review Press, 1983.

Sommer, Doris. "Who Can Tell? Filling in Blanks for Cirilo Villaverde." Hawley 88–107.

Sontag, Susan. *Illness as Metaphor and AIDS and Its Metaphors.* 1978, 1989. New York: Doubleday, 1990.

Spalter-Roth, Roberta, and Ronnee Schreiber. "Outsider Issues and Insider Tactics: Strategic Tensions in the Women's Policy Network during the 1980s." Ferree and Martin 105–27.

Spencer, Jane. *The Rise of the Woman Novelist: From Aphra Behn to Jane Austen.* 1986. Oxford: Blackwell, 1989.

Spillers, Hortense J. "Black, White, and in Color, or Learning How to Paint: Toward an Intramural Protocol of Reading." *New Historical Literary Study: Essays on Reproducing Texts, Representing History.* Eds. Jeffrey N. Cox and Larry J. Reynolds. Princeton, NJ: Princeton University Press, 1993. 267–91.

Spillers, Hortense J. "*Chosen Place, Timeless People:* Some Figurations on the New World." Pryse and Spillers 151–75.

Spivak, Gayatri Chakravorty. "French Feminism Revisited: Ethics and Politics." Butler and Scott 54–85.

Spivak, Gayatri Chakravorty. "Three Feminist Readings: McCullers, Drabble, Habermas." *Union Seminary Quarterly Review* 35.1–2 (1979–80): 15–34.

Sprengnether, Madelon. *The Spectral Mother: Freud, Feminism, and Psychoanalysis.* Ithaca, NY: Cornell University Press, 1990.

Stacey, Jackie, and Lynne Pearce. "The Heart of the Matter: Feminists Revisit Romance." Pearce and Stacey 11–45.

Steady, Filomina Chioma. "Women and Collective Action: Female Models in Transition." James and Busia 90–101.

Steady, Filomina Chioma, ed. *The Black Woman Cross-Culturally.* Cambridge, MA: Schenkman, 1981.

Stewart, Susan. *Crimes of Writing.* New York: Oxford University Press, 1991.

Stimpson, Catharine R. "Atwood Woman." *Nation* 31 May 1986: 764–67.

Stovel, Bruce. "Subjective to Objective: A Career Pattern in Jane Austen, George Eliot, and Contemporary Women Novelists." *Ariel* 18 (1987): 53–61.

Stovel, Nora Foster. "'A Feminine Ending?': Symbolism as Closure in the Novels of Margaret Drabble." *English Studies in Canada* 15 (March 1989): 80–93.

Stovel, Nora Foster. "From Wordsworth to Bennett: The Development of Margaret Drabble's Fiction." *International Fiction Review* 15 (1988): 130–40.

Sturgeon, Noël. *Ecofeminist Natures: Race, Gender, Feminist Theory, and Political Action.* New York: Routledge, 1997.

Sudarkasa, Niara. "Female Employment and Family Organization in West Africa." Steady, *Black* 49–63.

Sulieman, Susan Rubin. *Authoritarian Fictions: The Ideological Novel as a Literary Genre.* New York: Columbia University Press, 1983.

Sunstein, Cass R., ed. *Feminism & Political Theory.* Chicago: University of Chicago Press, 1990.

Sutton, Constance, and Susan Makiesky-Barrow. "Social Inequality and Sexual Status in Barbados." Steady, *Black* 469–98.

Swerdlow, Amy. "Pure Milk, Not Poison: Women Strike for Peace and the Test Ban Treaty of 1963." Harris and King 225–37.

Swift, Jonathan. *A Tale of a Tub with Other Early Works, 1696–1707.* Ed. Herbert Davis. Oxford: Blackwell, 1957.

Temple-Thurston, Barbara. "Nadine Gordimer: The Artist as *A Sport of Nature.*" *Studies in 20ᵗʰ Century Literature* 15 (1991): 175–84.

Theweleit, Klaus. "The Bomb's Womb and the Genders of War (War Goes on Preventing Women from Becoming the Mothers of Invention)." Cooke and Woollacott 283–315.

Thomas, Brook. *The New Historicism: And Other Old-Fashioned Topics.* Princeton, NJ: Princeton University Press, 1991.

Thompson, John B. *Studies in the Theory of Ideology.* Berkeley: University of California Press, 1984.

Thorne, Barrie. "Feminism and the Family: Two Decades of Thought." Thorne, *Rethinking* 3–30.

Thorne, Barrie, ed. *Rethinking the Family: Some Feminist Questions.* Boston: Northwestern University Press, 1992.

Thurman, Judith. "Choosing a Place." *New Yorker* 29 June 1987: 87–90.

Tiffin, Chris, and Alan Lawson, eds. *De-Scribing Empire: Post-colonialism and Textuality.* London: Routledge, 1994.

Tilly, Louise A., and Patricia Gurin, eds. *Women, Politics, and Change.* New York: Russell Sage Foundation, 1990.

Todd, Janet. *The Sign of Angelica: Women, Writing, and Fiction, 1660–1800.* London: Virago, 1989.

Tohidi, Nayereh. "Gender and Islamic Fundamentalism: Feminist Politics in Iran." Mohanty et al. 251–67.

Trask, Haunani-Kay. *Eros and Power: The Promise of Feminist Theory.* Philadelphia: University of Pennsylvania Press, 1986.

Trebilcot, Joyce, ed. *Mothering: Essays in Feminist Theory.* Totowa, NJ: Rowman and Allanheld, 1984.

Trescott, Jacqueline. "The Daughter of the Mother Poets." *Washington Post* 8 October 1991: C1-C2.

Troester, Rosalie Riegle. "Turbulence and Tenderness: Mothers, Daughters, and 'Othermothers' in Paule Marshall's *Brown Girl, Brownstone.*" *Sage* 1 (Fall 1984): 13–16.

Tronto, Joan C. *Moral Boundaries: A Political Argument for an Ethic of Care.* New York: Routledge, 1993.

Turim, Maureen. "The Erotic in Asian Cinema." Gibson and Gibson 81–89.

van Boheemen, Christine. *The Novel as Family Romance: Language, Gender, and Authority from Fielding to Joyce.* Ithaca, NY: Cornell University Press, 1987.

Vance, Carole S., ed. *Pleasure and Danger: Exploring Female Sexuality.* Boston: Routledge, 1984.

VanSpanckeren, Kathryn, and Jan Garden Castro, eds. *Margaret Atwood: Vision and Forms.* Carbondale, IL: Southern Illinois University Press, 1988.

Verba, Sidney. "Women in American Politics." Tilly and Gurin 555–72.

Veyne, Paul. *Writing History.* Trans. Mina Moore-Rinvolucri. 1971. Middletown, CT: Wesleyan University Press, 1984.

Vickers, Jill. "The Intellectual Origins of the Women's Movements in Canada." Backhouse and Flaherty 39–60.

Visel, Robin. "Othering the Self: Nadine Gordimer's Colonial Heroines." *Ariel* 19.4 (1988): 33–41.

Wade, Michael. "*A Sport of Nature:* Identity and Repression of the Jewish Subject." B. King 155–72.

Wade-Gayles, Gloria. *No Crystal Stair: Visions of Race and Gender in Black Women's Fiction.* 1984. Cleveland: Pilgrim Press, 1997.

Wade-Gayles, Gloria. "The Truths of Our Mothers' Lives: Mother-Daughter Relationships in Black Women's Fiction." *Sage* 1.2 (1984): 8–12.

Wagner, Kathrin. *Rereading Nadine Gordimer.* Bloomington: Indiana University Press, 1994.

Walkowitz, Judith, with Myra Jehlen and Bell Chevigny. "Patrolling the Borders: Feminist Historiography and the New Historicism." *Radical History Review* 43 (1989): 23–43

Wall, Cheryl, ed. *Changing Our Own Words.* New Brunswick, NJ: Rutgers University Press, 1989.

Wallace, Michelle. "The Politics of Location: Cinema/Theory/Literature/Ethnicity/Sexuality/ Me." *Framework* 36 (1989): 42–55.

Wallace, Michelle. "Variations on Negation and the Heresy of Black Feminist Creativity." Gates, *Reading* 52–67.

Wallerstein, Immanuel. "The National and the Universal: Can There Be Such a Thing as World Culture?" A. King 81–105.

Wardlow, Grant. *Political Terrorism: Theory, Tactics, and Counter-measures.* 2nd ed. 1989. Cambridge: Cambridge University Press, 1990.

Wartenberg, Thomas E. *The Forms of Power: From Domination to Transformation.* Philadelphia: Temple University Press, 1990.

Washington, Mary Helen. "I Sign My Mother's Name: Alice Walker, Dorothy West, Paule Marshall." Perry and Brownley 142–63.

Watson, Barbara Bellow. "On Power and the Literary Text." *Signs* 1 (1975): 111–18.

Watson, Sophie, ed. *Playing the State: Australian Feminist Interventions.* London: Verso, 1990.

Watt, Ian. *The Rise of the Novel: Studies in Defoe, Richardson and Fielding.* 1957. Berkeley: University of California Press, 1967.

Waugh, Patricia. *Feminine Fictions: Revisiting the Postmodern.* London: Routledge, 1989.

Weber, Max. *Economy and Society: An Outline of Interpretive Sociology.* Eds. Guenther Roth and Claus Wittich. 3 vols. New York: Bedminster Press, 1968.

Weed, Elizabeth, ed. *Coming to Terms: Feminism, Theory, Politics.* New York: Routledge, 1989.

Weinhouse, Linda. "The Deconstruction of Victory: Gordimer's *A Sport of Nature.*" *Research in African Literatures* 21.2 (1990): 91–100.

Weir, Lorna. "Women and the State: A Conference for Feminist Activists." *Feminist Review* 26 (July 1987): 93–103.

Weiss, Linda. *The Myth of the Powerless State.* Ithaca, NY: Cornell University Press, 1998.

Welchman, John C. "The Philosophical Brothel." *Rethinking Borders.* Ed. Welchman. Minneapolis: University of Minnesota Press, 1996. 160–86.

West, Robin. *Caring for Justice.* New York: New York University Press, 1997.

Weston, Kath. "The Politics of Gay Families." Thorne, *Rethinking* 119–39.

White, Stephen K. *Political Theory and Postmodernism.* Cambridge: Cambridge University Press, 1991.

Whittier, Gayle. "Mistresses and Madonnas in the Novels of Margaret Drabble." *Gender and Literary Voice.* Ed. Janet Todd. New York: Holmes and Meier, 1980. 197–213.

Whittier, Nancy. *Feminist Generations: The Persistence of the Radical Women's Movement.* Philadelphia: Temple University Press, 1995.

Wicke, Jennifer. "Through a Glass Darkly: Pornography's Academic Market." Gibson and Gibson 62–80.

Wilentz, Gay. *Binding Cultures: Black Women Writers in Africa and the Diaspora.* Bloomington: Indiana University Press, 1992.

Williams, John. "Return of a Native Daughter: An Interview with Paule Marshall and Maryse Condé." *Sage* 3.2 (1986): 52–53.

Williams, Linda. *Hard Core: Power, Pleasure, and the "Frenzy of the Visible."* Berkeley: University of California Press, 1989.

Willis, Ellen. "Radical Feminism and Feminist Radicalism." Sayres et al. 91–118.

Willis, Susan. *Specifying: Black Women Writing the American Experience.* Madison: University of Wisconsin Press, 1987.

Wilson, Anna. "Audre Lorde and the African-American Tradition: When the Family Is Not Enough." Munt 75–93.

Wilson, Geraldine L. "The Self/Group Actualization of Black Women." Rodgers-Rose 301–14.

Wilson, Sharon R. "Camera Images in Margaret Atwood's Novels." Mendez-Egle 29–57.

Wilson, Sharon R. "Turning Life into Popular Art: *Bodily Harm*'s Life-Tourist." *Studies in Canadian Literature* 10.1–2 (1985): 136–45.

Wilson, Sharon Rose. *Margaret Atwood's Fairy-Tale Sexual Politics.* Jackson: University Press of Mississippi, 1993.

Winnett, Susan. "Making Metaphors/Moving On: *Burger's Daughter* and *A Sport of Nature.*" B. King 140–54.

Wittig, Monique. *The Straight Mind and Other Essays.* Boston: Beacon Press, 1992.

Wong, Shelley Sunn. "Unnaming the Same: Theresa Hak Kynug Cha's *DICTEE.*" *Feminist Measures: Soundings in Poetry and Theory.* Eds. Lynn Keller and Cristanne Miller. Ann Arbor: University of Michigan Press, 1994. 43–68.

Woolf, Virginia. *A Room of One's Own.* 1929. New York: Harcourt, n.d.

Woolf, Virginia. *Three Guineas.* 1938. New York: Harcourt, n.d.

Yeager, Patricia. *Honey-Mad Women: Emancipatory Strategies in Women's Writing.* New York: Columbia University Press, 1988.

Yeatman, Anna. *Bureaucrats, Technocrats, Femocrats: Essays on the Contemporary Australian State.* Sydney: Allen, 1990.

Yeatman, Anna. *Postmodern Revisionings of the Political.* New York: Routledge, 1994.

Yelin, Louise. "Decolonizing the Novel: Nadine Gordimer's *A Sport of Nature* and British Literary Traditions." *Decolonizing Tradition: New Views of Twentieth-Century "British" Literary Canons.* Ed. Karen Lawrence. Urbana: University of Illinois Press, 1992. 191–211.

Yglesias, Helen. "Rescuing a Reputation." *Women's Review of Books* 12.5 (February 1995): 7.

Young, Iris Marion. "Impartiality and the Civic Public: Some Implications of the Feminist Critiques of Moral and Political Theory." *Feminism as Critique: On the Politics of Gender.* Eds. Seyla Benhabib and Drucilla Cornell. Minneapolis: University of Minnesota Press, 1987. 57–76.

Young, Iris Marion. "The Ideal of Community and the Politics of Difference." Nicholson, *Feminism* 300–23.

Young, Iris Marion. *Justice and the Politics of Difference.* Princeton, NJ: Princeton University Press, 1990.

Young, Iris Marion. "Polity and Group Difference: A Critique of the Ideal of Universal Citizenship." Sunstein 117–41.

Yuval-Davis, Nira. "Identity Politics and Women's Ethnicity." Moghadam 408–24.

Zimmerman, Bonnie. "Lesbians Like This and That: Some Notes on Lesbian Criticism for the Nineties." Munt 1–15.

Zimmerman, Bonnie. *The Safe Sea of Women: Lesbian Fiction, 1969–1989.* Boston: Beacon Press, 1990.

Zimmerman, Bonnie. "What Has Never Been: An Overview of Lesbian Feminist Literary Criticism." Showalter, *New* 200–224.

Index